Maid Sama!

Hiro Fujiwara

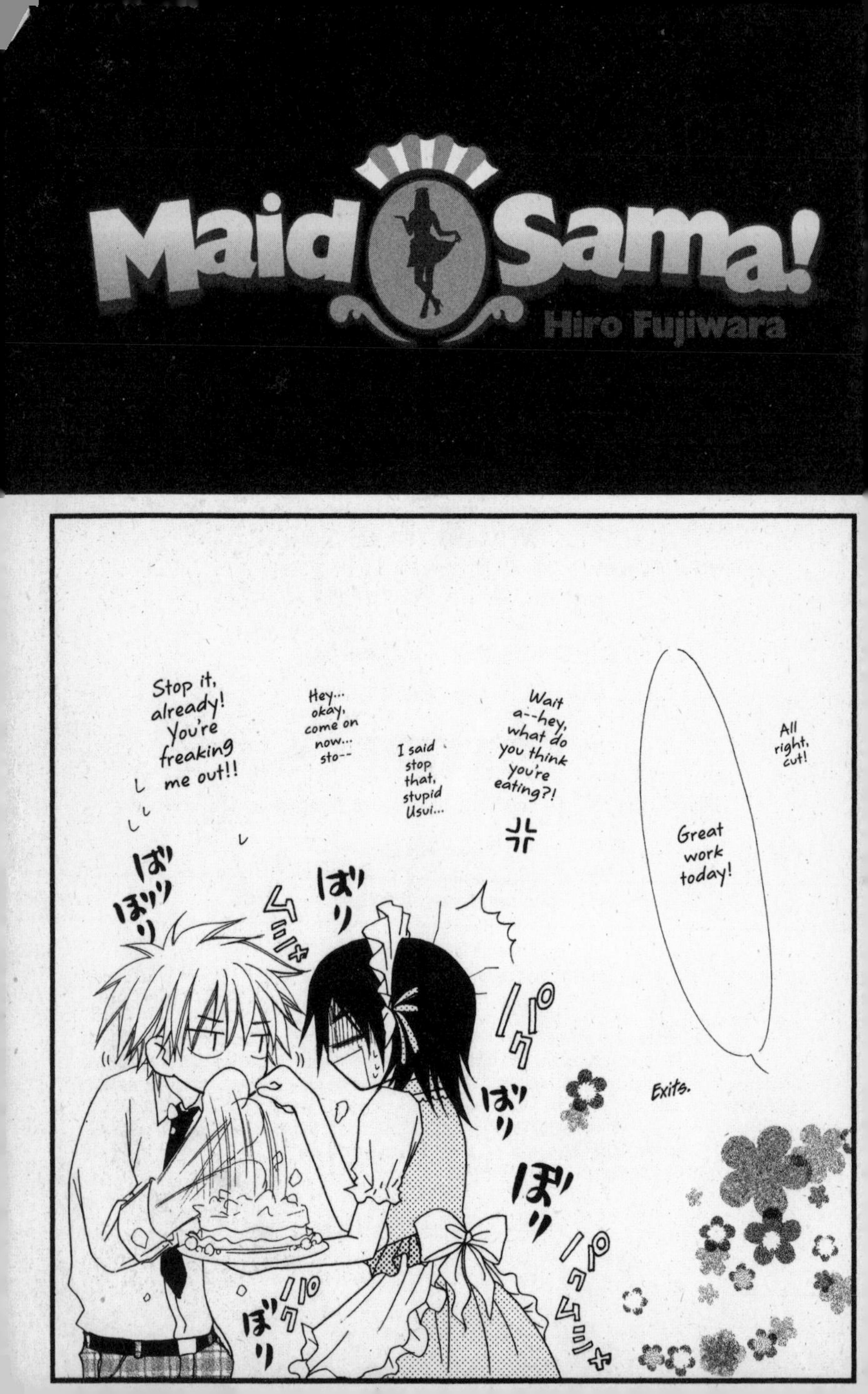
All right, cut!
Great work today!
Exits.
Wait a--hey, what do you think you're eating?!
I said stop that, stupid Usui...
Hey... okay, come on now... sto--
Stop it, already! You're freaking me out!!

Maid Sama! Volume 5
Created by Hiro Fujiwara

Translation - Su Mon Han
English Adaptation - Karen S. Ahlstrom
Retouch and Lettering - Star Print Brokers
Production Artist - Rui Kyo
Graphic Designer - Louis Csontos

Editor - Lillian Diaz-Przybyl
Print Production Manager - Lucas Rivera
Managing Editor - Vy Nguyen
Senior Designer - Louis Csontos
Art Director - Al-Insan Lashley
Director of Sales and Manufacturing - Allyson De Simone
Associate Publisher - Marco F. Pavia
President and C.O.O. - John Parker
C.E.O. and Chief Creative Officer - Stu Levy

A  Manga

TOKYOPOP Inc.
5900 Wilshire Blvd. Suite 2000
Los Angeles, CA 90036

E-mail: info@TOKYOPOP.com
Come visit us online at www.TOKYOPOP.com

ISBN: 978-1-4278-1689-4

First TOKYOPOP printing: July 2010
10 9 8 7 6 5 4 3 2 1
Printed in the USA

Maid Sama!

Hiro Fujiwara

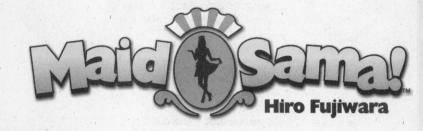

Vol. 5

by
Hiro Fujiwara

TOKYOPOP®

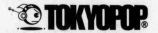

HAMBURG // LONDON // LOS ANGELES // TOKYO

♡ WELCOME HOME, MASTER! ♡

Please allow me to introduce all the ladies and gentlemen who appeared in the previous volume.♥

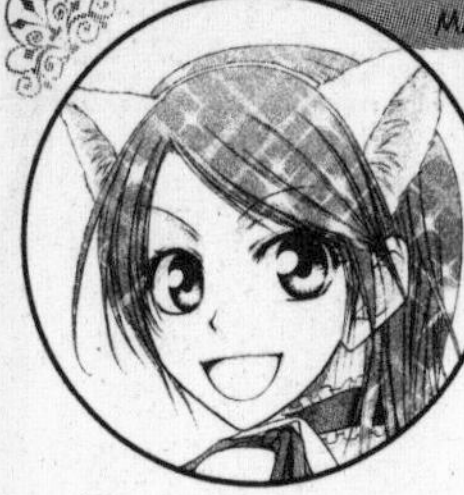

Maid

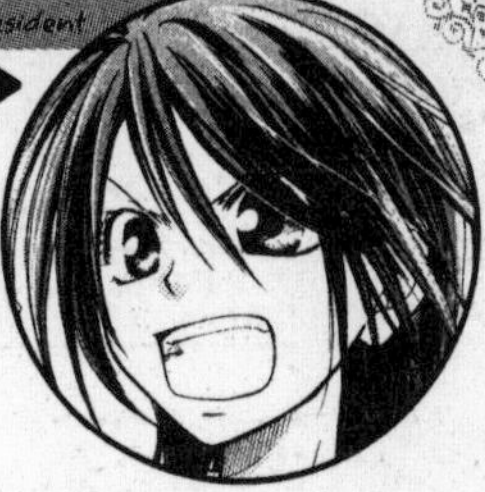

President

MISAKI AYUZAWA (HIGH SCHOOL JUNIOR)

AN INDOMITABLE STUDENT COUNCIL PRESIDENT BY DAY, BUT A WAITRESS AT A MAID CAFE BY NIGHT!! BRILLIANT BOTH IN ACADEMICS AND ATHLETICS, HER SPECIALTY IS AIKIDO (ALL ACHIEVED THROUGH MASSIVE HARD WORK AND DEDICATION). AT WORK, THEY CALL HER MISA-CHAN-- A SMART, COOL-HEADED MAID!

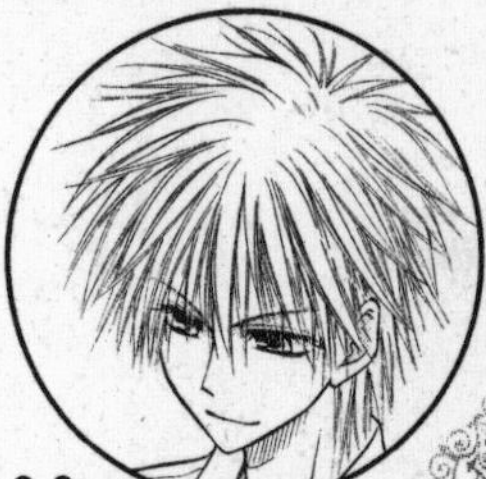

TAKUMI USUI (HIGH SCHOOL JUNIOR)

THE SCHOOL HEARTTHROB. HE ACCIDENTALLY DISCOVERED MISAKI'S SECRET AND, INTRIGUED, HAS TAKEN TO FOLLOWING HER AROUND. HE'S SUPER SMART, GREAT AT SPORTS, AS GORGEOUS AS THEY COME AND UNBEATABLE IN A FIGHT--THE PERFECT MAN. BUT AS FAR AS MISAKI'S CONCERNED, HE'S ALSO THE DEMON KING OF SEXUAL HARASSMENT. LATELY, HE'S BECOME MAID LATTE'S #1 CUSTOMER.

SEIKA HIGH SCHOOL

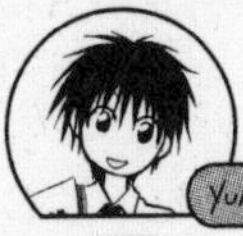

Yukimura

THE VICE PRESIDENT OF THE STUDENT COUNCIL. HIDDEN IN MISAKI'S SHADOW, HE ALWAYS TRIES TO DO HIS BEST.

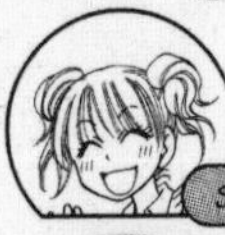

Sakura

ONE OF MISAKI'S PRECIOUS FEW FEMALE CLASSMATES. "MISAKI, WE LOVE YOU!"♥

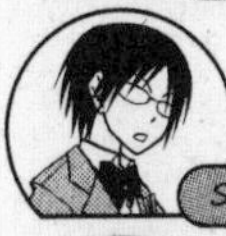

Shizuko

A FRIEND OF MISAKI AND SAKURA. SHE'S ALWAYS COOL AND LEVELHEADED.

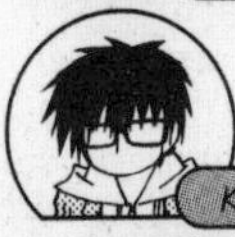

Kanou

A FIRST-YEAR STUDENT PROFICIENT IN HYPNOTISM. HE'S UNCOMFORTABLE WITH WOMEN.

The Idiot Trio

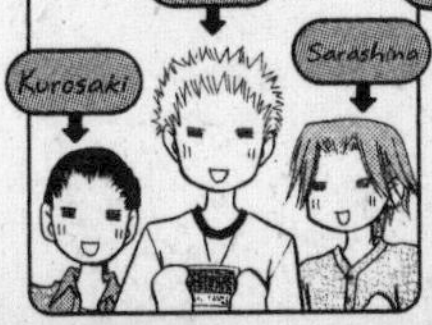
Shirokawa
Kurosaki
Sarashina

FORMERLY OPPOSED TO THE PRESIDENT, THESE THREE DISCOVERED MISAKI'S SECRET AND ENDED UP BECOMING HUGE FANS OF MISA-CHAN.

Cafe Maid Latte

MISAKI'S PART-TIME JOB--THE STAFF ALL EAGERLY AWAIT YOUR RETURN, MASTER. ♥

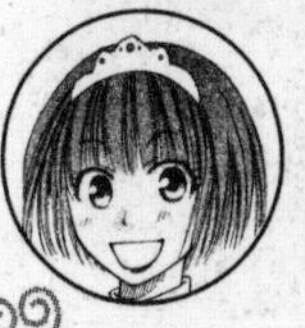

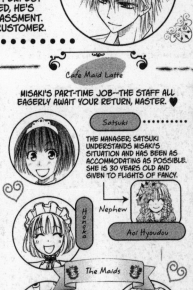

Satsuki

THE MANAGER; SATSUKI UNDERSTANDS MISAKI'S SITUATION AND HAS BEEN AS ACCOMMODATING AS POSSIBLE. SHE IS 30 YEARS OLD AND GIVEN TO FLIGHTS OF FANCY.

Nephew

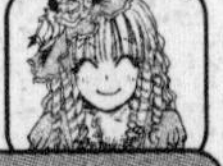

Aoi Hyoudou

The Maids

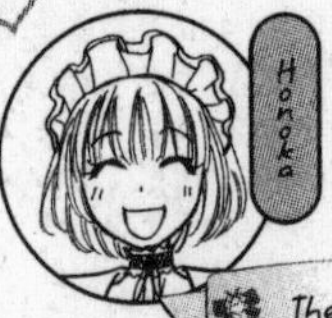

Honoka

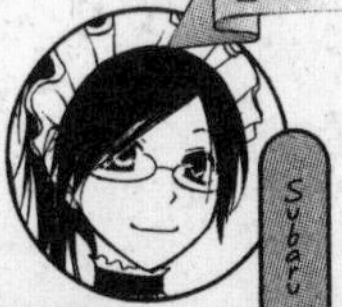

Subaru

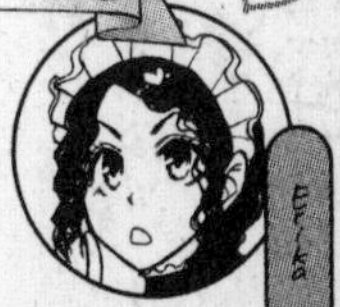

Erika

Other

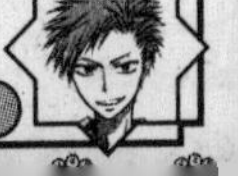

STUDENT COUNCIL PRESIDENT OF THE OBSCENELY RICH MIYABI GAOKA ACADEMY.

Tora Igarashi

♡ NOW, PLEASE ALLOW ME TO SUMMARIZE THE EVENTS OF THE PREVIOUS VOLUME. ♡

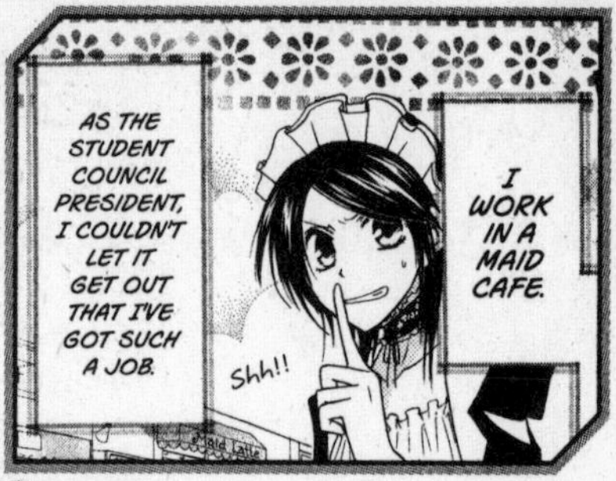

I WORK IN A MAID CAFE.
AS THE STUDENT COUNCIL PRESIDENT, I COULDN'T LET IT GET OUT THAT I'VE GOT SUCH A JOB.
Shh!!

MISAKI, THE STUDENT COUNCIL PRESIDENT OF THE PREVIOUSLY ALL-MALE SEIKA HIGH SCHOOL, SPENDS HER DAYS VALIANTLY BATTLING TO PROTECT THE FEMALE STUDENT BODY AND KEEP THE BOYS FROM RUNNING AMOK. HOWEVER, BRAVE MISAKI HAS A LITTLE SECRET--SHE WORKS AT A MAID CAFE! NOW CONSTANTLY TAILED BY USUI--WHO DISCOVERED HER SECRET BY ACCIDENT--MISAKI MUST FIND A WAY TO CONTINUE HER CRAZY DOUBLE LIFE AS A MAID AND A PRESIDENT! ♥

WHILE MISAKI WAS JUGGLING ALL THIS, SEIKA HIGH SCHOOL HELD AN OPEN HOUSE EVENT TO ATTRACT GRADUATING MIDDLE SCHOOLERS TO SEIKA. WITH THE HELP OF USUI AND FIRST-YEAR STUDENT KANOU, THE GIRLS WERE ABLE TO PUT ON A MAID CAFÉ-LIKE DINING HALL EVENT. THE FEMALE PROSPECTIVE STUDENTS REACTED SO FAVORABLY THAT WE HAVE A FEELING THERE WILL BE MANY MORE GIRLS STARTING AT SEIKA IN THE NEW SCHOOL YEAR!

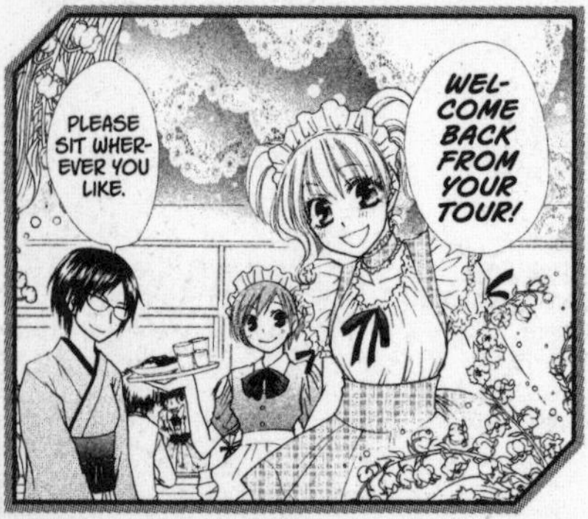

WEL-COME BACK FROM YOUR TOUR!
PLEASE SIT WHER-EVER YOU LIKE.

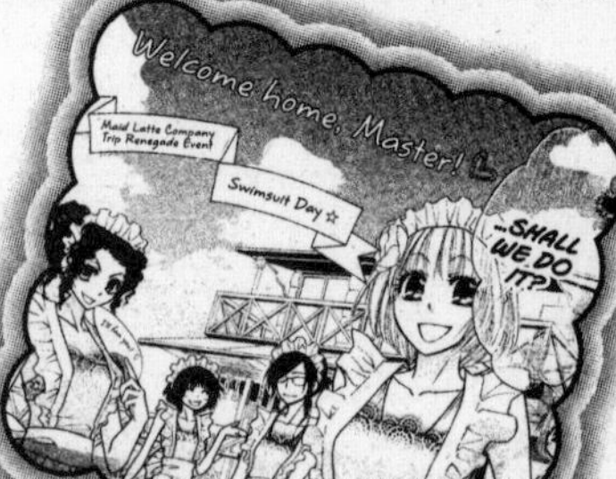

Welcome home, Master! ♥
Maid Latte Company Trip Renegade Event
Swimsuit Day ☆
...SHALL WE DO IT?

MEANWHILE, THE ENTIRE STAFF OF MAID LATTE PLUS USUI HEADED TO THE BEACH FOR A COMPANY TRIP! THINGS BEGAN HEATING UP AT THEIR BEACHSIDE INN WHEN ALL THE GIRLS DRESSED UP AS SWIMSUIT-CLAD MAIDS. ♥ THEN, MISAKI AND USUI FACE OFF AS OPPONENTS DURING A BEACH VOLLEYBALL TOURNAMENT! HOWEVER, DURING THE FINAL ROUND, USUI GETS INJURED...PROTECTING MISAKI!

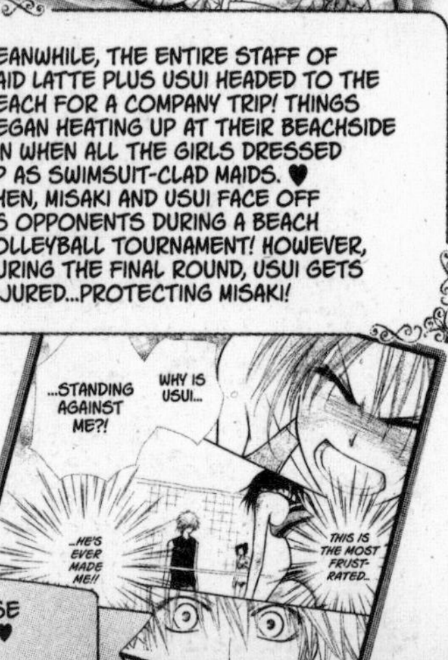

WHY IS USUI...
...STANDING AGAINST ME?!
THIS IS THE MOST FRUST-RATED...
...HE'S EVER MADE ME!!

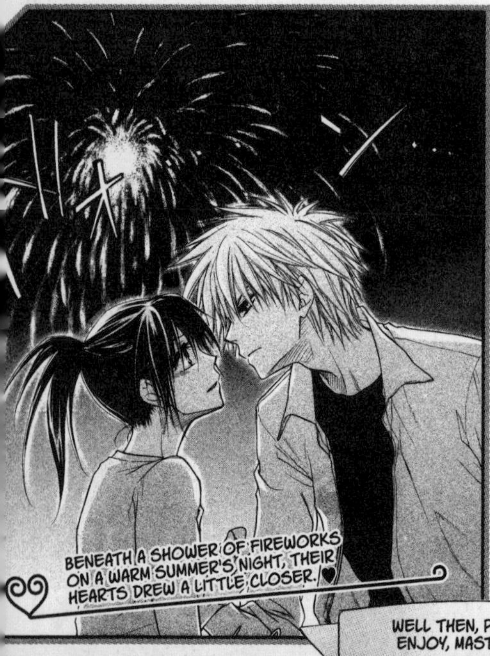

BENEATH A SHOWER OF FIREWORKS ON A WARM SUMMER'S NIGHT, THEIR HEARTS DREW A LITTLE CLOSER. ♥

WELL THEN, PLEASE ENJOY, MASTER! ♥

Cafe Maid Latte

5

— CONTENTS —

Cafe Maid Latte

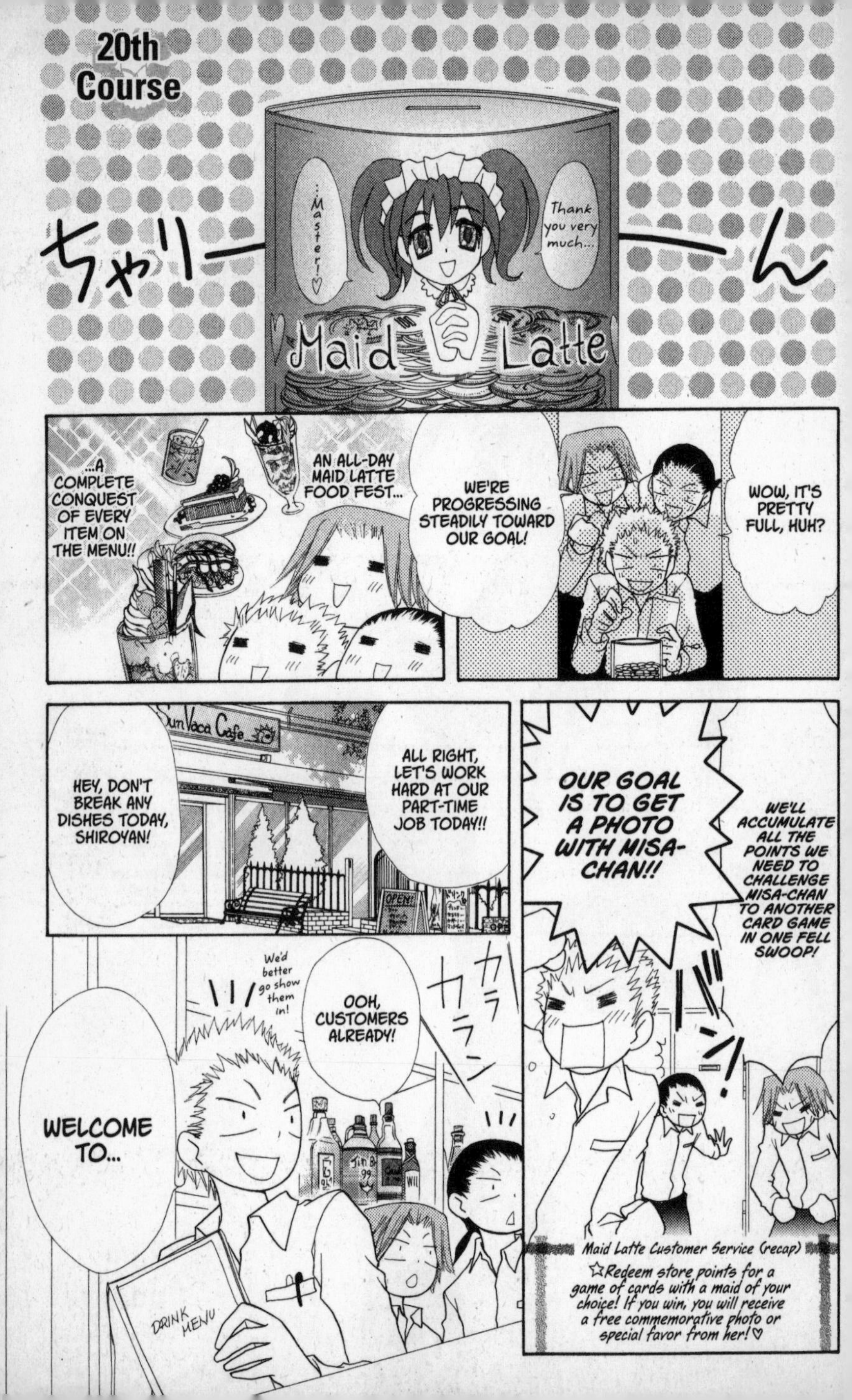
20th Course
ちゃりーーん
Thank you very much...
...Master!♡
Maid Latte
WOW, IT'S PRETTY FULL, HUH?
WE'RE PROGRESSING STEADILY TOWARD OUR GOAL!
AN ALL-DAY MAID LATTE FOOD FEST...
...A COMPLETE CONQUEST OF EVERY ITEM ON THE MENU!!
OUR GOAL IS TO GET A PHOTO WITH MISA-CHAN!!
WE'LL ACCUMULATE ALL THE POINTS WE NEED TO CHALLENGE MISA-CHAN TO ANOTHER CARD GAME IN ONE FELL SWOOP!
ドーン!
Maid Latte Customer Service (recap)
☆Redeem store points for a game of cards with a maid of your choice! If you win, you will receive a free commemorative photo or special favor from her!♡
Sun Vaca Cafe
ALL RIGHT, LET'S WORK HARD AT OUR PART-TIME JOB TODAY!!
HEY, DON'T BREAK ANY DISHES TODAY, SHIROYAN!
OPEN!
カラン カラン
OOH, CUSTOMERS ALREADY!
We'd better go show them in!
WELCOME TO...
DRINK MENU

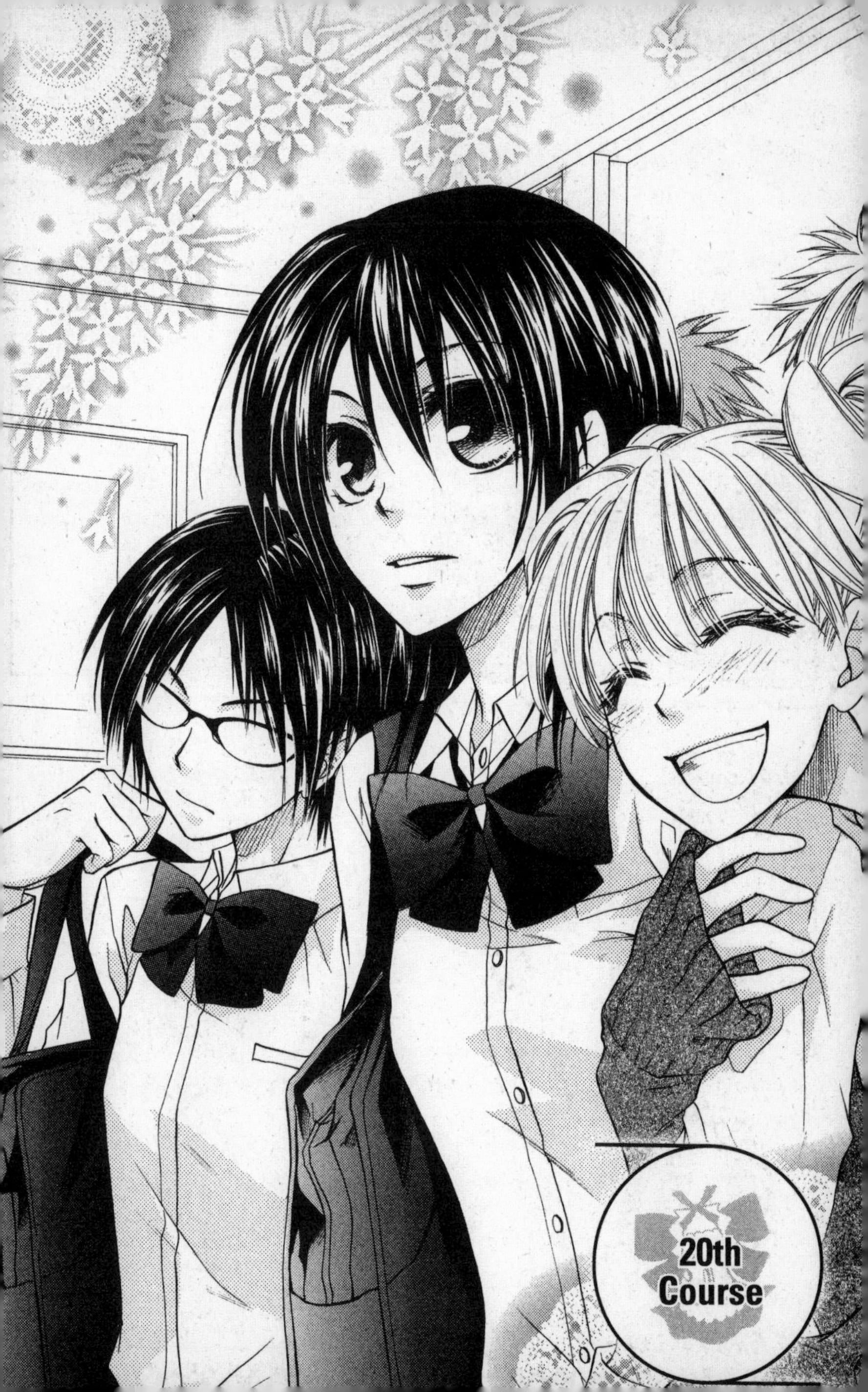
20th Course

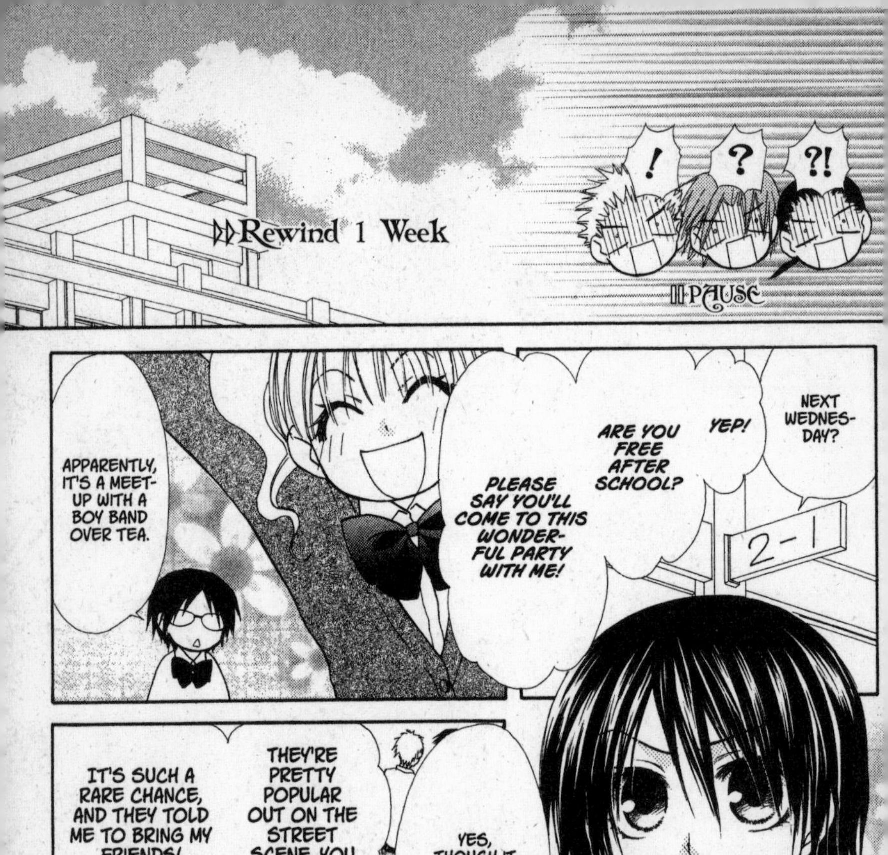
!
?
?!
PAUSE
Rewind 1 Week
NEXT WEDNESDAY?
YEP!
ARE YOU FREE AFTER SCHOOL?
PLEASE SAY YOU'LL COME TO THIS WONDERFUL PARTY WITH ME!
2-1
APPARENTLY, IT'S A MEET-UP WITH A BOY BAND OVER TEA.
BOY BAND?
YES, THOUGH IT SEEMS THEY'RE ALSO STUDENTS AT YUMESAKI HIGH SCHOOL.
They're only an amateur band.
THEY'RE PRETTY POPULAR OUT ON THE STREET SCENE, YOU KNOW!
IT'S SUCH A RARE CHANCE, AND THEY TOLD ME TO BRING MY FRIENDS! ♡

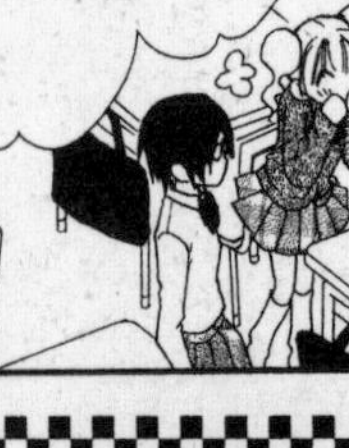

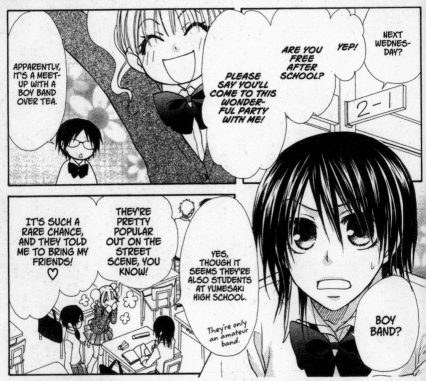

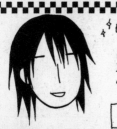

Extraneous Question Corner

Question 1

Hello, I'm the author. I was thinking I'd use these spaces to answer the questions I've received from readers.

Right off the bat, a question that really fills in the gaps...

Q: Which do you prefer on your fried eggs: Worcestershire sauce, or soy sauce?

Hi, there. I'm Fujiwara.

A: Salt and pepper.

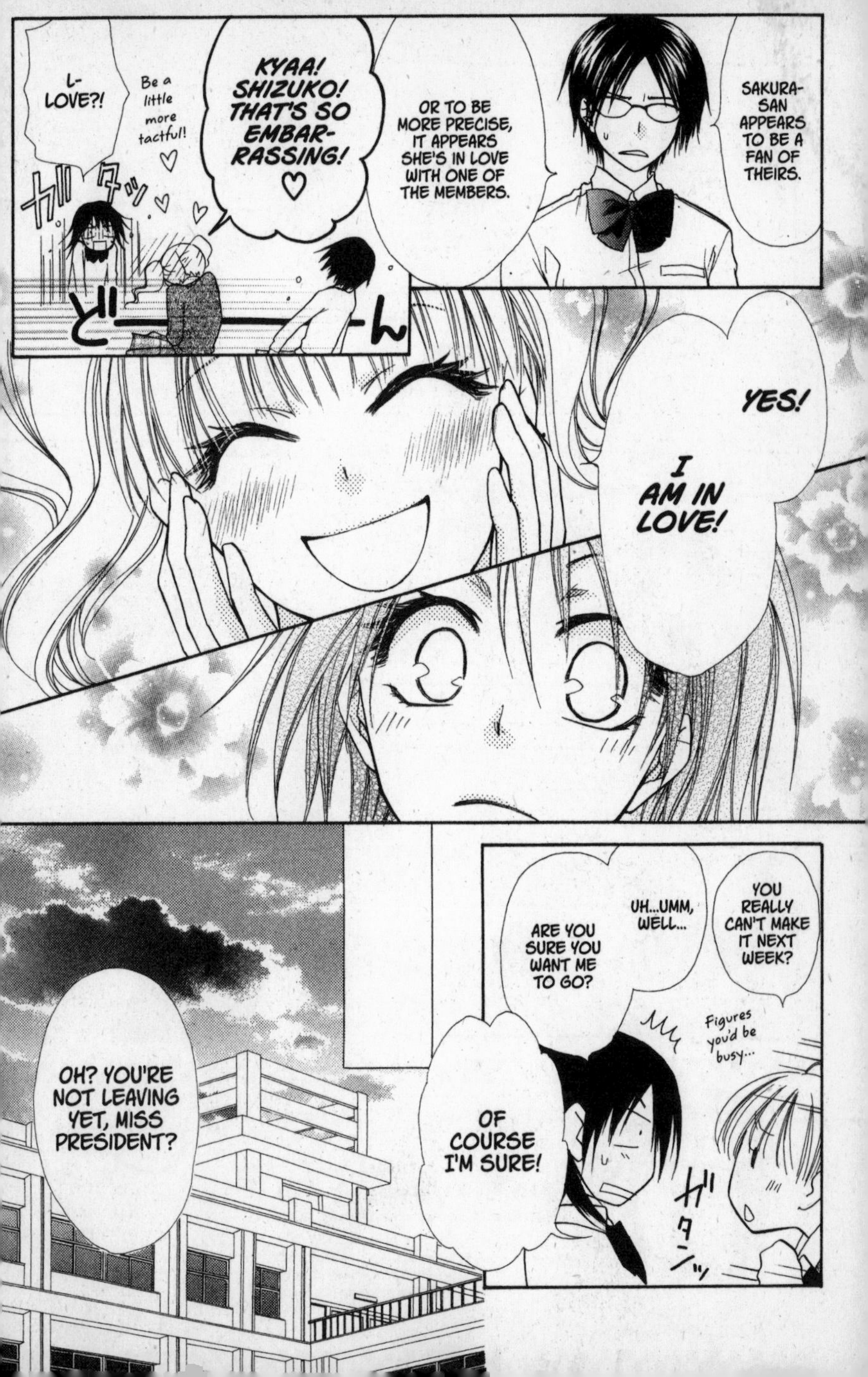
SAKURA-SAN APPEARS TO BE A FAN OF THEIRS.
OR TO BE MORE PRECISE, IT APPEARS SHE'S IN LOVE WITH ONE OF THE MEMBERS.
KYAA! SHIZUKO! THAT'S SO EMBARRASSING! ♡
Be a little more tactful! ♡
L-LOVE?!
YES!
I AM IN LOVE!
YOU REALLY CAN'T MAKE IT NEXT WEEK?
UH...UMM, WELL...
ARE YOU SURE YOU WANT ME TO GO?
Figures you'd be busy...
OF COURSE I'M SURE!
OH? YOU'RE NOT LEAVING YET, MISS PRESIDENT?

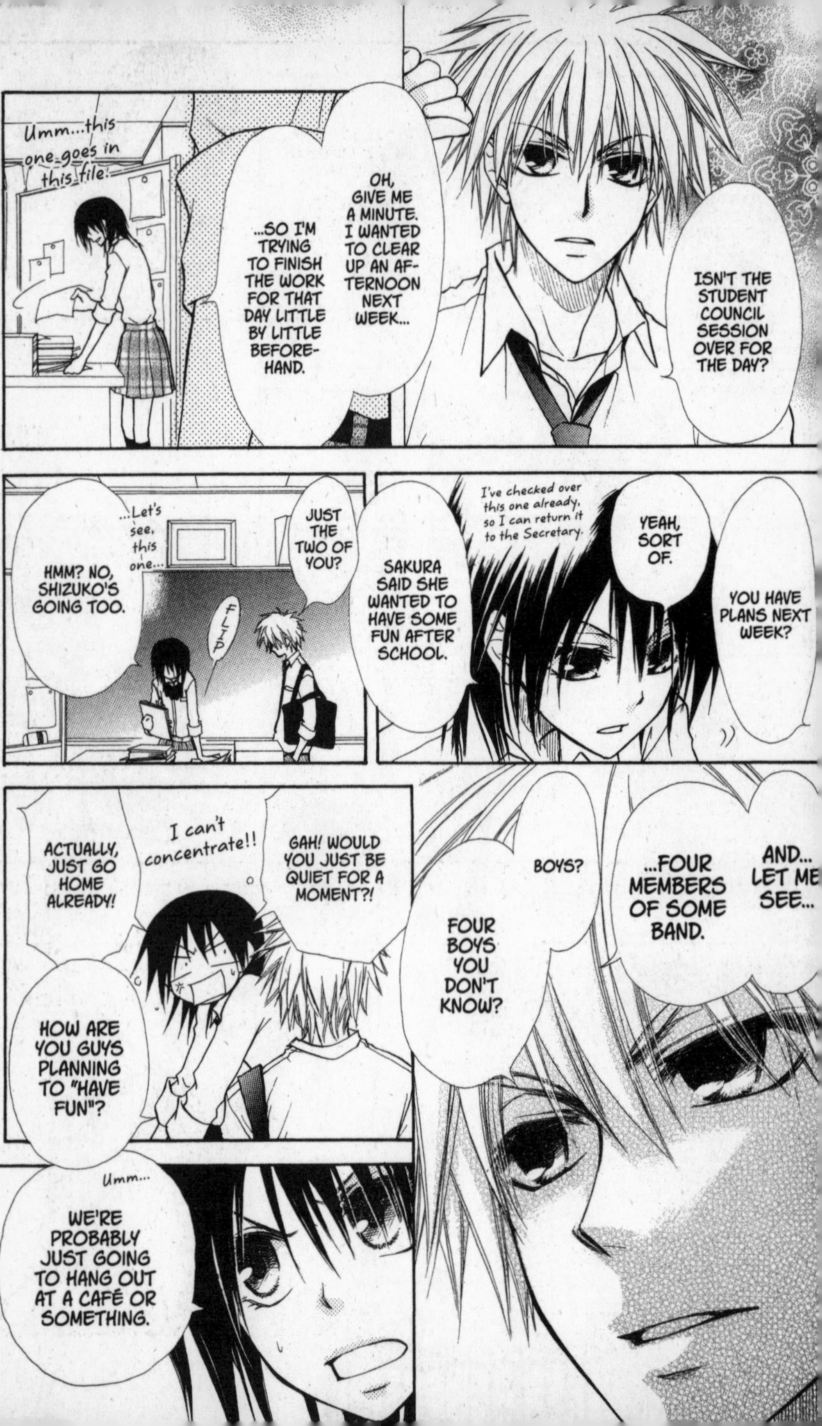
ISN'T THE STUDENT COUNCIL SESSION OVER FOR THE DAY?
OH, GIVE ME A MINUTE. I WANTED TO CLEAR UP AN AFTERNOON NEXT WEEK...
...SO I'M TRYING TO FINISH THE WORK FOR THAT DAY LITTLE BY LITTLE BEFOREHAND.
Umm...this one goes in this file.
YOU HAVE PLANS NEXT WEEK?
YEAH, SORT OF.
I've checked over this one already, so I can return it to the Secretary.
SAKURA SAID SHE WANTED TO HAVE SOME FUN AFTER SCHOOL.
JUST THE TWO OF YOU?
HMM? NO, SHIZUKO'S GOING TOO.
...Let's see, this one...
FLIP
AND... LET ME SEE...
...FOUR MEMBERS OF SOME BAND.
BOYS?
FOUR BOYS YOU DON'T KNOW?
GAH! WOULD YOU JUST BE QUIET FOR A MOMENT?!
I can't concentrate!!
ACTUALLY, JUST GO HOME ALREADY!
HOW ARE YOU GUYS PLANNING TO "HAVE FUN"?
Umm...
WE'RE PROBABLY JUST GOING TO HANG OUT AT A CAFÉ OR SOMETHING.

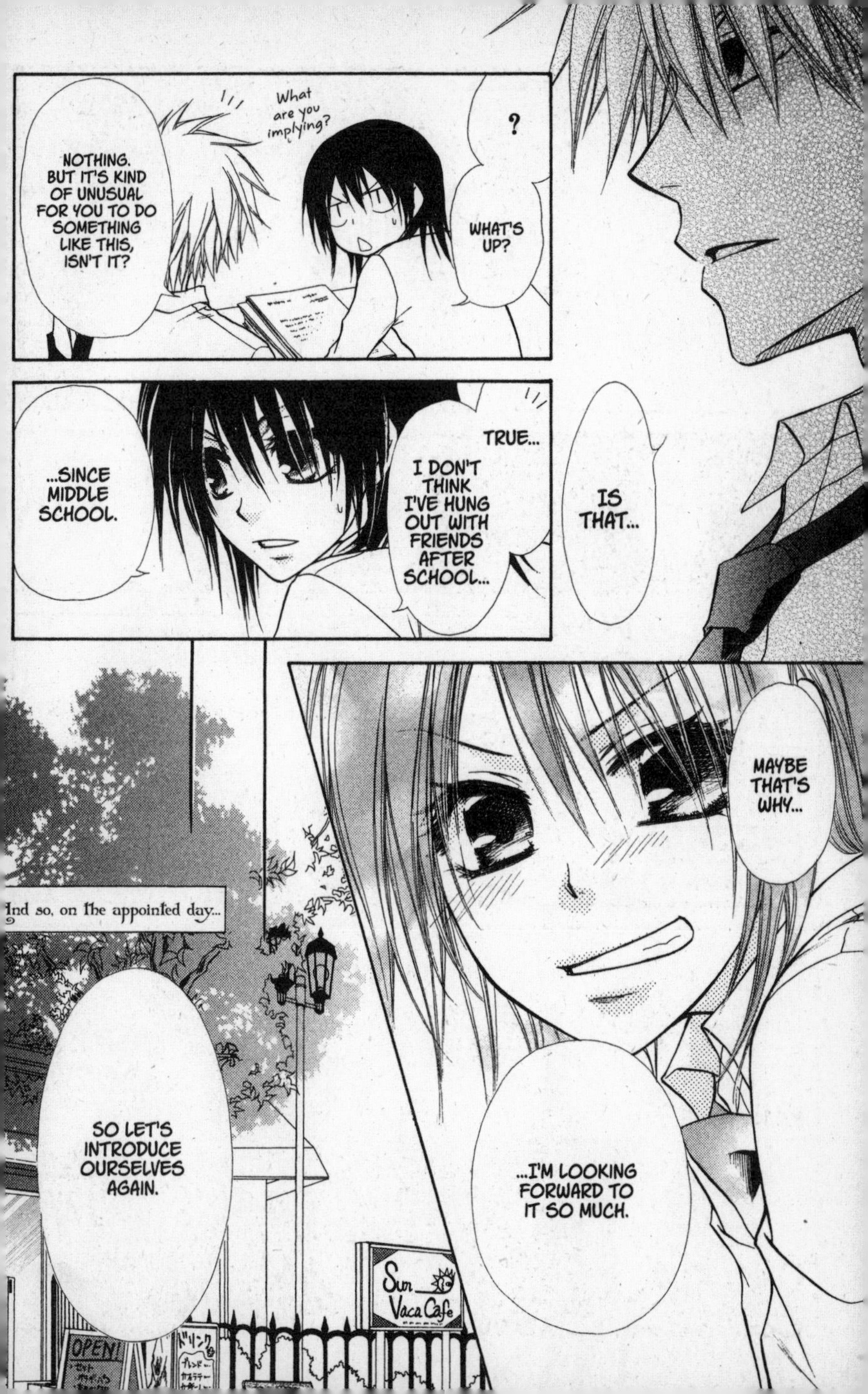
?
WHAT'S UP?
NOTHING. BUT IT'S KIND OF UNUSUAL FOR YOU TO DO SOMETHING LIKE THIS, ISN'T IT?
What are you implying?
TRUE...
I DON'T THINK I'VE HUNG OUT WITH FRIENDS AFTER SCHOOL...
...SINCE MIDDLE SCHOOL.
IS THAT...
MAYBE THAT'S WHY...
...I'M LOOKING FORWARD TO IT SO MUCH.
And so, on the appointed day...
SO LET'S INTRODUCE OURSELVES AGAIN.
Sun Vaca Cafe
OPEN!

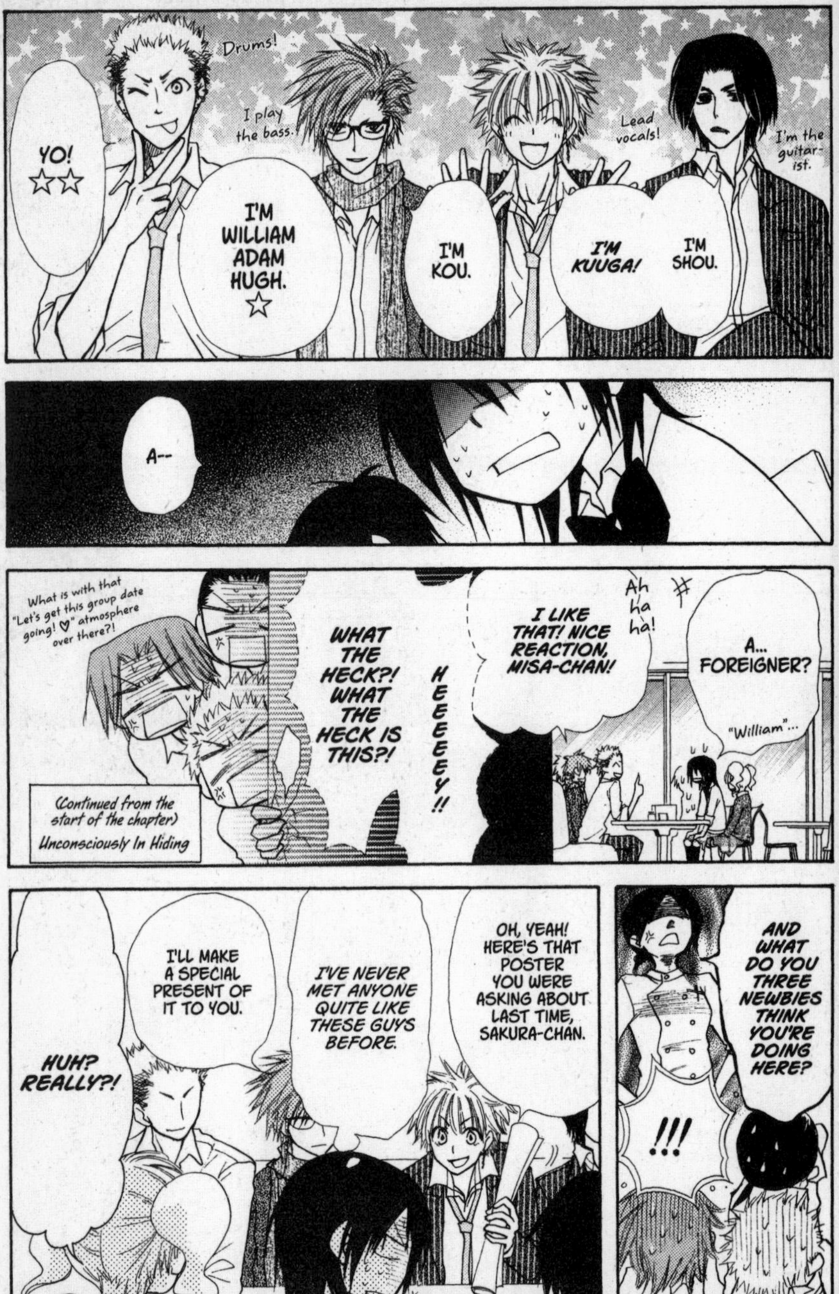
I'm the guitarist.
I'M SHOU.
Lead vocals!
I'M KUUGA!
I'M KOU.
I play the bass.
I'M WILLIAM ADAM HUGH. ☆
Drums!
YO! ☆☆
A--
A... FOREIGNER?
"William"...
Ah ha ha!
I LIKE THAT! NICE REACTION, MISA-CHAN!
HEEEEEY!!
WHAT THE HECK?! WHAT THE HECK IS THIS?!
What is with that "Let's get this group date going! ♡" atmosphere over there?!
(Continued from the start of the chapter) Unconsciously In Hiding
AND WHAT DO YOU THREE NEWBIES THINK YOU'RE DOING HERE?
!!!
OH, YEAH! HERE'S THAT POSTER YOU WERE ASKING ABOUT LAST TIME, SAKURA-CHAN.
I'VE NEVER MET ANYONE QUITE LIKE THESE GUYS BEFORE.
I'LL MAKE A SPECIAL PRESENT OF IT TO YOU.
HUH? REALLY?!

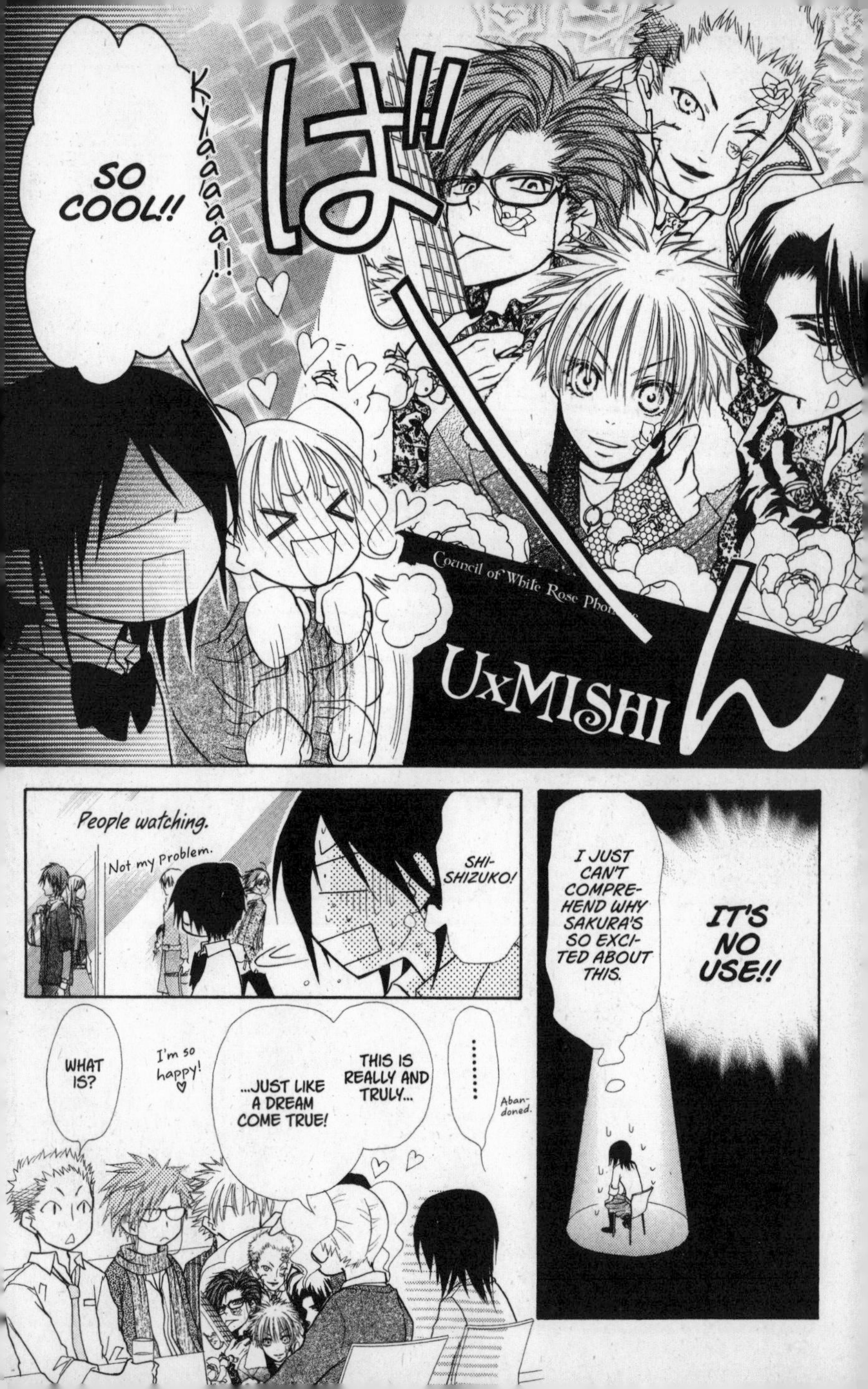
ば
ん
Council of White Rose Pho
UxMISHI
Kyaaaaaa!!
SO COOL!!
IT'S NO USE!!
I JUST CAN'T COMPREHEND WHY SAKURA'S SO EXCITED ABOUT THIS.
SHI-SHIZUKO!
People watching.
Not my Problem.
......
Aban-doned.
THIS IS REALLY AND TRULY...
...JUST LIKE A DREAM COME TRUE!
I'm so happy! ♡
WHAT IS?

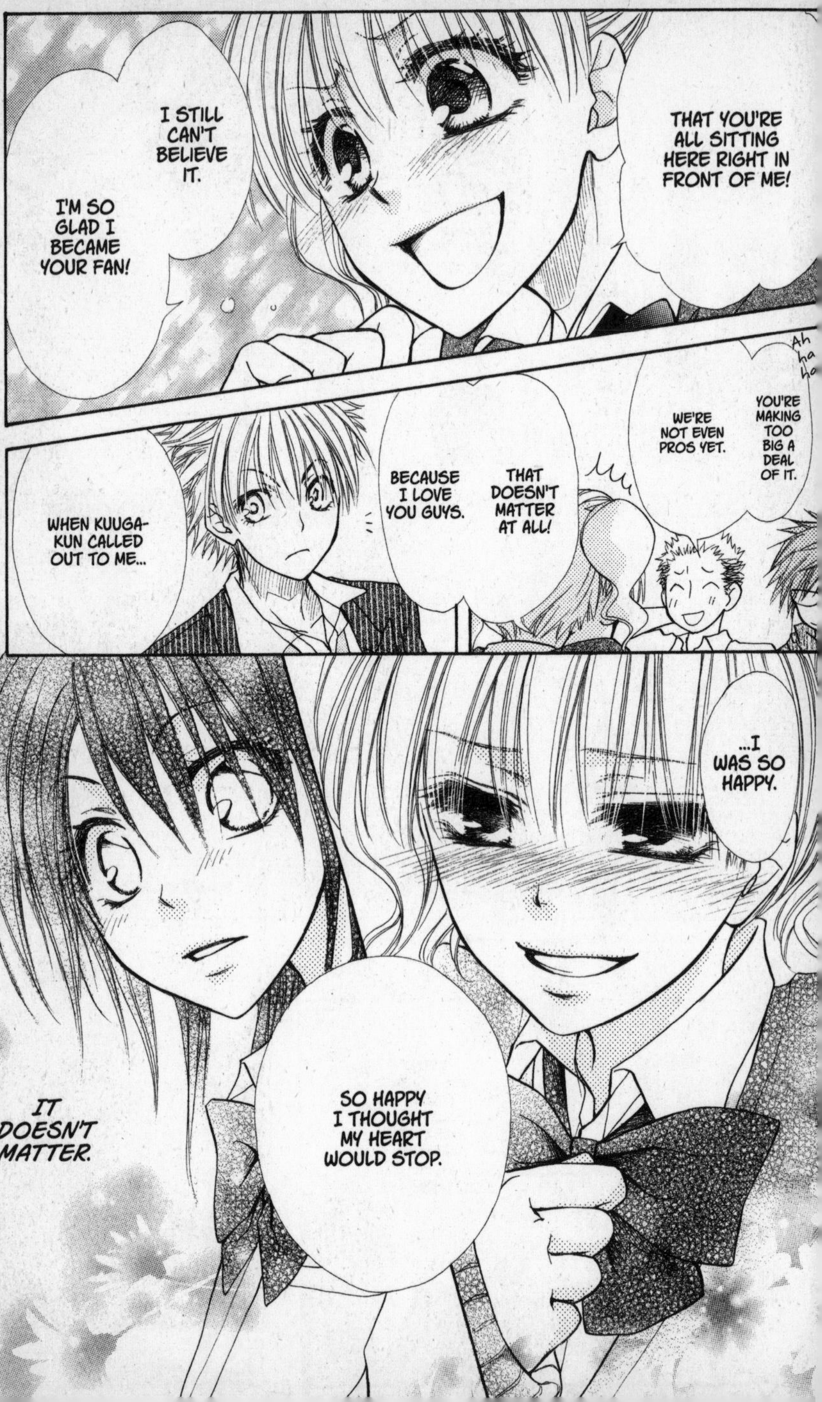
I STILL CAN'T BELIEVE IT.
THAT YOU'RE ALL SITTING HERE RIGHT IN FRONT OF ME!
I'M SO GLAD I BECAME YOUR FAN!
Ah ha ha
YOU'RE MAKING TOO BIG A DEAL OF IT.
WE'RE NOT EVEN PROS YET.
THAT DOESN'T MATTER AT ALL!
BECAUSE I LOVE YOU GUYS.
WHEN KUUGA-KUN CALLED OUT TO ME...
...I WAS SO HAPPY.
SO HAPPY I THOUGHT MY HEART WOULD STOP.
IT DOESN'T MATTER.

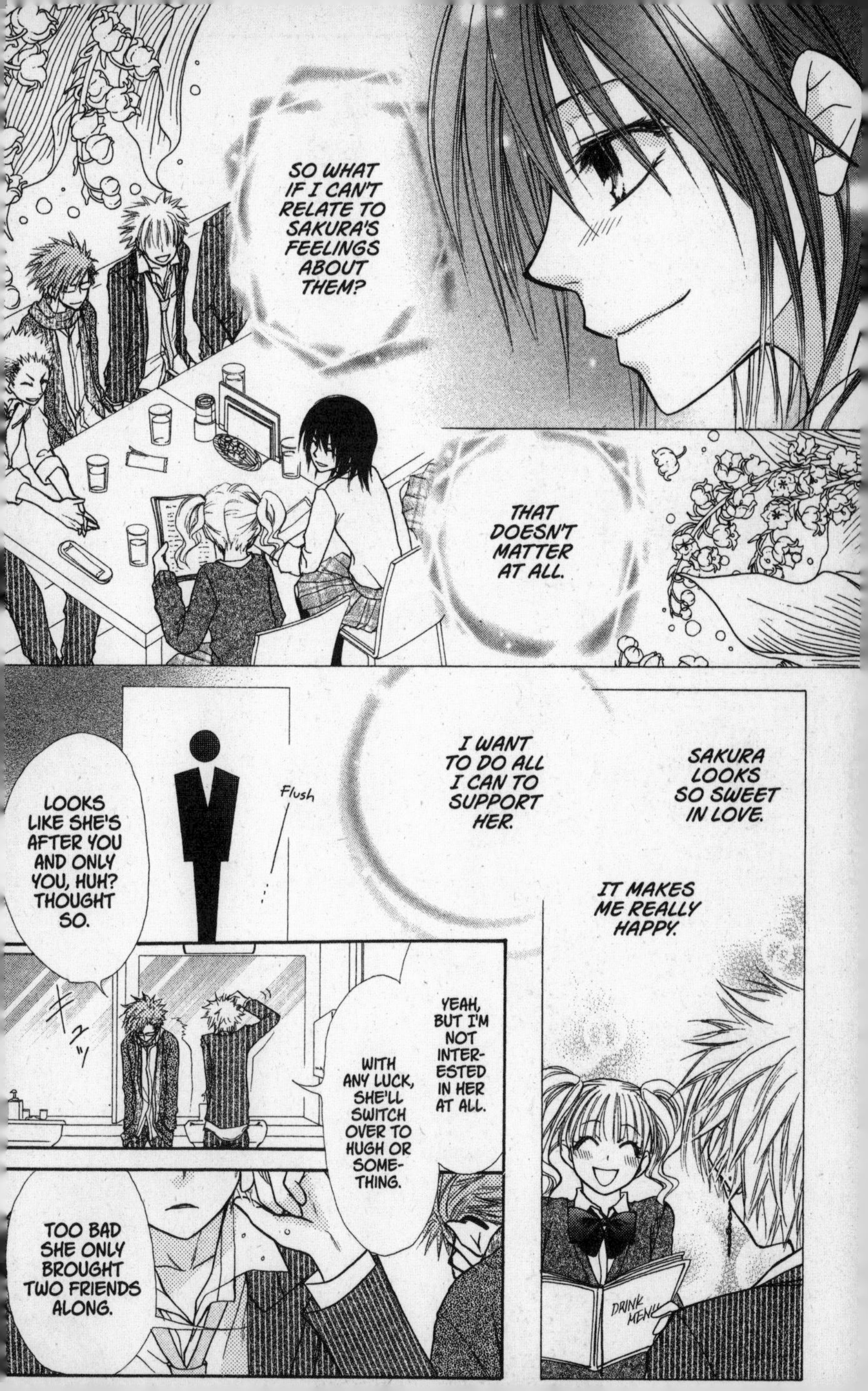
SO WHAT IF I CAN'T RELATE TO SAKURA'S FEELINGS ABOUT THEM?
THAT DOESN'T MATTER AT ALL.
SAKURA LOOKS SO SWEET IN LOVE.
IT MAKES ME REALLY HAPPY.
I WANT TO DO ALL I CAN TO SUPPORT HER.
DRINK MENU
Flush
LOOKS LIKE SHE'S AFTER YOU AND ONLY YOU, HUH? THOUGHT SO.
YEAH, BUT I'M NOT INTER-ESTED IN HER AT ALL.
WITH ANY LUCK, SHE'LL SWITCH OVER TO HUGH OR SOME-THING.
TOO BAD SHE ONLY BROUGHT TWO FRIENDS ALONG.

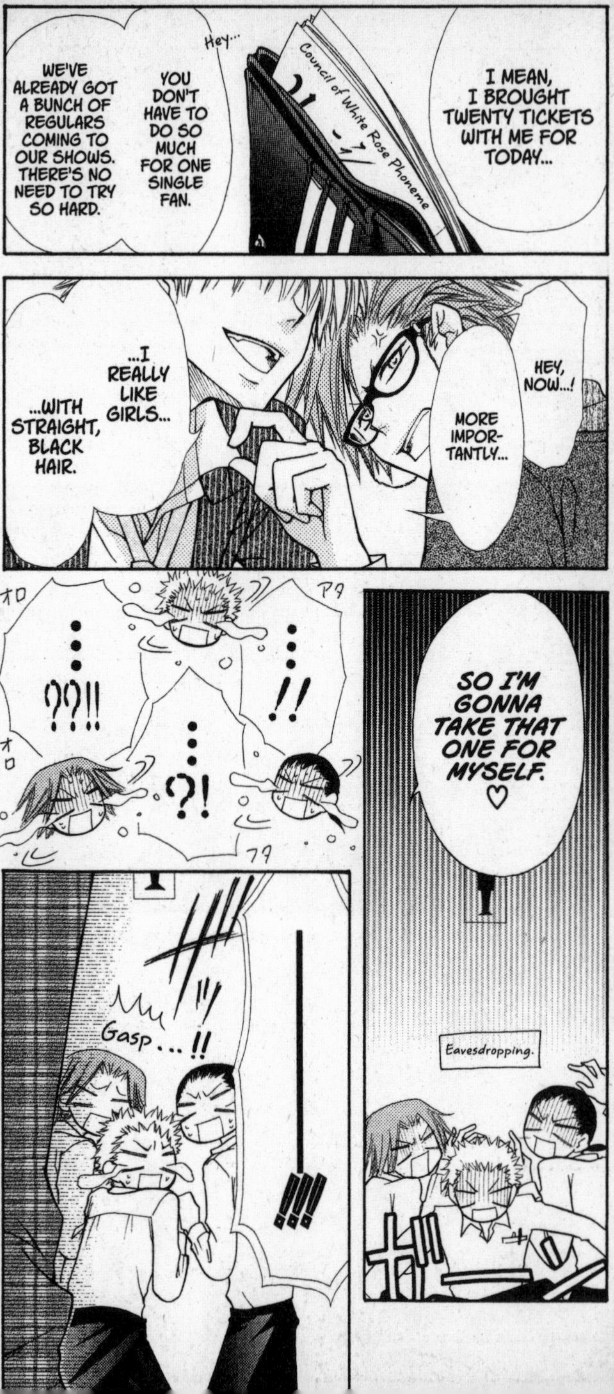
I MEAN, I BROUGHT TWENTY TICKETS WITH ME FOR TODAY...
Council of White Rose Phoneme
Hey...
YOU DON'T HAVE TO DO SO MUCH FOR ONE SINGLE FAN.
WE'VE ALREADY GOT A BUNCH OF REGULARS COMING TO OUR SHOWS. THERE'S NO NEED TO TRY SO HARD.
HEY, NOW...!
MORE IMPORTANTLY...
...I REALLY LIKE GIRLS...
...WITH STRAIGHT, BLACK HAIR.
SO I'M GONNA TAKE THAT ONE FOR MYSELF. ♡
Eavesdropping.
...!!
...??!!
...?!
Gasp...!!
!!!!

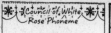

Council of White Rose Phoneme

UxMISHI

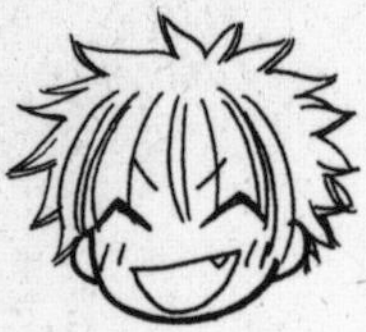

Vocalist

Kuuga (age 16)

Yumesaki High 1st Year
A self-centered, free-spirited individual.

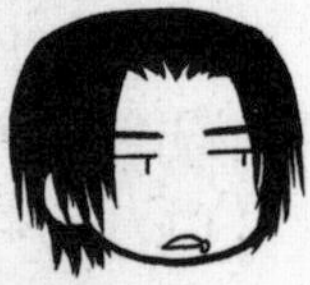

Guitarist

Shou (age 16)

Yumesaki High 1st Year
Another free spirit who moves at his own pace.

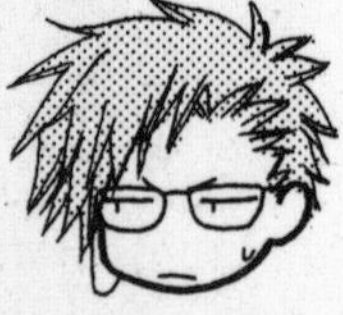

Bassist

Kou (age 17)

Yumesaki High 2nd Year
A cautious type, wise to the ways of the world.

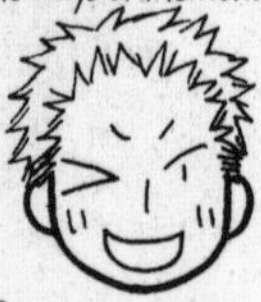

Drums

William Adam Hugh (age 17)

Yumesaki High 2nd Year
A hapless but good-hearted person.

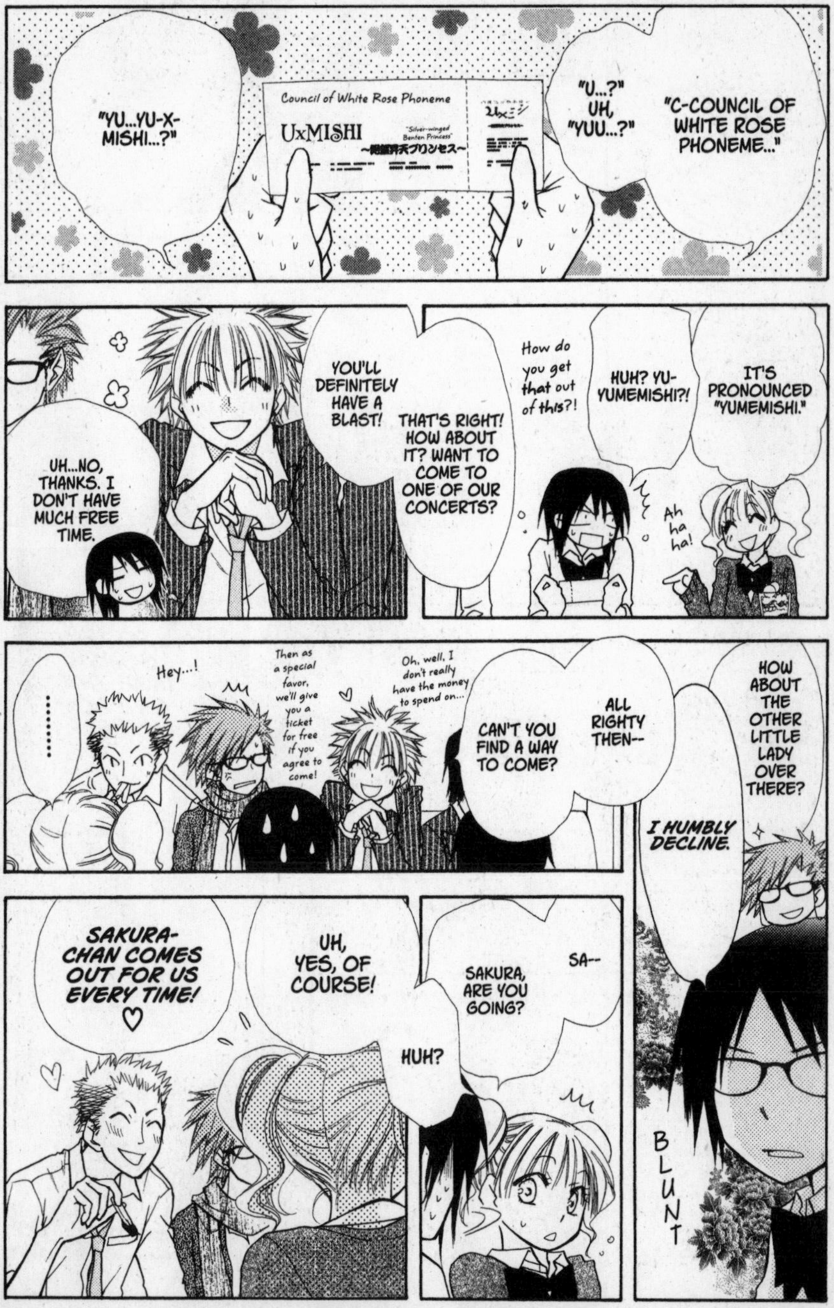
"C-COUNCIL OF WHITE ROSE PHONEME..."
"U...?" UH, "YUU...?"
Council of White Rose Phoneme
UxMISHI
"Silver-winged Benten Princess"
"YU...YU-X-MISHI...?"
IT'S PRONOUNCED "YUMEMISHI."
Ah ha ha!
HUH? YU-YUMEMISHI?!
How do you get that out of this?!
THAT'S RIGHT! HOW ABOUT IT? WANT TO COME TO ONE OF OUR CONCERTS?
YOU'LL DEFINITELY HAVE A BLAST!
UH...NO, THANKS. I DON'T HAVE MUCH FREE TIME.
HOW ABOUT THE OTHER LITTLE LADY OVER THERE?
I HUMBLY DECLINE.
BLUNT
ALL RIGHTY THEN--
CAN'T YOU FIND A WAY TO COME?
Oh, well, I don't really have the money to spend on...
Then as a special favor, we'll give you a ticket for free if you agree to come!
Hey...!
....
SA--
SAKURA, ARE YOU GOING?
HUH?
UH, YES, OF COURSE!
SAKURA-CHAN COMES OUT FOR US EVERY TIME! ♡

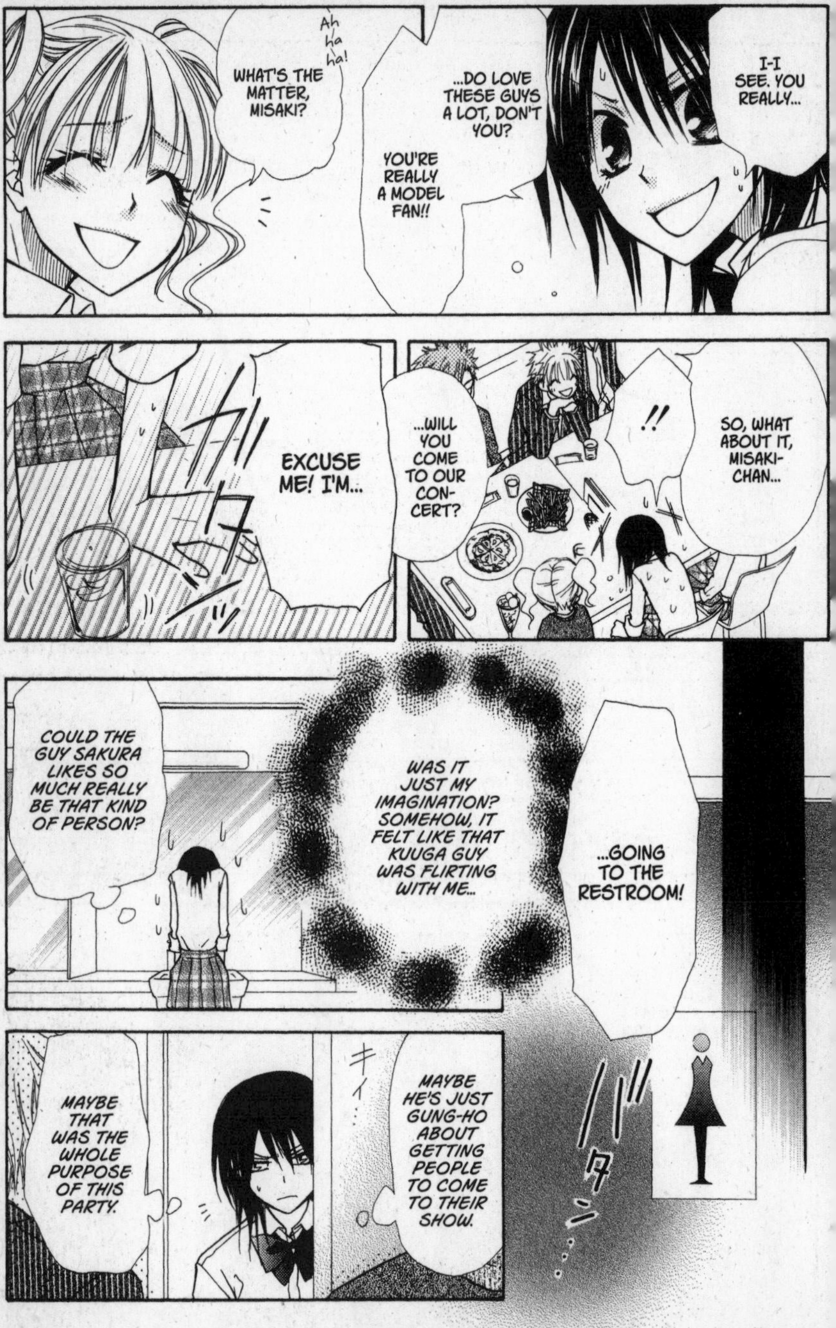
I-I SEE. YOU REALLY...
...DO LOVE THESE GUYS A LOT, DON'T YOU?
YOU'RE REALLY A MODEL FAN!!
Ah ha ha!
WHAT'S THE MATTER, MISAKI?
SO, WHAT ABOUT IT, MISAKI-CHAN...
!!
...WILL YOU COME TO OUR CON-CERT?
EXCUSE ME! I'M...
...GOING TO THE RESTROOM!
WAS IT JUST MY IMAGINATION? SOMEHOW, IT FELT LIKE THAT KUUGA GUY WAS FLIRTING WITH ME...
COULD THE GUY SAKURA LIKES SO MUCH REALLY BE THAT KIND OF PERSON?
MAYBE HE'S JUST GUNG-HO ABOUT GETTING PEOPLE TO COME TO THEIR SHOW.
MAYBE THAT WAS THE WHOLE PURPOSE OF THIS PARTY.

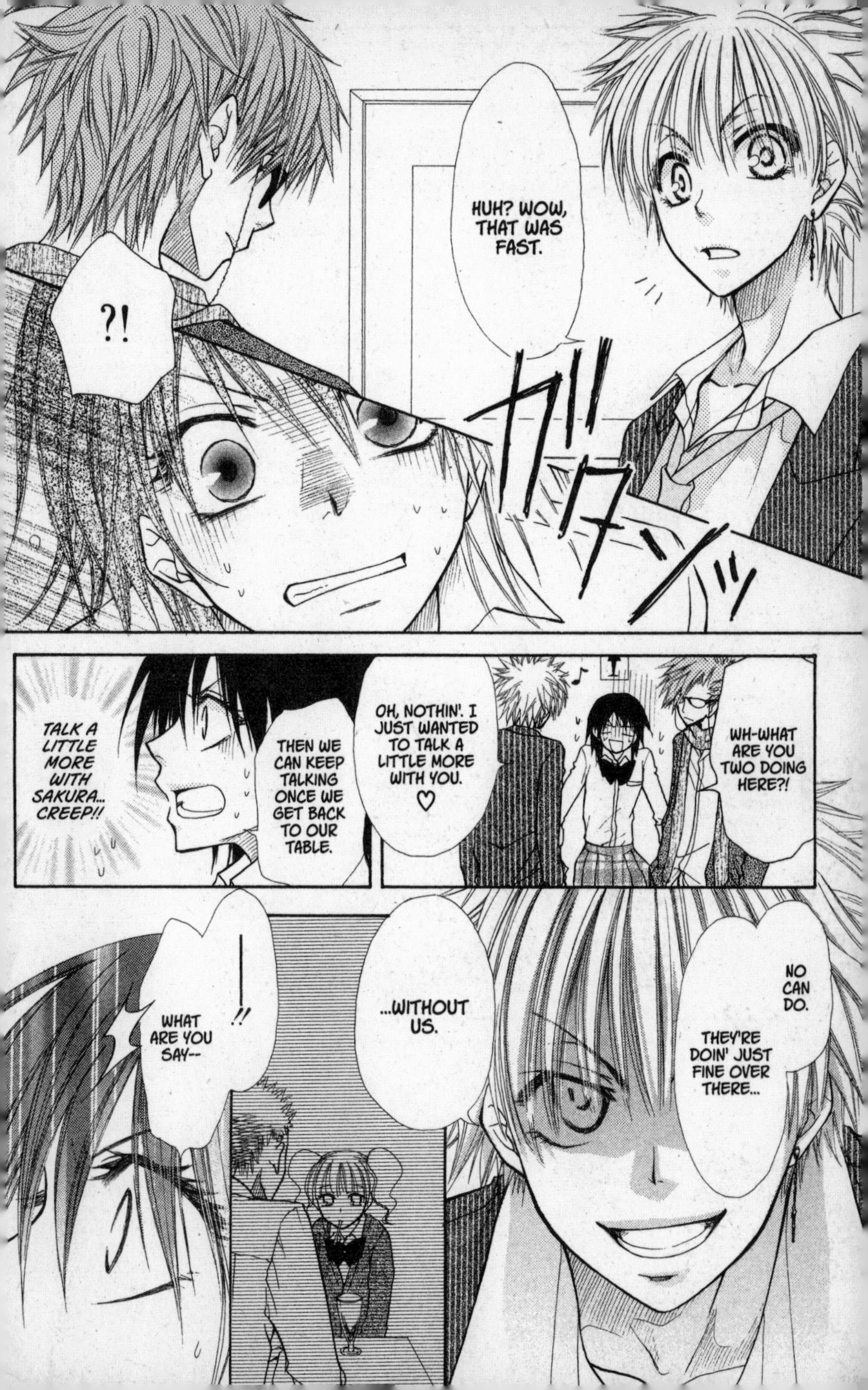
HUH? WOW, THAT WAS FAST.
?!
ガタンッ
WH-WHAT ARE YOU TWO DOING HERE?!
OH, NOTHIN'. I JUST WANTED TO TALK A LITTLE MORE WITH YOU. ♡
THEN WE CAN KEEP TALKING ONCE WE GET BACK TO OUR TABLE.
TALK A LITTLE MORE WITH SAKURA... CREEP!!
NO CAN DO.
THEY'RE DOIN' JUST FINE OVER THERE...
...WITHOUT US.
—!!
WHAT ARE YOU SAY--

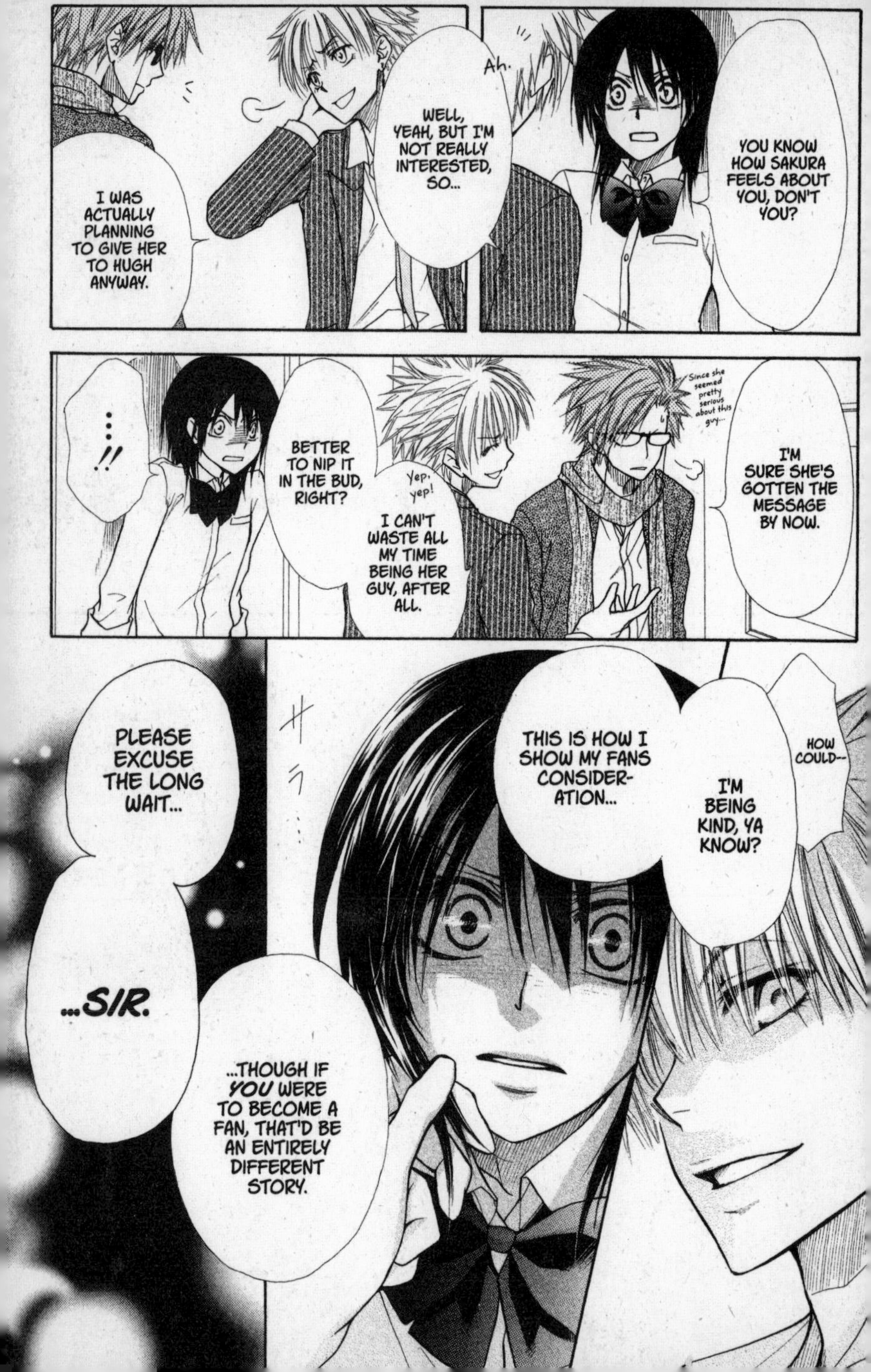
YOU KNOW HOW SAKURA FEELS ABOUT YOU, DON'T YOU?
Ah.
WELL, YEAH, BUT I'M NOT REALLY INTERESTED, SO...
I WAS ACTUALLY PLANNING TO GIVE HER TO HUGH ANYWAY.
I'M SURE SHE'S GOTTEN THE MESSAGE BY NOW.
Since she seemed pretty serious about this guy...
BETTER TO NIP IT IN THE BUD, RIGHT?
Yep, yep!
I CAN'T WASTE ALL MY TIME BEING HER GUY, AFTER ALL.
...!!
HOW COULD--
I'M BEING KIND, YA KNOW?
THIS IS HOW I SHOW MY FANS CONSIDER-ATION...
...THOUGH IF *YOU* WERE TO BECOME A FAN, THAT'D BE AN ENTIRELY DIFFERENT STORY.
ガラ
PLEASE EXCUSE THE LONG WAIT...
...**SIR.**

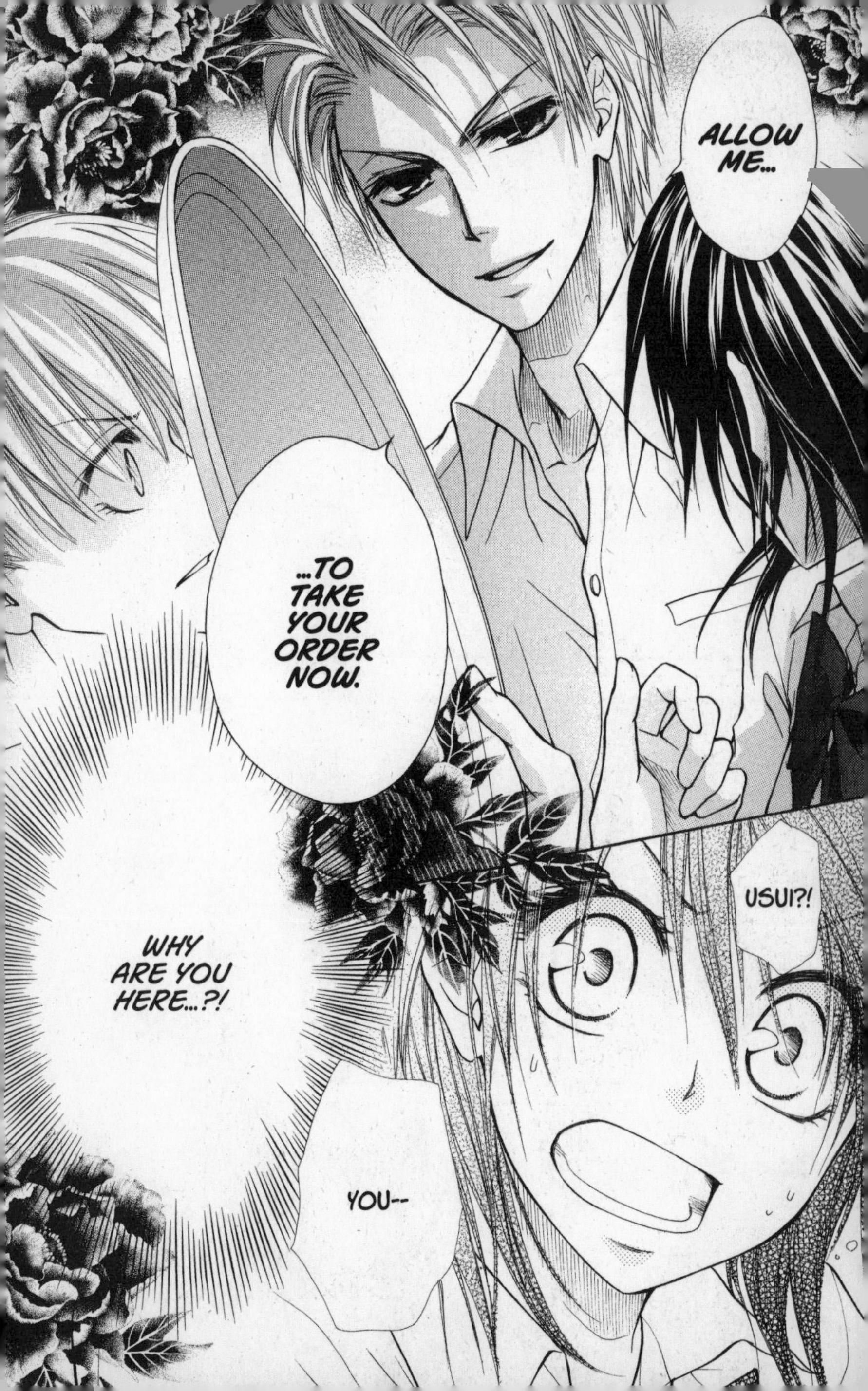
ALLOW ME...
...TO TAKE YOUR ORDER NOW.
USUI?!
YOU--
WHY ARE YOU HERE...?!

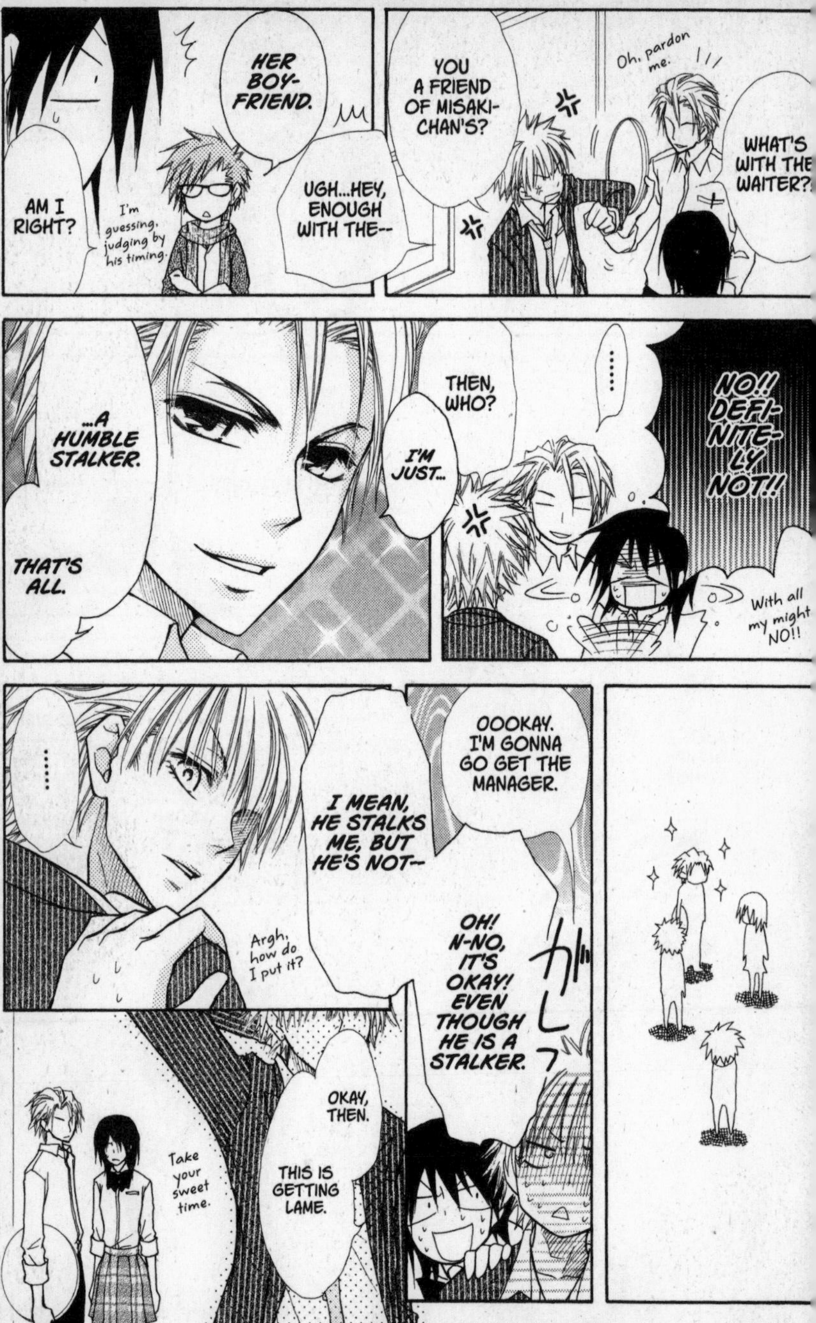
Oh, pardon me.
WHAT'S WITH THE WAITER?!
YOU A FRIEND OF MISAKI-CHAN'S?
UGH...HEY, ENOUGH WITH THE--
HER BOY-FRIEND.
I'm guessing, judging by his timing.
AM I RIGHT?
......
NO!! DEFI-NITE-LY NOT!!
With all my might NO!!
THEN, WHO?
I'M JUST...
...A HUMBLE STALKER.
THAT'S ALL.
OOOKAY. I'M GONNA GO GET THE MANAGER.
OH! N-NO, IT'S OKAY! EVEN THOUGH HE IS A STALKER.
......
I MEAN, HE STALKS ME, BUT HE'S NOT--
Argh, how do I put it?
OKAY, THEN.
THIS IS GETTING LAME.
Take your sweet time.

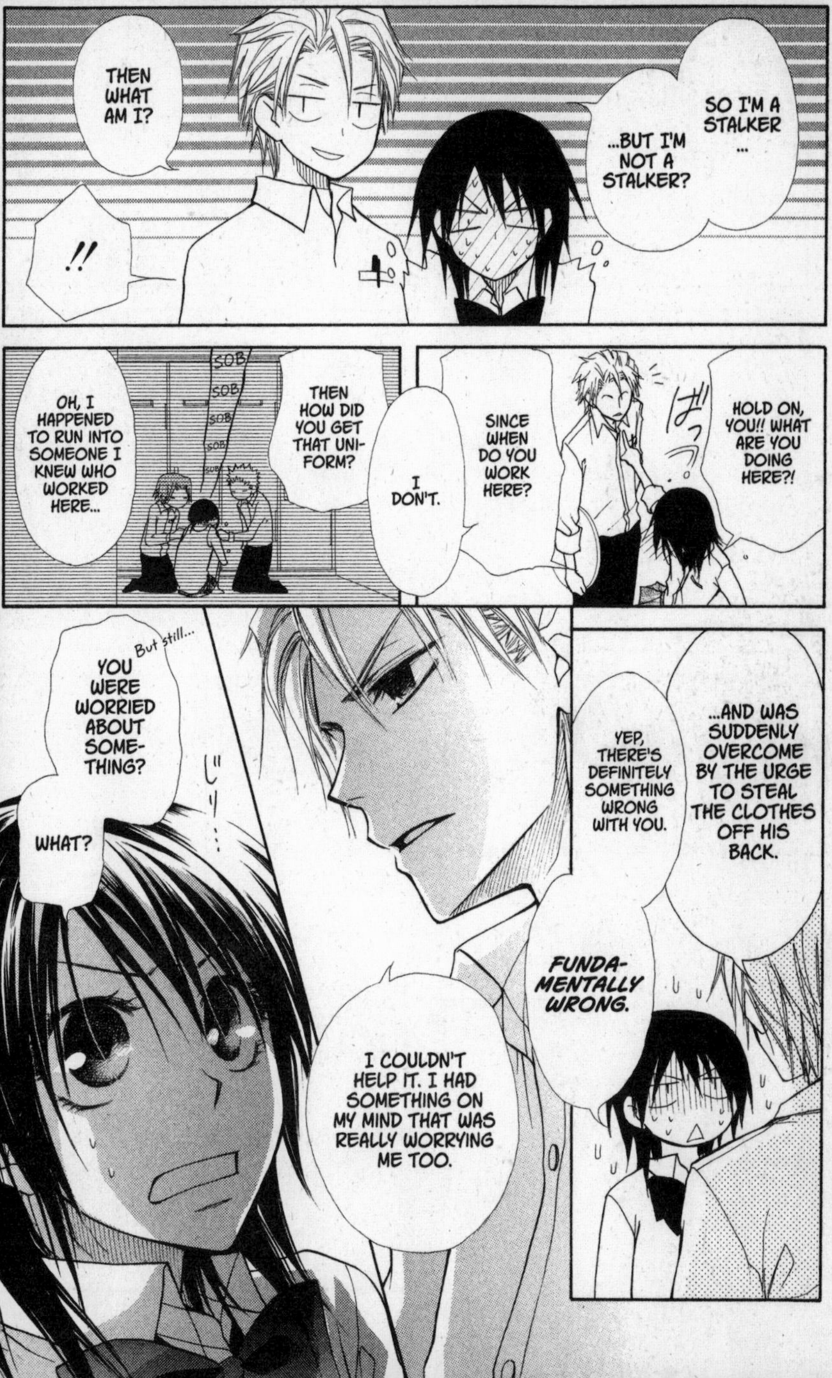
SO I'M A STALKER ...
...BUT I'M NOT A STALKER?
THEN WHAT AM I?
!!
HOLD ON, YOU!! WHAT ARE YOU DOING HERE?!
ばっ
SINCE WHEN DO YOU WORK HERE?
I DON'T.
THEN HOW DID YOU GET THAT UNIFORM?
SOB SOB SOB SOB SOB
OH, I HAPPENED TO RUN INTO SOMEONE I KNEW WHO WORKED HERE...
...AND WAS SUDDENLY OVERCOME BY THE URGE TO STEAL THE CLOTHES OFF HIS BACK.
YEP, THERE'S DEFINITELY SOMETHING WRONG WITH YOU.
FUNDAMENTALLY WRONG.
I COULDN'T HELP IT. I HAD SOMETHING ON MY MIND THAT WAS REALLY WORRYING ME TOO.
じり...
But still...
YOU WERE WORRIED ABOUT SOMETHING?
WHAT?

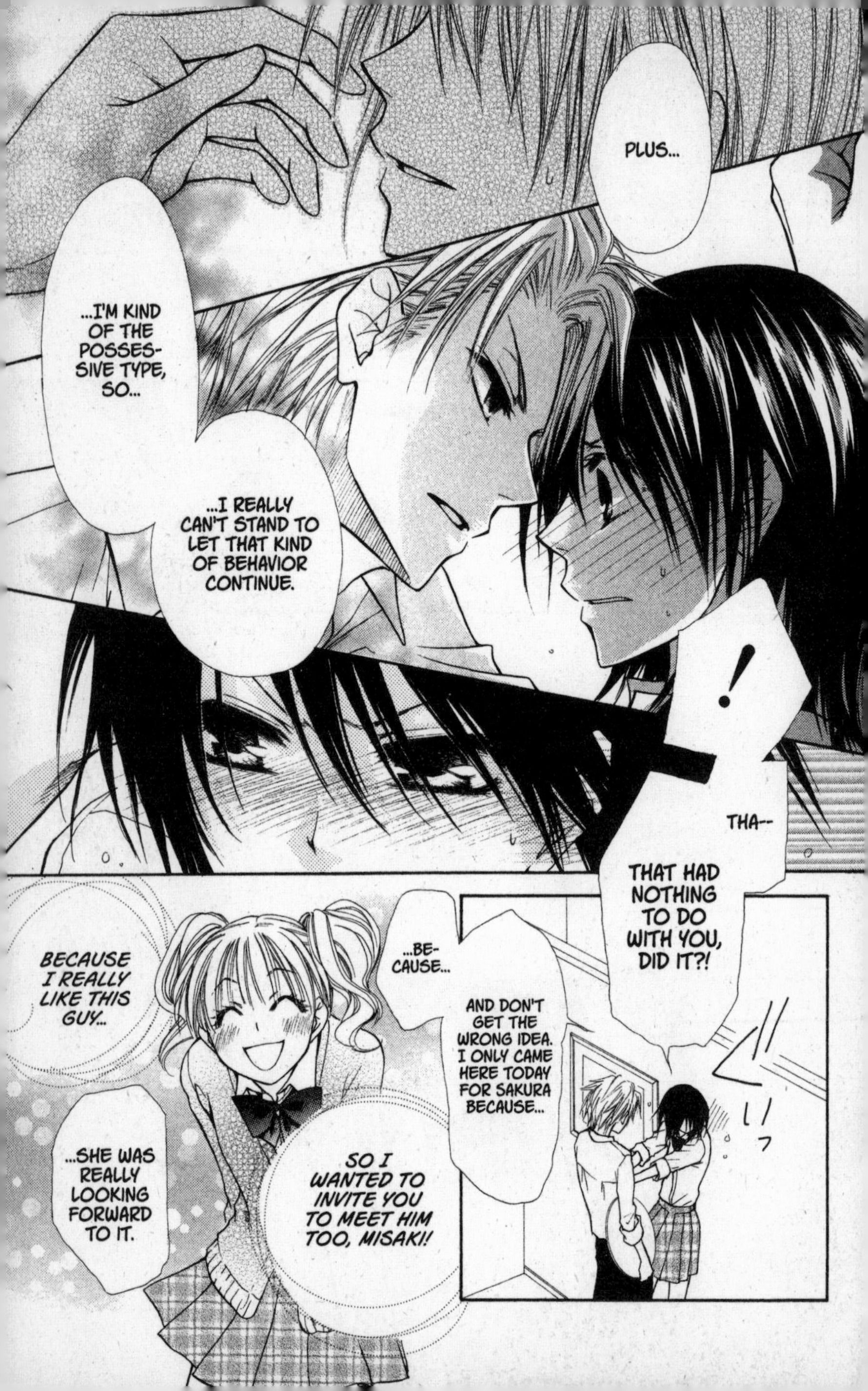
PLUS...
...I'M KIND OF THE POSSESSIVE TYPE, SO...
...I REALLY CAN'T STAND TO LET THAT KIND OF BEHAVIOR CONTINUE.
!
THA--
THAT HAD NOTHING TO DO WITH YOU, DID IT?!
AND DON'T GET THE WRONG IDEA. I ONLY CAME HERE TODAY FOR SAKURA BECAUSE...
...BE-CAUSE...
...SHE WAS REALLY LOOKING FORWARD TO IT.
BECAUSE I REALLY LIKE THIS GUY...
SO I WANTED TO INVITE YOU TO MEET HIM TOO, MISAKI!

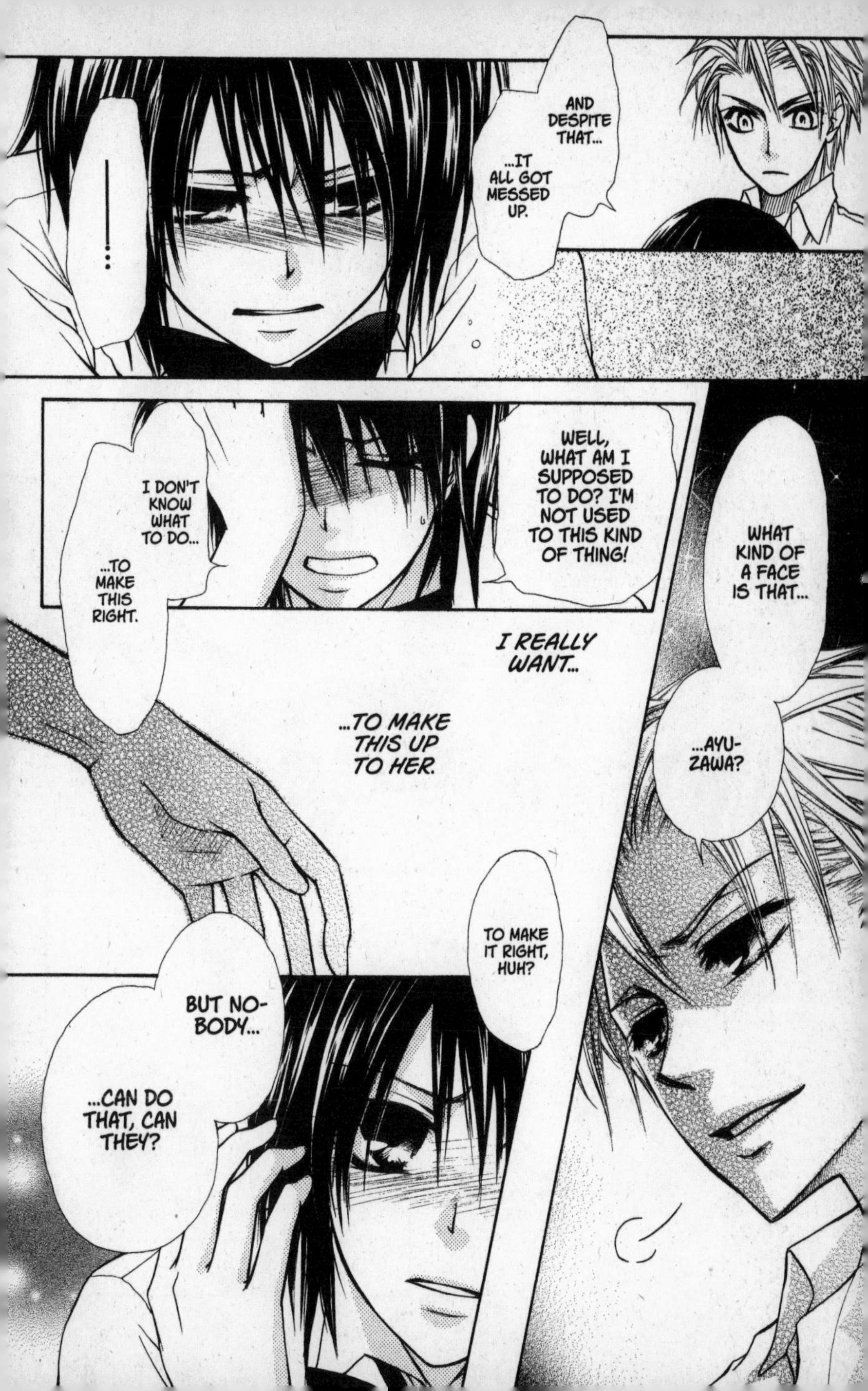
AND DESPITE THAT...
...IT ALL GOT MESSED UP.
......
WHAT KIND OF A FACE IS THAT...
...AYU-ZAWA?
TO MAKE IT RIGHT, HUH?
WELL, WHAT AM I SUPPOSED TO DO? I'M NOT USED TO THIS KIND OF THING!
I DON'T KNOW WHAT TO DO...
...TO MAKE THIS RIGHT.
I REALLY WANT...
...TO MAKE THIS UP TO HER.
BUT NO-BODY...
...CAN DO THAT, CAN THEY?

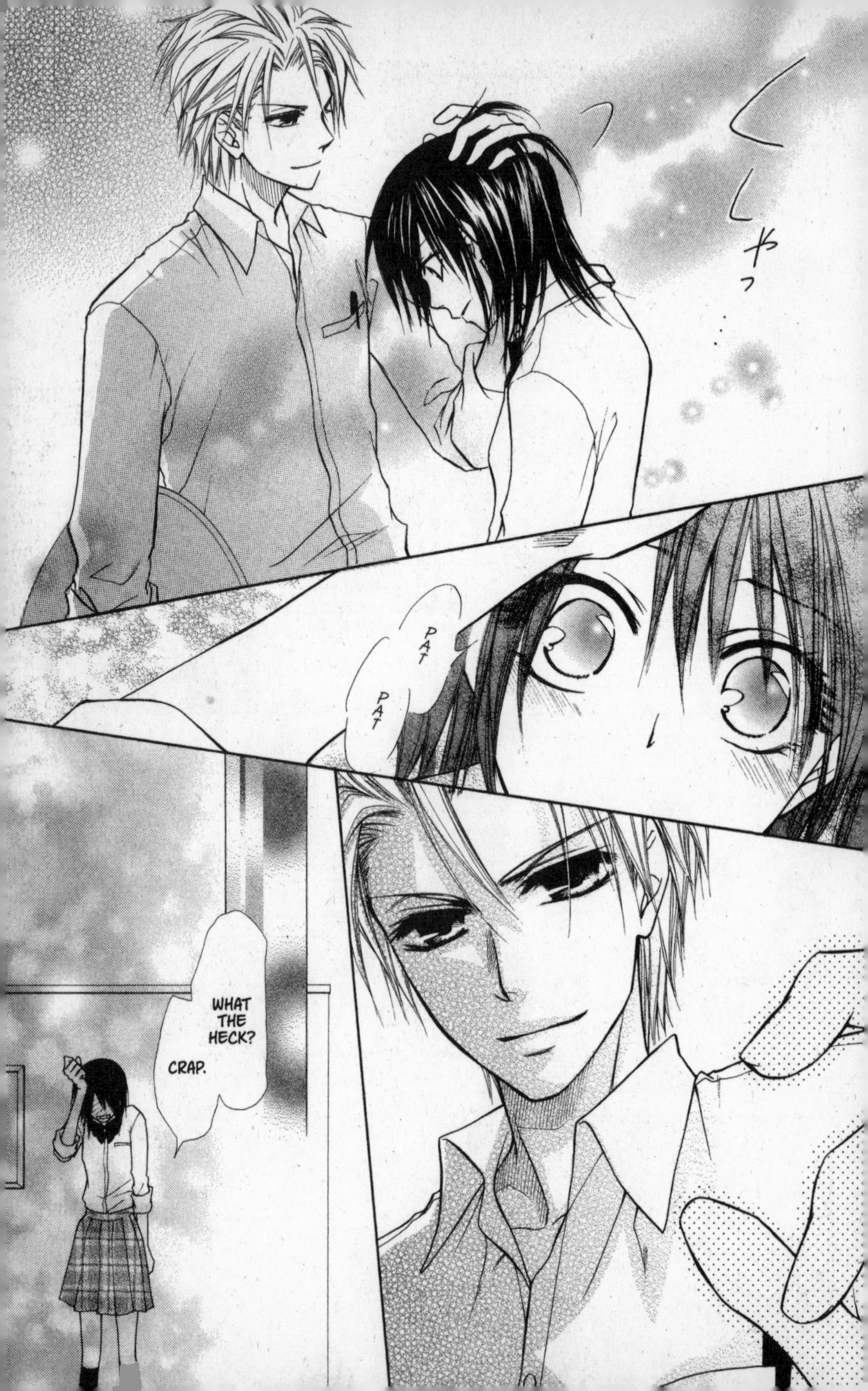
くしゃっ…
PAT PAT
WHAT THE HECK?
CRAP.

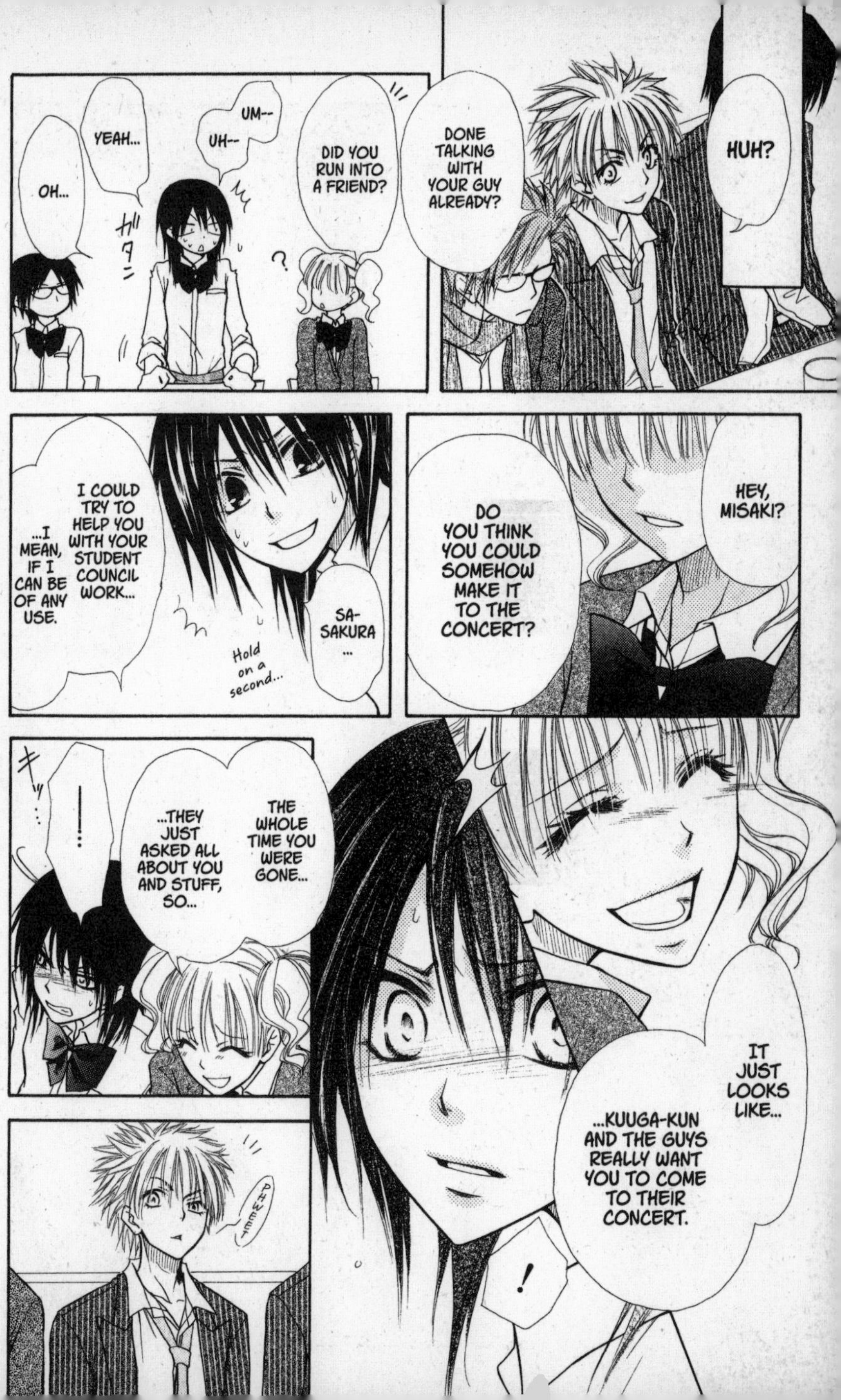
HUH?
DONE TALKING WITH YOUR GUY ALREADY?
DID YOU RUN INTO A FRIEND?
UM-- UH--
YEAH...
OH...
HEY, MISAKI?
DO YOU THINK YOU COULD SOMEHOW MAKE IT TO THE CONCERT?
SA-SAKURA...
Hold on a second...
I COULD TRY TO HELP YOU WITH YOUR STUDENT COUNCIL WORK...
...I MEAN, IF I CAN BE OF ANY USE.
IT JUST LOOKS LIKE...
...KUUGA-KUN AND THE GUYS REALLY WANT YOU TO COME TO THEIR CONCERT.
!
THE WHOLE TIME YOU WERE GONE...
...THEY JUST ASKED ALL ABOUT YOU AND STUFF, SO...
!...
PHWEET

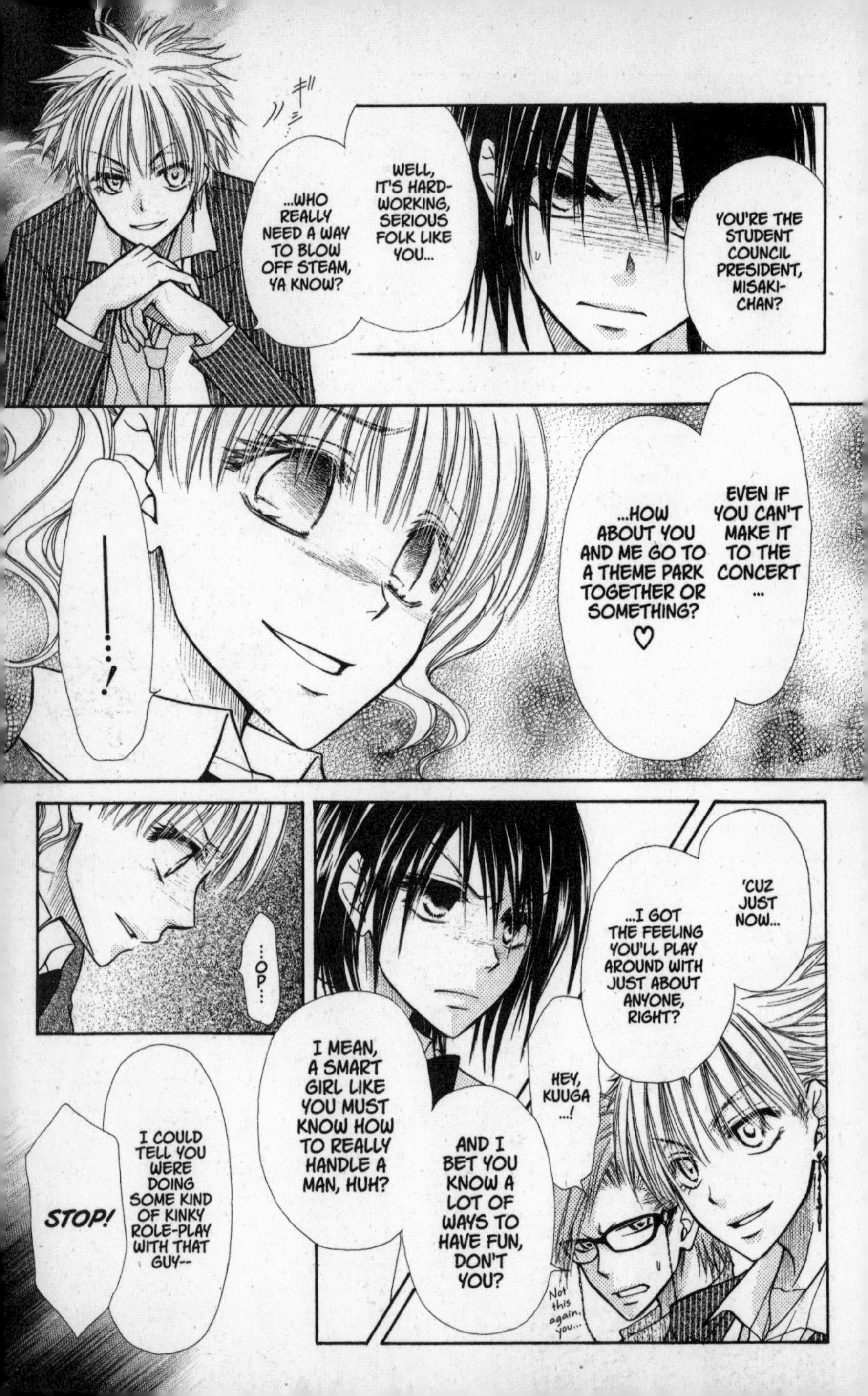
YOU'RE THE STUDENT COUNCIL PRESIDENT, MISAKI-CHAN?
WELL, IT'S HARD-WORKING, SERIOUS FOLK LIKE YOU...
...WHO REALLY NEED A WAY TO BLOW OFF STEAM, YA KNOW?
EVEN IF YOU CAN'T MAKE IT TO THE CONCERT ...
...HOW ABOUT YOU AND ME GO TO A THEME PARK TOGETHER OR SOMETHING? ♡
...!
'CUZ JUST NOW...
...I GOT THE FEELING YOU'LL PLAY AROUND WITH JUST ABOUT ANYONE, RIGHT?
HEY, KUUGA ...!
I MEAN, A SMART GIRL LIKE YOU MUST KNOW HOW TO REALLY HANDLE A MAN, HUH?
AND I BET YOU KNOW A LOT OF WAYS TO HAVE FUN, DON'T YOU?
Not this again, you...
...OP...
I COULD TELL YOU WERE DOING SOME KIND OF KINKY ROLE-PLAY WITH THAT GUY--
STOP!

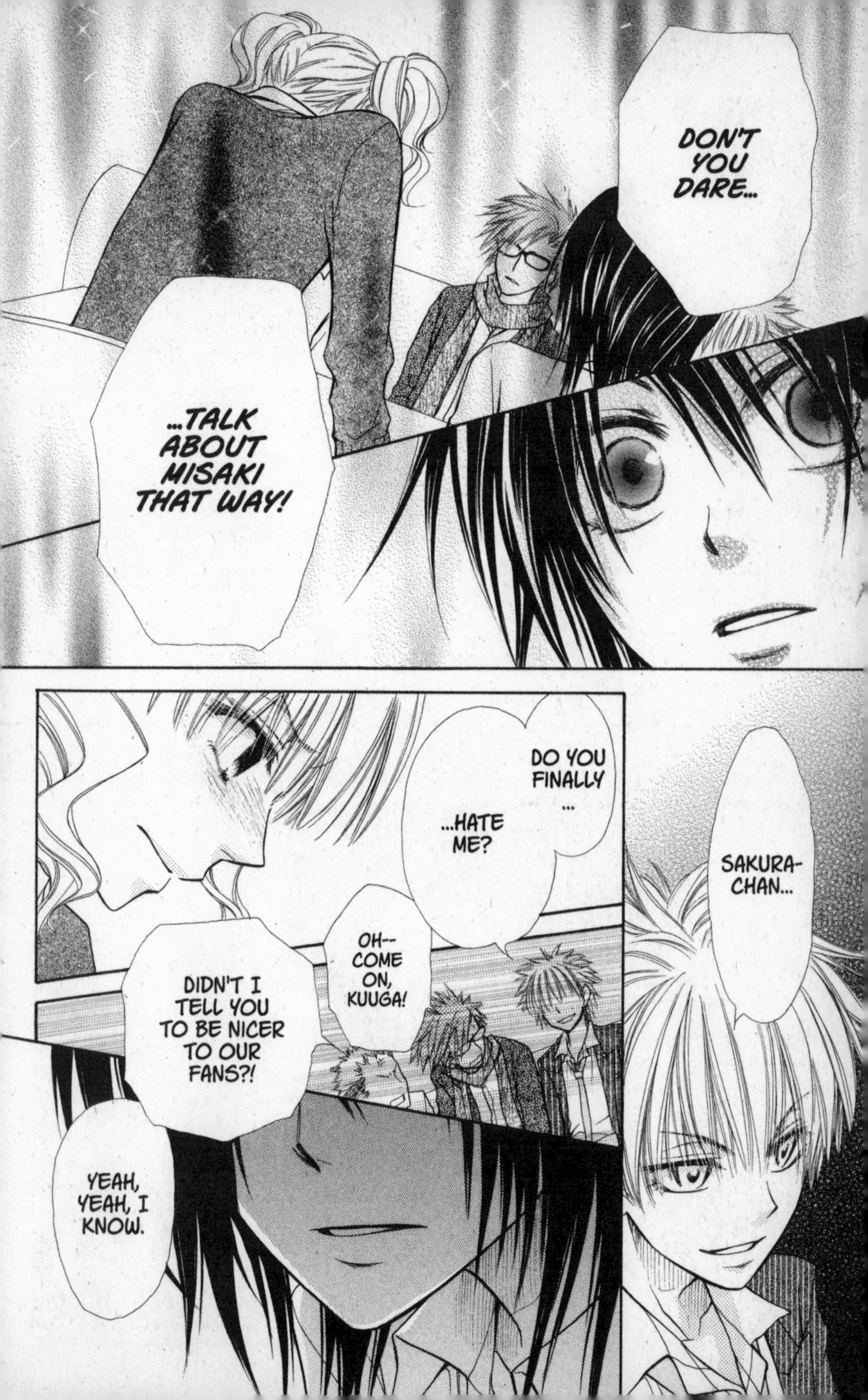
DON'T YOU DARE...
...TALK ABOUT MISAKI THAT WAY!
SAKURA-CHAN...
DO YOU FINALLY ...
...HATE ME?
OH-- COME ON, KUUGA!
DIDN'T I TELL YOU TO BE NICER TO OUR FANS?!
YEAH, YEAH, I KNOW.

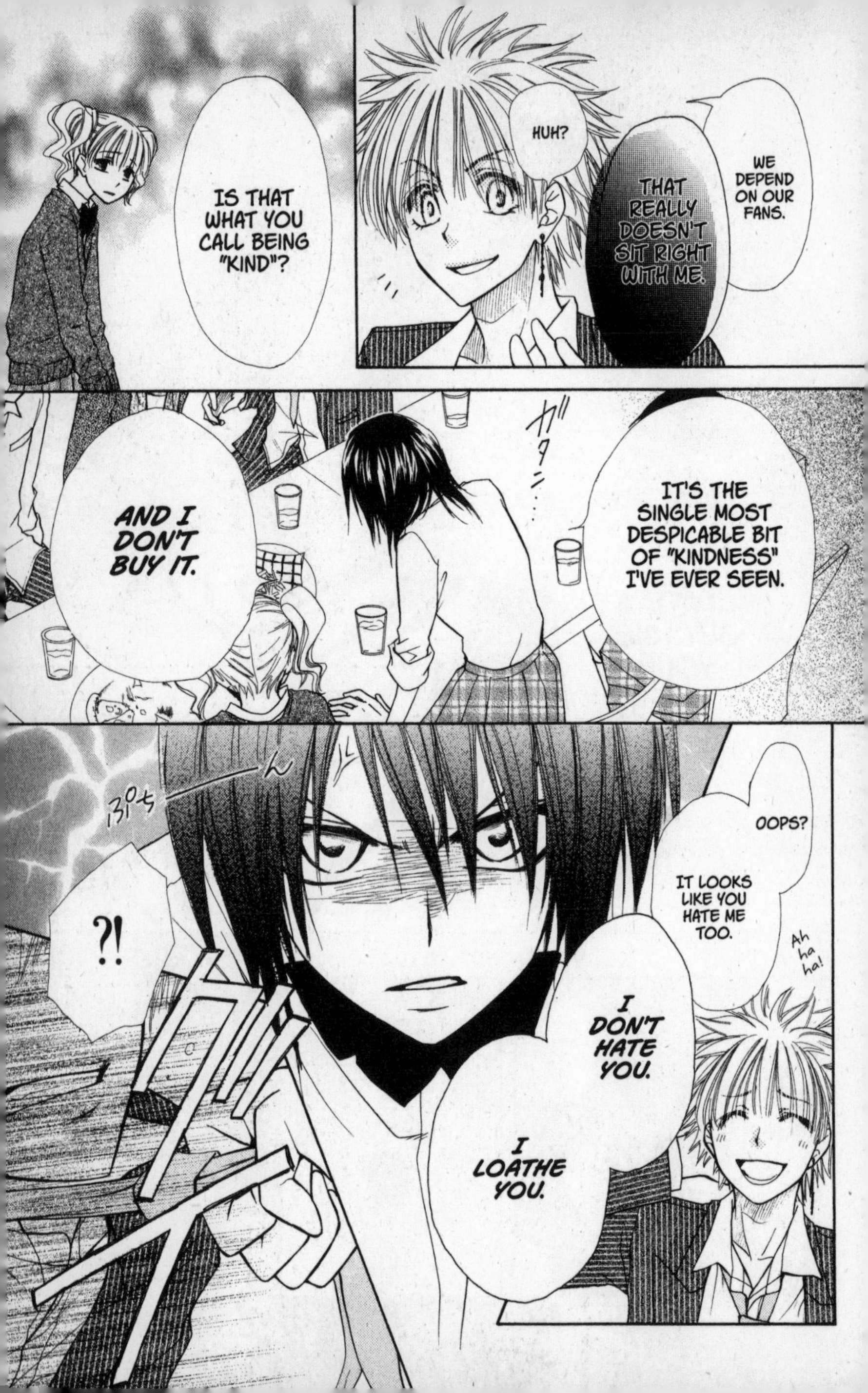

WE DEPEND ON OUR FANS.
HUH?
THAT REALLY DOESN'T SIT RIGHT WITH ME.
IS THAT WHAT YOU CALL BEING "KIND"?
ガタン
IT'S THE SINGLE MOST DESPICABLE BIT OF "KINDNESS" I'VE EVER SEEN.
AND I DON'T BUY IT.
OOPS?
IT LOOKS LIKE YOU HATE ME TOO.
Ah ha ha!
I DON'T HATE YOU.
I LOATHE YOU.
ぷち—ん
?!

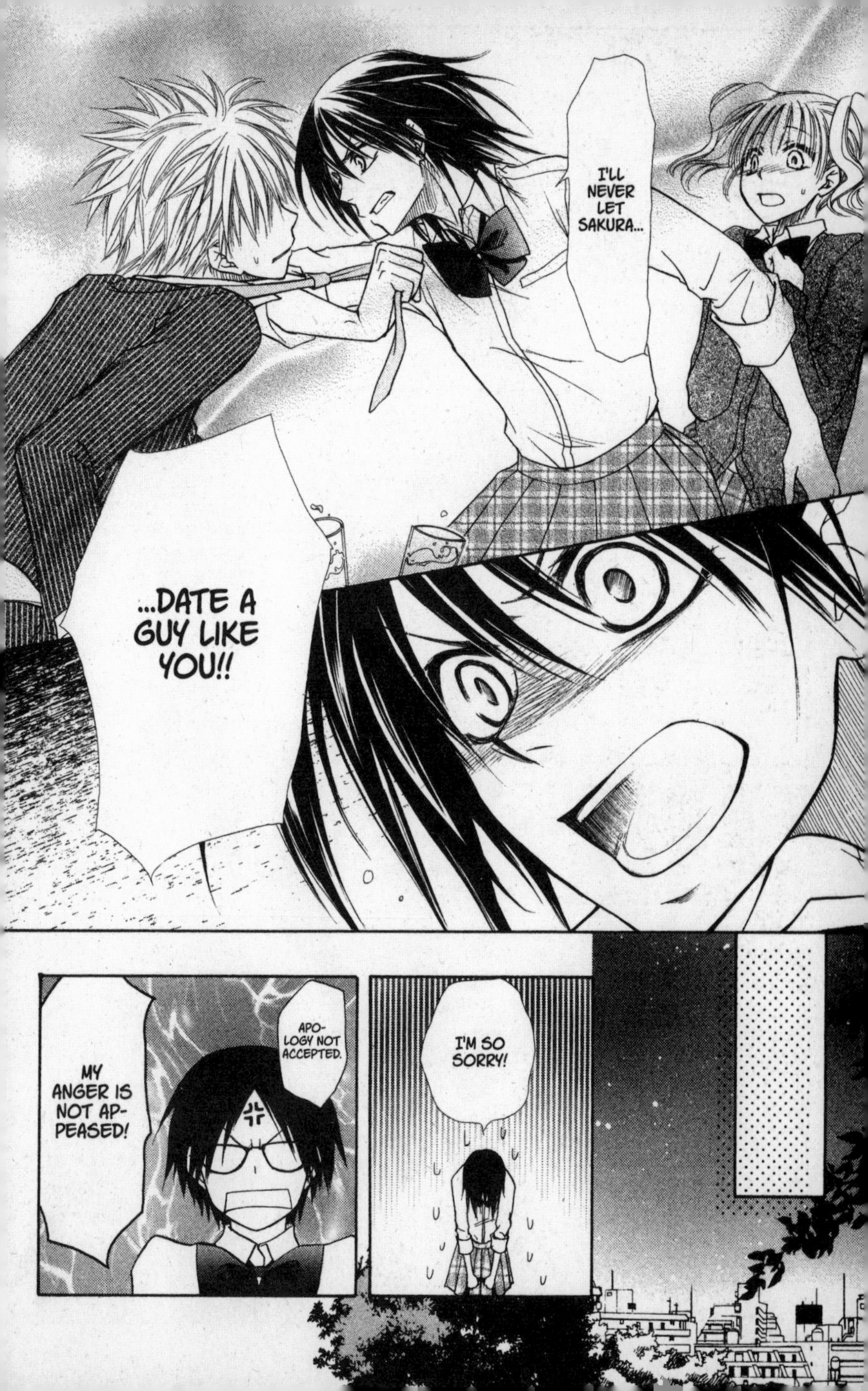
I'LL NEVER LET SAKURA...
...DATE A GUY LIKE YOU!!
I'M SO SORRY!
APO-LOGY NOT ACCEPTED.
MY ANGER IS NOT AP-PEASED!

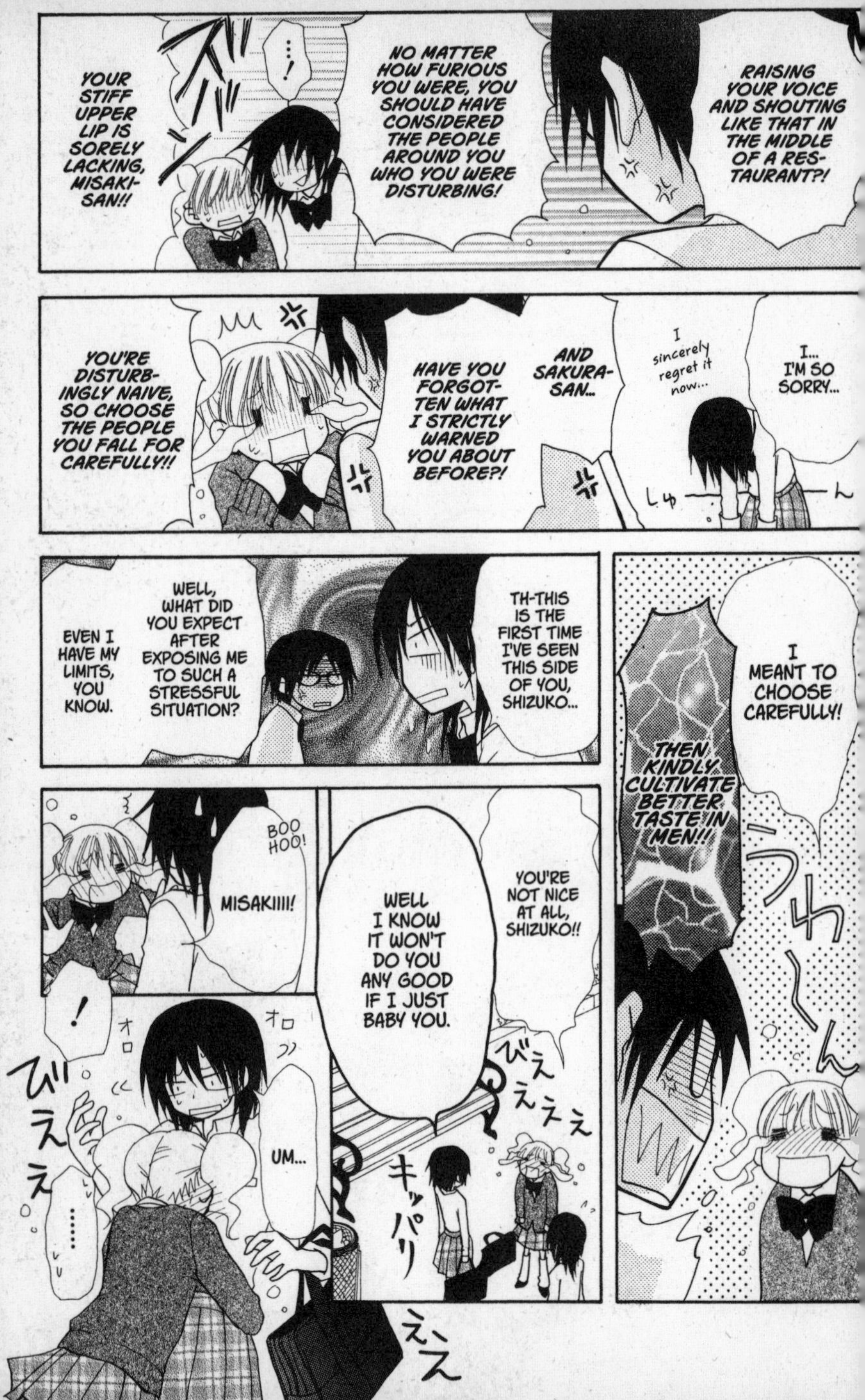
RAISING YOUR VOICE AND SHOUTING LIKE THAT IN THE MIDDLE OF A RES-TAURANT?!
NO MATTER HOW FURIOUS YOU WERE, YOU SHOULD HAVE CONSIDERED THE PEOPLE AROUND YOU WHO YOU WERE DISTURBING!
...!
YOUR STIFF UPPER LIP IS SORELY LACKING, MISAKI-SAN!!
I... I'M SO SORRY...
しゅーーん
I sincerely regret it now...
AND SAKURA-SAN...
HAVE YOU FORGOT-TEN WHAT I STRICTLY WARNED YOU ABOUT BEFORE?!
YOU'RE DISTURB-INGLY NAIVE, SO CHOOSE THE PEOPLE YOU FALL FOR CAREFULLY!!
I MEANT TO CHOOSE CAREFULLY!
THEN KINDLY CULTIVATE BETTER TASTE IN MEN!!
TH-THIS IS THE FIRST TIME I'VE SEEN THIS SIDE OF YOU, SHIZUKO...
WELL, WHAT DID YOU EXPECT AFTER EXPOSING ME TO SUCH A STRESSFUL SITUATION?
EVEN I HAVE MY LIMITS, YOU KNOW.
YOU'RE NOT NICE AT ALL, SHIZUKO!!
WELL I KNOW IT WON'T DO YOU ANY GOOD IF I JUST BABY YOU.
キッパリ
BOO HOO!
MISAKIIII!
!
UM...
......

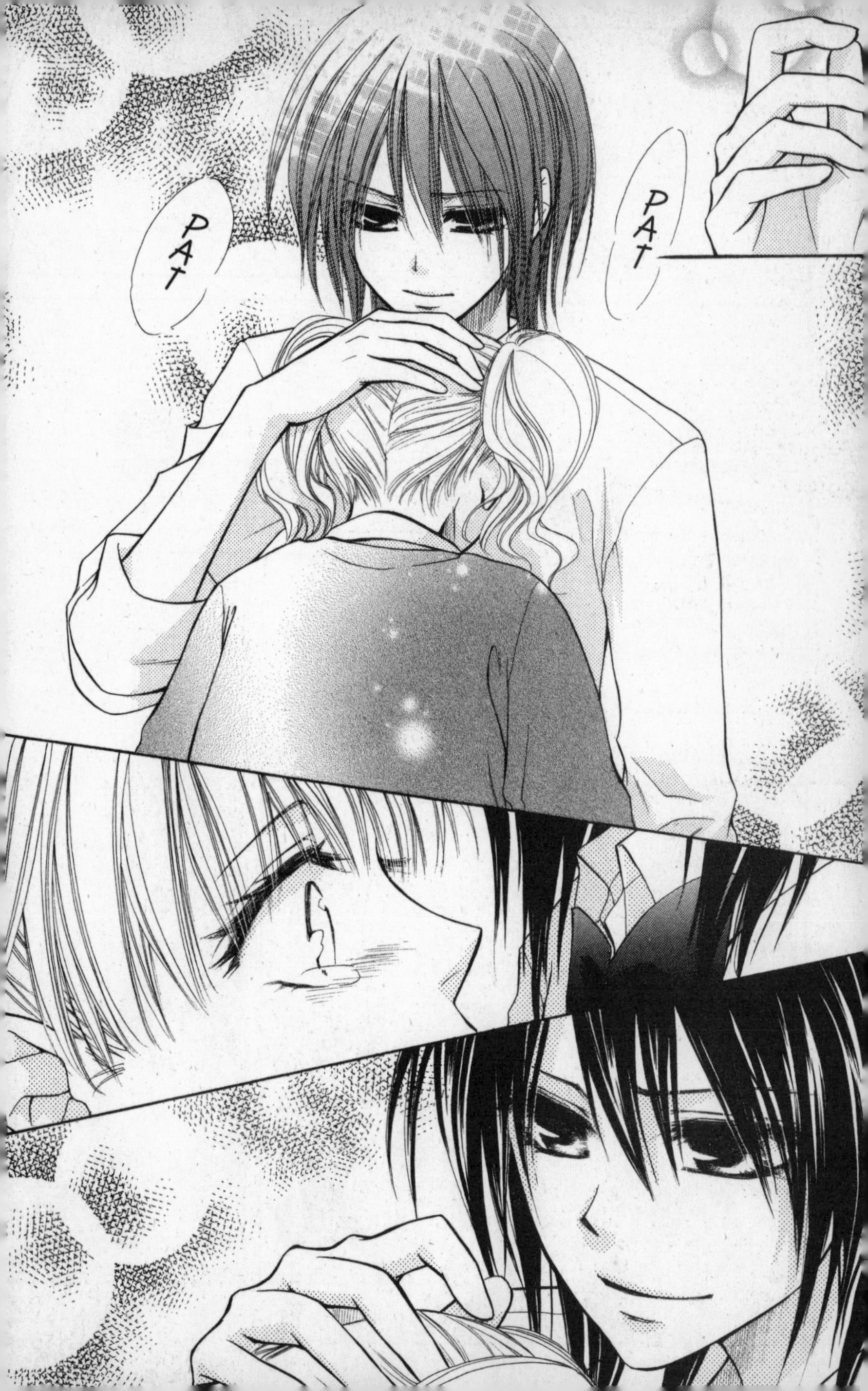
PAT
PAT

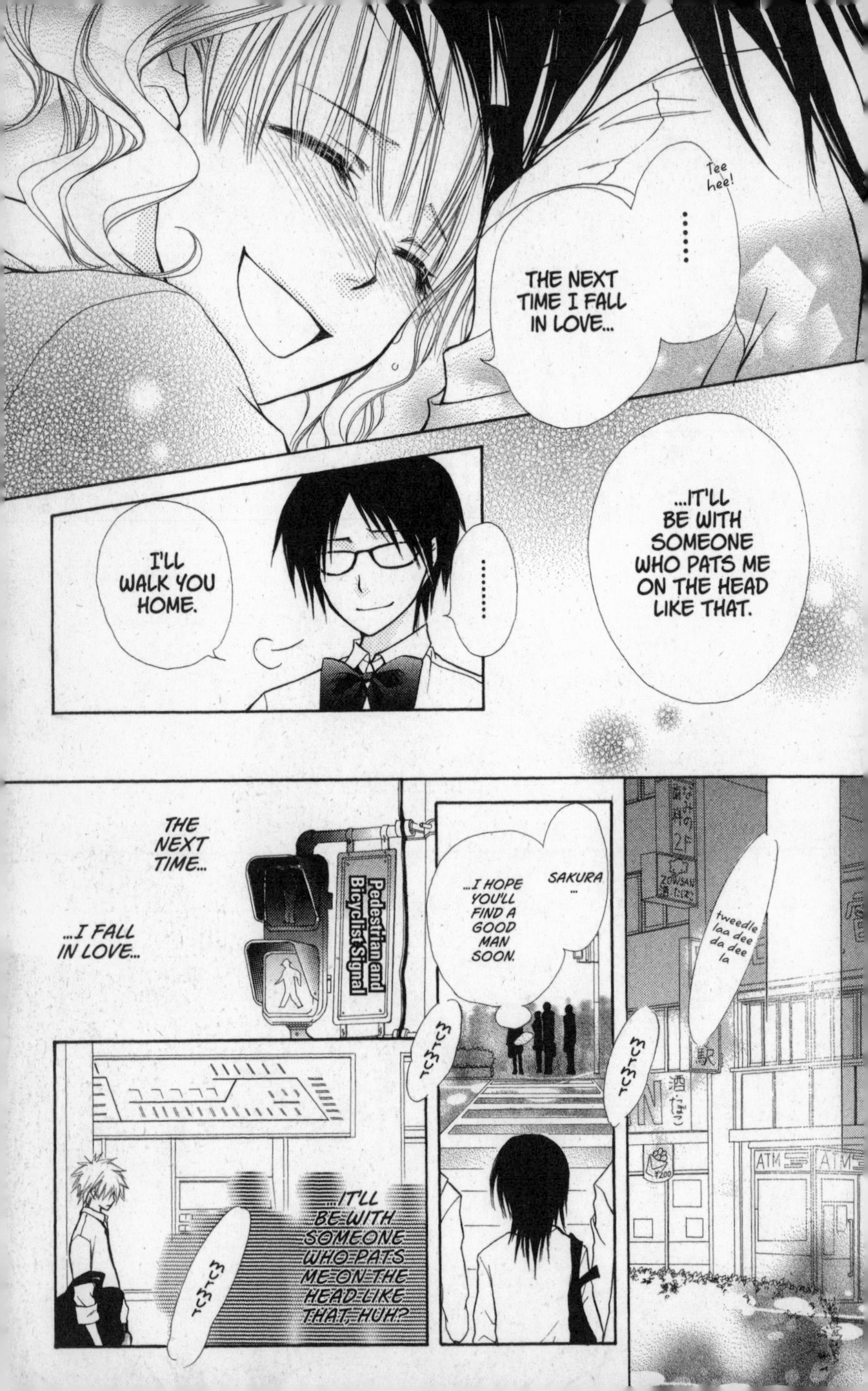
Tee hee!
......
THE NEXT TIME I FALL IN LOVE...
...IT'LL BE WITH SOMEONE WHO PATS ME ON THE HEAD LIKE THAT.
....
I'LL WALK YOU HOME.
tweedle laa dee da dee la
SAKURA ...
...I HOPE YOU'LL FIND A GOOD MAN SOON.
murmur
murmur
THE NEXT TIME...
...I FALL IN LOVE...
Pedestrian and Bicyclist Signal
...IT'LL BE WITH SOMEONE WHO PATS ME ON THE HEAD LIKE THAT, HUH?
murmur

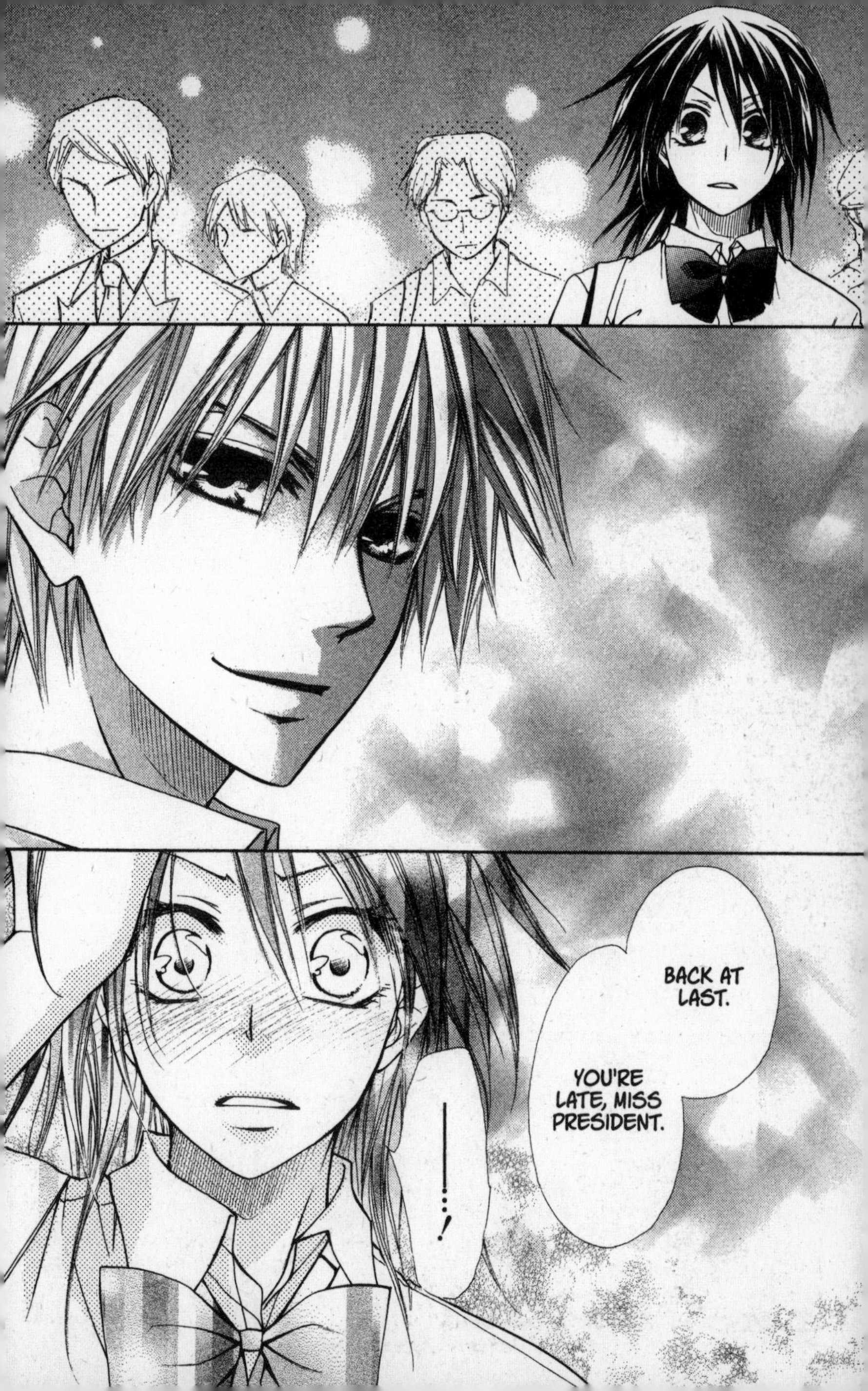
BACK AT LAST.
YOU'RE LATE, MISS PRESIDENT.
...!

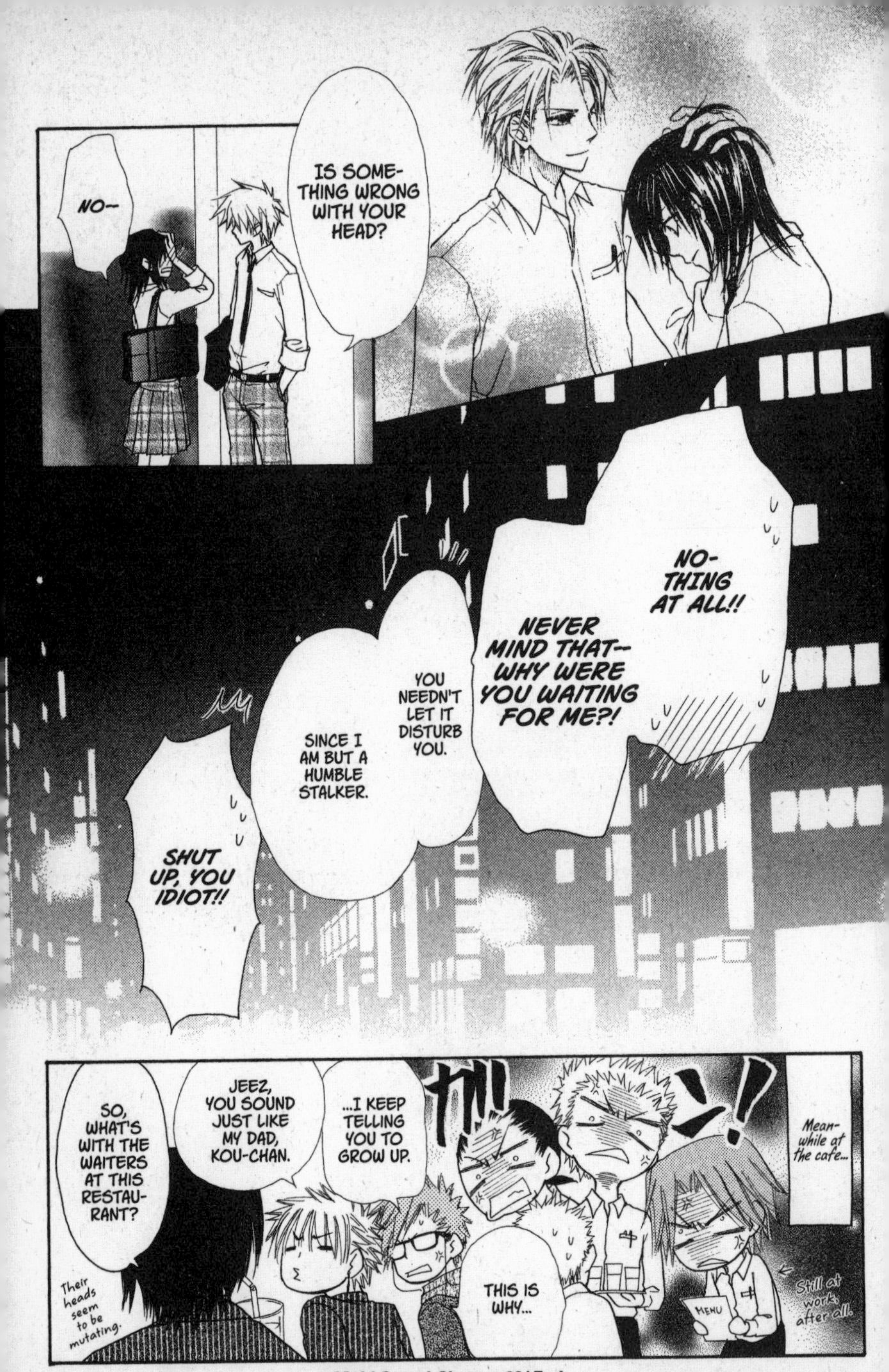
IS SOME-THING WRONG WITH YOUR HEAD?
NO--
NO-THING AT ALL!!
NEVER MIND THAT-- WHY WERE YOU WAITING FOR ME?!
YOU NEEDN'T LET IT DISTURB YOU.
SINCE I AM BUT A HUMBLE STALKER.
SHUT UP, YOU IDIOT!!
Mean-while at the cafe...
Still at work, after all.
...I KEEP TELLING YOU TO GROW UP.
JEEZ, YOU SOUND JUST LIKE MY DAD, KOU-CHAN.
SO, WHAT'S WITH THE WAITERS AT THIS RESTAU-RANT?
THIS IS WHY...
MENU
Their heads seem to be mutating.

Maid Sama! Chapter 20/ End

Q&A time...

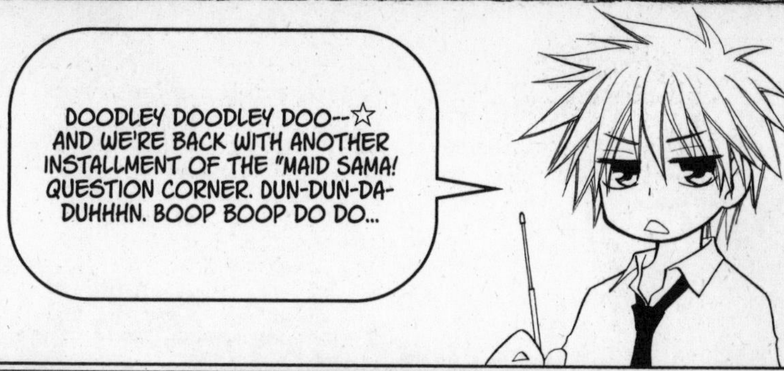
DOODLEY DOODLEY DOO--☆ AND WE'RE BACK WITH ANOTHER INSTALLMENT OF THE "MAID SAMA! QUESTION CORNER. DUN-DUN-DA-DUHHHN. BOOP BOOP DO DO...

: WAIT A--U-USUI-SAN?! ARE YOU ALL RIGHT?! HANG IN THERE!!

: ***HEH, HANG ONTO WHAT? ANYWAY, LET'S GET TO THE FIRST QUESTION.***

: WAH! NOT IN THE MOOD FOR SMALL TALK, I GUESS! WH-WH-WHAT'S WITH USUI-SAN TODAY?

—·—·—·—·—·—·—·—·—·—·—·—

QUESTION 1: WHAT IS YUKIMURA'S TYPE?

: LITTLE 6-MONTH-OLD "EVERYONE'S PET" YUKIMURA-KUN, THIS QUESTION IS FOR YOU.

: ***HMPH! I-I'M NOT A PET!!*** BUT, IS THIS REALLY A QUESTION FOR ME?! F-F-FOR A NOBODY LIKE ME!

: IF YOU DON'T HURRY AND ANSWER, YOU'LL WASTE THE SPACE WE HAVE HERE.

: TH-TH-TH-THAT'S RIGHT! I'M SORRY! UM... M-MY TYPE...? TYPE...UM, MY TYPE...?

: ***GORILLAS.***

: TH-THAT'S RIGHT, GORIL--***HEY, WAIT A--WAAAAH! WHAT ARE YOU SAYING, USUI-SAN?!***

: WELL, THEN--ON TO THE NEXT QUESTION.

: W-W-WAIT...!!

—·—·—·—·—·—·—·—·—·—·—·—

QUESTION 2: WHY DOES USUI HARASS YUKIMURA?

: BECAUSE IT'S FUN.

: WHA--USUI-SAAAAN!!

WE LOVE TO RECEIVE YOUR
QUESTIONS, REQUESTS, ETC,
SO PLEASE SEND THEM IN TO:
HIRO FUJIWARA
C/O TOKYOPOP INC.
5900 WILSHIRE BLVD.
SUITE 2000
LOS ANGELES, CA
90036

QUESTION 3: WHAT KIND OF RELATIONSHIP DO USUI AND YUKIMURA HAVE?

: MASTER AND PET.

: P-PLEASE TAKE THIS MORE SERIOUSLY, USUI-SAN!

: SURE. RIGHT. SORRY ABOUT THAT. I WAS MISTAKEN.

: PHEW...F-FINALLY, WE CAN TALK SERIOUSLY--

: WE'RE MASTER AND *PUPPY.*

: OHH, FORGET IT! I JUST DON'T UNDERSTAND THIS ANYMORE!!

QUESTION 4: HAS YUKIMURA EVER INVITED A MAN TO "PLEASE $*#+ ME?" BEFORE?

: WELL, LOOK AT THAT, YUKIMURA. EVEN THE READERS
THINK YOU'RE *THAT KIND OF GUY.*

: I-I'VE NEVER INVITED ANYONE TO DO ANYTHING LIKE THAT!! WHAT ARE
YOU ALL SAYING?! I DON'T UNDERSTAND THIS AT ALL! WAAAAHH!

: AH, HERE'S A FITTING QUESTION.

QUESTION 5: WHAT IS A "SEDUCTIVE UKE?"

: YUKIMURA.

: ME?! WHAT IS THIS "SEDUCTIVE UKE" THING?! WHAT DOES IT MEAN?!

 : THERE, YOU'RE DOING IT RIGHT NOW...IF YOU WANT TO KNOW MORE,
SHALL I *GO OVER EVERY, LITTLE DETAIL BIT BY BIT...*

 : WAH! Y-YOU'RE TOO CLOSE, USUI-SAN! WAAH! P-
PLEASE, DON'T COME ANY CLOSER!!

 : THERE'S NOTHING TO BE AFRAID OF, YUKIMURA...COME HERE...

 : Y-YOU REALLY ARE ACTING STRANGE TODAY, USUI-SAN!!
WAAAH...! I-I...I...!
*I THINK I'M ABOUT TO WET MY PANTS,
SO PLEASE EXCUSE ME!!*

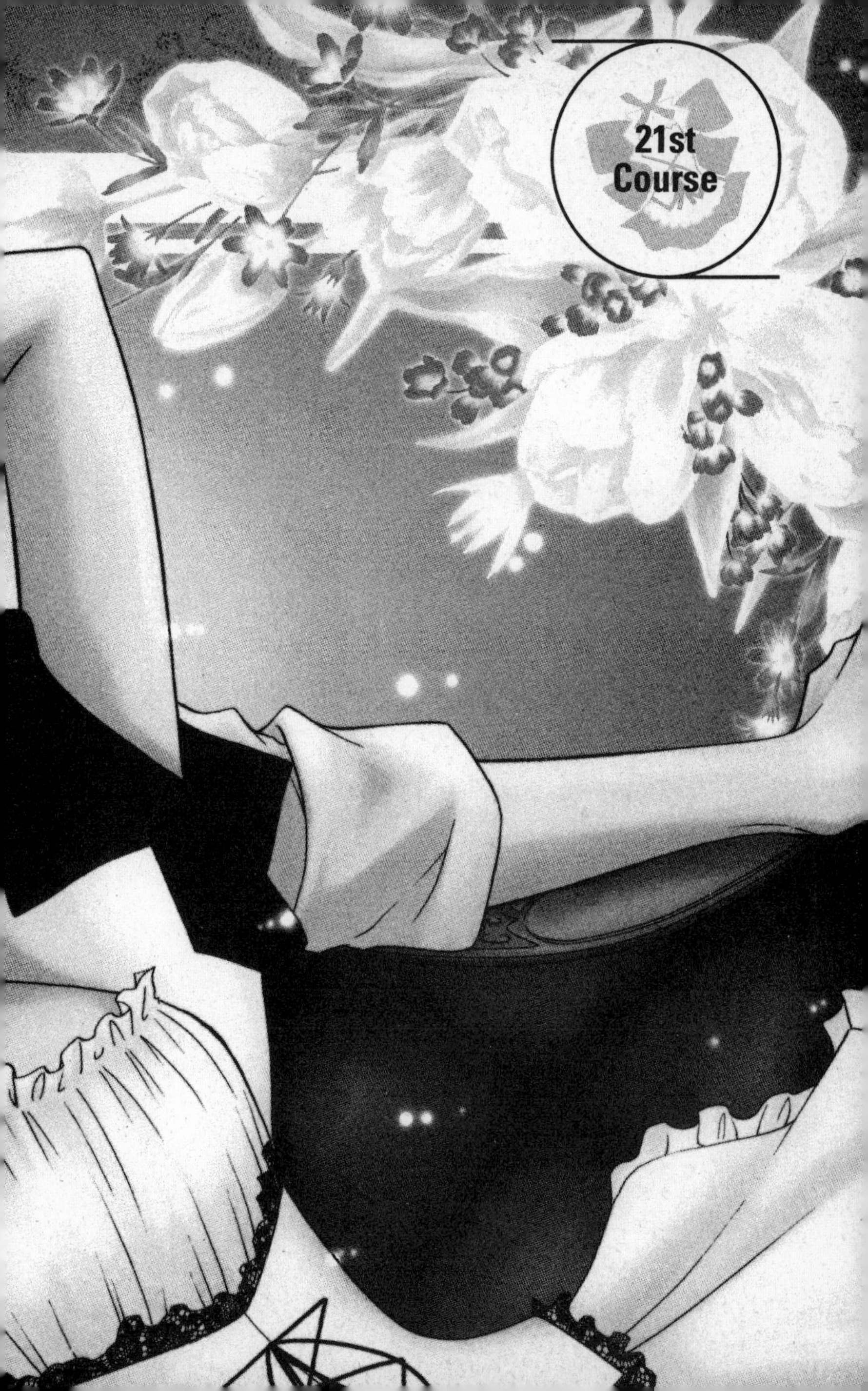
21st Course

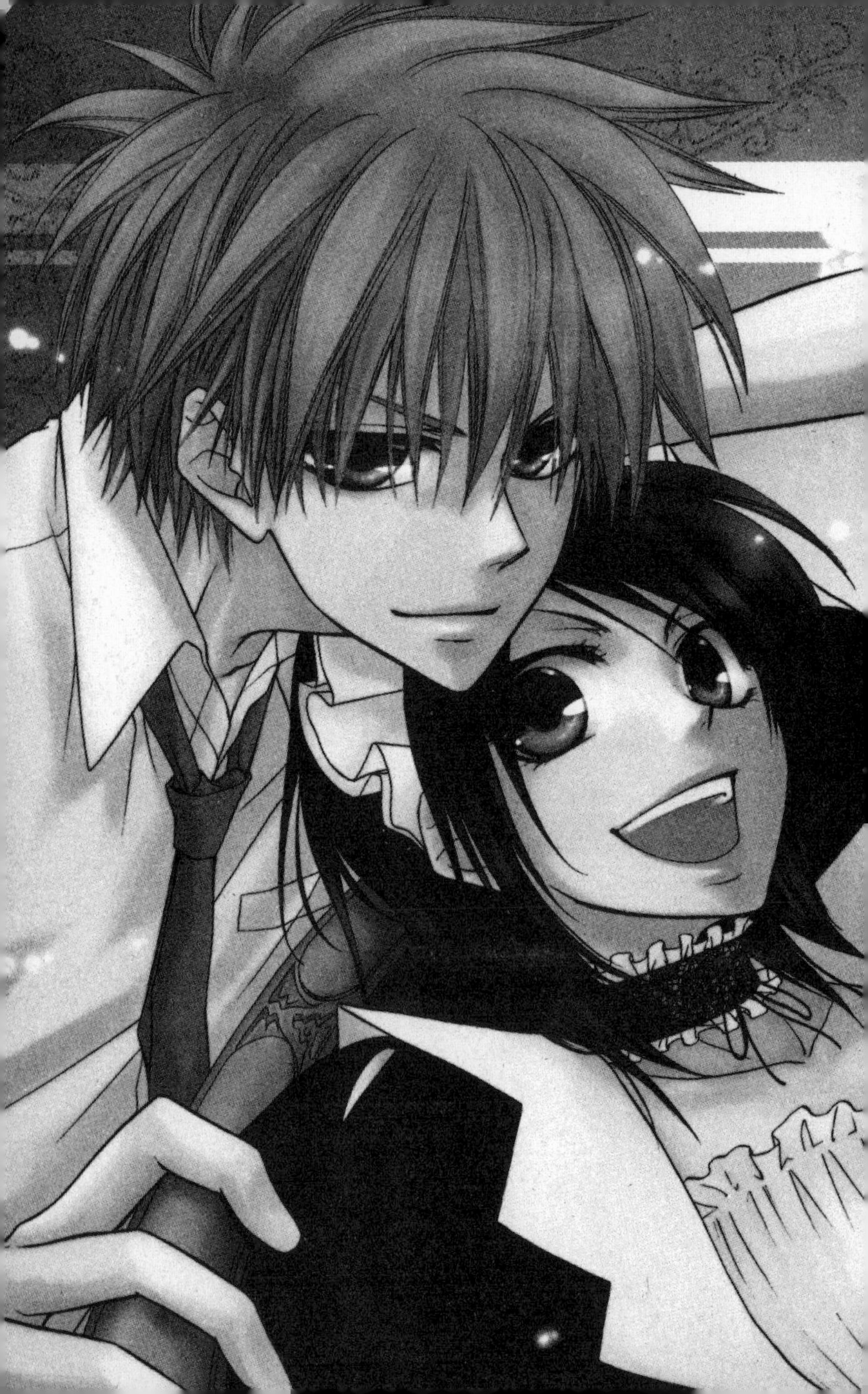

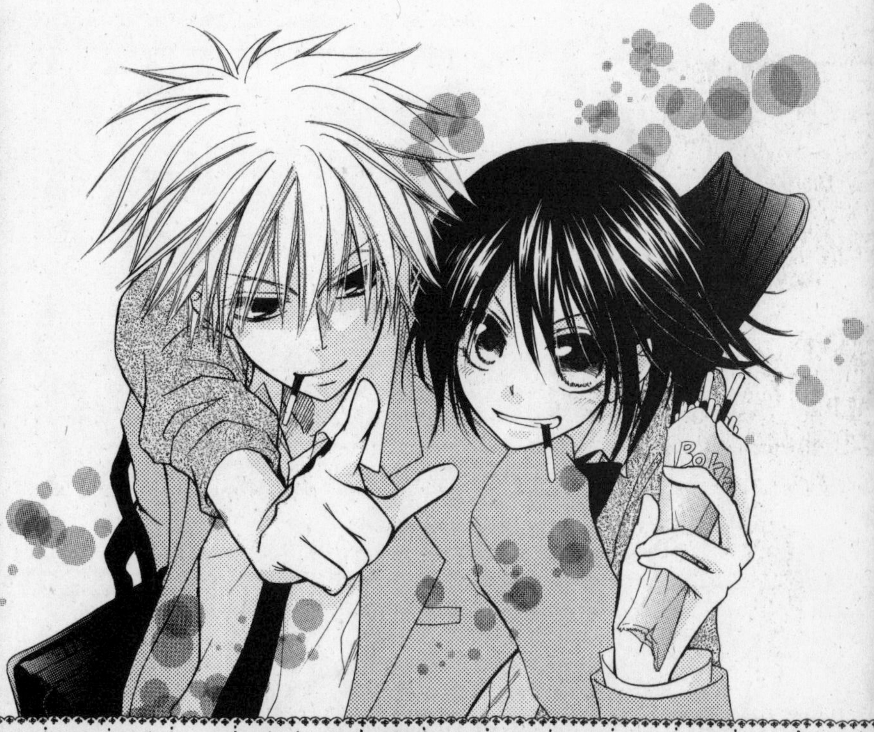

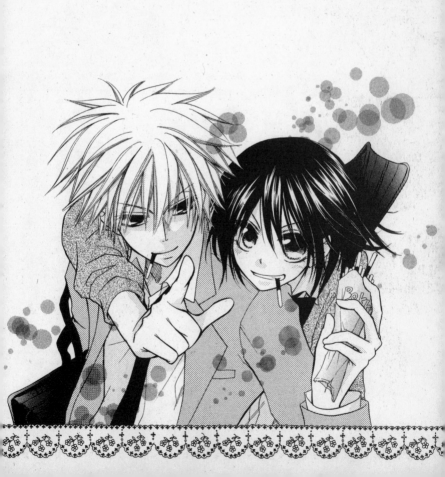

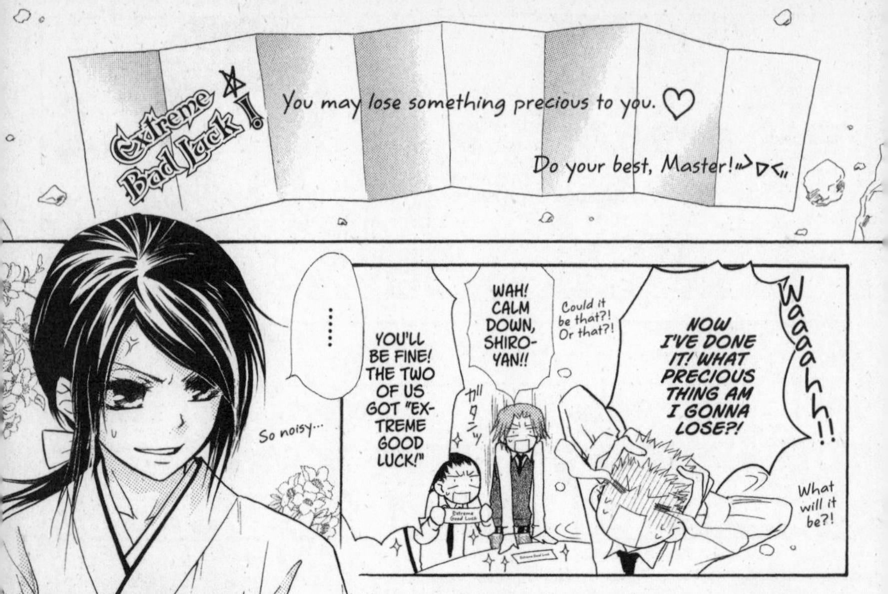
Extreme Bad Luck!
You may lose something precious to you. ♡
Do your best, Master!
Waaaahh!!
NOW I'VE DONE IT! WHAT PRECIOUS THING AM I GONNA LOSE?!
What will it be?!
Could it be that?! Or that?!
WAH! CALM DOWN, SHIRO-YAN!!
YOU'LL BE FINE! THE TWO OF US GOT "EXTREME GOOD LUCK!"
Extreme Good Luck
......
SO WHAT IF YOU GUYS GOT GOOD LUCK? IT'S GOT NOTHING TO DO WITH ME!!
Are you rubbing it in?! Jerks!!
PLEASE QUIET DOWN, MASTERS.
THEY'RE ONLY HOMEMADE FORTUNE COOKIES.
Completely non-superstitious.
So noisy...
Today at Maid Latte, it's
♡ Miko Day ♡

Miko are Shinto shrine priestesses (a popular fetish with some otaku). They attend to the shrine's upkeep and also tell fortunes and sell good luck charms.

Extraneous Question Corner

Question 2

Q: How old were you when you started drawing manga? And why did you start?

A: I actually went over this in volume 1, so I'll just summarize here. I started drawing manga seriously in my second year of middle school. I'm trying hard to remember what exactly caused me to start, but I really can't recall.

I've wanted to grow up to be a Manga-ka since elementary school.

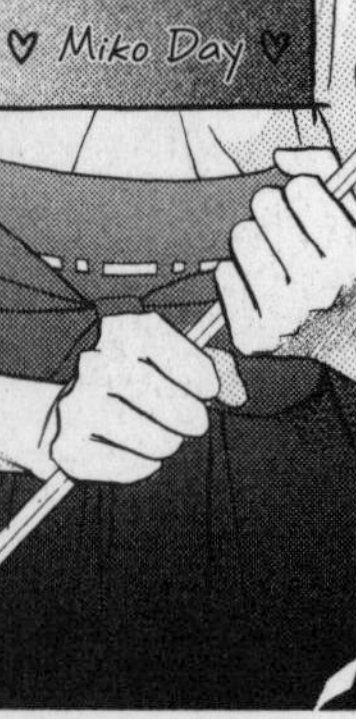

My favorite motto is "You become good at something **because** you love it."

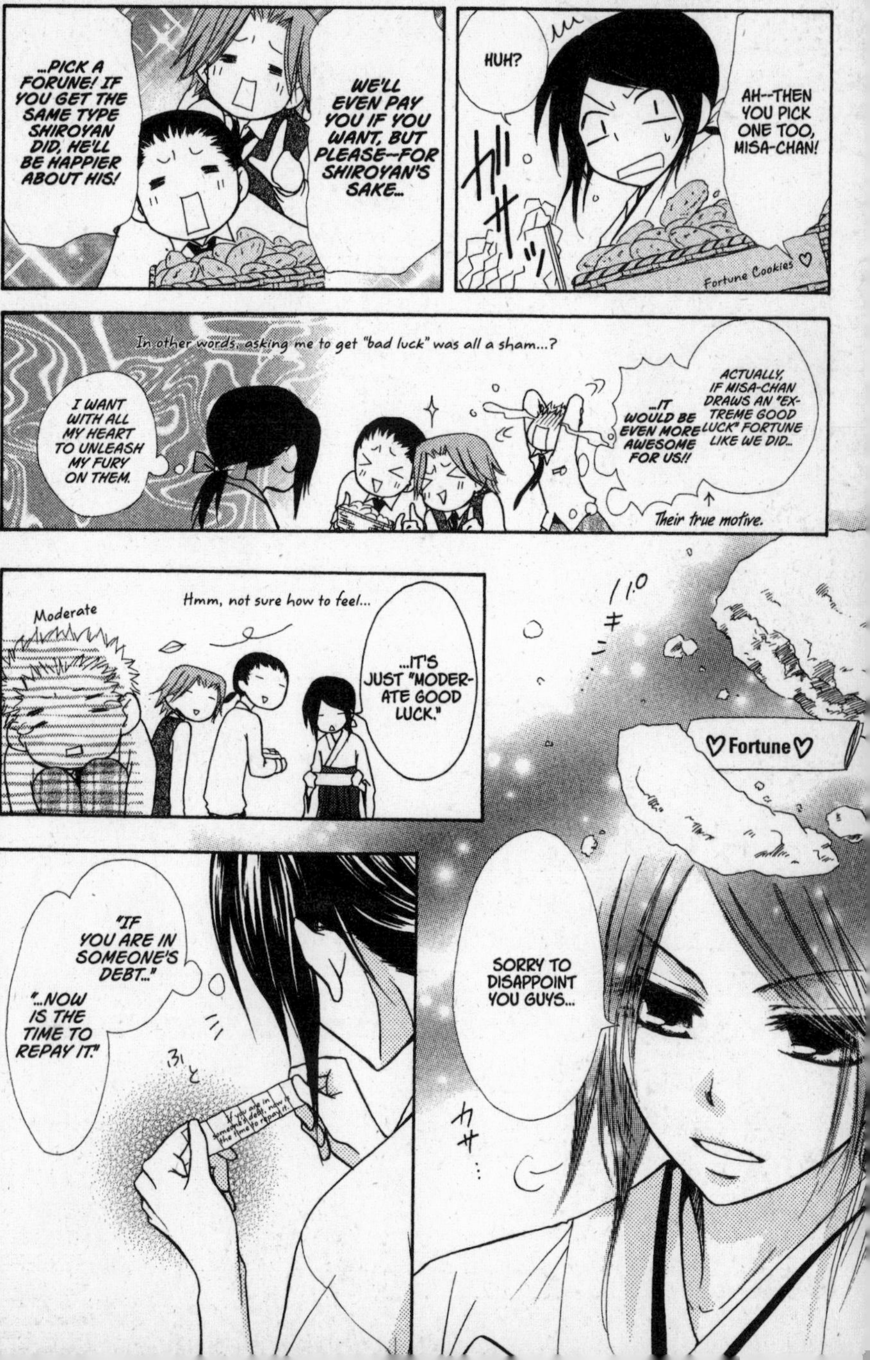
AH--THEN YOU PICK ONE TOO, MISA-CHAN!
HUH?
Fortune Cookies ♡
WE'LL EVEN PAY YOU IF YOU WANT, BUT PLEASE--FOR SHIROYAN'S SAKE...
...PICK A FORUNE! IF YOU GET THE SAME TYPE SHIROYAN DID, HE'LL BE HAPPIER ABOUT HIS!
ACTUALLY, IF MISA-CHAN DRAWS AN "EXTREME GOOD LUCK" FORTUNE LIKE WE DID...
...IT WOULD BE EVEN MORE AWESOME FOR US!!
Their true motive.
In other words, asking me to get "bad luck" was all a sham...?
I WANT WITH ALL MY HEART TO UNLEASH MY FURY ON THEM.
♡Fortune♡
SORRY TO DISAPPOINT YOU GUYS...
...IT'S JUST "MODERATE GOOD LUCK."
Hmm, not sure how to feel...
Moderate
"IF YOU ARE IN SOMEONE'S DEBT..."
"...NOW IS THE TIME TO REPAY IT."
If you are in someone's debt, now is the time to repay it.

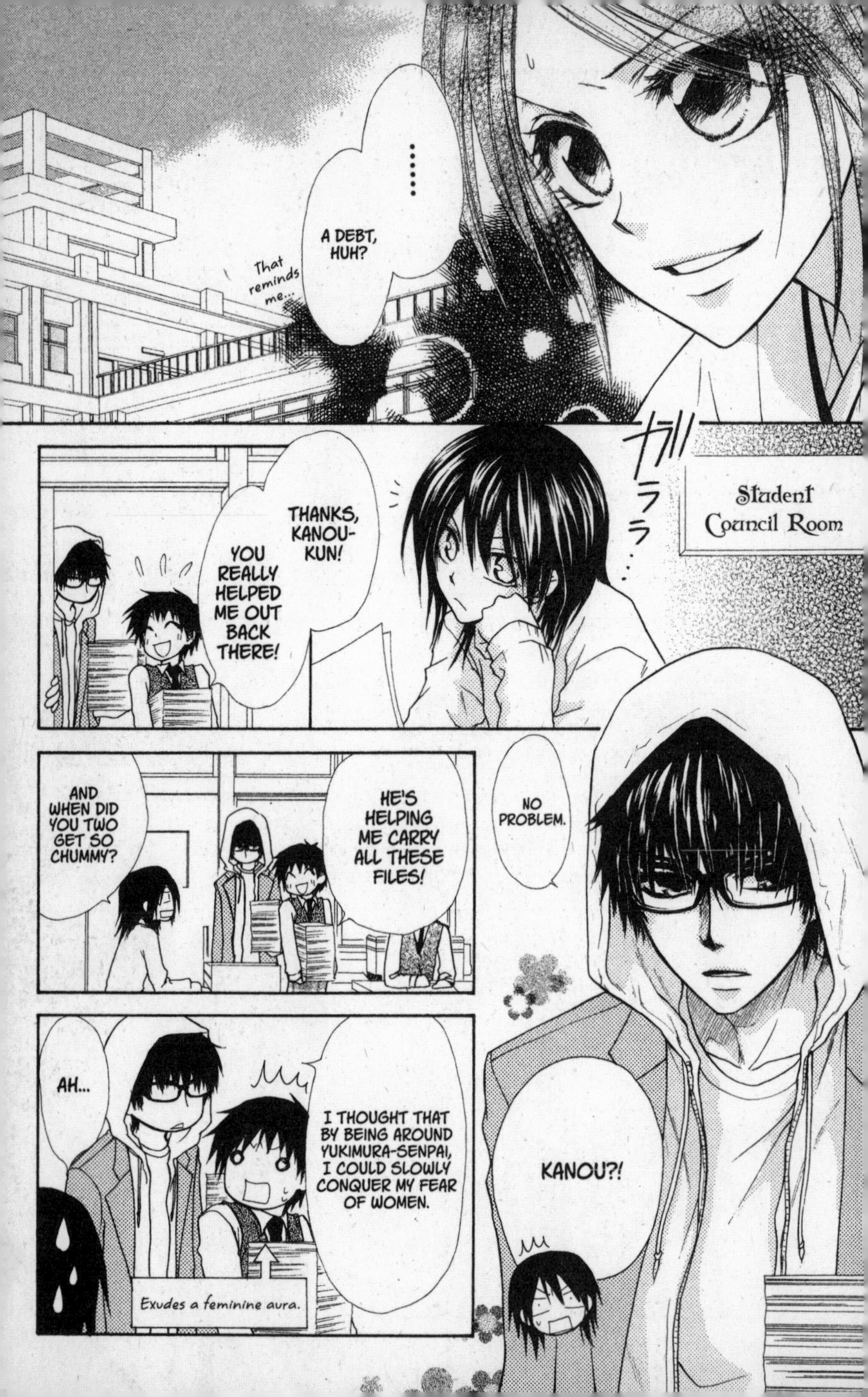

......
A DEBT, HUH?
That reminds me...
ガララ…
Student Council Room
THANKS, KANOU-KUN! YOU REALLY HELPED ME OUT BACK THERE!
NO PROBLEM.
KANOU?!
HE'S HELPING ME CARRY ALL THESE FILES!
AND WHEN DID YOU TWO GET SO CHUMMY?
I THOUGHT THAT BY BEING AROUND YUKIMURA-SENPAI, I COULD SLOWLY CONQUER MY FEAR OF WOMEN.
AH...
Exudes a feminine aura.

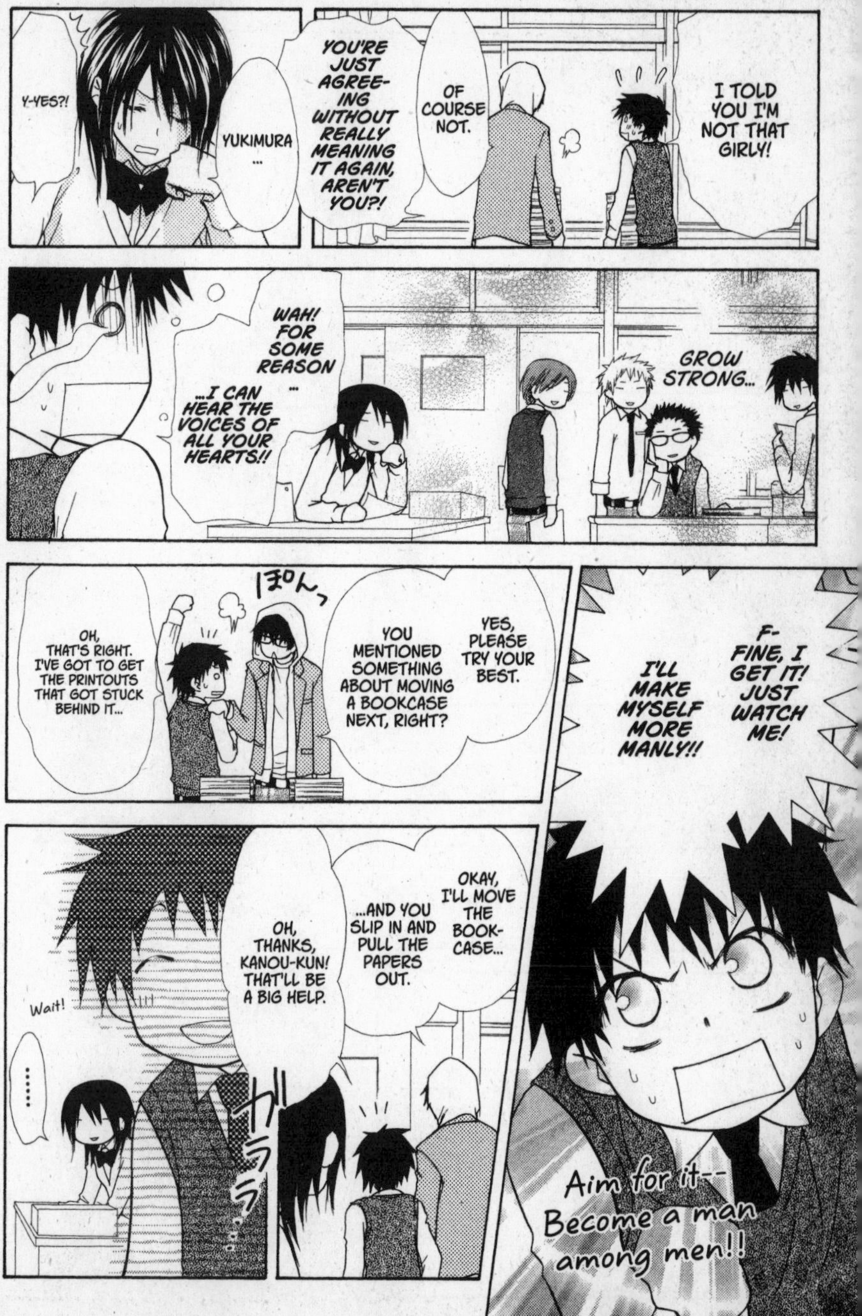
I TOLD YOU I'M NOT THAT GIRLY!
OF COURSE NOT.
YOU'RE JUST AGREEING WITHOUT REALLY MEANING IT AGAIN, AREN'T YOU?!
YUKIMURA ...
Y-YES?!
GROW STRONG...
WAH! FOR SOME REASON ...
...I CAN HEAR THE VOICES OF ALL YOUR HEARTS!!
F-FINE, I GET IT! JUST WATCH ME!
I'LL MAKE MYSELF MORE MANLY!!
Aim for it-- Become a man among men!!
YES, PLEASE TRY YOUR BEST.
ぽんっ
YOU MENTIONED SOMETHING ABOUT MOVING A BOOKCASE NEXT, RIGHT?
OH, THAT'S RIGHT. I'VE GOT TO GET THE PRINTOUTS THAT GOT STUCK BEHIND IT...
OKAY, I'LL MOVE THE BOOKCASE...
...AND YOU SLIP IN AND PULL THE PAPERS OUT.
OH, THANKS, KANOU-KUN! THAT'LL BE A BIG HELP.
ガララ...
Wait!
......

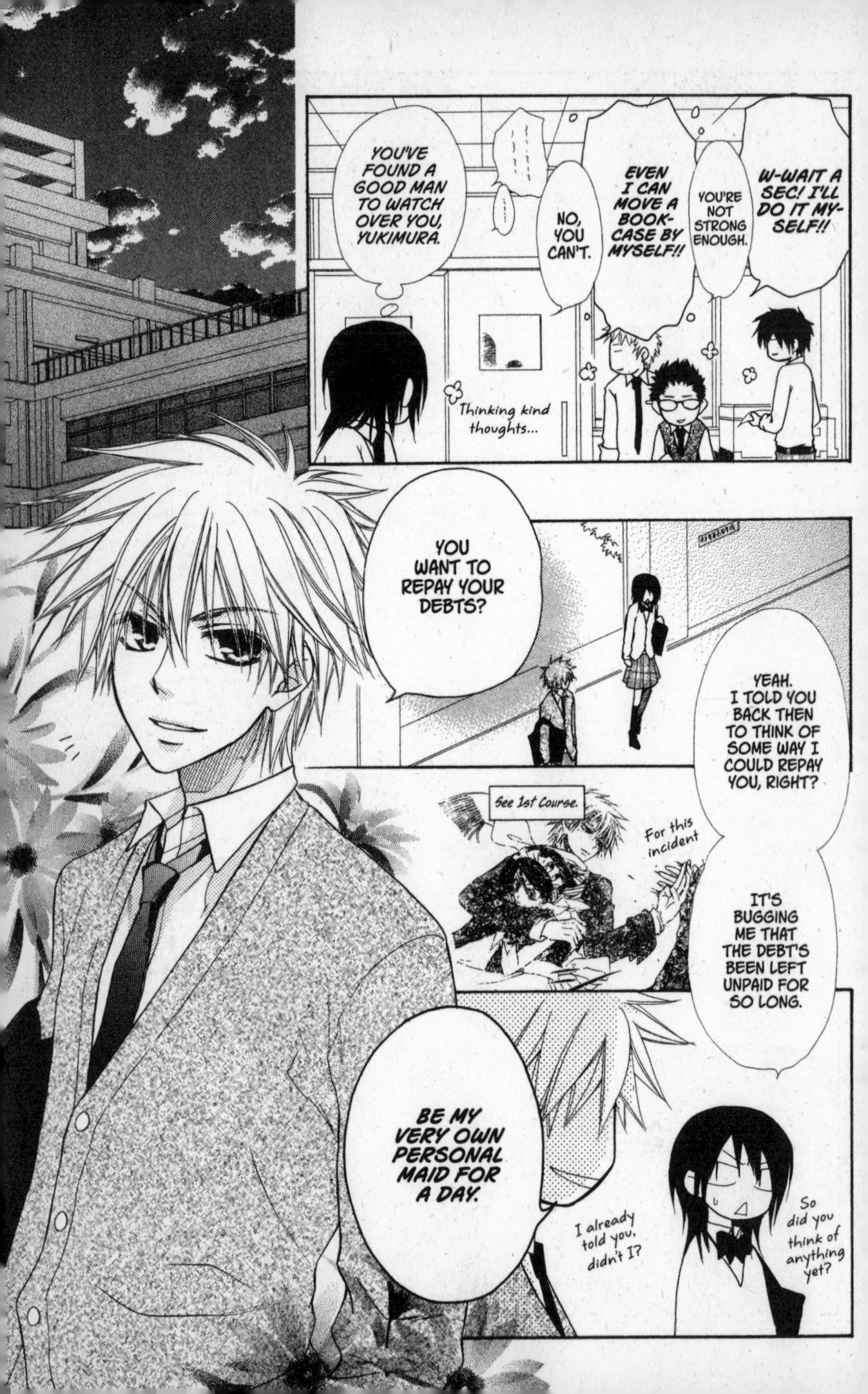
W-WAIT A SEC! I'LL DO IT MYSELF!!
YOU'RE NOT STRONG ENOUGH.
EVEN I CAN MOVE A BOOK-CASE BY MYSELF!!
NO, YOU CAN'T.
YOU'VE FOUND A GOOD MAN TO WATCH OVER YOU, YUKIMURA.
Thinking kind thoughts...
YOU WANT TO REPAY YOUR DEBTS?
YEAH. I TOLD YOU BACK THEN TO THINK OF SOME WAY I COULD REPAY YOU, RIGHT?
See 1st Course.
For this incident
IT'S BUGGING ME THAT THE DEBT'S BEEN LEFT UNPAID FOR SO LONG.
So did you think of anything yet?
I already told you, didn't I?
BE MY VERY OWN PERSONAL MAID FOR A DAY.

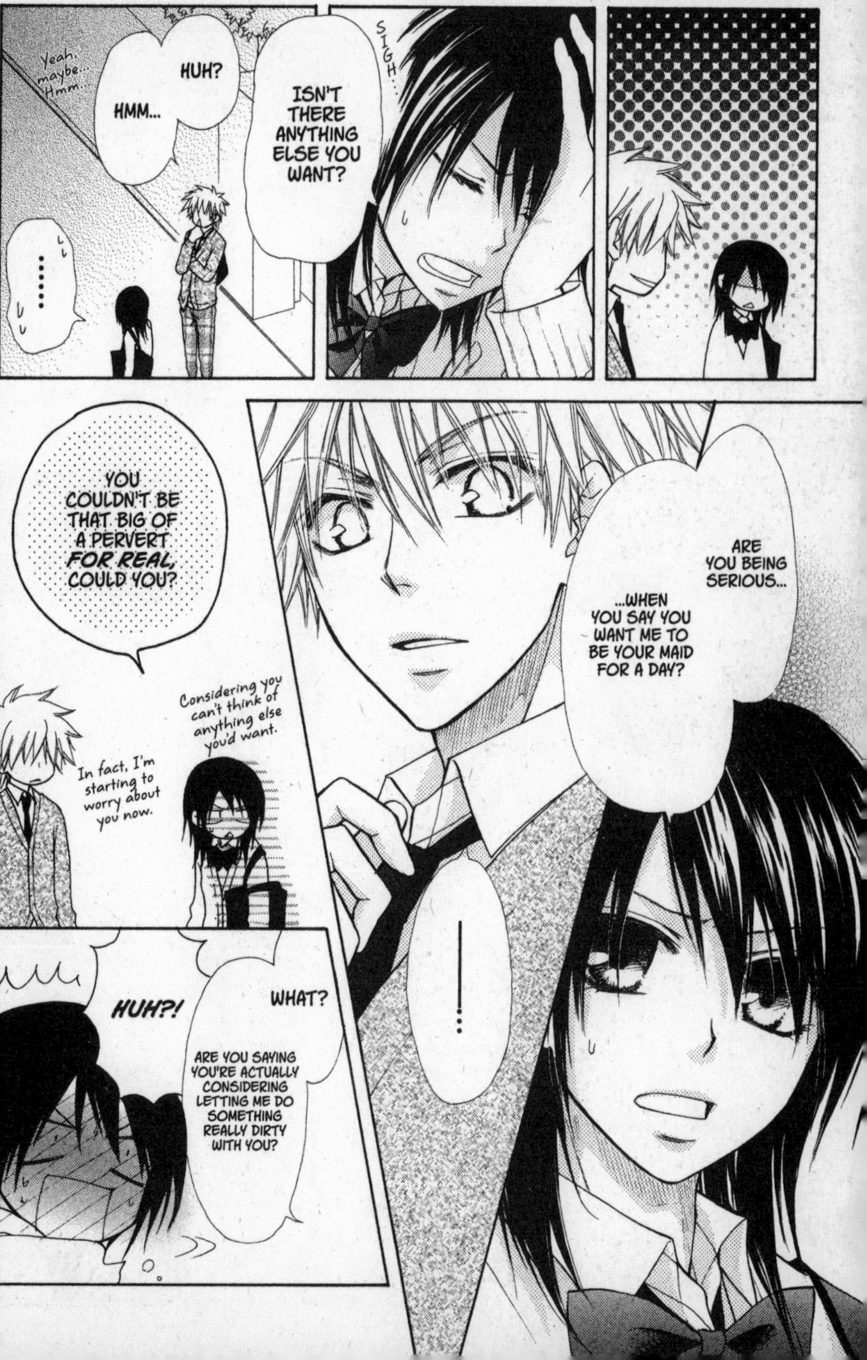
SIGH...
ISN'T THERE ANYTHING ELSE YOU WANT?
HUH?
HMM...
Yeah, maybe... Hmm...
......
ARE YOU BEING SERIOUS...
...WHEN YOU SAY YOU WANT ME TO BE YOUR MAID FOR A DAY?
......
YOU COULDN'T BE THAT BIG OF A PERVERT *FOR REAL,* COULD YOU?
Considering you can't think of anything else you'd want.
In fact, I'm starting to worry about you now.
WHAT?
ARE YOU SAYING YOU'RE ACTUALLY CONSIDERING LETTING ME DO SOMETHING REALLY DIRTY WITH YOU?
HUH?!

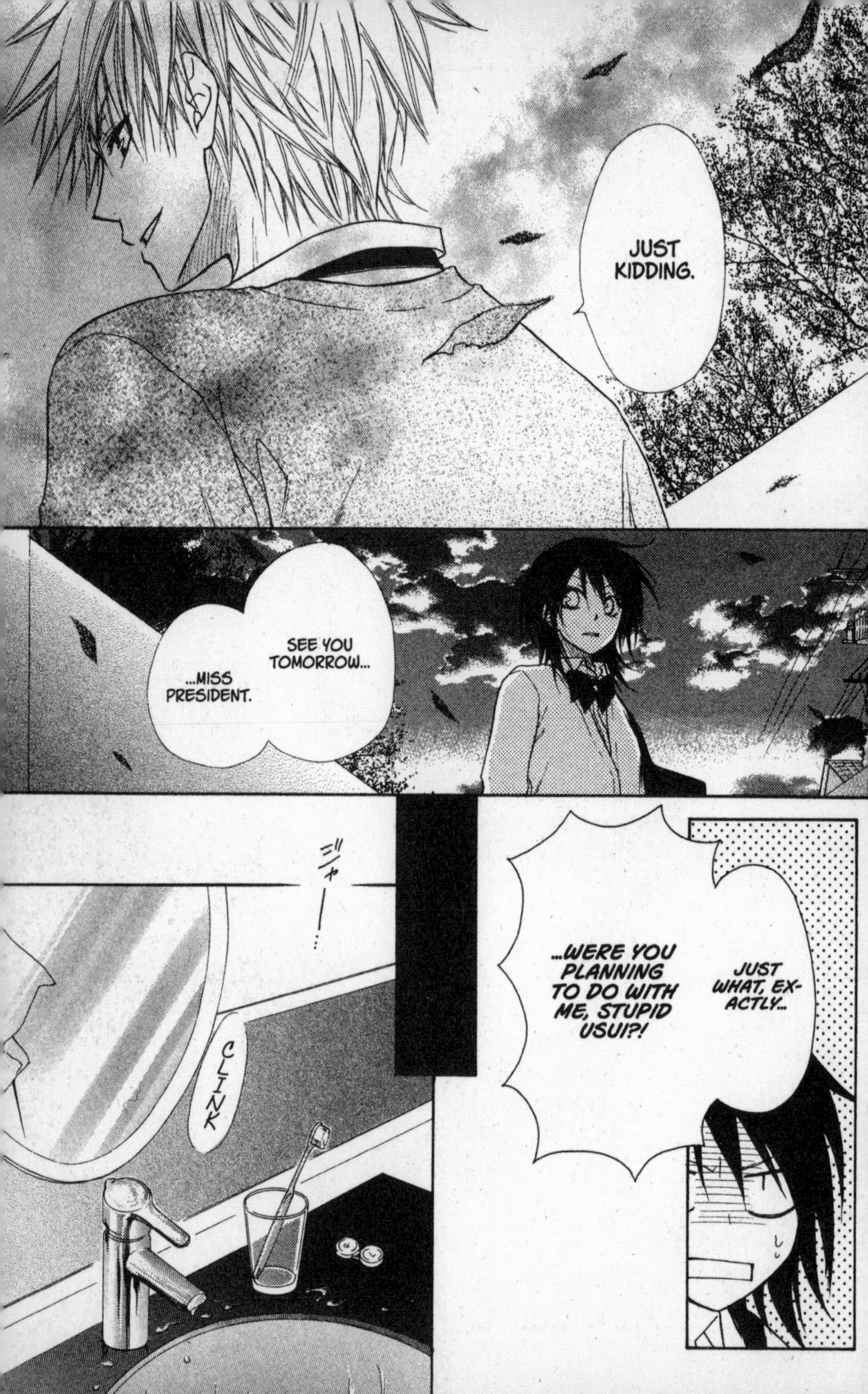
JUST KIDDING.
SEE YOU TOMORROW...
...MISS PRESIDENT.
JUST WHAT, EXACTLY...
...WERE YOU PLANNING TO DO WITH ME, STUPID USUI?!
ジャー…
CLINK

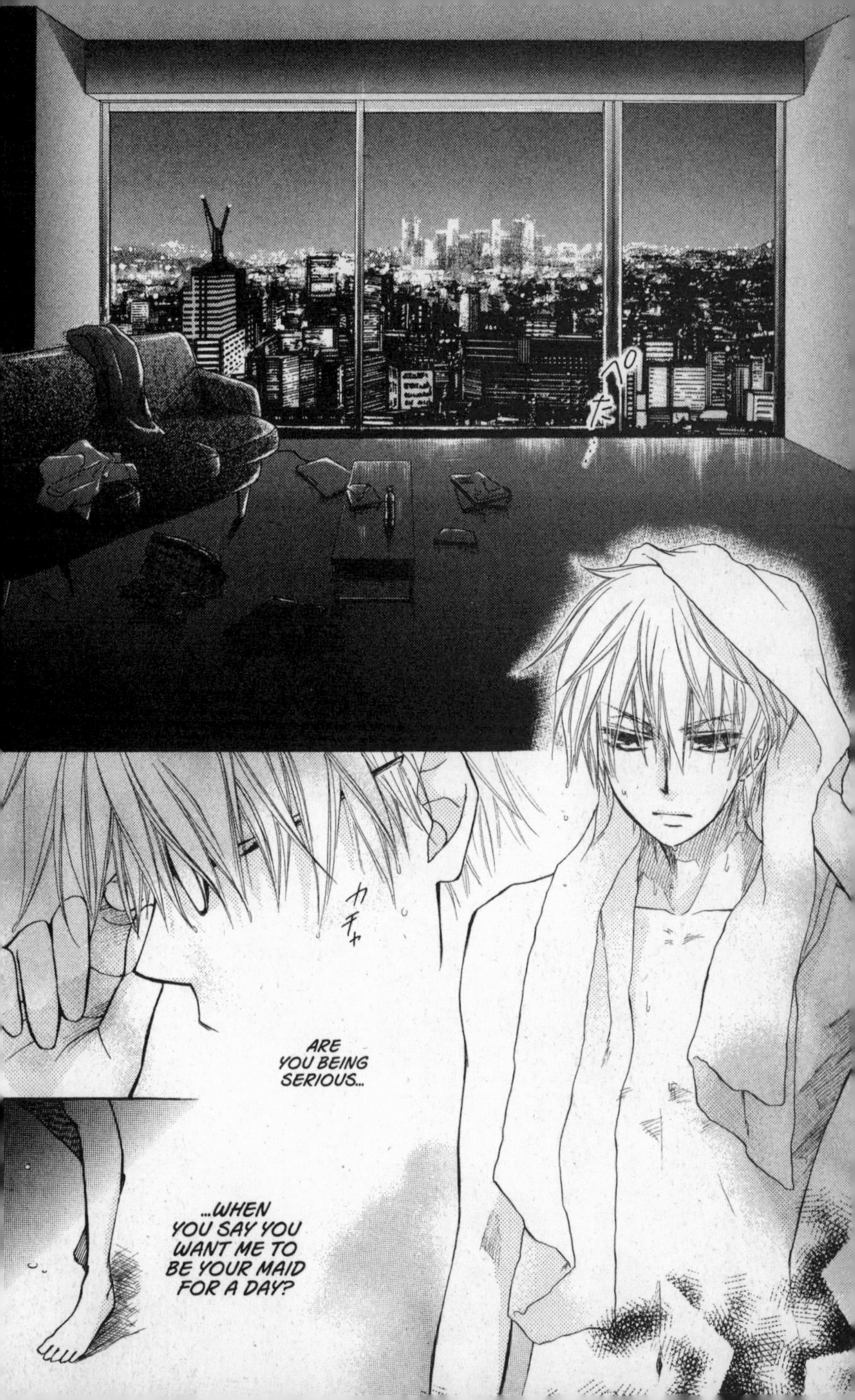
カチャ
ARE YOU BEING SERIOUS...
...WHEN YOU SAY YOU WANT ME TO BE YOUR MAID FOR A DAY?

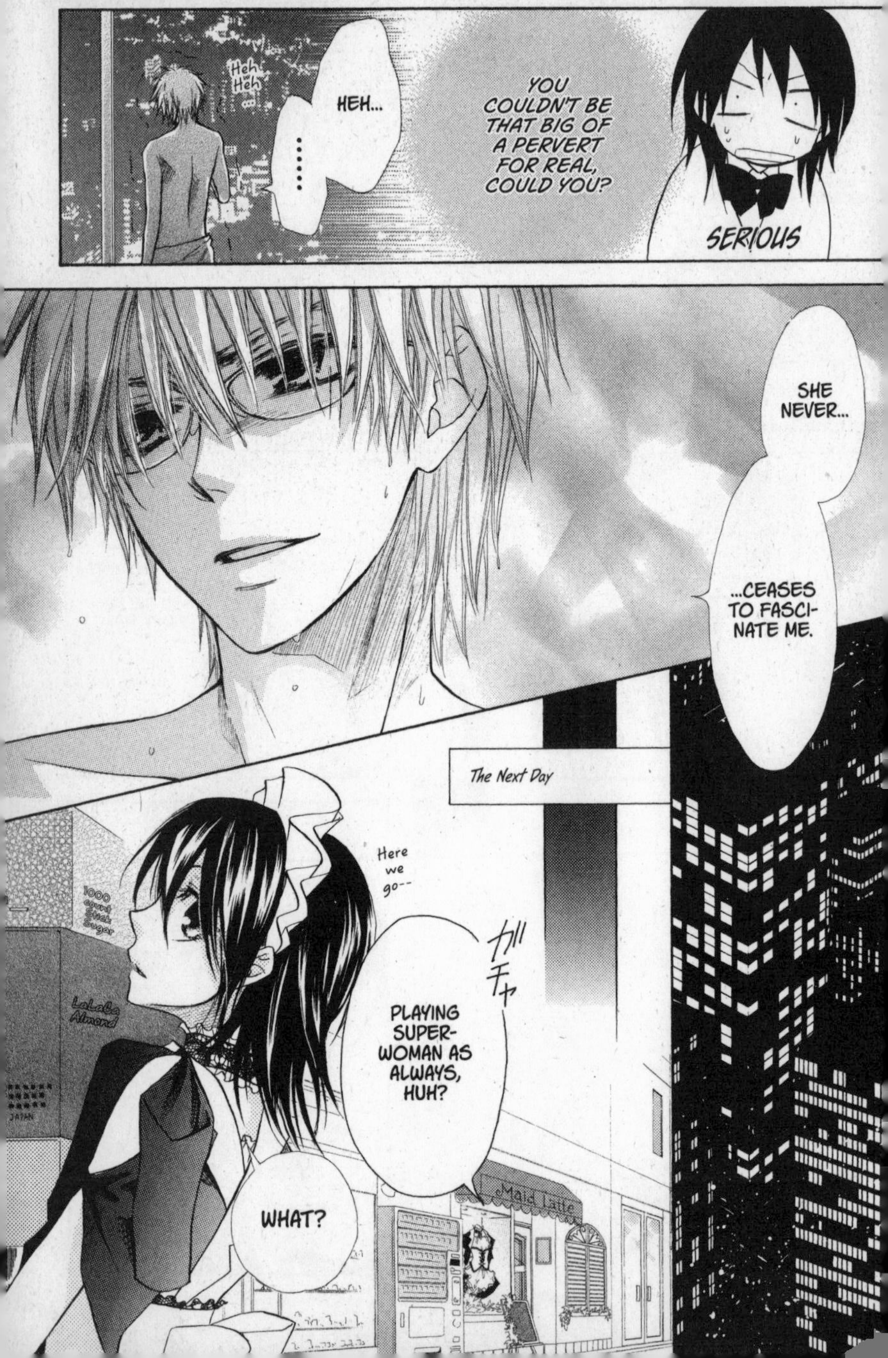
YOU COULDN'T BE THAT BIG OF A PERVERT FOR REAL, COULD YOU?
SERIOUS
HEH...
Heh Heh
......
SHE NEVER...
...CEASES TO FASCINATE ME.
The Next Day
Here we go--
ガチャ
1000 count Stick Sugar
PLAYING SUPER-WOMAN AS ALWAYS, HUH?
WHAT?
Maid Latte

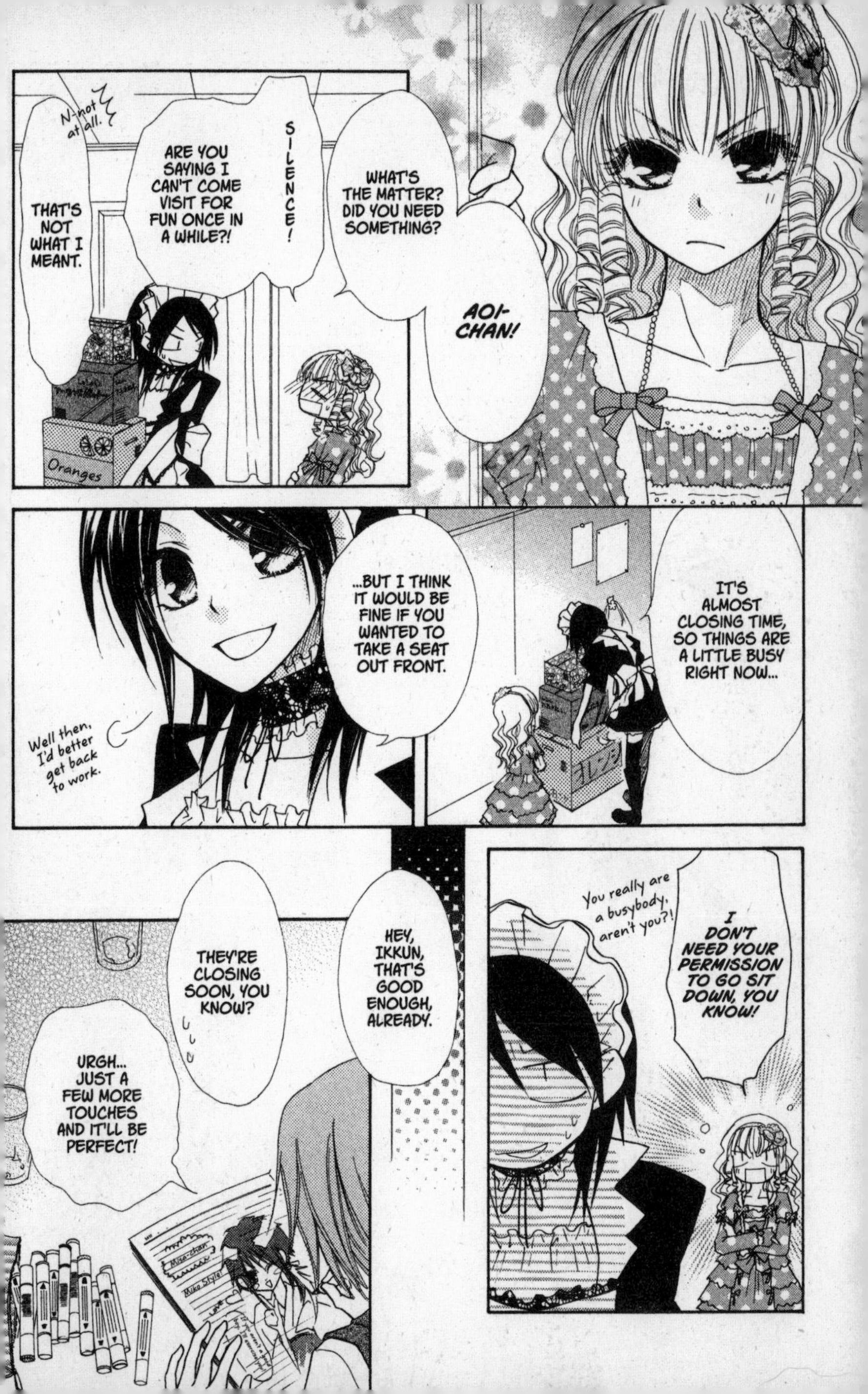
AOI-CHAN!
WHAT'S THE MATTER? DID YOU NEED SOMETHING?
SILENCE!
ARE YOU SAYING I CAN'T COME VISIT FOR FUN ONCE IN A WHILE?!
N-not at all.
THAT'S NOT WHAT I MEANT.
Oranges
IT'S ALMOST CLOSING TIME, SO THINGS ARE A LITTLE BUSY RIGHT NOW...
...BUT I THINK IT WOULD BE FINE IF YOU WANTED TO TAKE A SEAT OUT FRONT.
Well then, I'd better get back to work.
I DON'T NEED YOUR PERMISSION TO GO SIT DOWN, YOU KNOW!
You really are a busybody, aren't you?!
HEY, IKKUN, THAT'S GOOD ENOUGH, ALREADY.
THEY'RE CLOSING SOON, YOU KNOW?
URGH... JUST A FEW MORE TOUCHES AND IT'LL BE PERFECT!
Misa-chan
Miko Style!

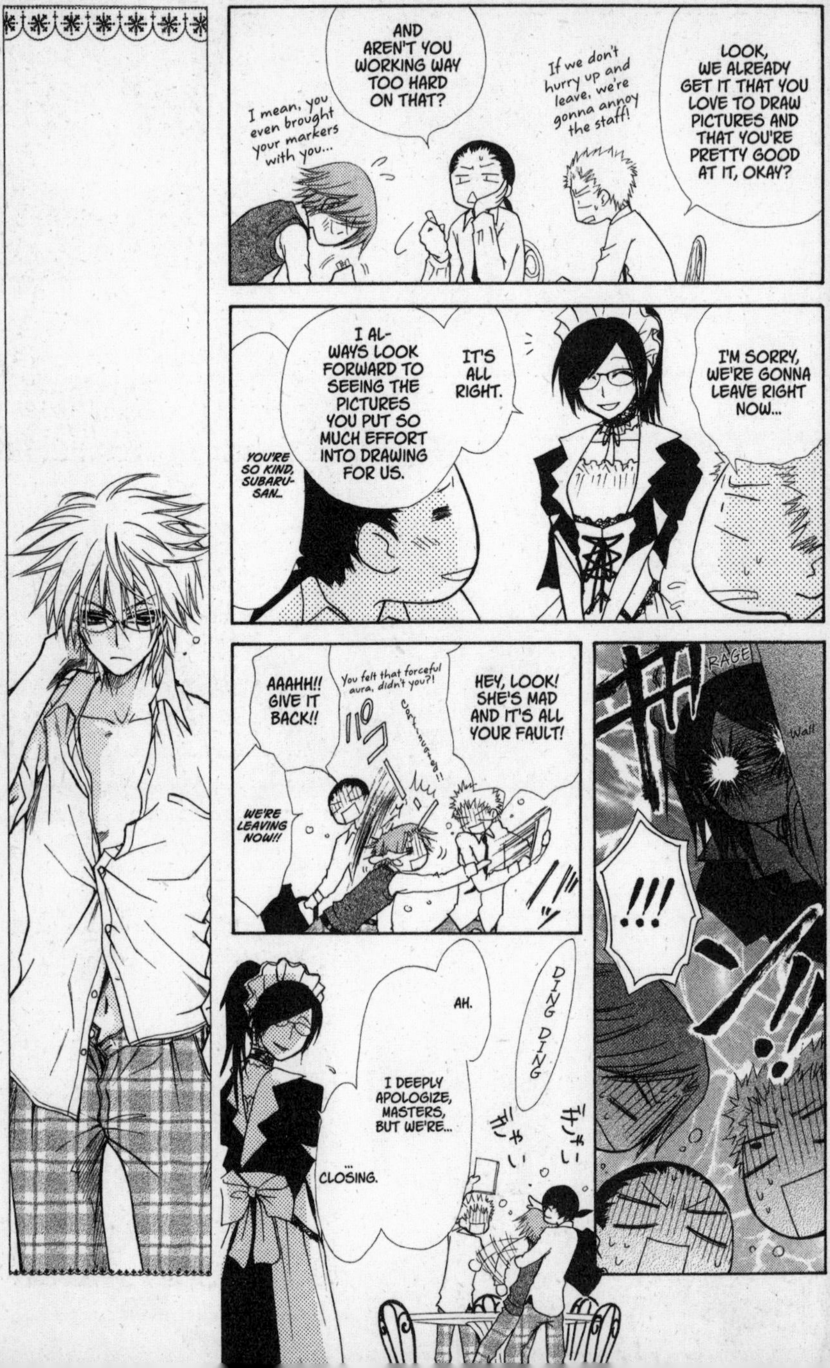
LOOK, WE ALREADY GET IT THAT YOU LOVE TO DRAW PICTURES AND THAT YOU'RE PRETTY GOOD AT IT, OKAY?
If we don't hurry up and leave, we're gonna annoy the staff!
AND AREN'T YOU WORKING WAY TOO HARD ON THAT?
I mean, you even brought your markers with you...
I'M SORRY, WE'RE GONNA LEAVE RIGHT NOW...
IT'S ALL RIGHT.
I ALWAYS LOOK FORWARD TO SEEING THE PICTURES YOU PUT SO MUCH EFFORT INTO DRAWING FOR US.
YOU'RE SO KIND, SUBARU-SAN...
RAGE
Wall
!!!
HEY, LOOK! SHE'S MAD AND IT'S ALL YOUR FAULT!
You felt that forceful aura, didn't you?!
Confiscated!!
AAAHH!! GIVE IT BACK!!
WE'RE LEAVING NOW!!
DING DING
AH.
I DEEPLY APOLOGIZE, MASTERS, BUT WE'RE...
... CLOSING.

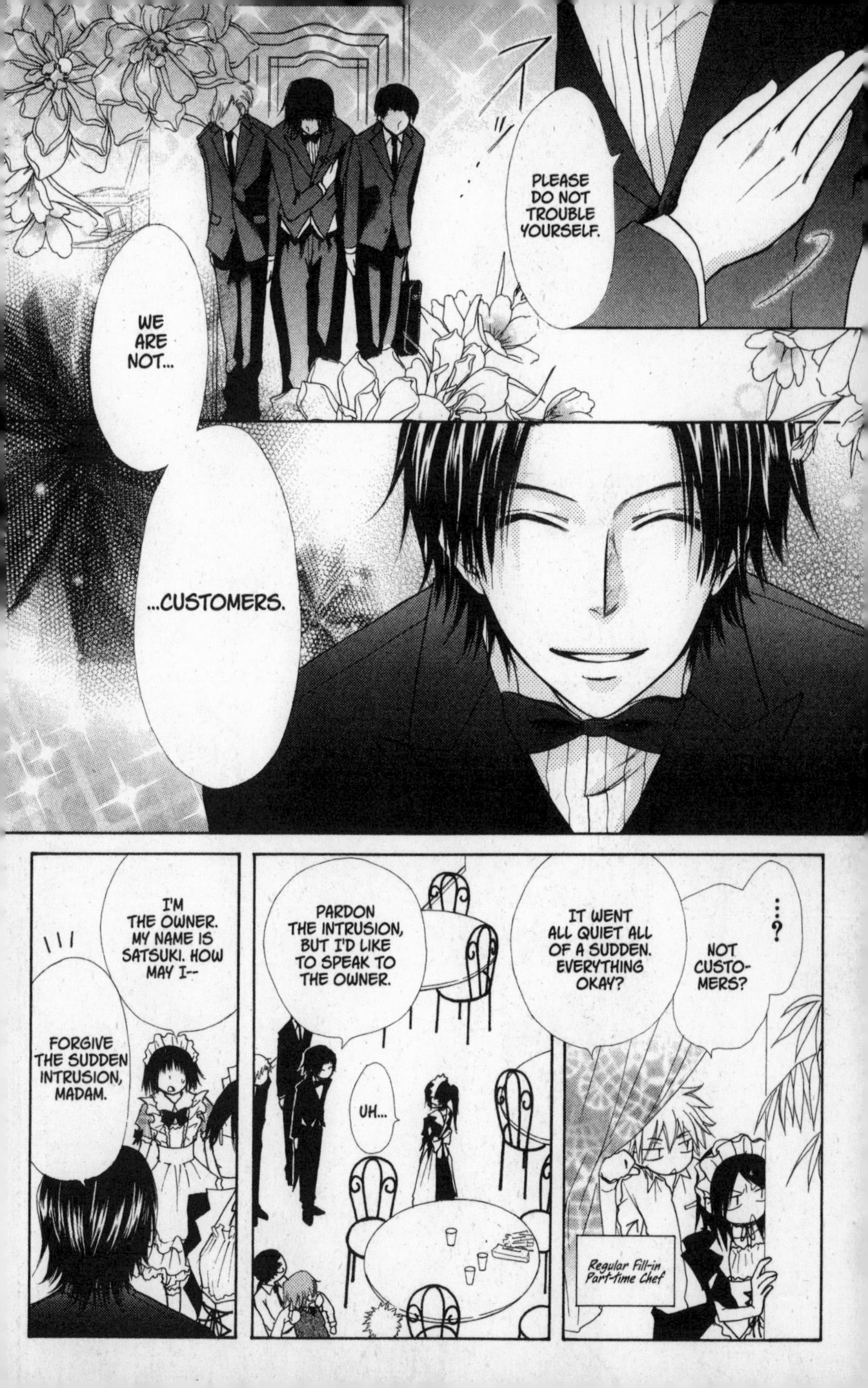
PLEASE DO NOT TROUBLE YOURSELF.
WE ARE NOT...
...CUSTOMERS.
...?
NOT CUSTO-MERS?
IT WENT ALL QUIET ALL OF A SUDDEN. EVERYTHING OKAY?
Regular Fill-in Part-time Chef
PARDON THE INTRUSION, BUT I'D LIKE TO SPEAK TO THE OWNER.
UH...
I'M THE OWNER. MY NAME IS SATSUKI. HOW MAY I--
FORGIVE THE SUDDEN INTRUSION, MADAM.

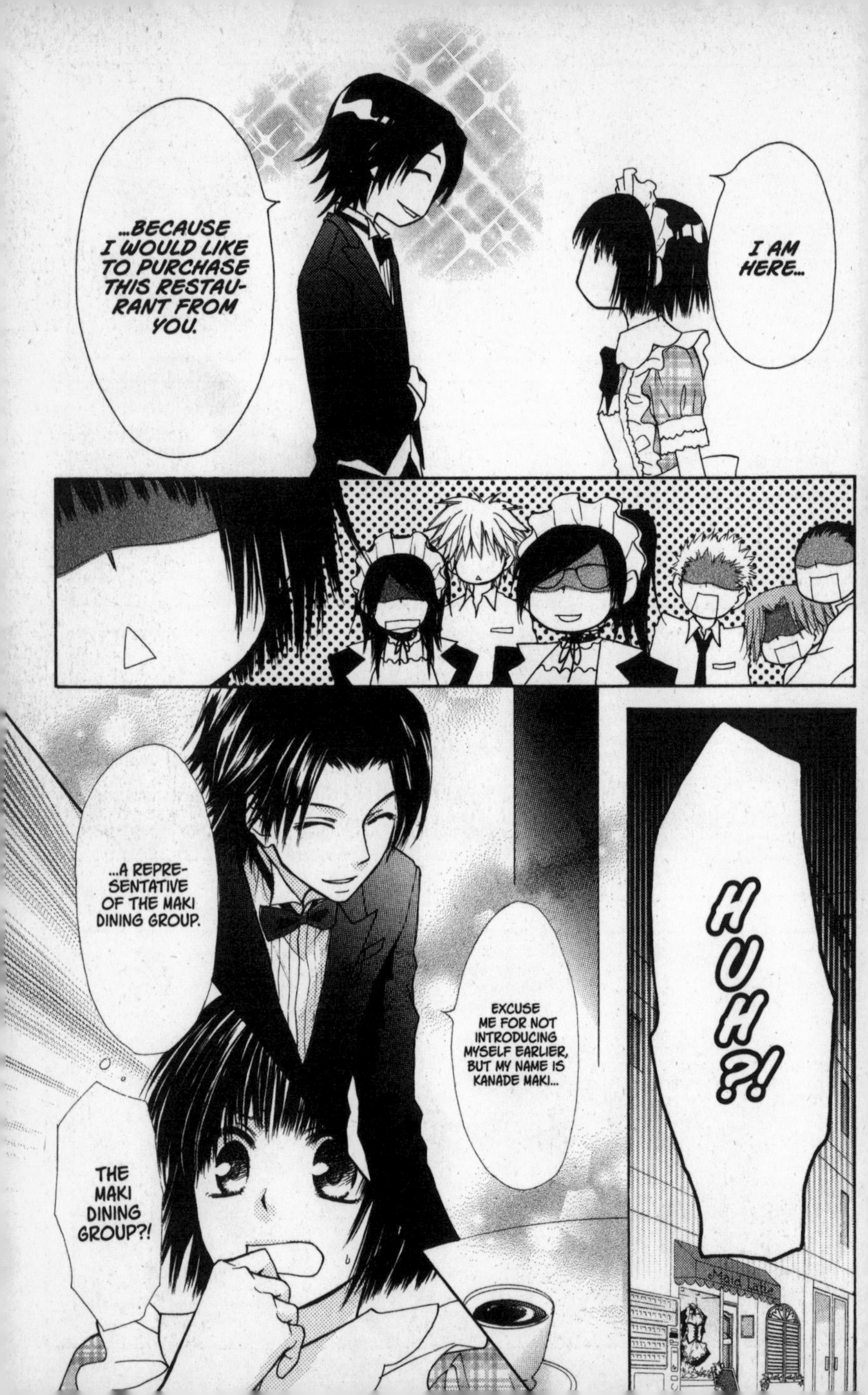
I AM HERE...
...BECAUSE I WOULD LIKE TO PURCHASE THIS RESTAU-RANT FROM YOU.
HUH?!
Maid Latte
EXCUSE ME FOR NOT INTRODUCING MYSELF EARLIER, BUT MY NAME IS KANADE MAKI...
...A REPRE-SENTATIVE OF THE MAKI DINING GROUP.
THE MAKI DINING GROUP?!

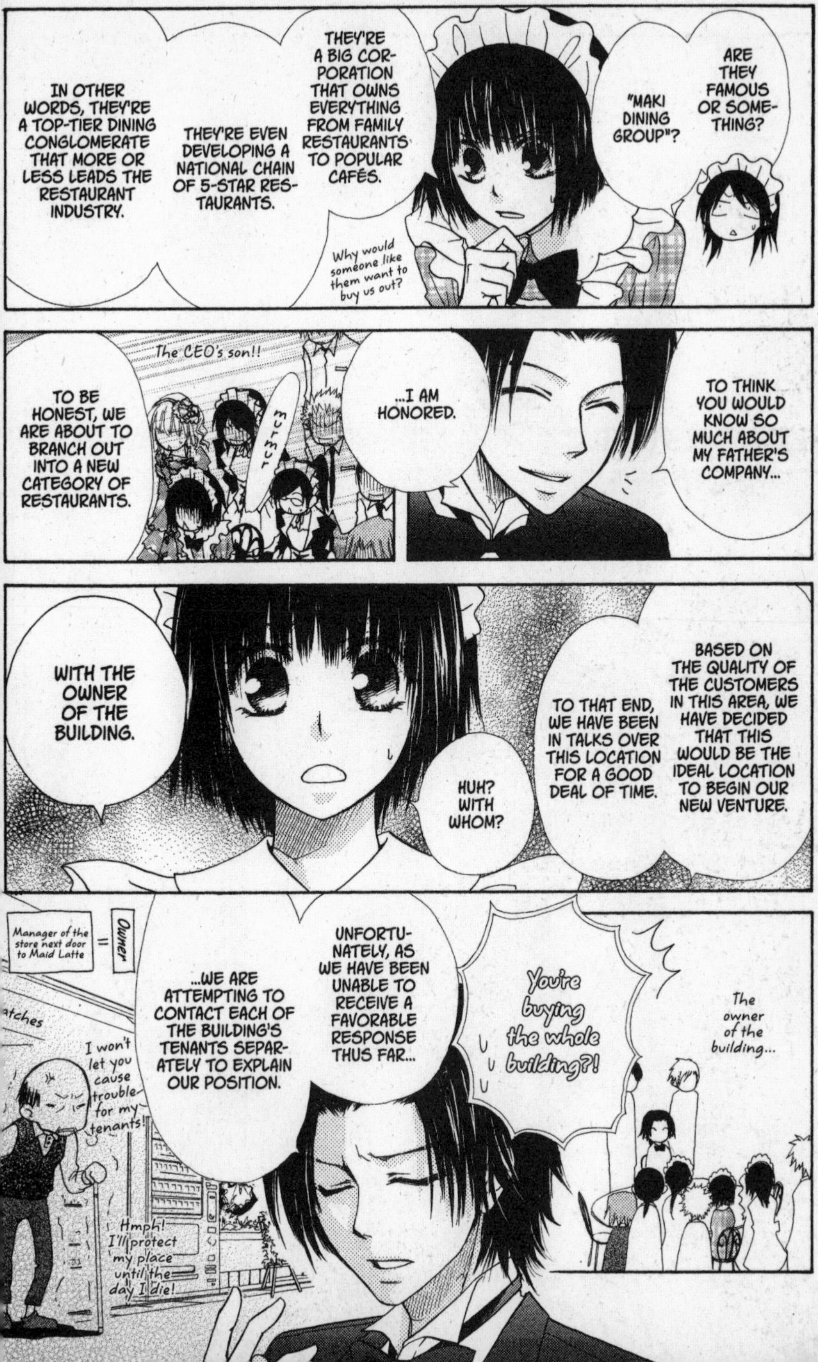
ARE THEY FAMOUS OR SOMETHING?
"MAKI DINING GROUP"?
THEY'RE A BIG CORPORATION THAT OWNS EVERYTHING FROM FAMILY RESTAURANTS TO POPULAR CAFÉS.
Why would someone like them want to buy us out?
THEY'RE EVEN DEVELOPING A NATIONAL CHAIN OF 5-STAR RESTAURANTS.
IN OTHER WORDS, THEY'RE A TOP-TIER DINING CONGLOMERATE THAT MORE OR LESS LEADS THE RESTAURANT INDUSTRY.
TO THINK YOU WOULD KNOW SO MUCH ABOUT MY FATHER'S COMPANY...
...I AM HONORED.
The CEO's son!!
murmur
TO BE HONEST, WE ARE ABOUT TO BRANCH OUT INTO A NEW CATEGORY OF RESTAURANTS.
BASED ON THE QUALITY OF THE CUSTOMERS IN THIS AREA, WE HAVE DECIDED THAT THIS WOULD BE THE IDEAL LOCATION TO BEGIN OUR NEW VENTURE.
TO THAT END, WE HAVE BEEN IN TALKS OVER THIS LOCATION FOR A GOOD DEAL OF TIME.
HUH? WITH WHOM?
WITH THE OWNER OF THE BUILDING.
The owner of the building...
You're buying the whole building?!
UNFORTUNATELY, AS WE HAVE BEEN UNABLE TO RECEIVE A FAVORABLE RESPONSE THUS FAR...
...WE ARE ATTEMPTING TO CONTACT EACH OF THE BUILDING'S TENANTS SEPARATELY TO EXPLAIN OUR POSITION.
Manager of the store next door to Maid Latte = Owner
I won't let you cause trouble for my tenants!
Hmph! I'll protect my place until the day I die!

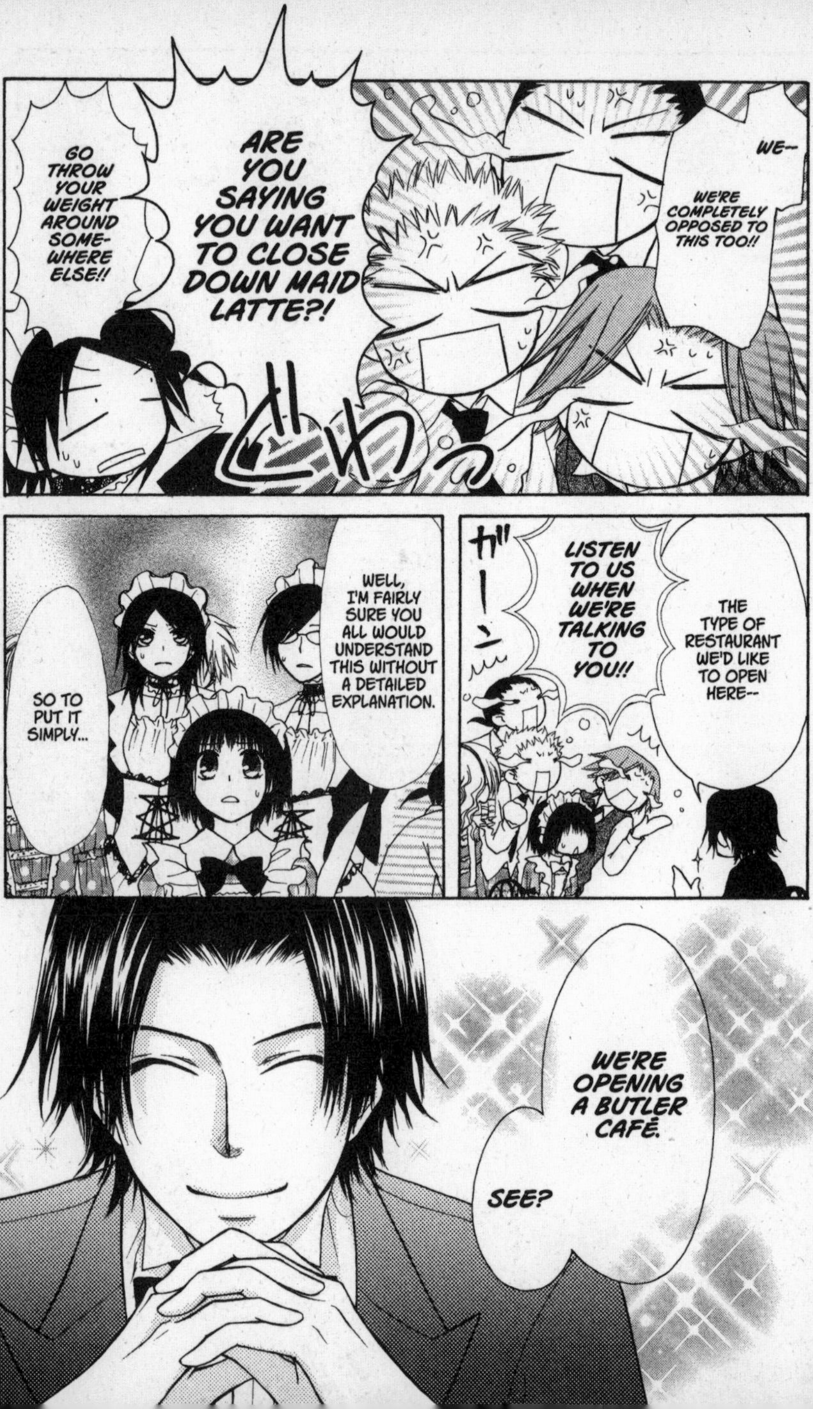
WE--
WE'RE COMPLETELY OPPOSED TO THIS TOO!!
ARE YOU SAYING YOU WANT TO CLOSE DOWN MAID LATTE?!
GO THROW YOUR WEIGHT AROUND SOME-WHERE ELSE!!
THE TYPE OF RESTAURANT WE'D LIKE TO OPEN HERE--
LISTEN TO US WHEN WE'RE TALKING TO YOU!!
WELL, I'M FAIRLY SURE YOU ALL WOULD UNDERSTAND THIS WITHOUT A DETAILED EXPLANATION.
SO TO PUT IT SIMPLY...
WE'RE OPENING A BUTLER CAFÉ.
SEE?

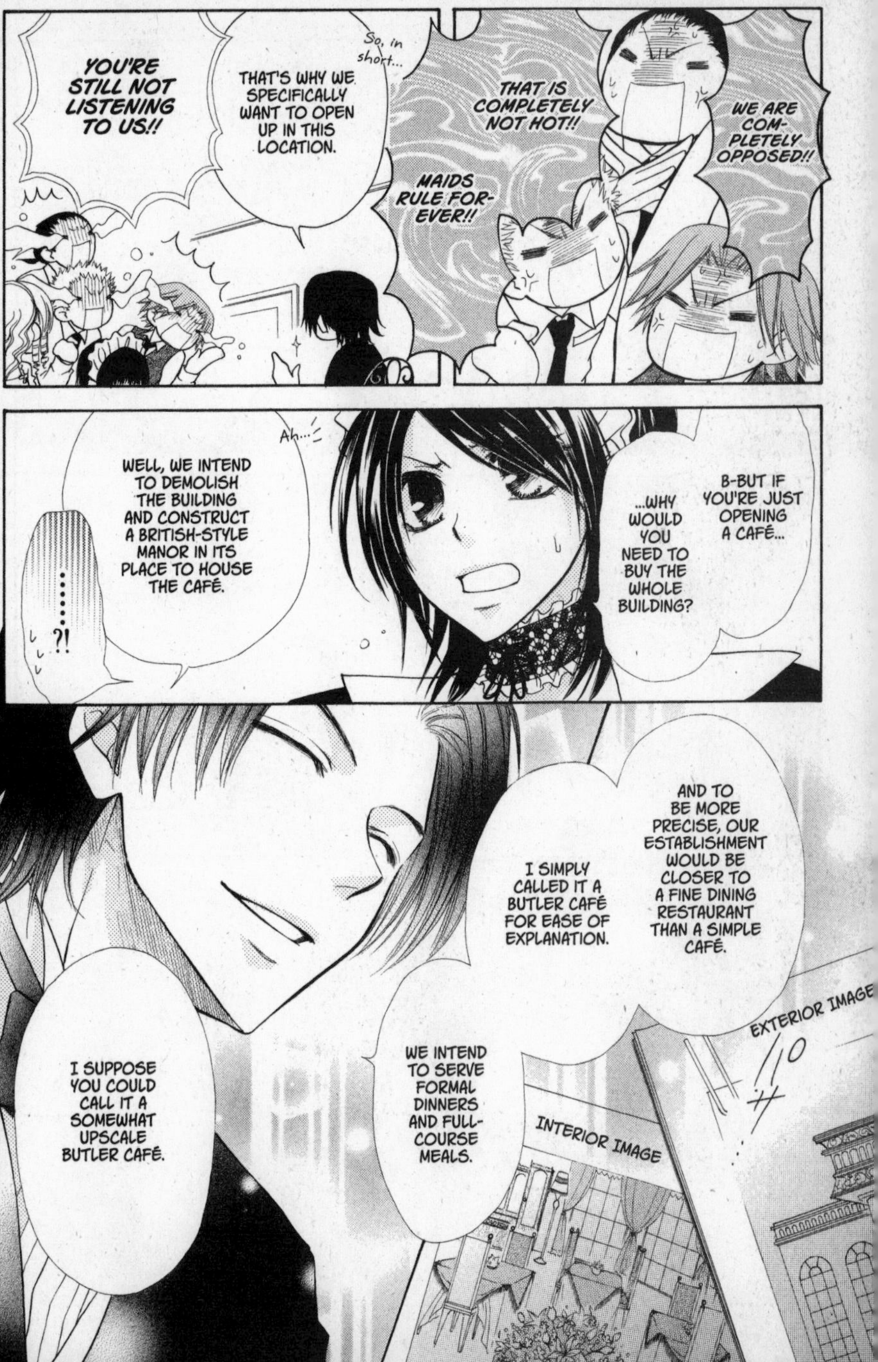
WE ARE COMPLETELY OPPOSED!!
THAT IS COMPLETELY NOT HOT!!
MAIDS RULE FOREVER!!
So, in short...
THAT'S WHY WE SPECIFICALLY WANT TO OPEN UP IN THIS LOCATION.
YOU'RE STILL NOT LISTENING TO US!!
B-BUT IF YOU'RE JUST OPENING A CAFÉ...
...WHY WOULD YOU NEED TO BUY THE WHOLE BUILDING?
Ah...
WELL, WE INTEND TO DEMOLISH THE BUILDING AND CONSTRUCT A BRITISH-STYLE MANOR IN ITS PLACE TO HOUSE THE CAFÉ.
......?!
AND TO BE MORE PRECISE, OUR ESTABLISHMENT WOULD BE CLOSER TO A FINE DINING RESTAURANT THAN A SIMPLE CAFÉ.
I SIMPLY CALLED IT A BUTLER CAFÉ FOR EASE OF EXPLANATION.
EXTERIOR IMAGE
WE INTEND TO SERVE FORMAL DINNERS AND FULL-COURSE MEALS.
INTERIOR IMAGE
I SUPPOSE YOU COULD CALL IT A SOMEWHAT UPSCALE BUTLER CAFÉ.

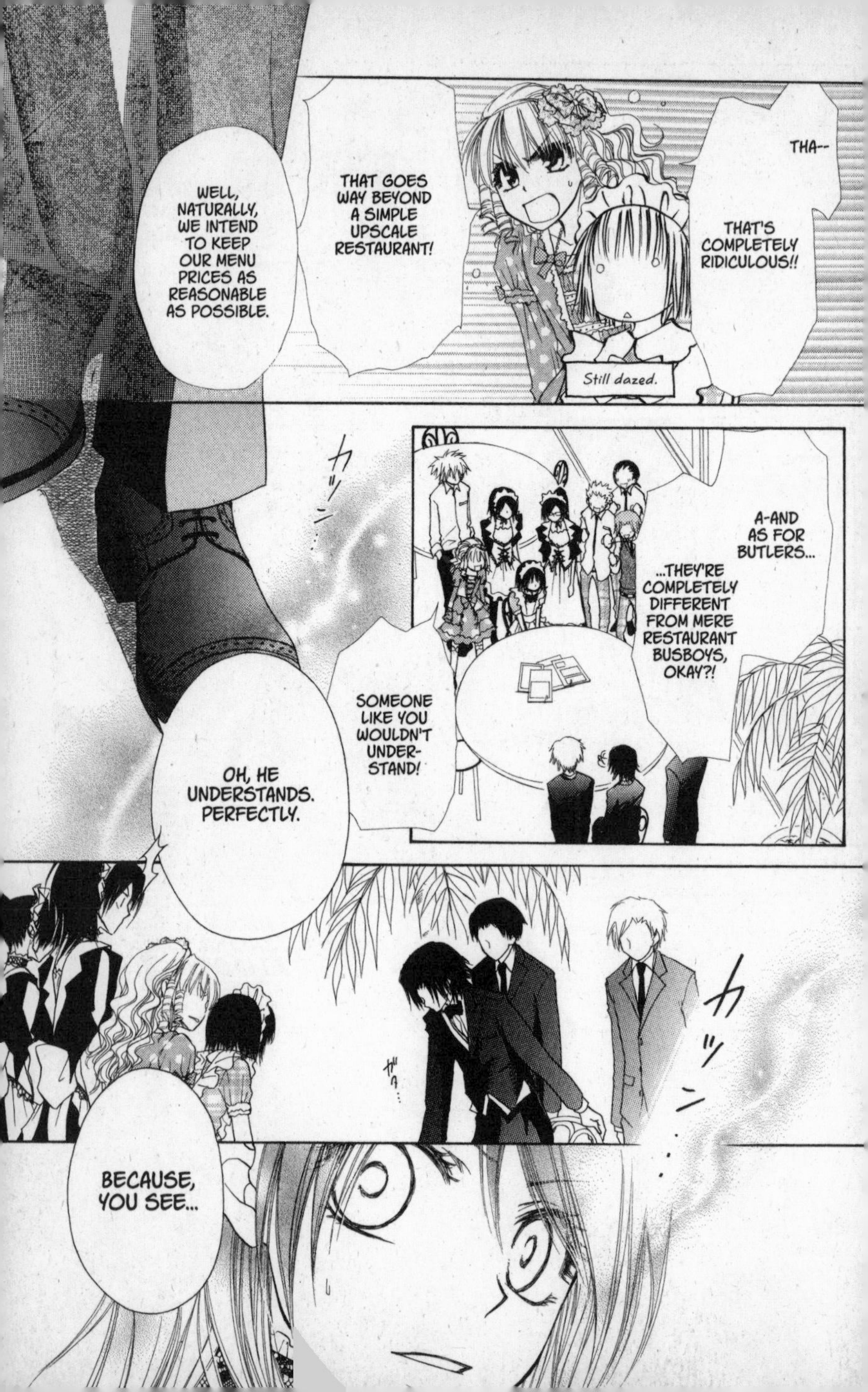
THA--
THAT'S COMPLETELY RIDICULOUS!!
THAT GOES WAY BEYOND A SIMPLE UPSCALE RESTAURANT!
Still dazed.
WELL, NATURALLY, WE INTEND TO KEEP OUR MENU PRICES AS REASONABLE AS POSSIBLE.
A-AND AS FOR BUTLERS...
...THEY'RE COMPLETELY DIFFERENT FROM MERE RESTAURANT BUSBOYS, OKAY?!
SOMEONE LIKE YOU WOULDN'T UNDER-STAND!
カツン…
OH, HE UNDERSTANDS. PERFECTLY.
カツン…
BECAUSE, YOU SEE...

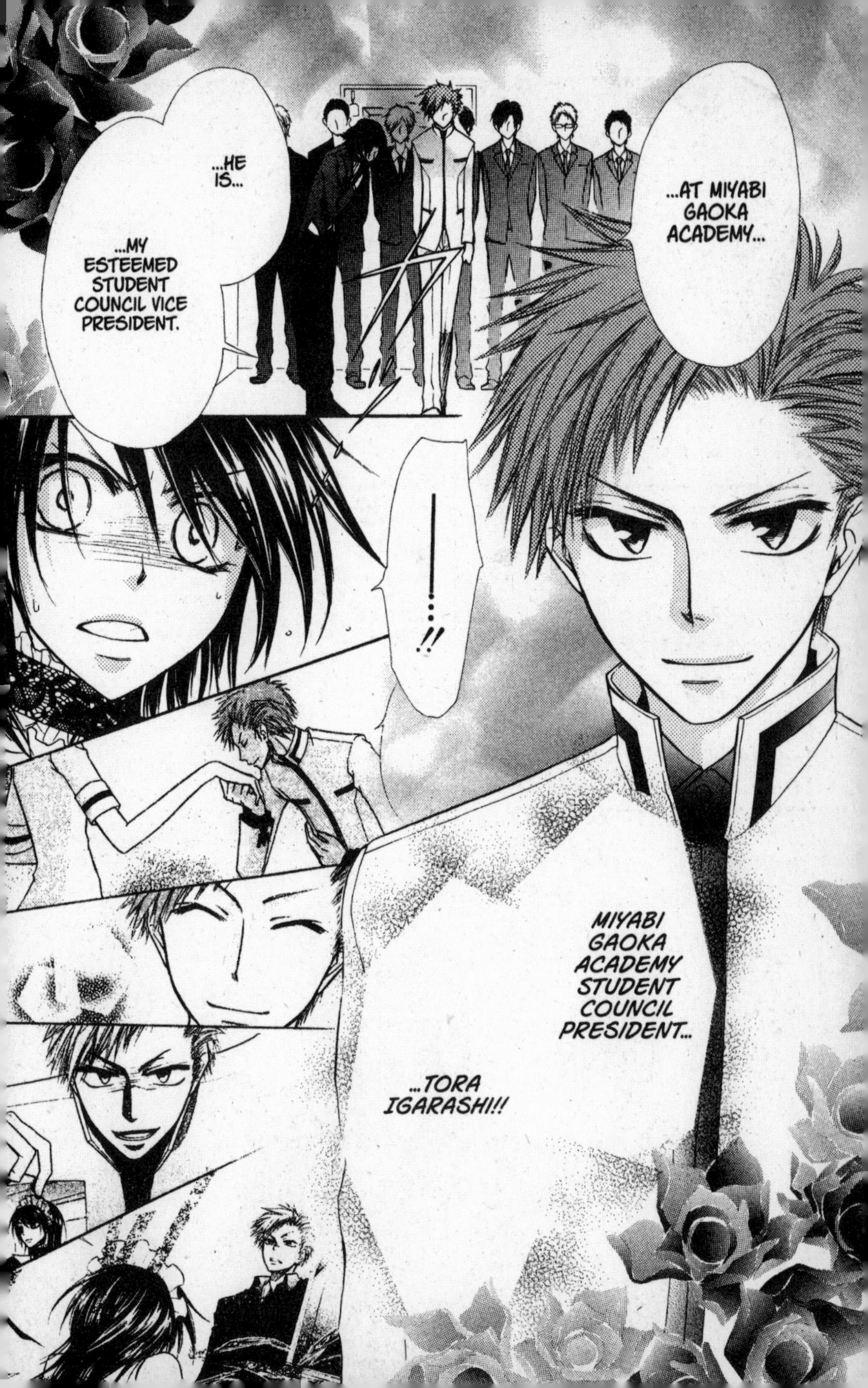
...AT MIYABI GAOKA ACADEMY...
...HE IS...
...MY ESTEEMED STUDENT COUNCIL VICE PRESIDENT.
—...!!
MIYABI GAOKA ACADEMY STUDENT COUNCIL PRESIDENT...
...TORA IGARASHI!!

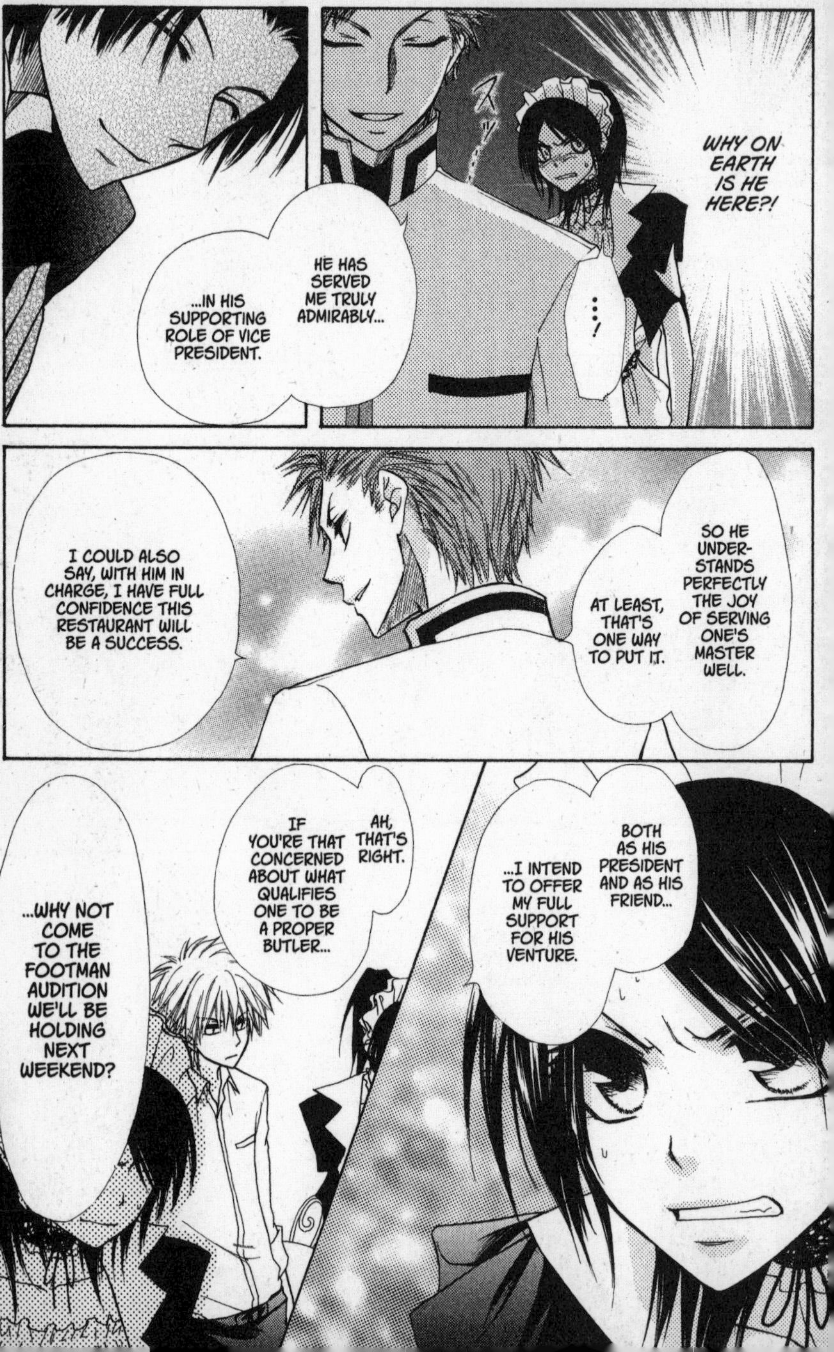
WHY ON EARTH IS HE HERE?!
...!
HE HAS SERVED ME TRULY ADMIRABLY...
...IN HIS SUPPORTING ROLE OF VICE PRESIDENT.
SO HE UNDERSTANDS PERFECTLY THE JOY OF SERVING ONE'S MASTER WELL.
AT LEAST, THAT'S ONE WAY TO PUT IT.
I COULD ALSO SAY, WITH HIM IN CHARGE, I HAVE FULL CONFIDENCE THIS RESTAURANT WILL BE A SUCCESS.
BOTH AS HIS PRESIDENT AND AS HIS FRIEND...
...I INTEND TO OFFER MY FULL SUPPORT FOR HIS VENTURE.
AH, THAT'S RIGHT.
IF YOU'RE THAT CONCERNED ABOUT WHAT QUALIFIES ONE TO BE A PROPER BUTLER...
...WHY NOT COME TO THE FOOTMAN AUDITION WE'LL BE HOLDING NEXT WEEKEND?

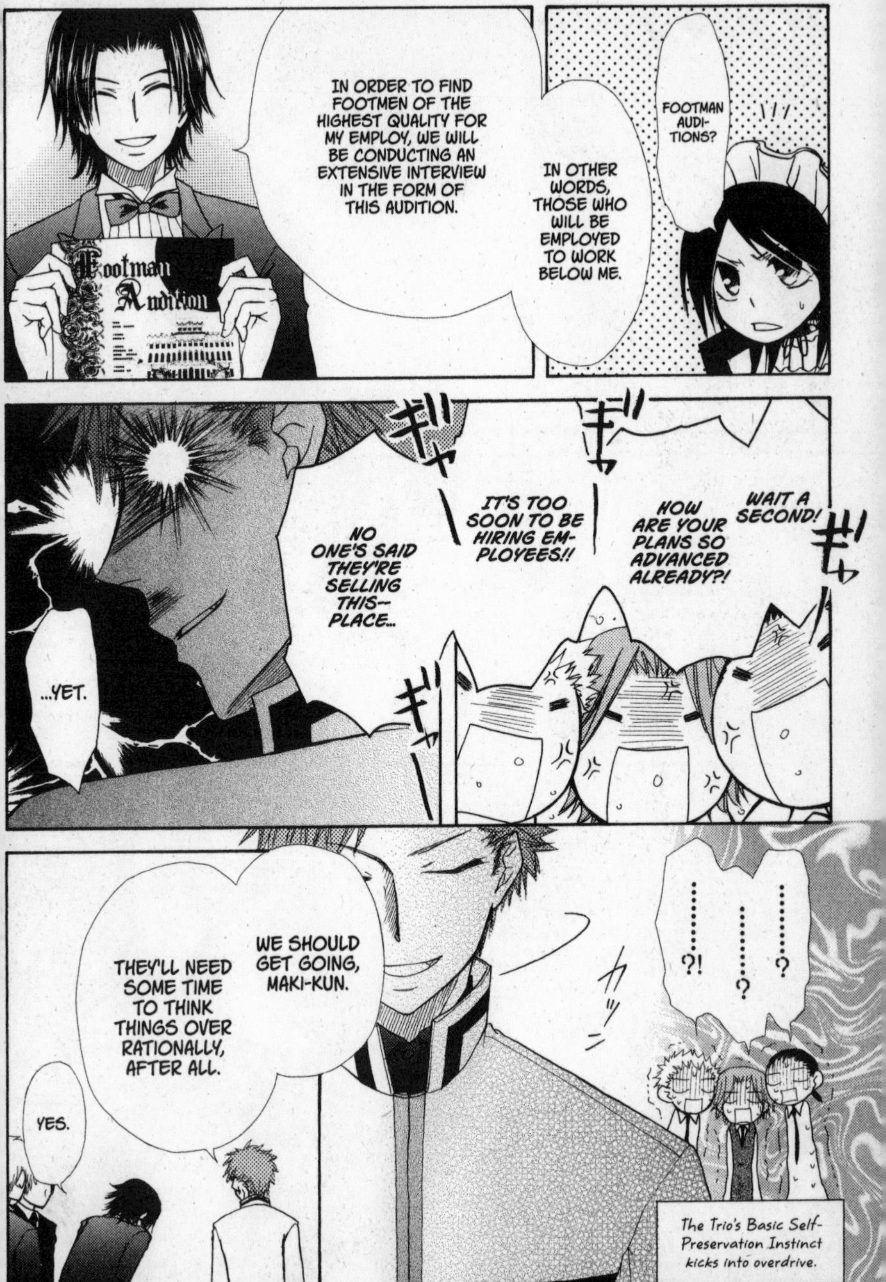
FOOTMAN AUDITIONS?
IN ORDER TO FIND FOOTMEN OF THE HIGHEST QUALITY FOR MY EMPLOY, WE WILL BE CONDUCTING AN EXTENSIVE INTERVIEW IN THE FORM OF THIS AUDITION.
IN OTHER WORDS, THOSE WHO WILL BE EMPLOYED TO WORK BELOW ME.
Footman Audition
ギャー
WAIT A SECOND!
HOW ARE YOUR PLANS SO ADVANCED ALREADY?!
ギャー
IT'S TOO SOON TO BE HIRING EM-PLOYEES!!
ギャー
NO ONE'S SAID THEY'RE SELLING THIS—PLACE...
ギャー
...YET.
......? ......? ......?!
The Trio's Basic Self-Preservation Instinct kicks into overdrive.
カツッ
WE SHOULD GET GOING, MAKI-KUN.
THEY'LL NEED SOME TIME TO THINK THINGS OVER RATIONALLY, AFTER ALL.
YES.

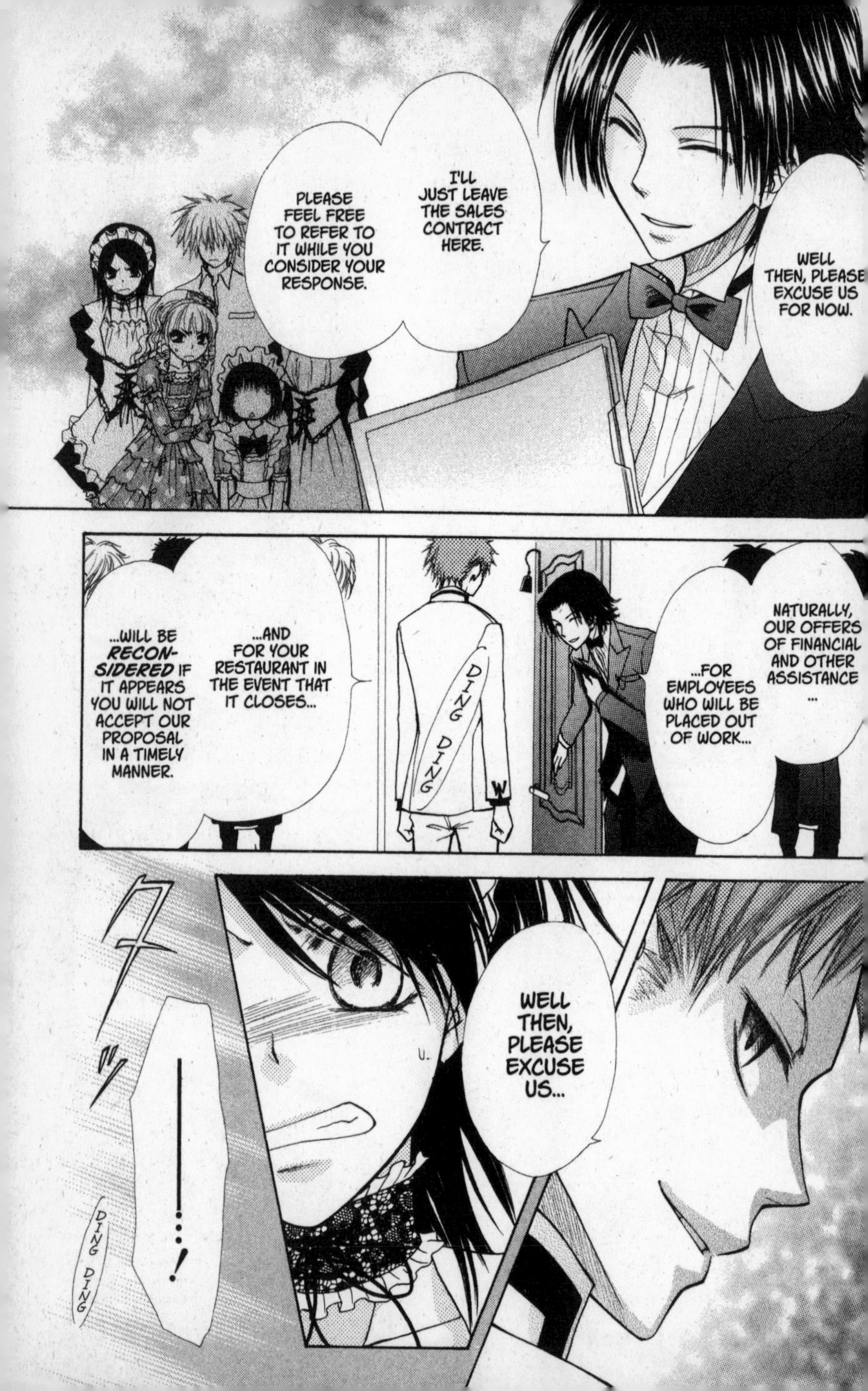
WELL THEN, PLEASE EXCUSE US FOR NOW.
I'LL JUST LEAVE THE SALES CONTRACT HERE.
PLEASE FEEL FREE TO REFER TO IT WHILE YOU CONSIDER YOUR RESPONSE.
NATURALLY, OUR OFFERS OF FINANCIAL AND OTHER ASSISTANCE ...
...FOR EMPLOYEES WHO WILL BE PLACED OUT OF WORK...
DING DING
...AND FOR YOUR RESTAURANT IN THE EVENT THAT IT CLOSES...
...WILL BE *RECONSIDERED* IF IT APPEARS YOU WILL NOT ACCEPT OUR PROPOSAL IN A TIMELY MANNER.
WELL THEN, PLEASE EXCUSE US...
...!
DING DING

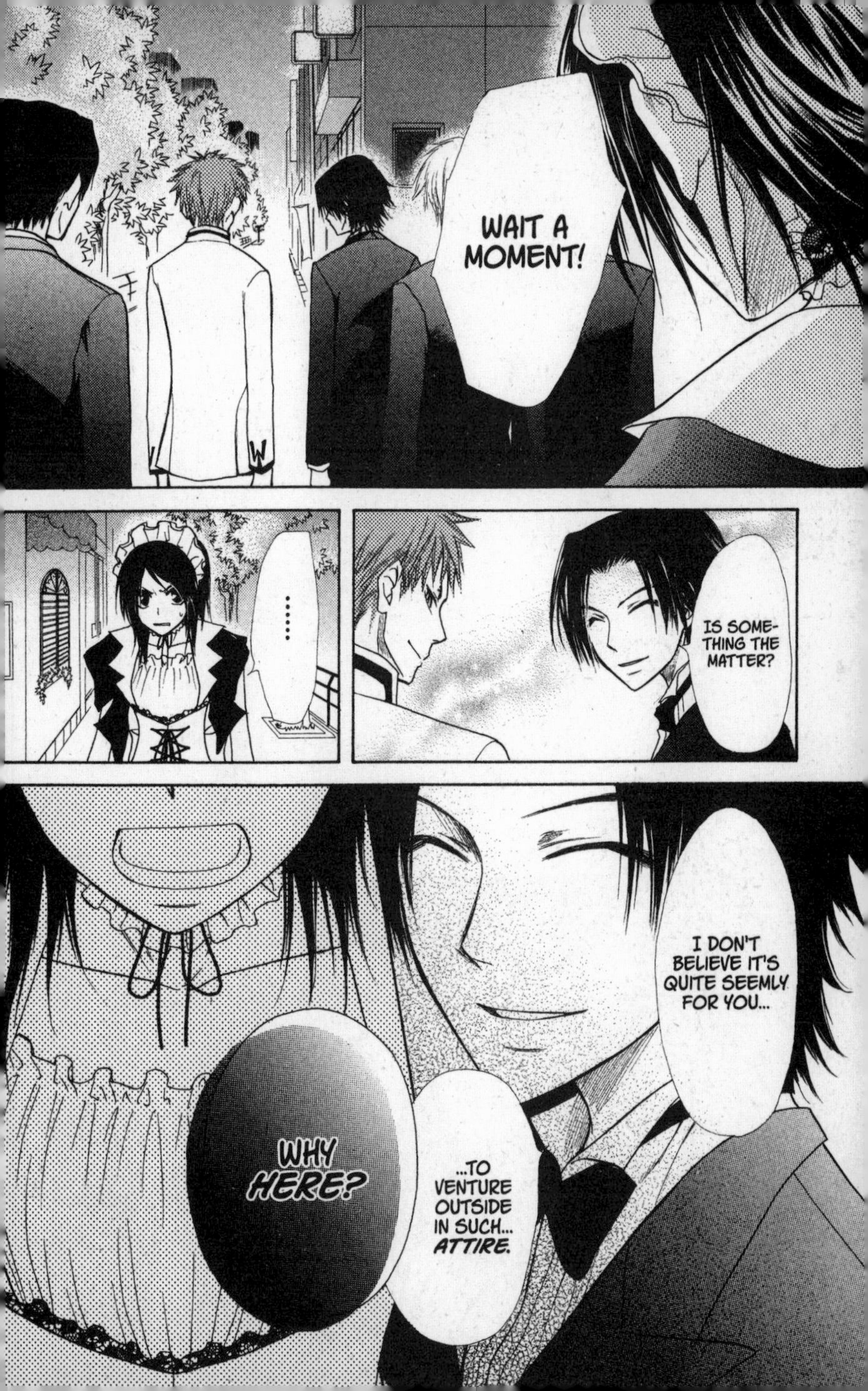
WAIT A MOMENT!
IS SOME-THING THE MATTER?
......
I DON'T BELIEVE IT'S QUITE SEEMLY FOR YOU...
...TO VENTURE OUTSIDE IN SUCH... *ATTIRE.*
WHY *HERE?*

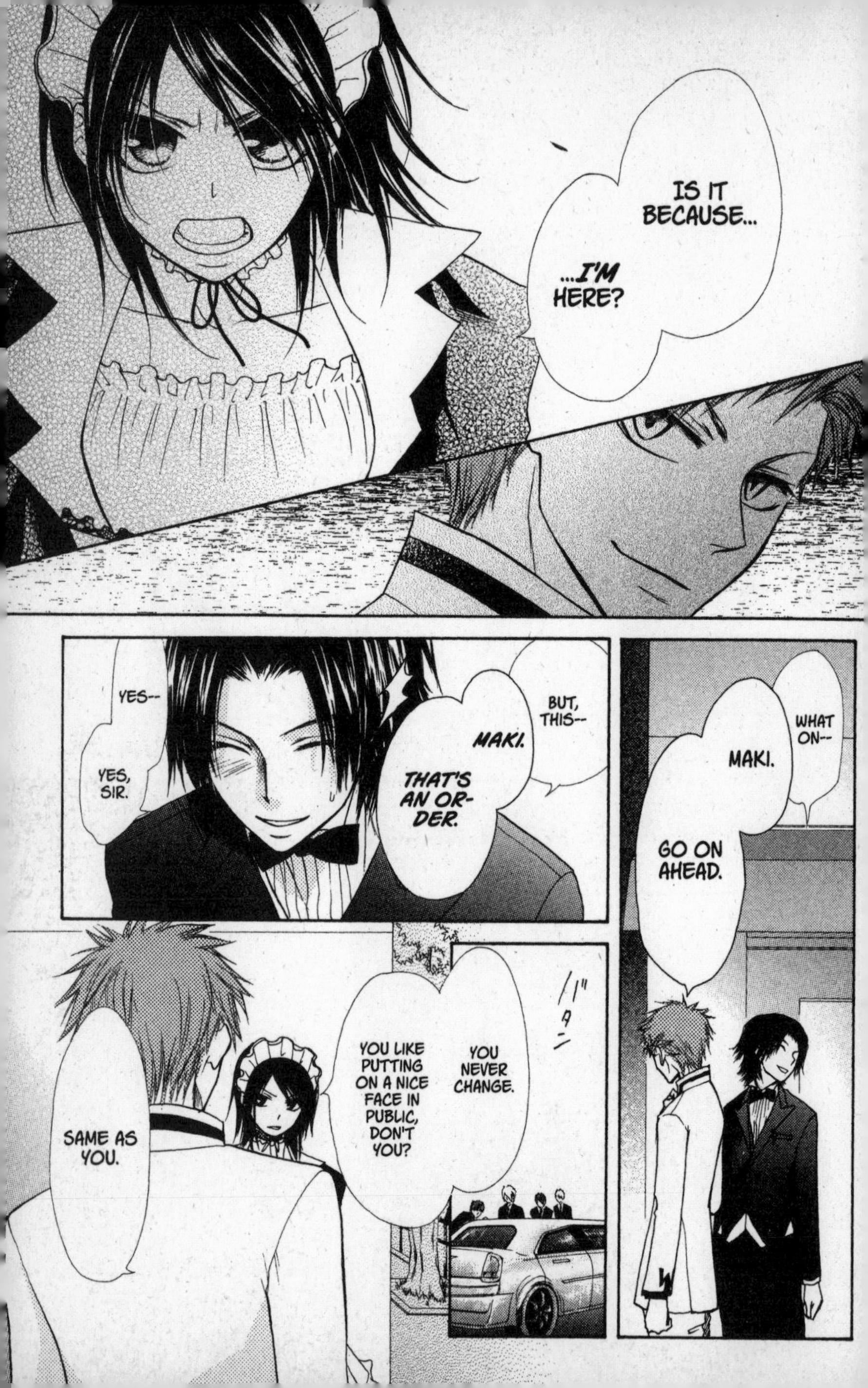
IS IT BECAUSE...
...I'M HERE?
WHAT ON--
MAKI.
GO ON AHEAD.
BUT, THIS--
MAKI.
THAT'S AN ORDER.
YES--
YES, SIR.
バタン
YOU NEVER CHANGE.
YOU LIKE PUTTING ON A NICE FACE IN PUBLIC, DON'T YOU?
SAME AS YOU.

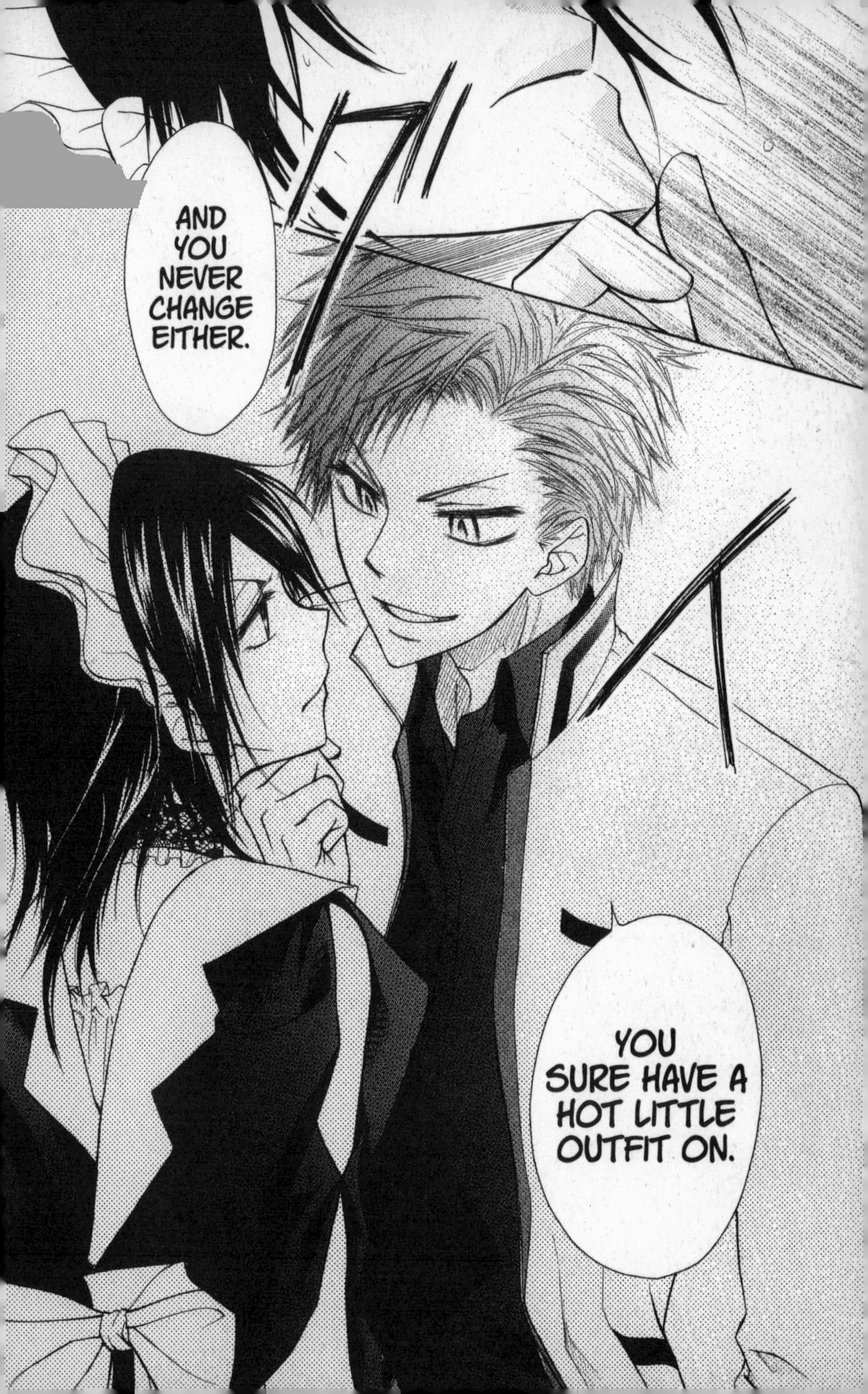
AND YOU NEVER CHANGE EITHER.
YOU SURE HAVE A HOT LITTLE OUTFIT ON.

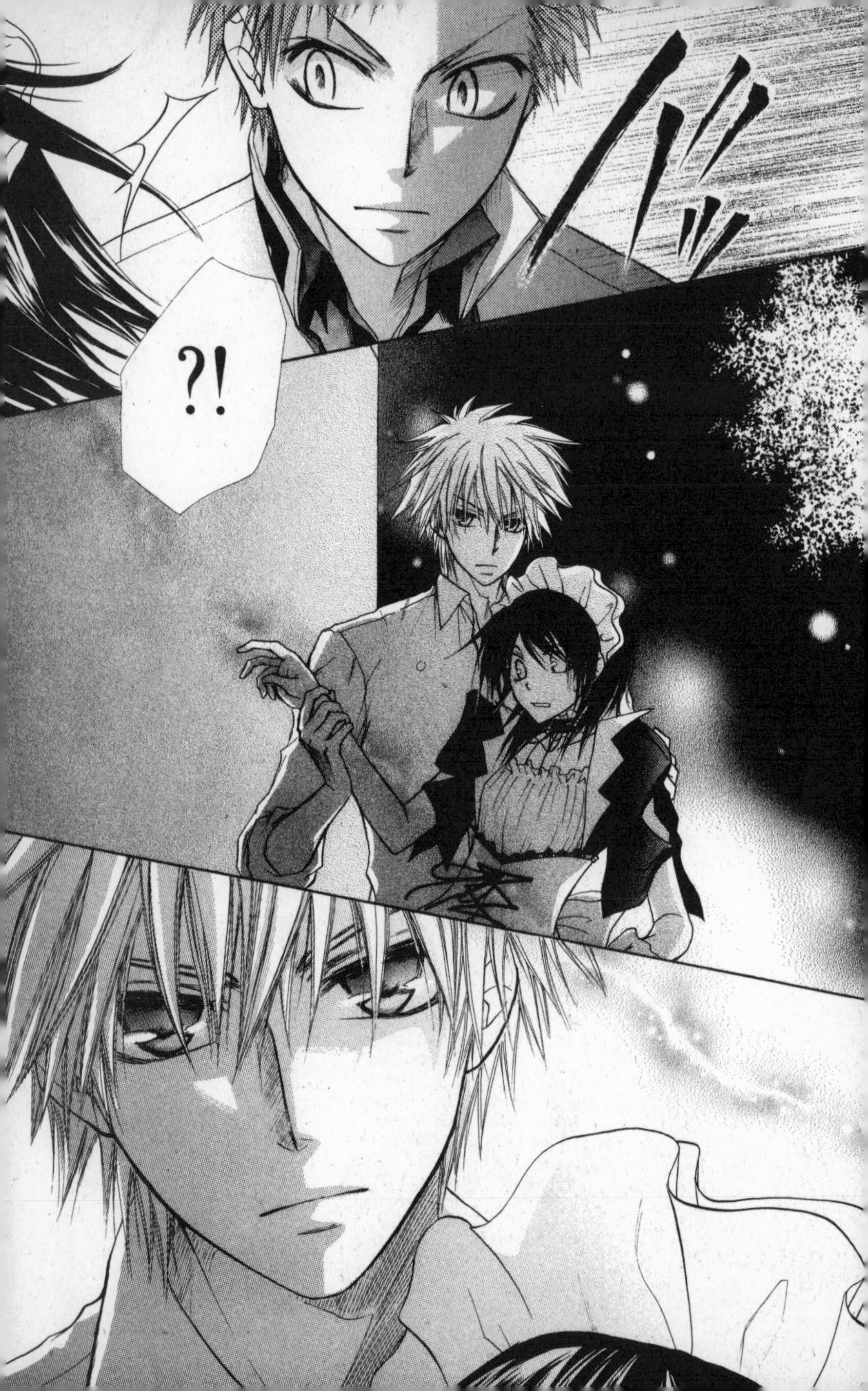
?!

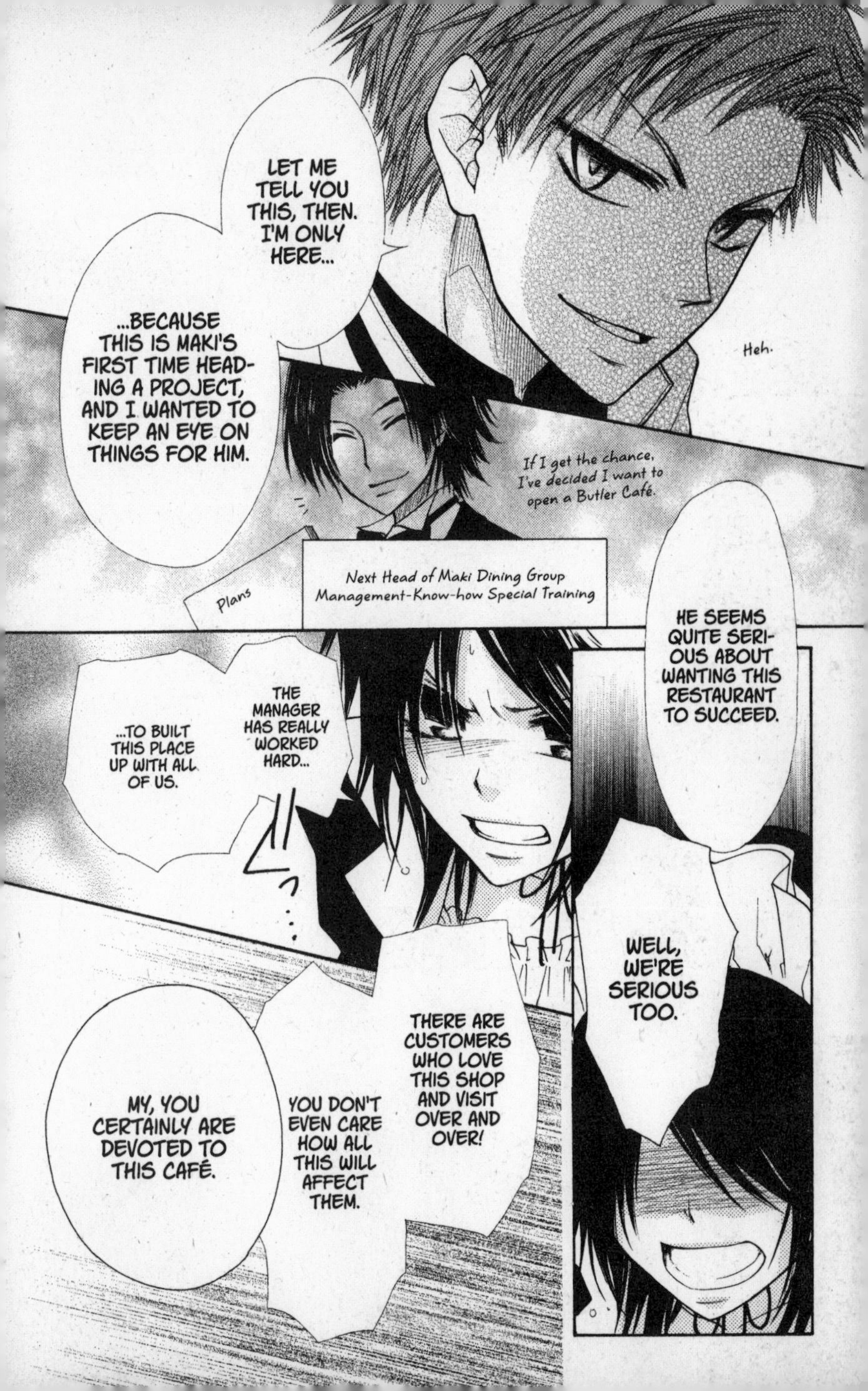

LET ME TELL YOU THIS, THEN. I'M ONLY HERE...
Heh.
...BECAUSE THIS IS MAKI'S FIRST TIME HEADING A PROJECT, AND I WANTED TO KEEP AN EYE ON THINGS FOR HIM.
If I get the chance, I've decided I want to open a Butler Café.
Next Head of Maki Dining Group Management-Know-how Special Training
Plans
HE SEEMS QUITE SERIOUS ABOUT WANTING THIS RESTAURANT TO SUCCEED.
THE MANAGER HAS REALLY WORKED HARD...
...TO BUILT THIS PLACE UP WITH ALL OF US.
WELL, WE'RE SERIOUS TOO.
THERE ARE CUSTOMERS WHO LOVE THIS SHOP AND VISIT OVER AND OVER!
YOU DON'T EVEN CARE HOW ALL THIS WILL AFFECT THEM.
MY, YOU CERTAINLY ARE DEVOTED TO THIS CAFÉ.

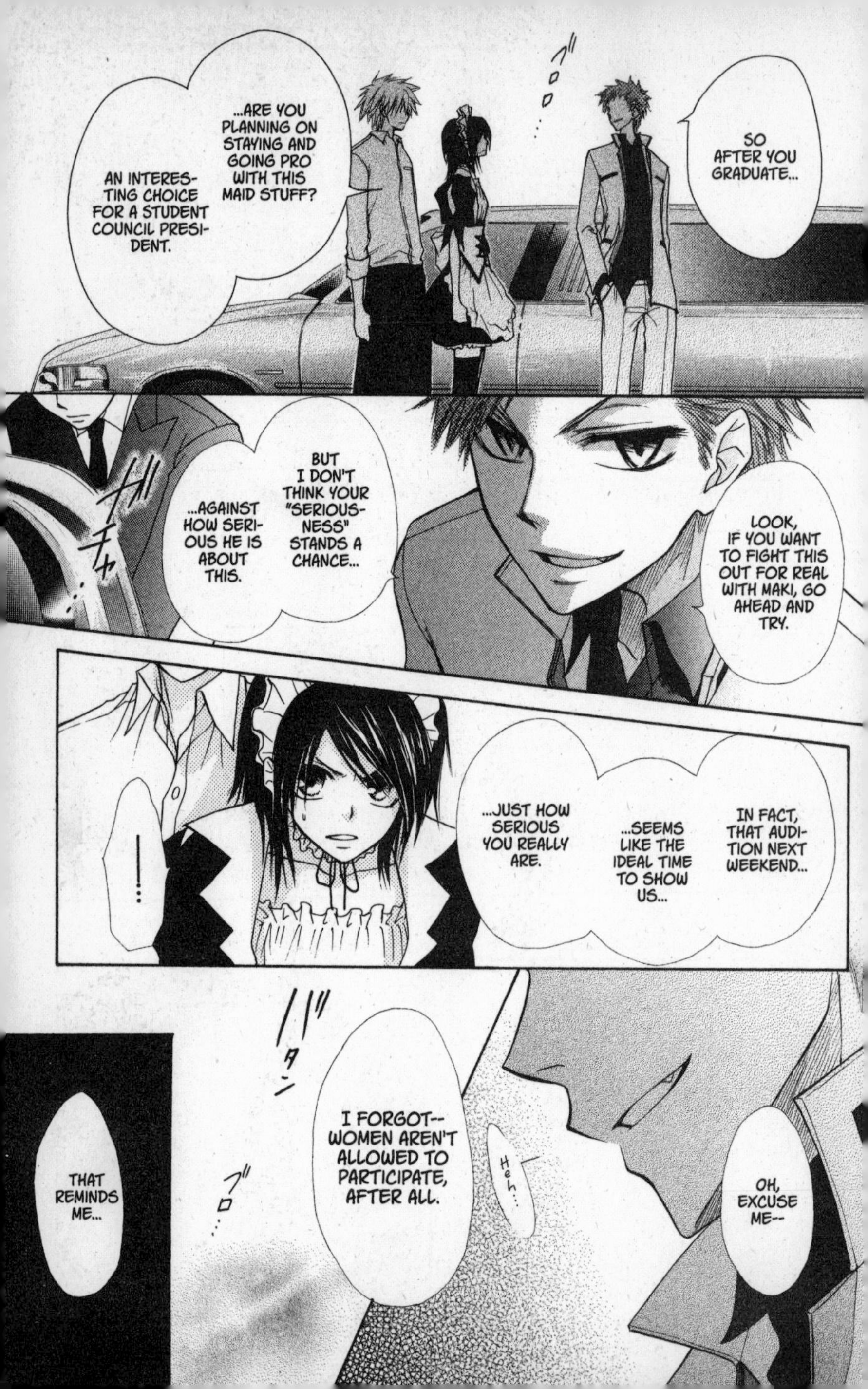
SO AFTER YOU GRADUATE...
ブロロ...
...ARE YOU PLANNING ON STAYING AND GOING PRO WITH THIS MAID STUFF?
AN INTERESTING CHOICE FOR A STUDENT COUNCIL PRESIDENT.
LOOK, IF YOU WANT TO FIGHT THIS OUT FOR REAL WITH MAKI, GO AHEAD AND TRY.
BUT I DON'T THINK YOUR "SERIOUSNESS" STANDS A CHANCE...
...AGAINST HOW SERIOUS HE IS ABOUT THIS.
ガチャ...
IN FACT, THAT AUDITION NEXT WEEKEND...
...SEEMS LIKE THE IDEAL TIME TO SHOW US...
...JUST HOW SERIOUS YOU REALLY ARE.
...!!
OH, EXCUSE ME--
Heh...
I FORGOT--WOMEN AREN'T ALLOWED TO PARTICIPATE, AFTER ALL.
バタン
ブロ...
THAT REMINDS ME...

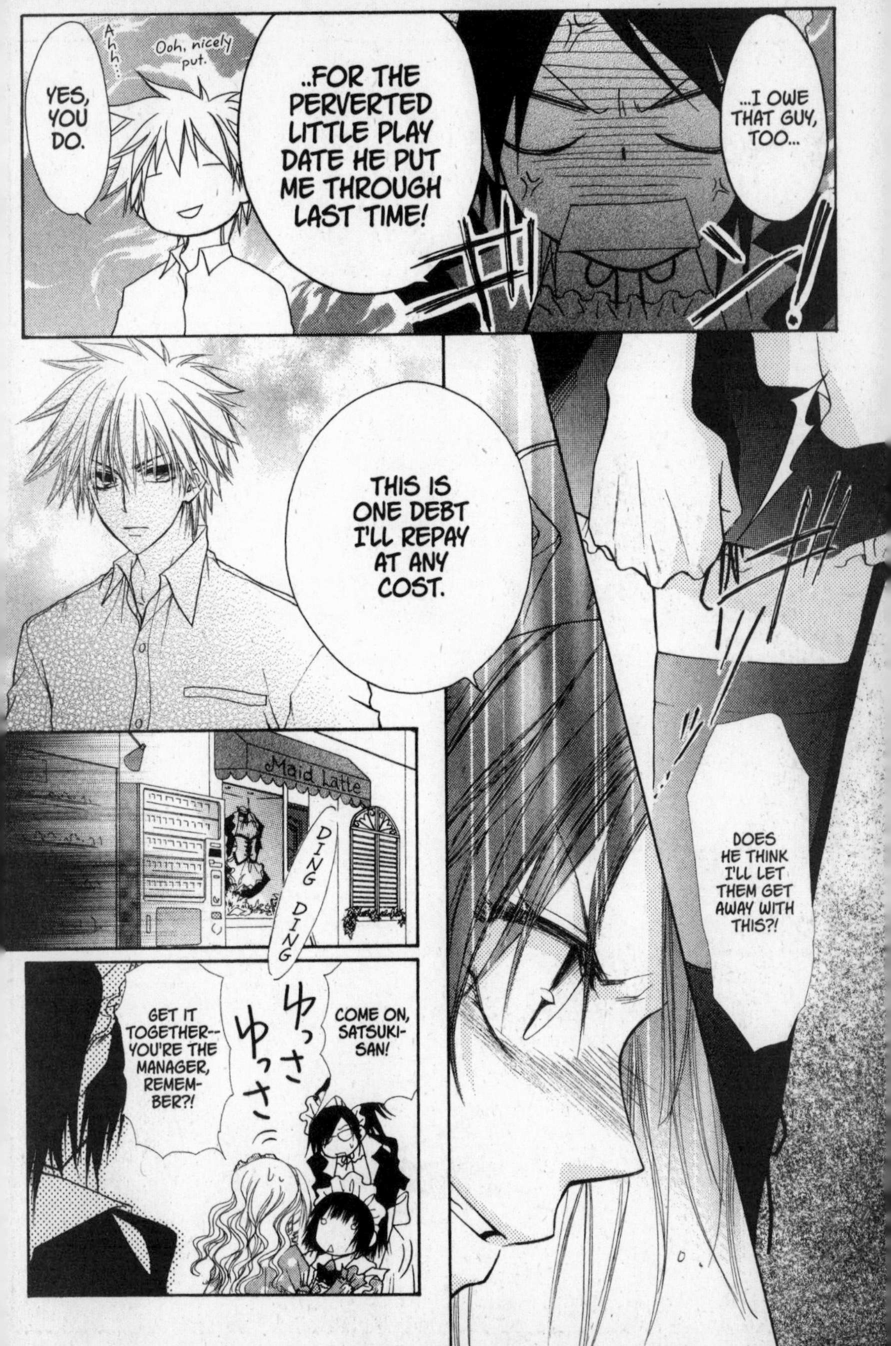

...I OWE THAT GUY, TOO...
..FOR THE PERVERTED LITTLE PLAY DATE HE PUT ME THROUGH LAST TIME!
Ooh, nicely put.
Ahh...
YES, YOU DO.
DOES HE THINK I'LL LET THEM GET AWAY WITH THIS?!
THIS IS ONE DEBT I'LL REPAY AT ANY COST.
Maid Latte
DING DING
ゆっさゆっさ
COME ON, SATSUKI-SAN!
GET IT TOGETHER--YOU'RE THE MANAGER, REMEMBER?!

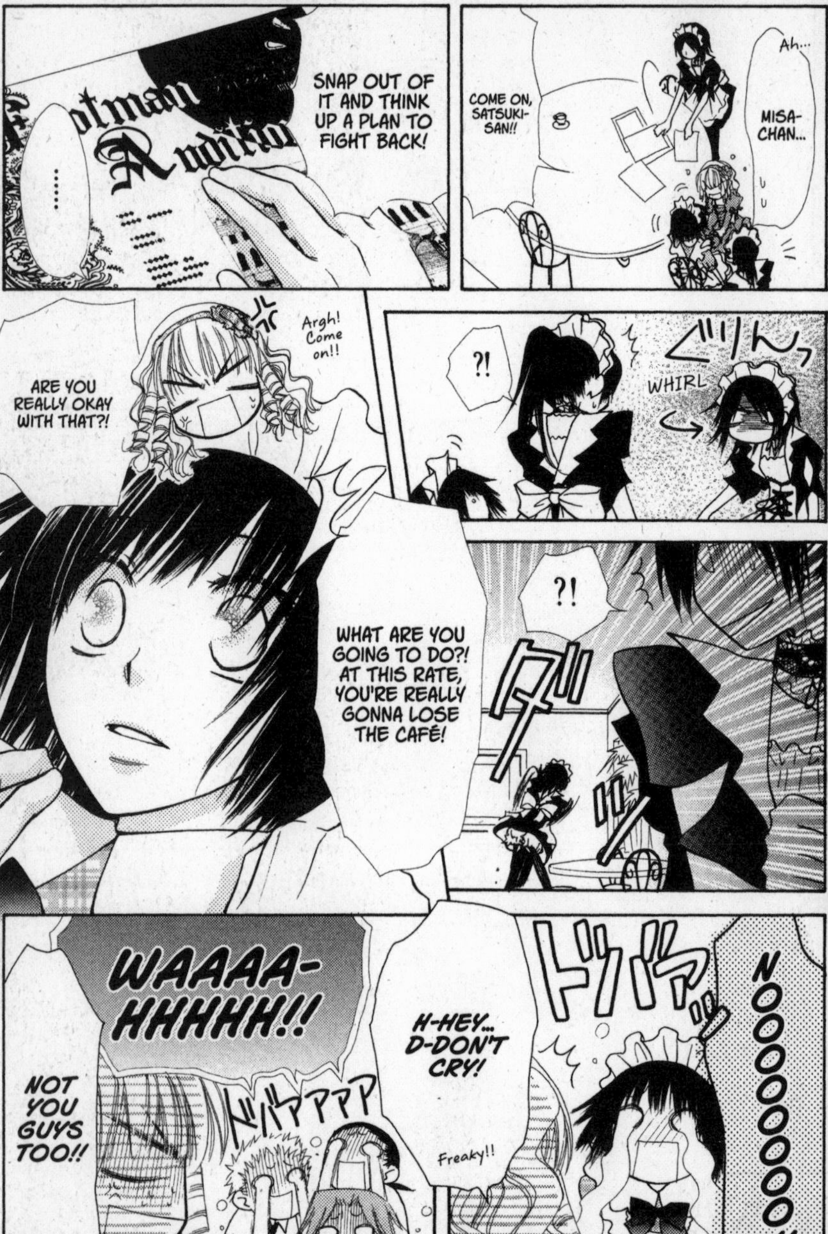
Ah...
MISA-CHAN...
COME ON, SATSUKI-SAN!!
SNAP OUT OF IT AND THINK UP A PLAN TO FIGHT BACK!
......
?!
ぐりんっ
WHIRL
?!
ダ
Argh! Come on!!
ARE YOU REALLY OKAY WITH THAT?!
WHAT ARE YOU GOING TO DO?! AT THIS RATE, YOU'RE REALLY GONNA LOSE THE CAFÉ!
NOOOOOOOOOO!!
ドバァ
H-HEY... D-DON'T CRY!
Freaky!!
WAAAAA-HHHHHH!!
ドバァァァァ
NOT YOU GUYS TOO!!

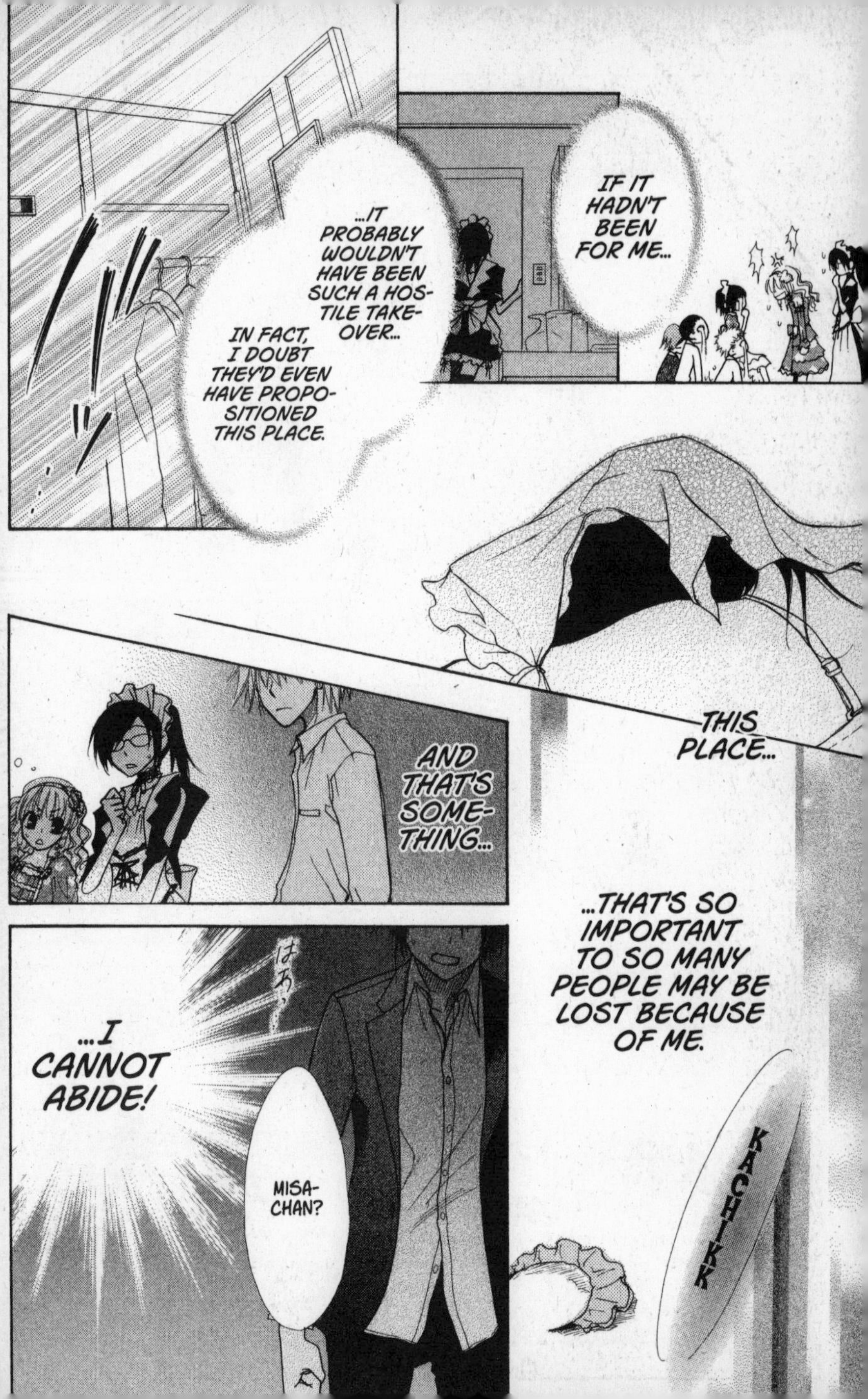
IF IT HADN'T BEEN FOR ME...
...IT PROBABLY WOULDN'T HAVE BEEN SUCH A HOS-TILE TAKE-OVER...
IN FACT, I DOUBT THEY'D EVEN HAVE PROPO-SITIONED THIS PLACE.
THIS PLACE...
AND THAT'S SOME-THING...
...THAT'S SO IMPORTANT TO SO MANY PEOPLE MAY BE LOST BECAUSE OF ME.
KACHIKK
MISA-CHAN?
はあ,
...I CANNOT ABIDE!

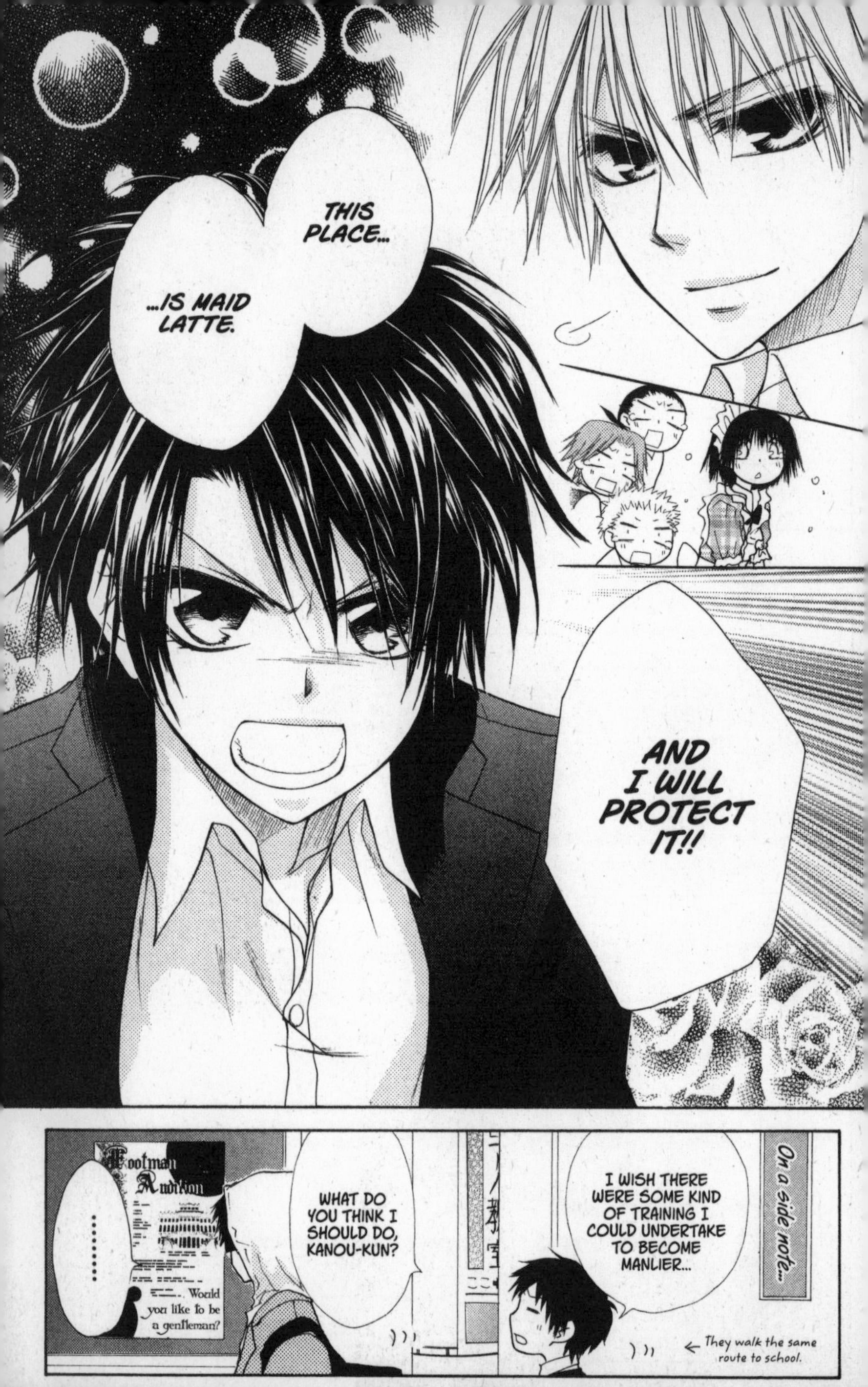
THIS PLACE...
...IS MAID LATTE.
AND I WILL PROTECT IT!!
On a side note...
I WISH THERE WERE SOME KIND OF TRAINING I COULD UNDERTAKE TO BECOME MANLIER...
← They walk the same route to school.
WHAT DO YOU THINK I SHOULD DO, KANOU-KUN?
......
Footman Audition
Would you like to be a gentleman?

...ABOUT THE EYESORE OF A Q+A PAGE YOU SAW LAST TIME... I DEEPLY APOLOGIZE FOR THAT. IT'S JUST THAT USUI SAID HE ACTUALLY FELT LIKE DOING IT FOR ONCE, SO I WENT AND LET HIM. THAT PERVERTED ALIEN SCUM SHALL BE SEVERELY PUNISHED. I PROMISE YOU!

 WELL, THEN! LET'S GET ON WITH THE QUESTIONS!

QUESTION 6: WILL THE IDIOT TRIO EVER BE DRAWN WITH PROPER PROPORTIONS AGAIN?

 WILL THEY, INDEED? AT LEAST FOR THIS PRESENT TIME, THE AUTHOR HAS EXPRESSED THAT *NO, SHE DOES NOT FEEL ANY INCLINATION WHATSOEVER TO DRAW THEM PROPERLY AGAIN.*

 WHA-WHA-WHAAAAAAAAAAAAAAAAAAAAAAAA?!

 W-W-W-WAIT A MINUTE!!

 SHOULDN'T YOU THINK OF THAT NOT AS A QUESTION, BUT AS A REQUEST AND *PUT IN PICTURE OF US DRAWN TO REALISTICALLY AND AWESOMELY AGAIN?!*

 JEEZ, IT'S YOU GUYS! I DON'T RECALL CALLING YOU OUT HERE, YOU KNOW.

 TH-THAT'S SO MEAN!!

 WE'RE YOUR PERSONAL CHEERING SQUAD, AFTER ALL!!

 ARGH, FINE, FINE, FINE. BUT *YOU'RE IN MY WAY RIGHT NOW,* SO GO ON, SHOO. SHOO!

SHE...SHE BRUSHED US OFF!!

 THEY REALLY ARE OBEDIENT LITTLE IDIOTS, AREN'T THEY? ER...WELL, THEN--WHAT'S THE NEXT QUESTION?

QUESTION 7: I'D REALLY LOVE IT IF SOMETHING LIKE AN USUI PHOTO COLLECTION EXISTED.

W-WAIT, WAIT, WAIT! ARE YOU BEING SERIOUS?! AND THAT'S NOT EVEN A QUESTION, IS IT?! EVEN IF YOU WERE WRITING IT IN AS A REQUEST, THAT ONE IS ABSOLUTELY DENIED! LOOK CLOSELY--WHAT BIT OF THAT PERVERTED ALIEN STALKER IS APPEALING, I ASK?! HE'S A *PERVERT* AND AN *ALIEN* PLUS A *STALKER,* GOT IT?! WHAT'S WORSE, HE'S A *DEMON KING OF SEXUAL HARASSMENT!* HE'S EVEN DONE THINGS TO OTHER MALES IN THE PAST. UH-OH, SPEAK OF THE DEVIL...

 M-MISS PRESIDENT...

 :YU-YUKIMURA...YOU'RE ALIVE...THERE, THERE, DON'T CRY ANYMORE...

 :I-I DON'T WANT TO DO THE Q&A CORNER ANYMORE...IT'S SCARY...

 :GROW...STRONG...

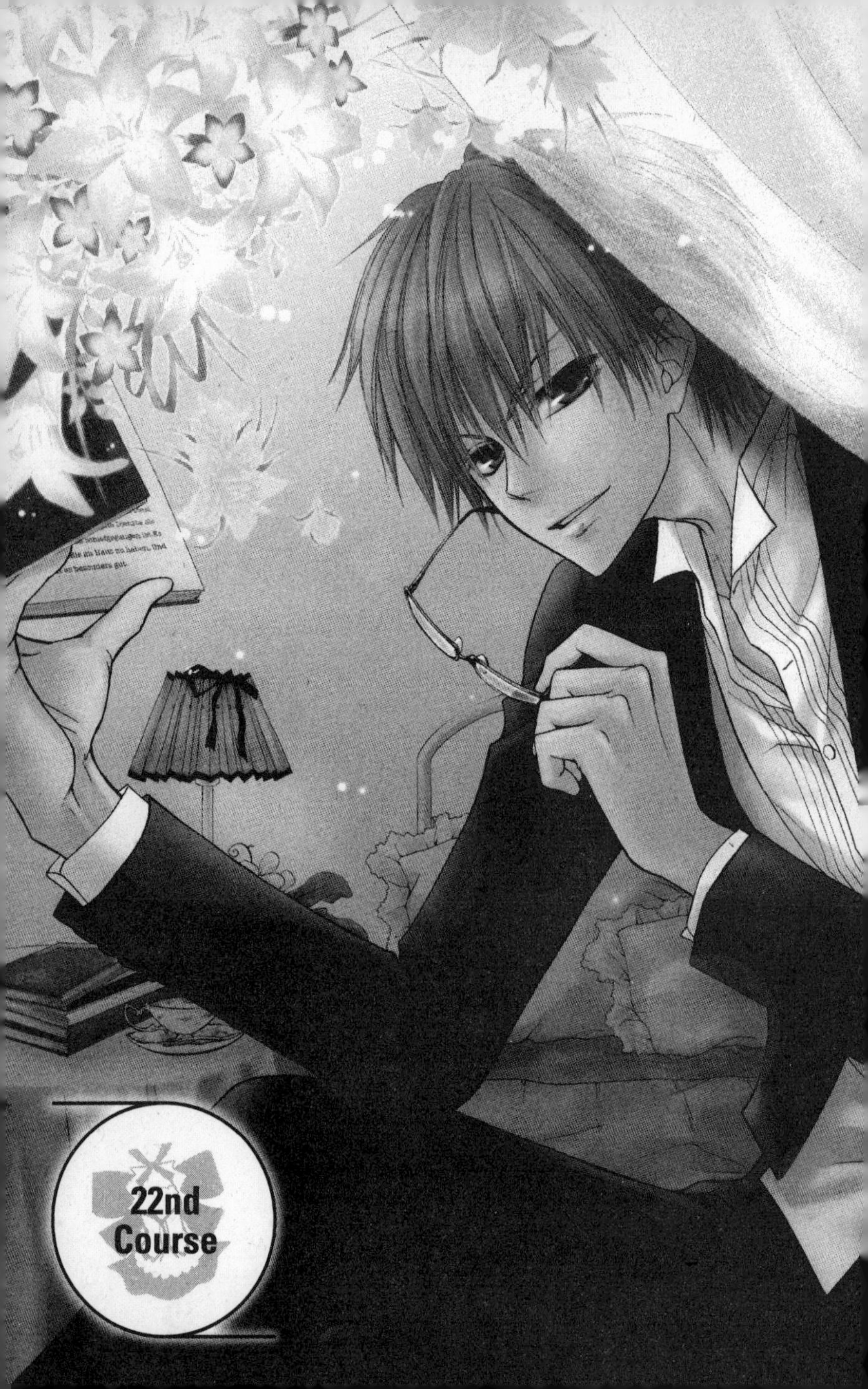
22nd
Course

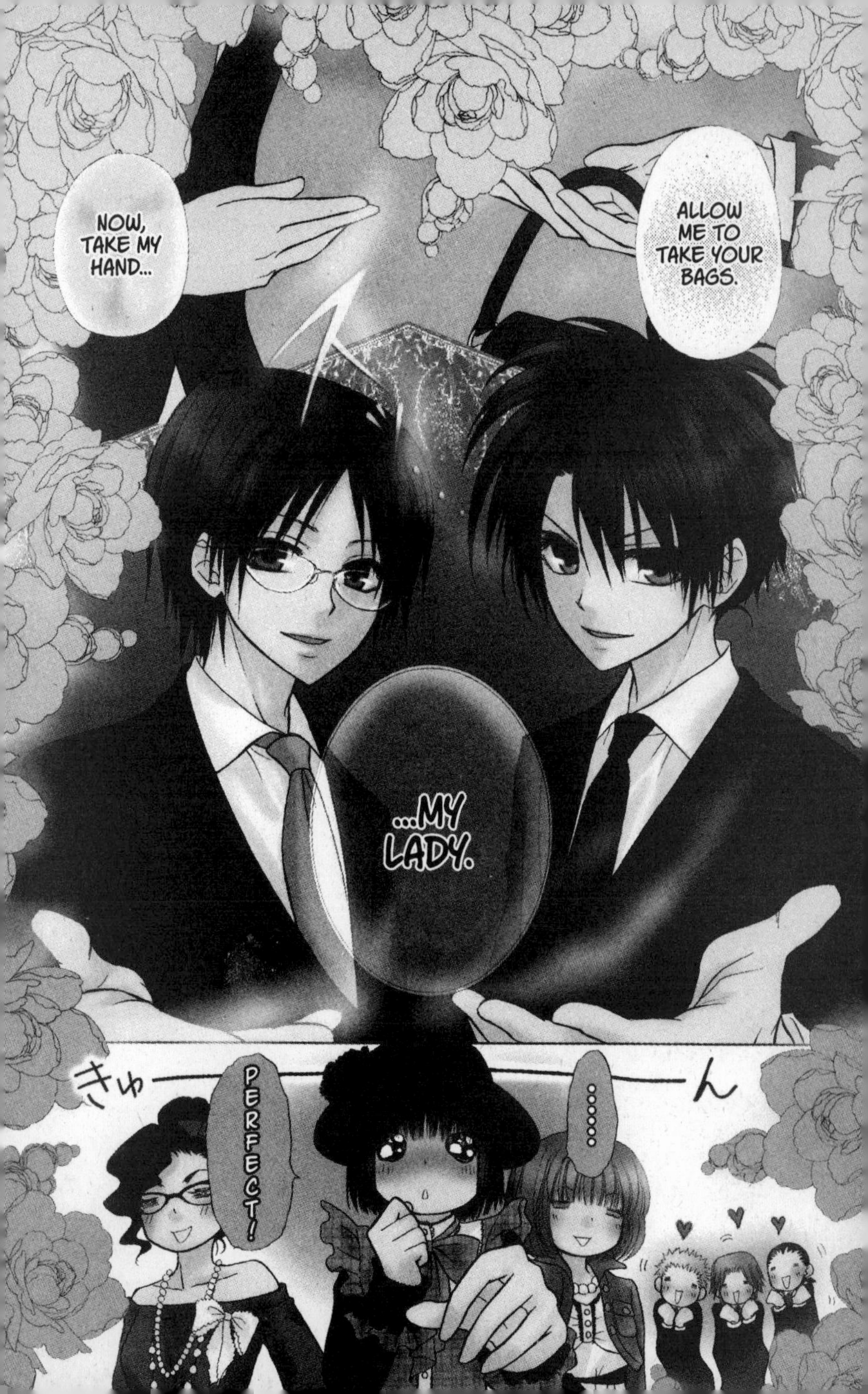
ALLOW ME TO TAKE YOUR BAGS.
NOW, TAKE MY HAND...
...MY LADY.
きゅーーーん
......
PERFECT!

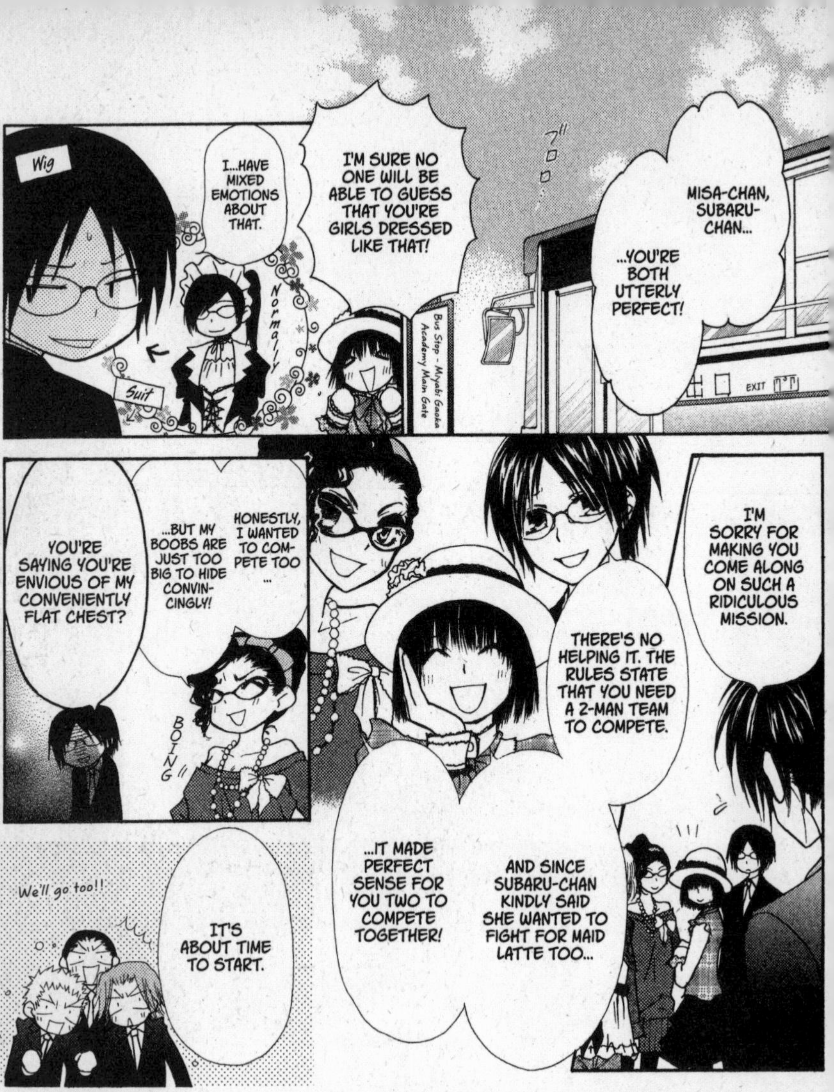
MISA-CHAN, SUBARU-CHAN...
...YOU'RE BOTH UTTERLY PERFECT!
EXIT
Bus Stop - Miyabi Gaoka Academy Main Gate
I'M SURE NO ONE WILL BE ABLE TO GUESS THAT YOU'RE GIRLS DRESSED LIKE THAT!
I...HAVE MIXED EMOTIONS ABOUT THAT.
Wig
Normally
Suit
I'M SORRY FOR MAKING YOU COME ALONG ON SUCH A RIDICULOUS MISSION.
THERE'S NO HELPING IT. THE RULES STATE THAT YOU NEED A 2-MAN TEAM TO COMPETE.
AND SINCE SUBARU-CHAN KINDLY SAID SHE WANTED TO FIGHT FOR MAID LATTE TOO...
...IT MADE PERFECT SENSE FOR YOU TWO TO COMPETE TOGETHER!
HONESTLY, I WANTED TO COMPETE TOO...
...BUT MY BOOBS ARE JUST TOO BIG TO HIDE CONVINCINGLY!
BOING
YOU'RE SAYING YOU'RE ENVIOUS OF MY CONVENIENTLY FLAT CHEST?
IT'S ABOUT TIME TO START.
We'll go too!!

Extraneous Question Corner

Question 3

Q. Please tell us about your life path from elementary school to the present.

A.
- I grew up frolicking in Mother Nature at an elementary school in the rapidly depopulating countryside.
- In middle school, I learned of the deep world of manga → The budding of my otaku nature.
- In high school, I went nuts playing contrabass → Latent otakuism.
- As a humanities major in university, I reveled in four years of absolute freedom → Otaku **explosion**. Upon graduating, I also made my debut as a manga artist, which brings us to the present day.

The most useful experience I had to prepare me to be a manga-ka was my time as a manga assistant during my university years.

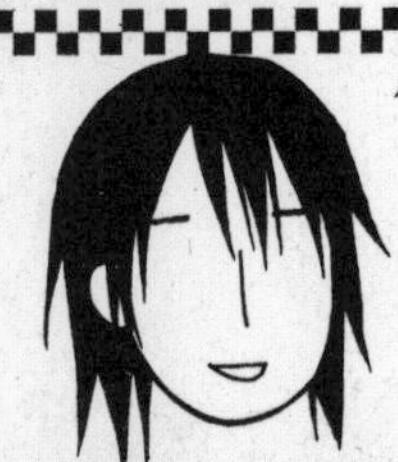

I've had absolutely zero official manga-drawing training.

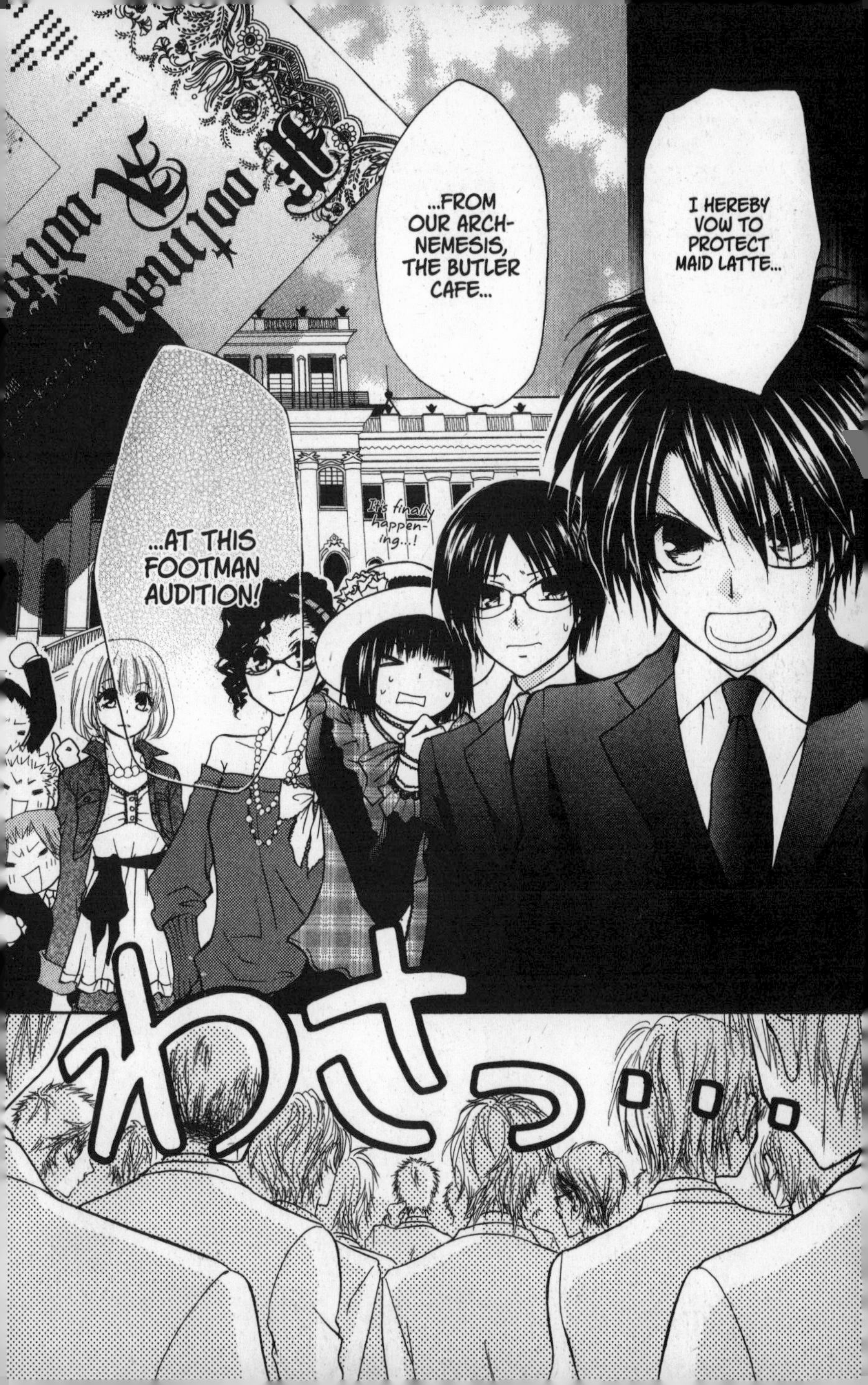
I HEREBY VOW TO PROTECT MAID LATTE...
...FROM OUR ARCH-NEMESIS, THE BUTLER CAFE...
It's finally happen-ing...!
...AT THIS FOOTMAN AUDITION!
わさっ...

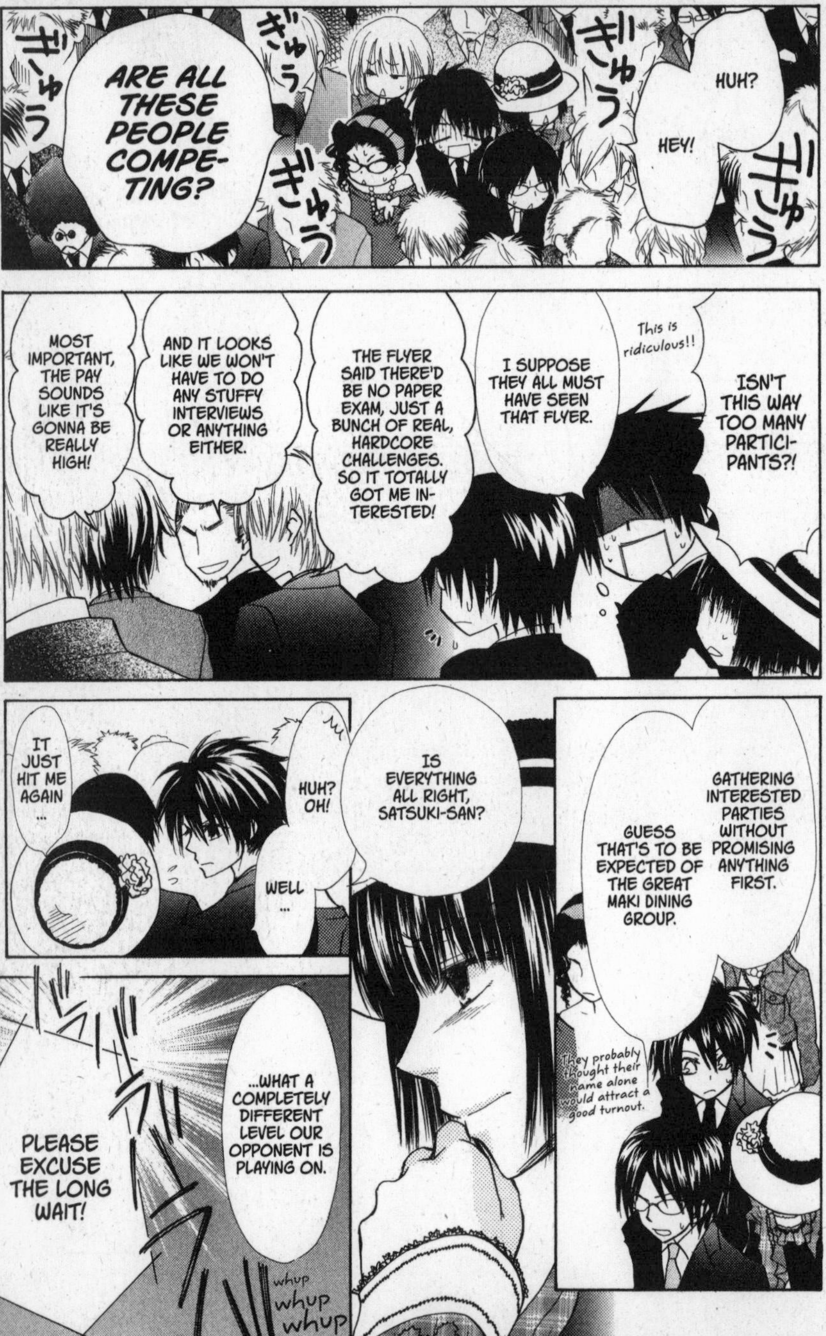
HUH?
HEY!
ぎゅう
ぎゅう
ぎゅう
ぎゅう
ぎゅう
ARE ALL THESE PEOPLE COMPETING?
ISN'T THIS WAY TOO MANY PARTICIPANTS?!
This is ridiculous!!
I SUPPOSE THEY ALL MUST HAVE SEEN THAT FLYER.
THE FLYER SAID THERE'D BE NO PAPER EXAM, JUST A BUNCH OF REAL, HARDCORE CHALLENGES. SO IT TOTALLY GOT ME INTERESTED!
AND IT LOOKS LIKE WE WON'T HAVE TO DO ANY STUFFY INTERVIEWS OR ANYTHING EITHER.
MOST IMPORTANT, THE PAY SOUNDS LIKE IT'S GONNA BE REALLY HIGH!
GATHERING INTERESTED PARTIES WITHOUT PROMISING ANYTHING FIRST.
GUESS THAT'S TO BE EXPECTED OF THE GREAT MAKI DINING GROUP.
They probably thought their name alone would attract a good turnout.
IS EVERYTHING ALL RIGHT, SATSUKI-SAN?
HUH? OH!
WELL ...
IT JUST HIT ME AGAIN ...
...WHAT A COMPLETELY DIFFERENT LEVEL OUR OPPONENT IS PLAYING ON.
PLEASE EXCUSE THE LONG WAIT!
whup whup whup

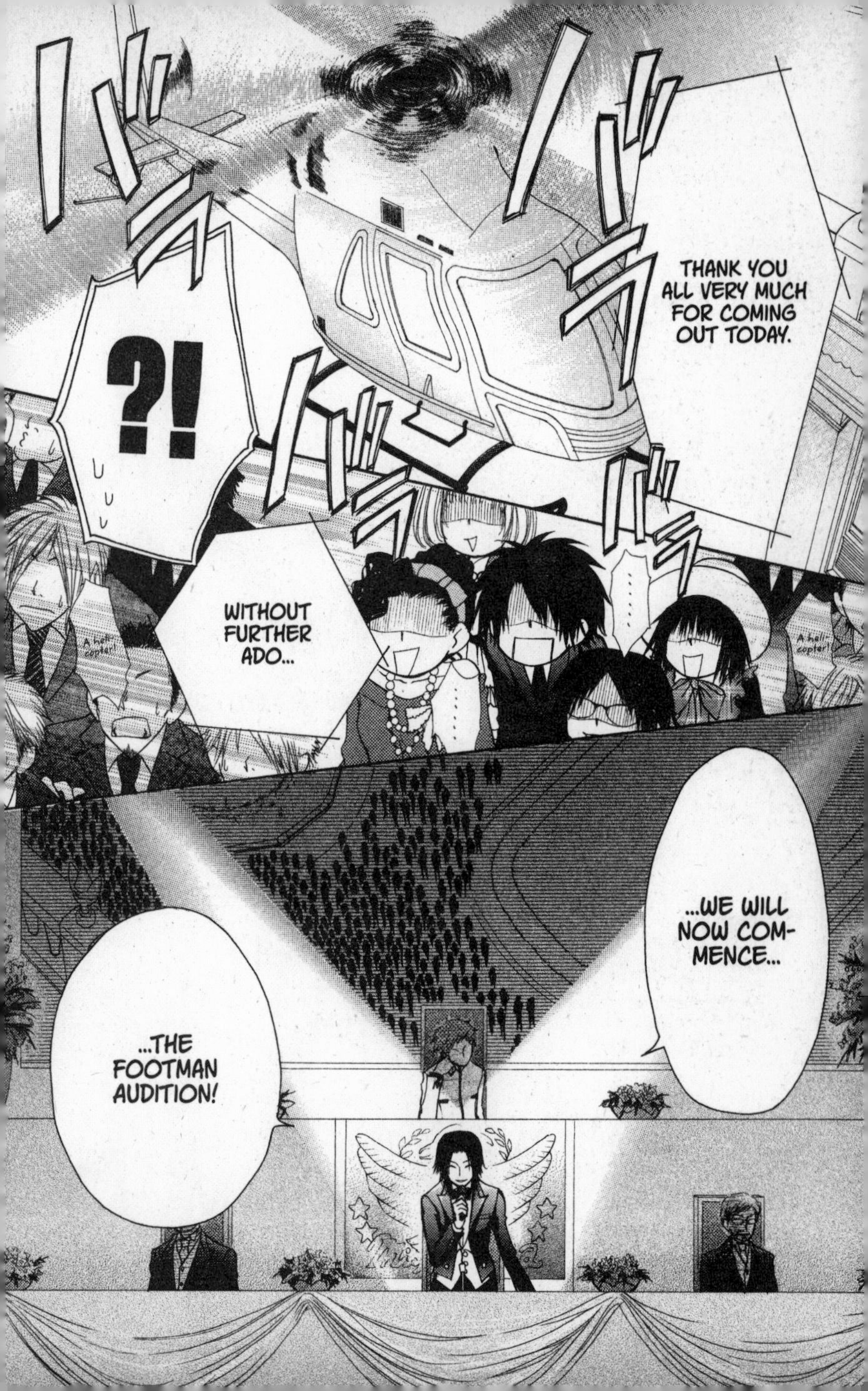
THANK YOU ALL VERY MUCH FOR COMING OUT TODAY.
?!
A heli-copter!
A heli-copter!
WITHOUT FURTHER ADO...
...WE WILL NOW COM-MENCE...
...THE FOOTMAN AUDITION!

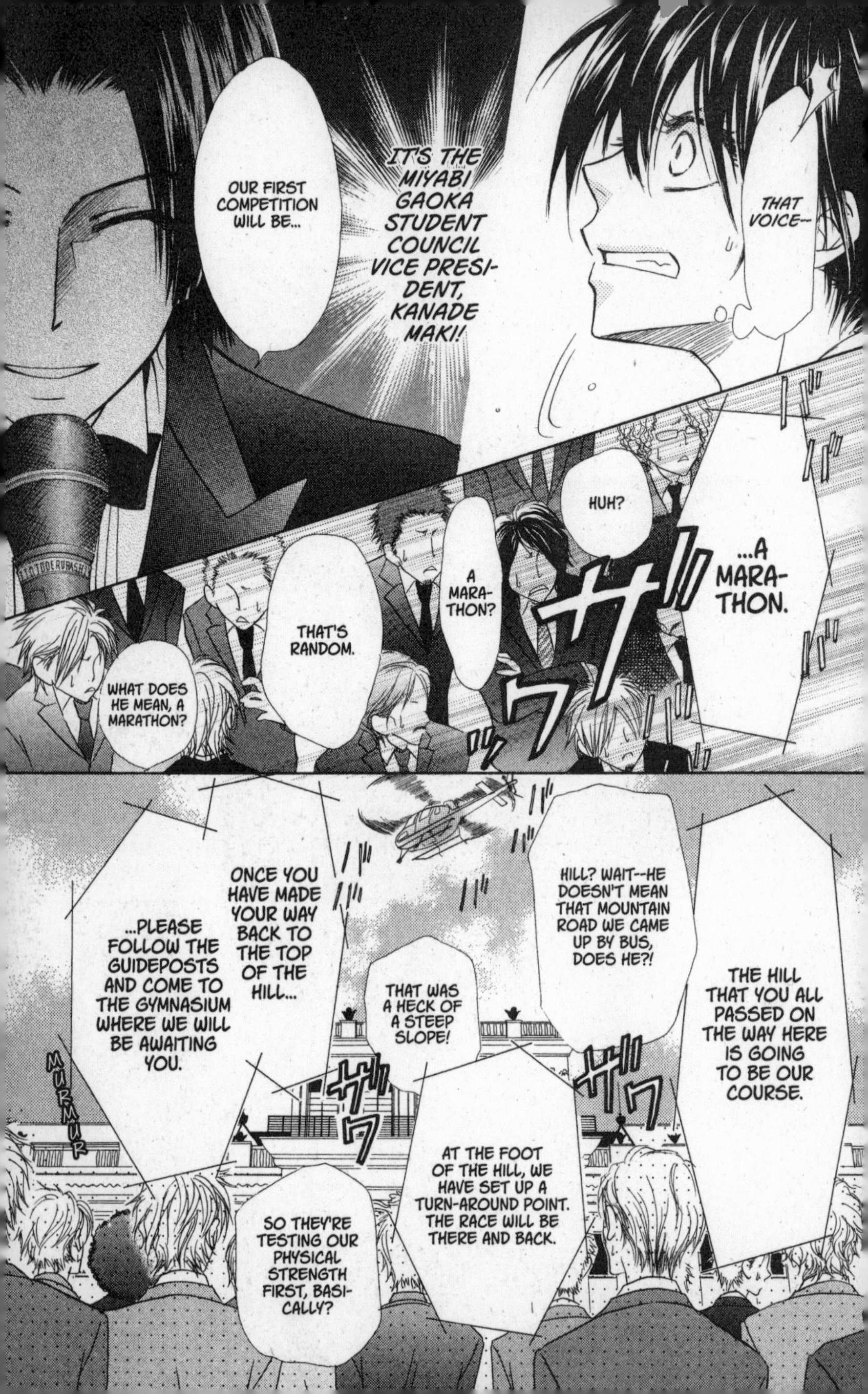
THAT VOICE--
IT'S THE MIYABI GAOKA STUDENT COUNCIL VICE PRESIDENT, KANADE MAKI!
OUR FIRST COMPETITION WILL BE...
...A MARATHON.
HUH?
A MARATHON?
THAT'S RANDOM.
WHAT DOES HE MEAN, A MARATHON?
THE HILL THAT YOU ALL PASSED ON THE WAY HERE IS GOING TO BE OUR COURSE.
HILL? WAIT--HE DOESN'T MEAN THAT MOUNTAIN ROAD WE CAME UP BY BUS, DOES HE?!
AT THE FOOT OF THE HILL, WE HAVE SET UP A TURN-AROUND POINT. THE RACE WILL BE THERE AND BACK.
THAT WAS A HECK OF A STEEP SLOPE!
ONCE YOU HAVE MADE YOUR WAY BACK TO THE TOP OF THE HILL...
...PLEASE FOLLOW THE GUIDEPOSTS AND COME TO THE GYMNASIUM WHERE WE WILL BE AWAITING YOU.
SO THEY'RE TESTING OUR PHYSICAL STRENGTH FIRST, BASICALLY?
MURMUR

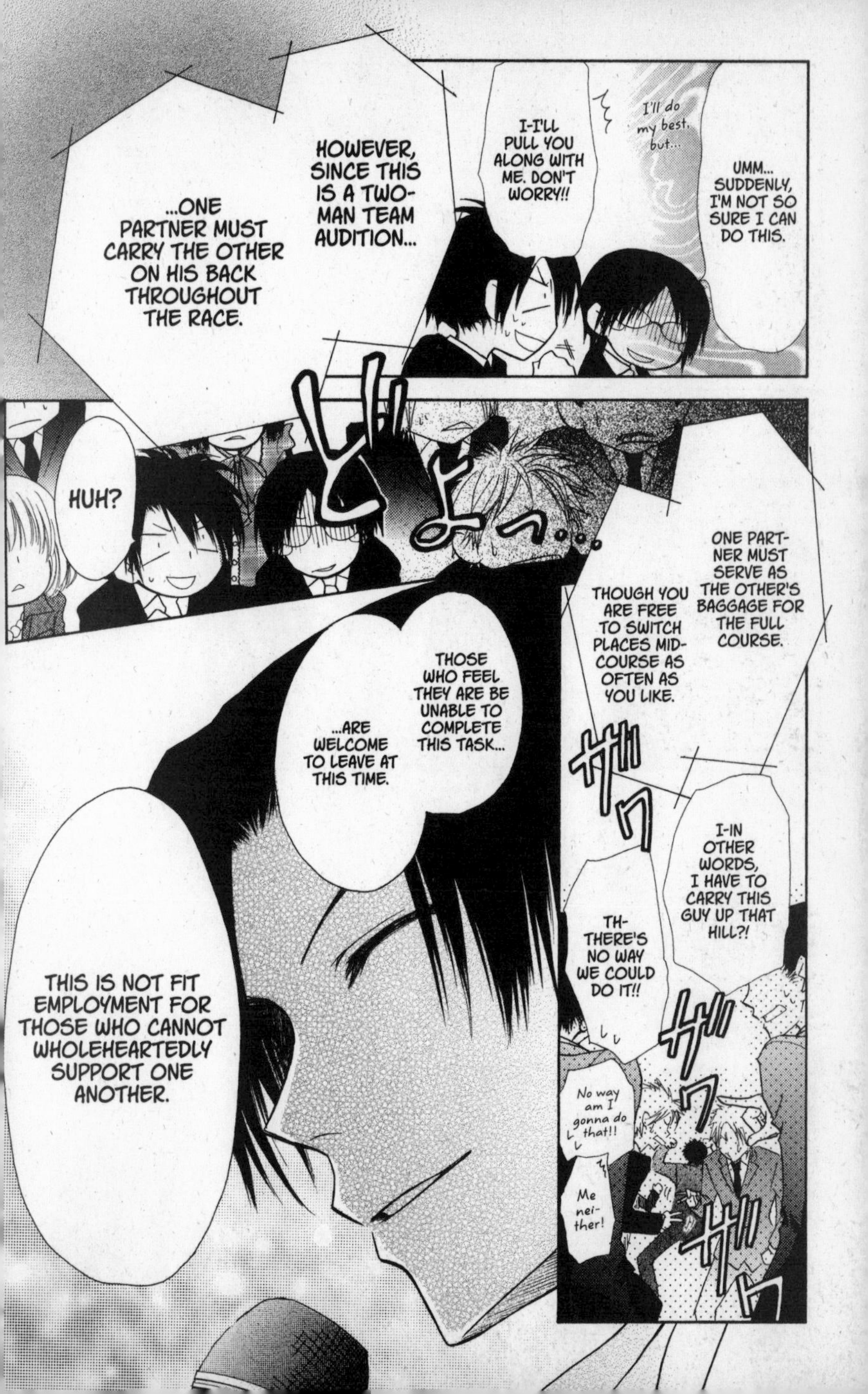

UMM... SUDDENLY, I'M NOT SO SURE I CAN DO THIS.
I'll do my best, but...
I-I'LL PULL YOU ALONG WITH ME. DON'T WORRY!!
HOWEVER, SINCE THIS IS A TWO-MAN TEAM AUDITION...
...ONE PARTNER MUST CARRY THE OTHER ON HIS BACK THROUGHOUT THE RACE.
どよっ...
HUH?
ONE PARTNER MUST SERVE AS THE OTHER'S BAGGAGE FOR THE FULL COURSE.
THOUGH YOU ARE FREE TO SWITCH PLACES MID-COURSE AS OFTEN AS YOU LIKE.
ザワ
I-IN OTHER WORDS, I HAVE TO CARRY THIS GUY UP THAT HILL?!
TH-THERE'S NO WAY WE COULD DO IT!!
ザワ
ザワ
No way am I gonna do that!!
Me neither!
THOSE WHO FEEL THEY ARE BE UNABLE TO COMPLETE THIS TASK...
...ARE WELCOME TO LEAVE AT THIS TIME.
THIS IS NOT FIT EMPLOYMENT FOR THOSE WHO CANNOT WHOLEHEARTEDLY SUPPORT ONE ANOTHER.

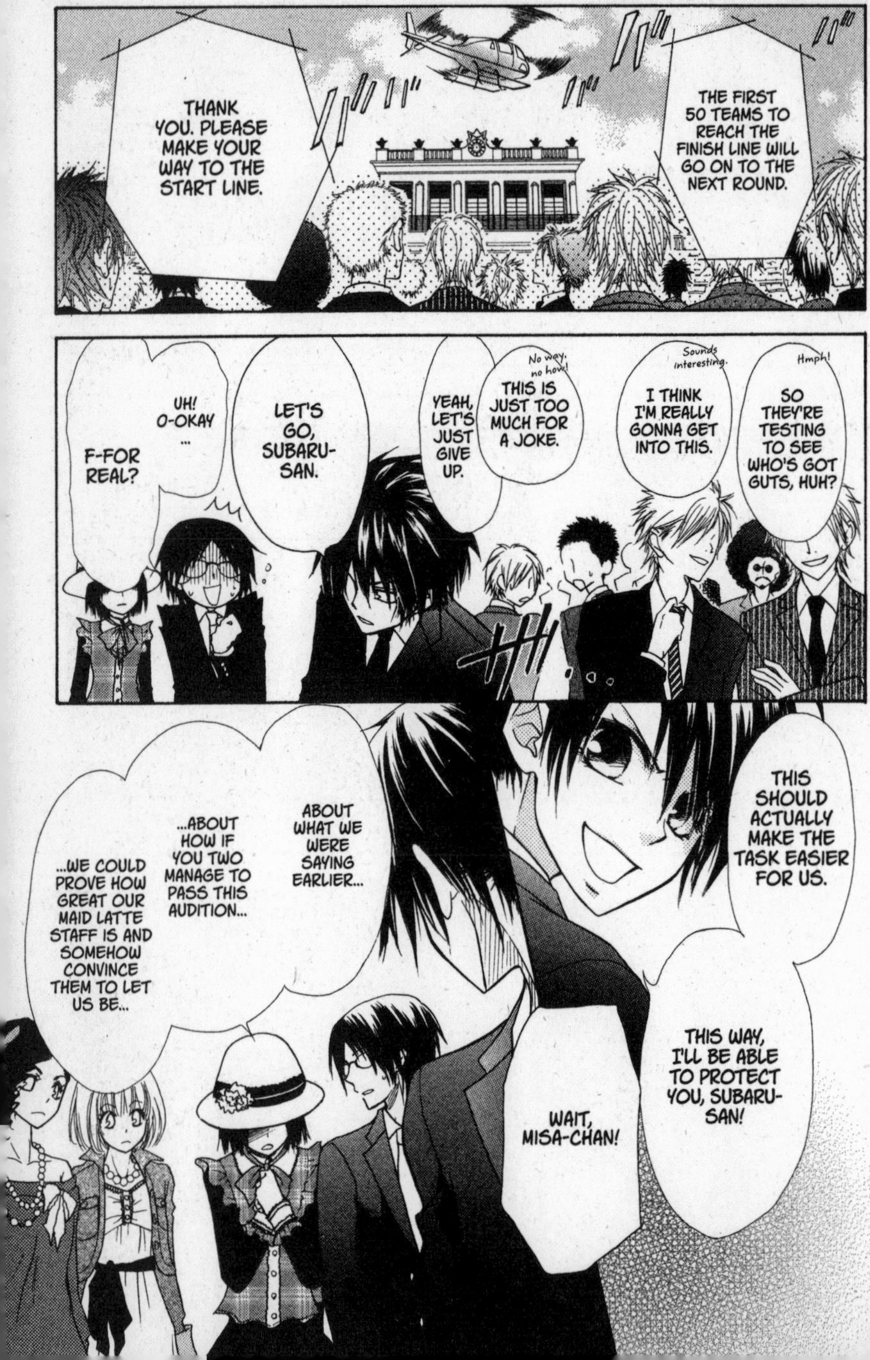
THE FIRST 50 TEAMS TO REACH THE FINISH LINE WILL GO ON TO THE NEXT ROUND.
THANK YOU. PLEASE MAKE YOUR WAY TO THE START LINE.
Hmph!
SO THEY'RE TESTING TO SEE WHO'S GOT GUTS, HUH?
Sounds interesting.
I THINK I'M REALLY GONNA GET INTO THIS.
No way, no how!
THIS IS JUST TOO MUCH FOR A JOKE.
YEAH, LET'S JUST GIVE UP.
LET'S GO, SUBARU-SAN.
UH! O-OKAY ...
F-FOR REAL?
THIS SHOULD ACTUALLY MAKE THE TASK EASIER FOR US.
ABOUT WHAT WE WERE SAYING EARLIER...
...ABOUT HOW IF YOU TWO MANAGE TO PASS THIS AUDITION...
...WE COULD PROVE HOW GREAT OUR MAID LATTE STAFF IS AND SOMEHOW CONVINCE THEM TO LET US BE...
THIS WAY, I'LL BE ABLE TO PROTECT YOU, SUBARU-SAN!
WAIT, MISA-CHAN!

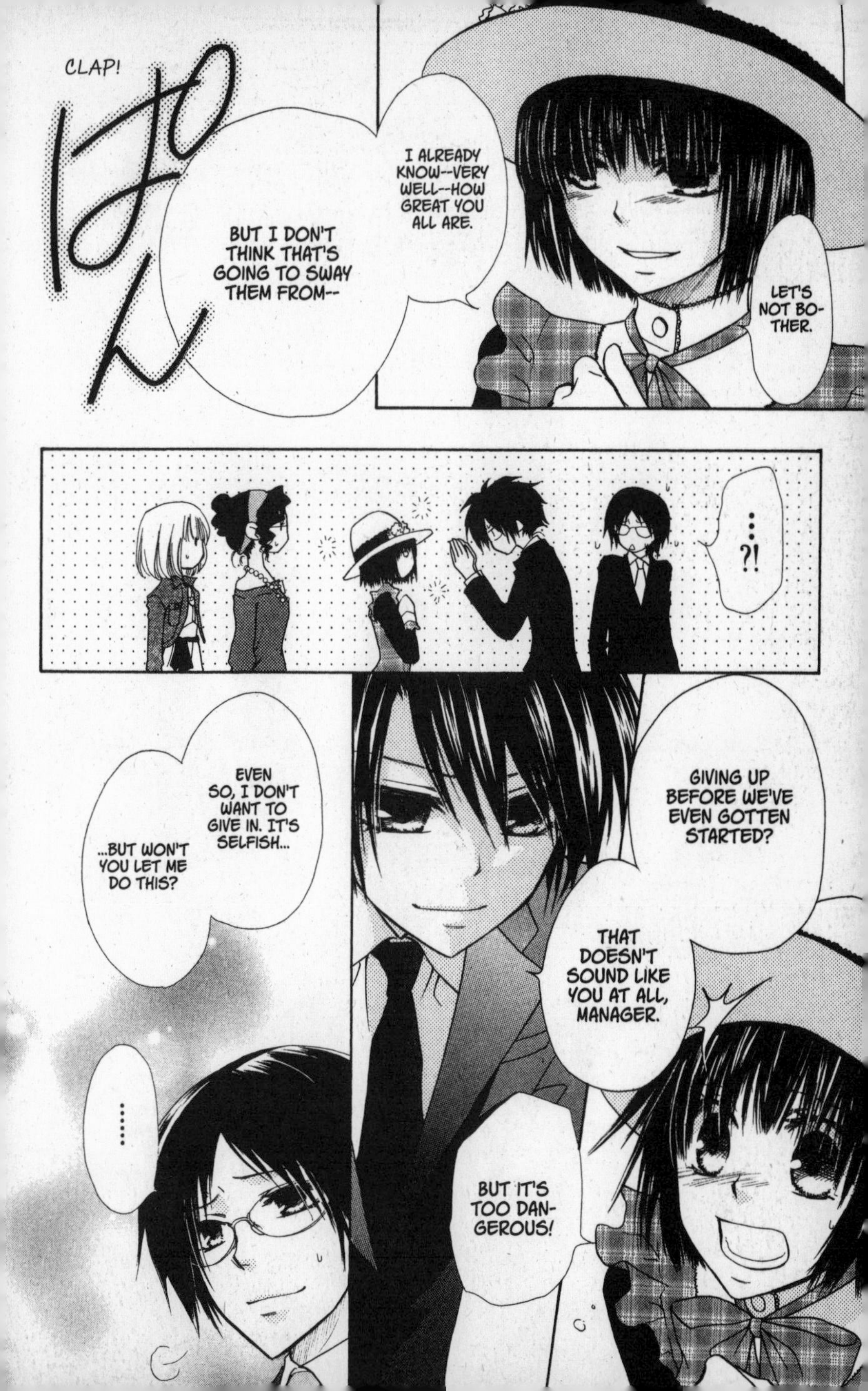
I ALREADY KNOW--VERY WELL--HOW GREAT YOU ALL ARE.
BUT I DON'T THINK THAT'S GOING TO SWAY THEM FROM--
LET'S NOT BO-THER.
CLAP!
...?!
GIVING UP BEFORE WE'VE EVEN GOTTEN STARTED?
THAT DOESN'T SOUND LIKE YOU AT ALL, MANAGER.
BUT IT'S TOO DAN-GEROUS!
EVEN SO, I DON'T WANT TO GIVE IN. IT'S SELFISH...
...BUT WON'T YOU LET ME DO THIS?
......

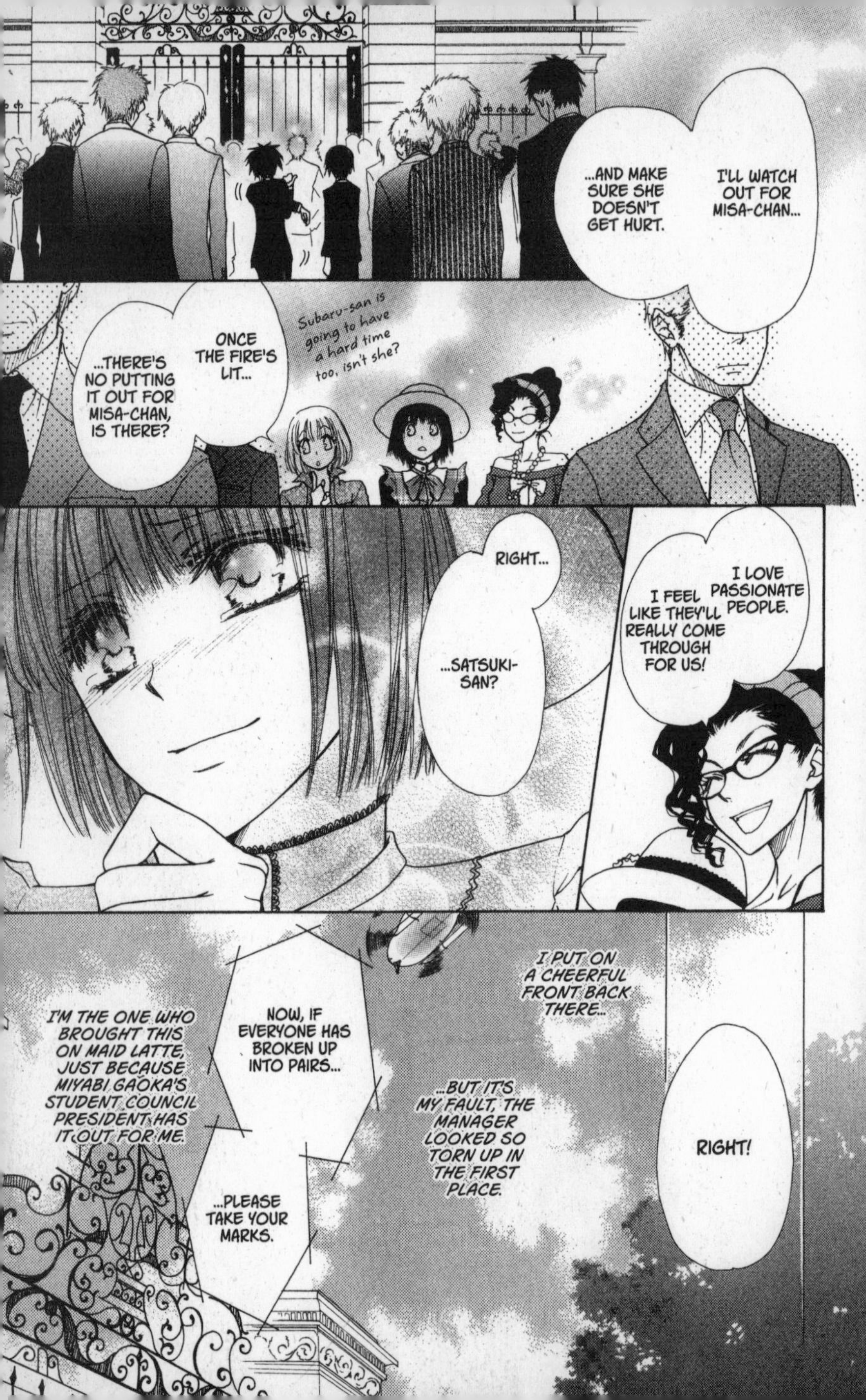
I'LL WATCH OUT FOR MISA-CHAN...
...AND MAKE SURE SHE DOESN'T GET HURT.
Subaru-san is going to have a hard time too, isn't she?
ONCE THE FIRE'S LIT...
...THERE'S NO PUTTING IT OUT FOR MISA-CHAN, IS THERE?
I LOVE PASSIONATE PEOPLE.
I FEEL LIKE THEY'LL REALLY COME THROUGH FOR US!
RIGHT...
...SATSUKI-SAN?
RIGHT!
I PUT ON A CHEERFUL FRONT BACK THERE...
...BUT IT'S MY FAULT, THE MANAGER LOOKED SO TORN UP IN THE FIRST PLACE.
NOW, IF EVERYONE HAS BROKEN UP INTO PAIRS...
...PLEASE TAKE YOUR MARKS.
I'M THE ONE WHO BROUGHT THIS ON MAID LATTE, JUST BECAUSE MIYABI GAOKA'S STUDENT COUNCIL PRESIDENT HAS IT OUT FOR ME.

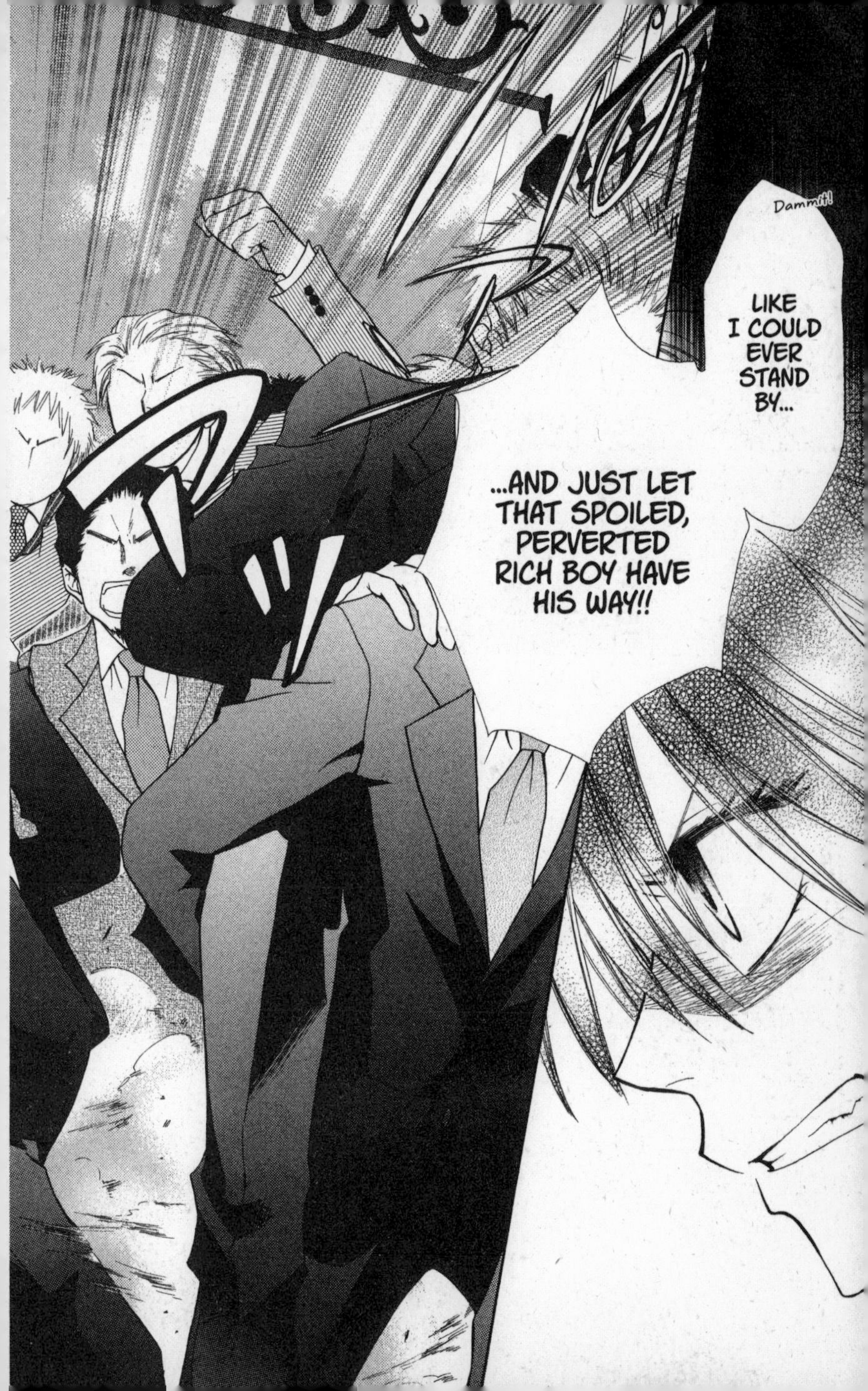
Dammit!
LIKE I COULD EVER STAND BY...
...AND JUST LET THAT SPOILED, PERVERTED RICH BOY HAVE HIS WAY!!

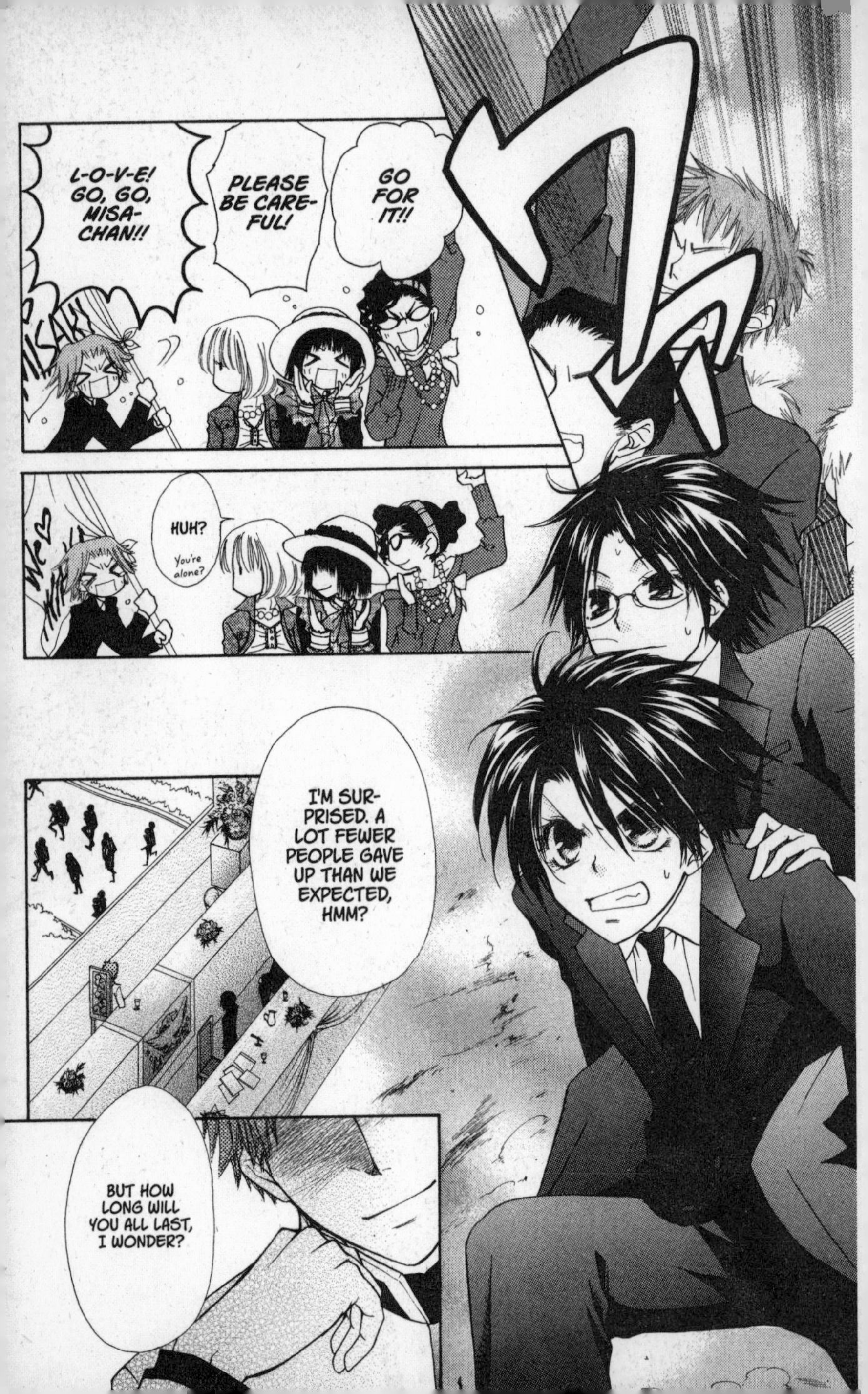
GO FOR IT!!
PLEASE BE CARE-FUL!
L-O-V-E! GO, GO, MISA-CHAN!!
MISAKI
HUH?
You're alone?
I'M SUR-PRISED. A LOT FEWER PEOPLE GAVE UP THAN WE EXPECTED, HMM?
BUT HOW LONG WILL YOU ALL LAST, I WONDER?

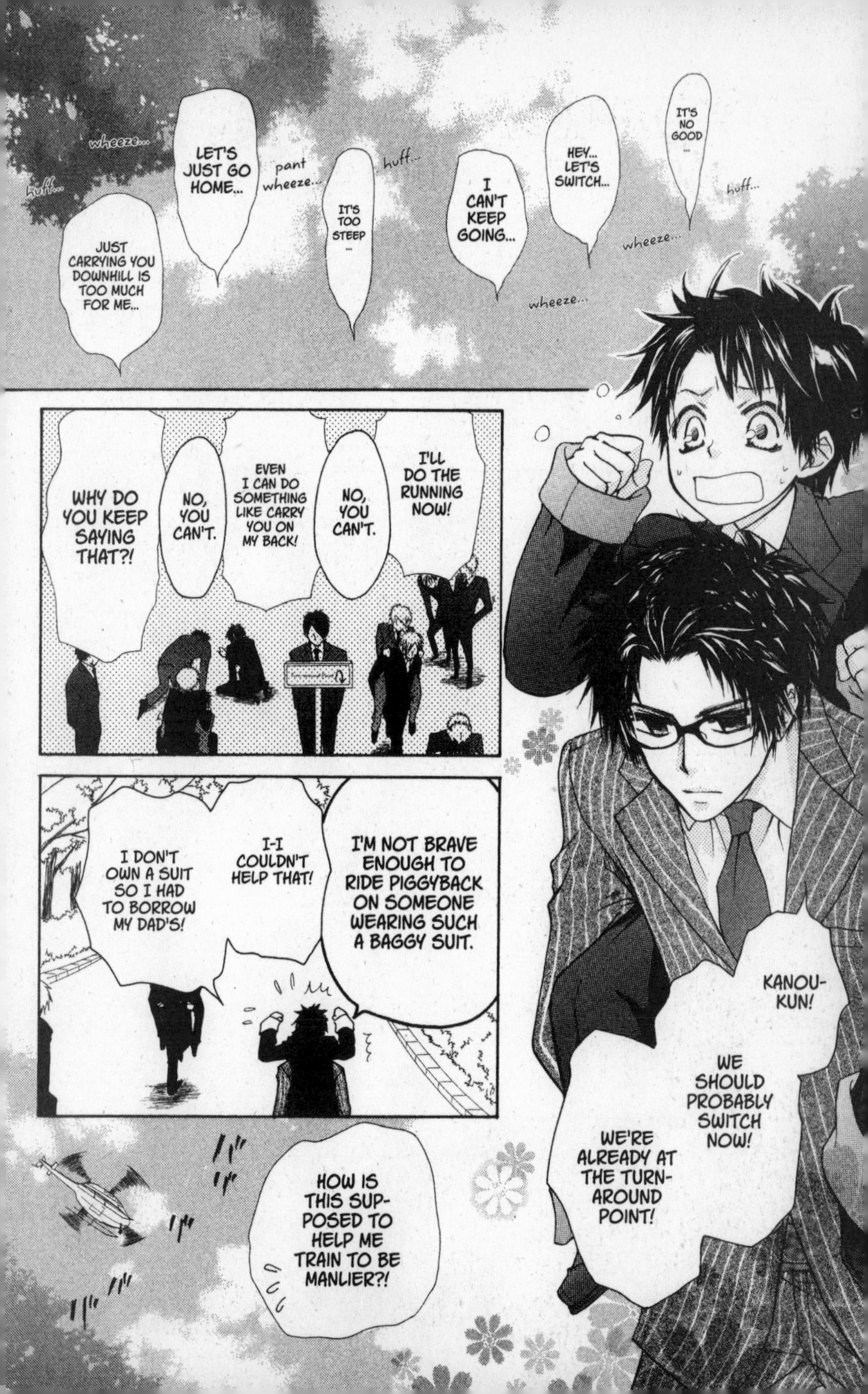
IT'S NO GOOD...
huff...
HEY... LET'S SWITCH...
wheeze...
I CAN'T KEEP GOING...
wheeze...
huff...
IT'S TOO STEEP...
pant wheeze...
LET'S JUST GO HOME...
wheeze...
huff...
JUST CARRYING YOU DOWNHILL IS TOO MUCH FOR ME...
KANOU-KUN!
WE SHOULD PROBABLY SWITCH NOW!
WE'RE ALREADY AT THE TURN-AROUND POINT!
I'LL DO THE RUNNING NOW!
NO, YOU CAN'T.
EVEN I CAN DO SOMETHING LIKE CARRY YOU ON MY BACK!
NO, YOU CAN'T.
WHY DO YOU KEEP SAYING THAT?!
I'M NOT BRAVE ENOUGH TO RIDE PIGGYBACK ON SOMEONE WEARING SUCH A BAGGY SUIT.
I-I COULDN'T HELP THAT!
I DON'T OWN A SUIT SO I HAD TO BORROW MY DAD'S!
HOW IS THIS SUPPOSED TO HELP ME TRAIN TO BE MANLIER?!

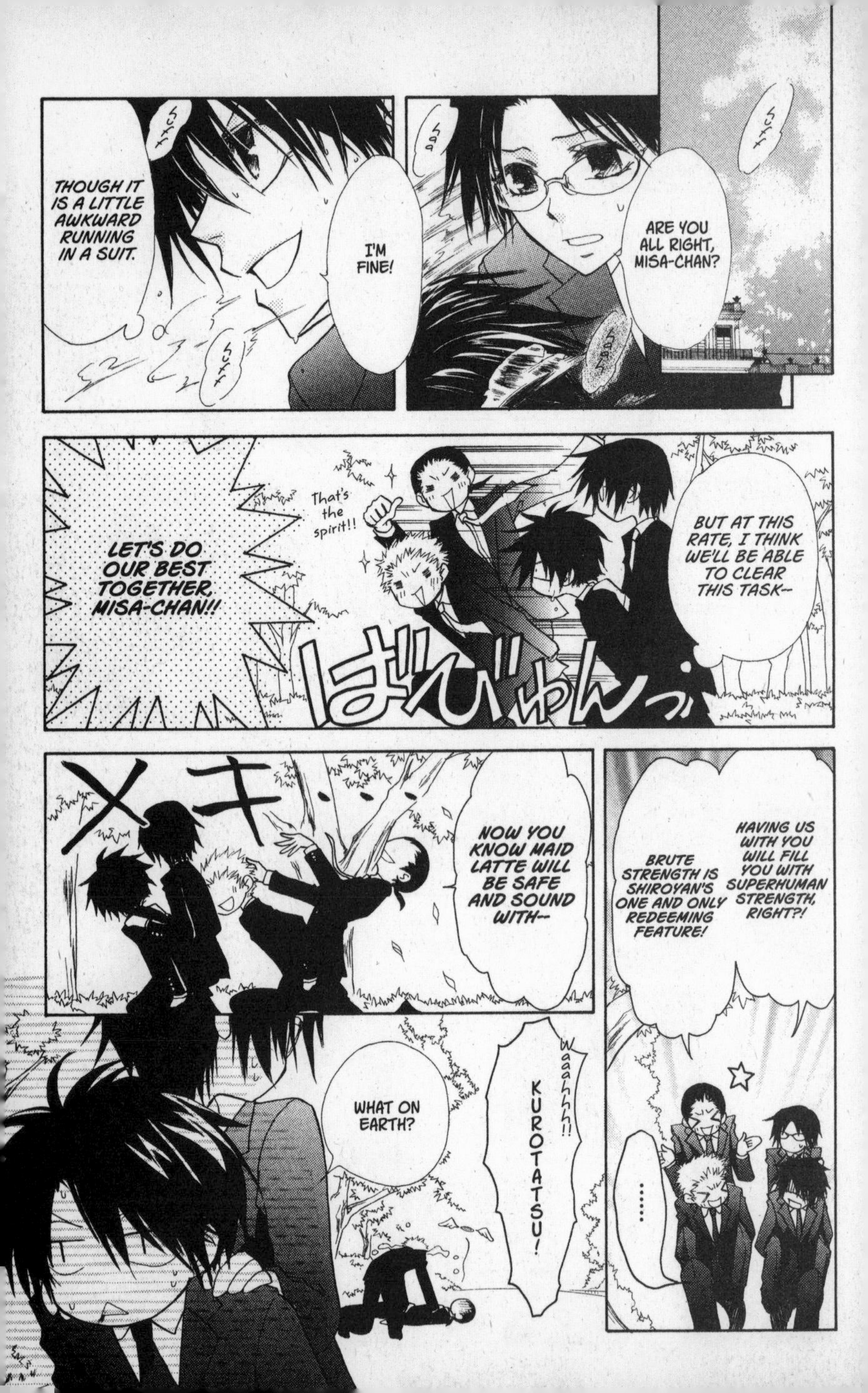
ARE YOU ALL RIGHT, MISA-CHAN?
I'M FINE!
THOUGH IT IS A LITTLE AWKWARD RUNNING IN A SUIT.
BUT AT THIS RATE, I THINK WE'LL BE ABLE TO CLEAR THIS TASK--
That's the spirit!!
LET'S DO OUR BEST TOGETHER, MISA-CHAN!!
ばんびゅんっ
HAVING US WITH YOU WILL FILL YOU WITH SUPERHUMAN STRENGTH, RIGHT?!
BRUTE STRENGTH IS SHIROYAN'S ONE AND ONLY REDEEMING FEATURE!
......
NOW YOU KNOW MAID LATTE WILL BE SAFE AND SOUND WITH--
メキ
KUROTATSU!
Waaahhh!!
WHAT ON EARTH?

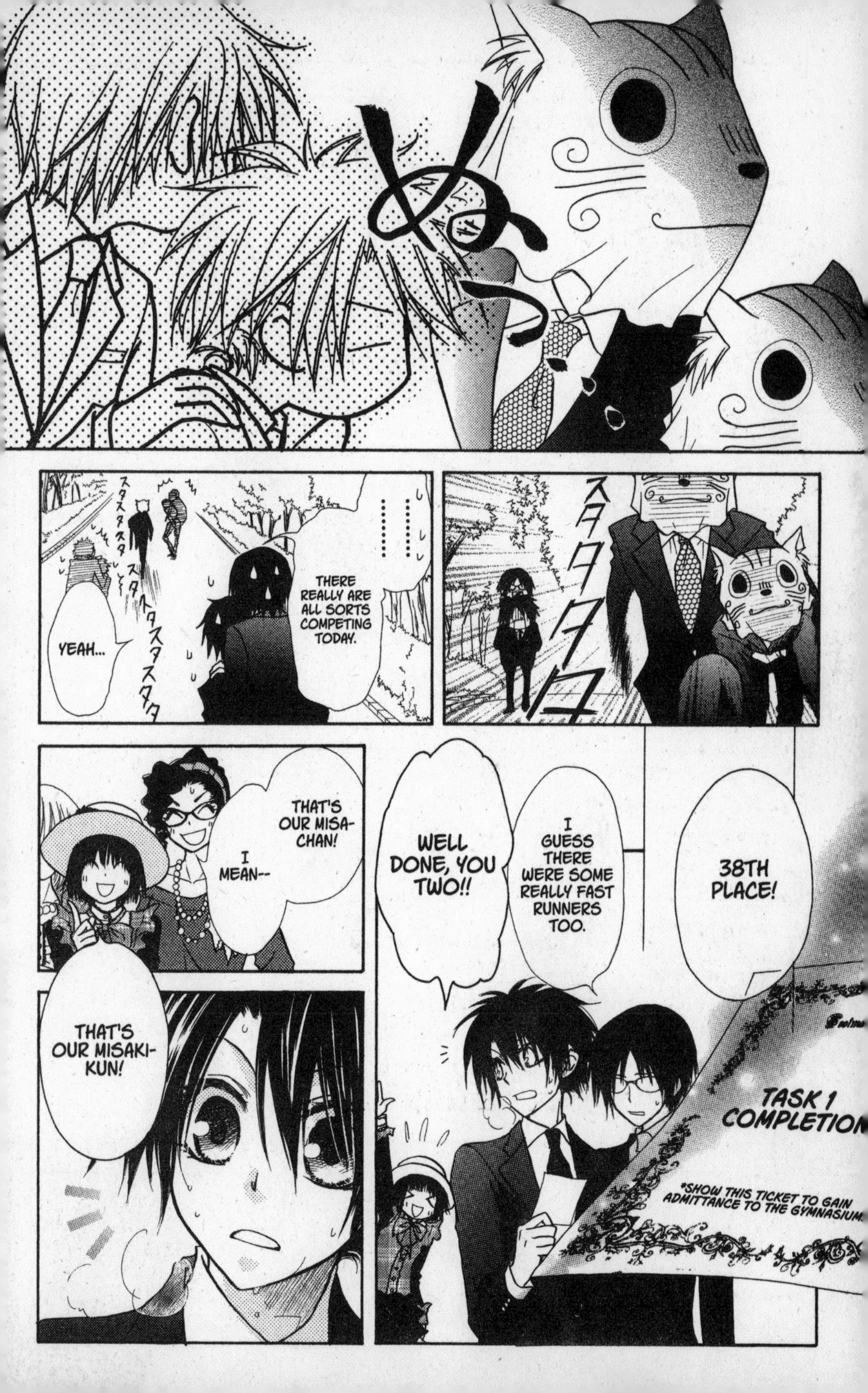
スタタタタ
......
THERE REALLY ARE ALL SORTS COMPETING TODAY.
YEAH...
38TH PLACE!
I GUESS THERE WERE SOME REALLY FAST RUNNERS TOO.
WELL DONE, YOU TWO!!
TASK 1 COMPLETION
*SHOW THIS TICKET TO GAIN ADMITTANCE TO THE GYMNASIUM.
THAT'S OUR MISA-CHAN!
I MEAN--
THAT'S OUR MISAKI-KUN!

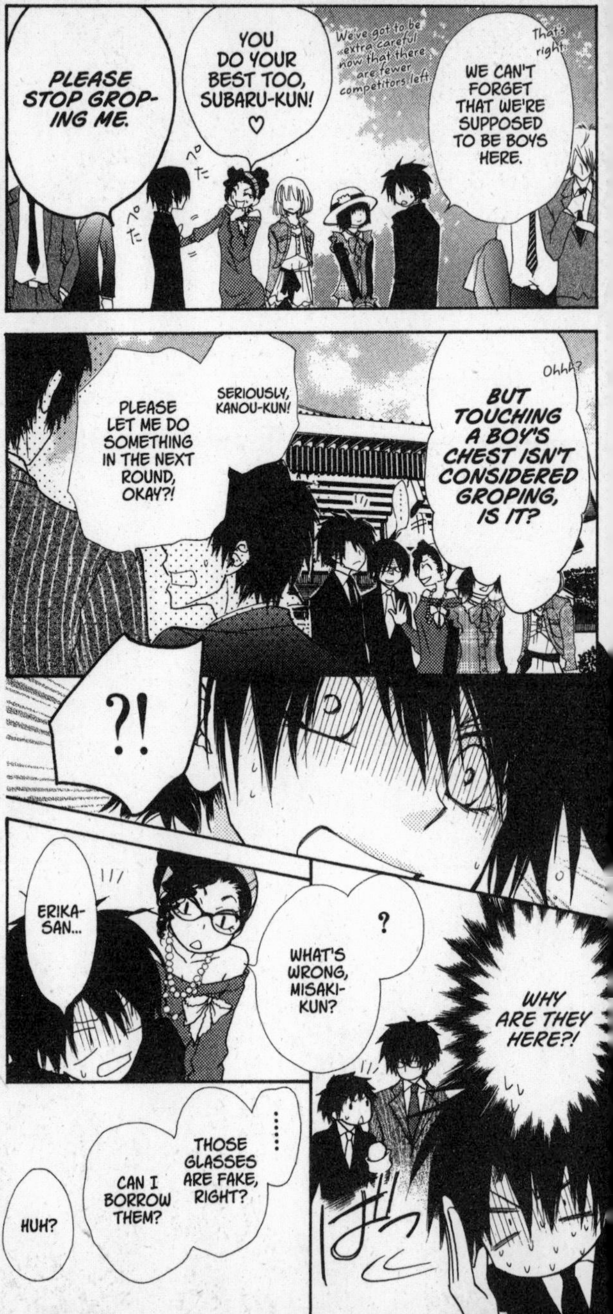
That's right.
WE CAN'T FORGET THAT WE'RE SUPPOSED TO BE BOYS HERE.
We've got to be extra careful now that there are fewer competitors left.
YOU DO YOUR BEST TOO, SUBARU-KUN! ♡
PLEASE STOP GROPING ME.
Ohhh?
BUT TOUCHING A BOY'S CHEST ISN'T CONSIDERED GROPING, IS IT?
SERIOUSLY, KANOU-KUN!
PLEASE LET ME DO SOMETHING IN THE NEXT ROUND, OKAY?!
?!
WHY ARE THEY HERE?!
?
WHAT'S WRONG, MISAKI-KUN?
ERIKA-SAN...
......
THOSE GLASSES ARE FAKE, RIGHT?
CAN I BORROW THEM?
HUH?

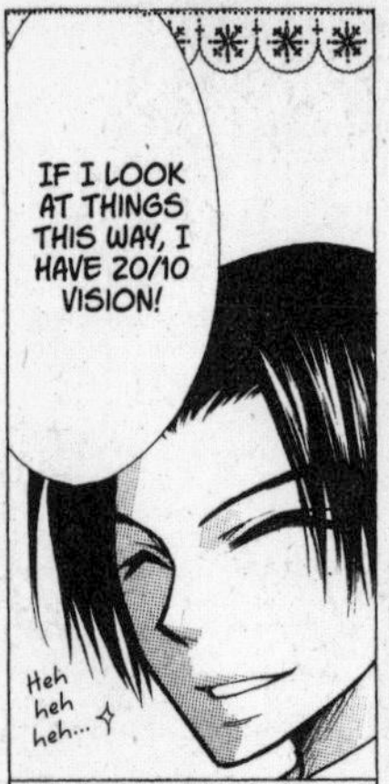
IF I LOOK AT THINGS THIS WAY, I HAVE 20/10 VISION!
Heh heh heh...

Name

Kanade Maki

Age (Class)

16 (Miyabi Gaoka Class II-A)

Blood Type

A

Height

178 cm (5ft 10in)

Weight

60 kg (132 lbs)

Special Skills

Shiatsu Massage

Likes

Servitude

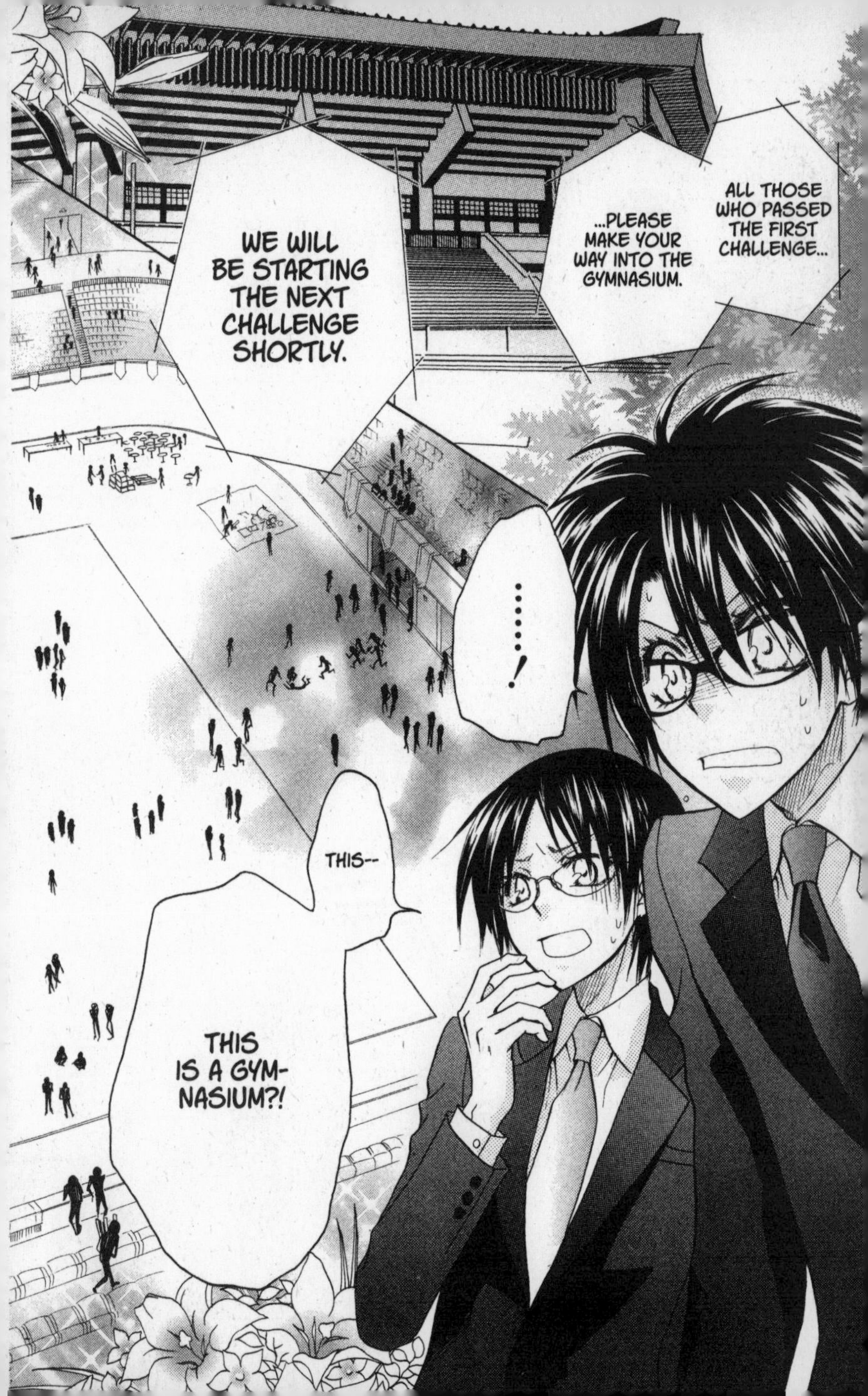
ALL THOSE WHO PASSED THE FIRST CHALLENGE...
...PLEASE MAKE YOUR WAY INTO THE GYMNASIUM.
WE WILL BE STARTING THE NEXT CHALLENGE SHORTLY.
......!
THIS--
THIS IS A GYMNASIUM?!

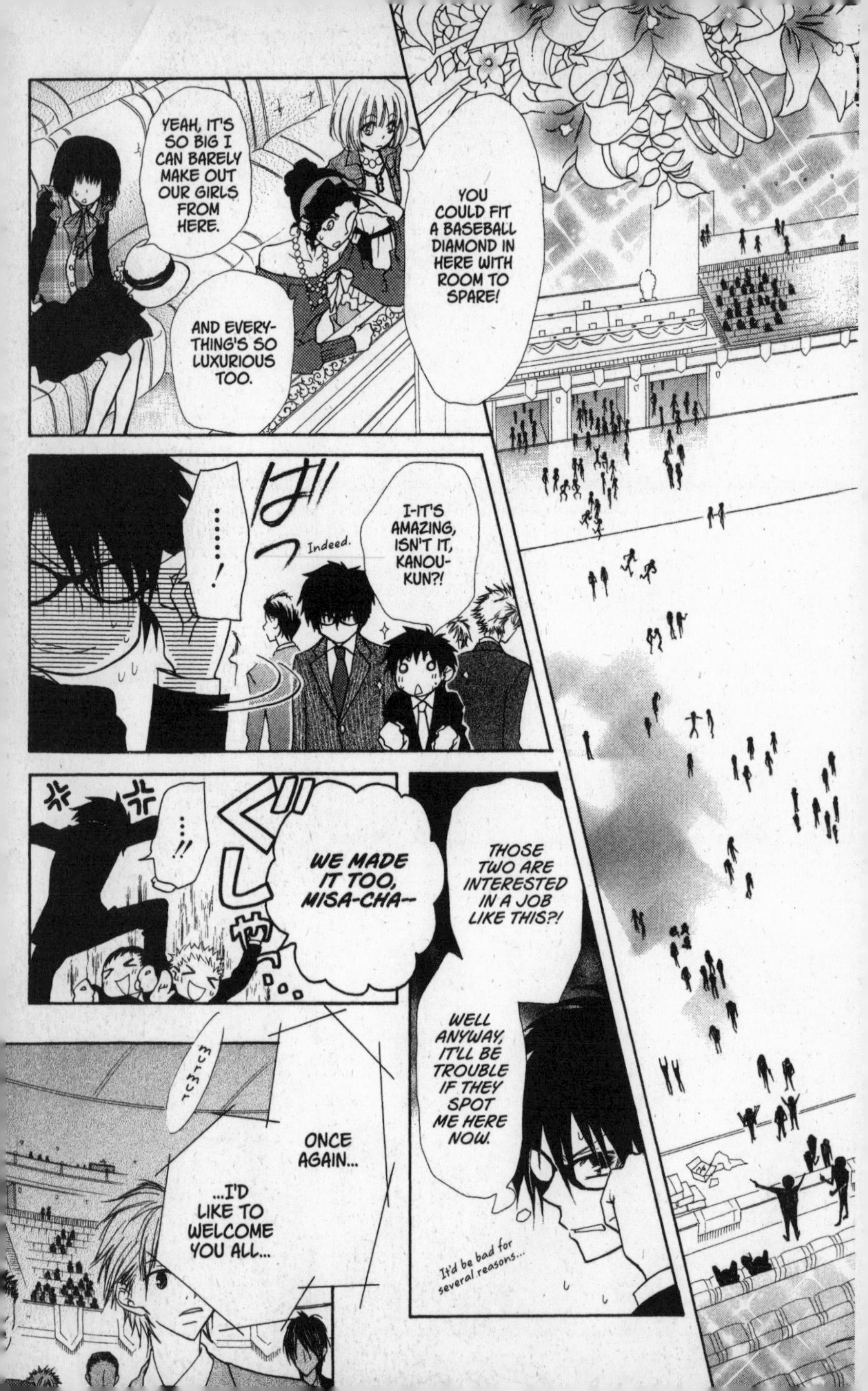
YOU COULD FIT A BASEBALL DIAMOND IN HERE WITH ROOM TO SPARE!
YEAH, IT'S SO BIG I CAN BARELY MAKE OUT OUR GIRLS FROM HERE.
AND EVERY-THING'S SO LUXURIOUS TOO.
I-IT'S AMAZING, ISN'T IT, KANOU-KUN?!
Indeed.
......!
THOSE TWO ARE INTERESTED IN A JOB LIKE THIS?!
WELL ANYWAY, IT'LL BE TROUBLE IF THEY SPOT ME HERE NOW.
It'd be bad for several reasons...
WE MADE IT TOO, MISA-CHA~
...!!
ONCE AGAIN...
...I'D LIKE TO WELCOME YOU ALL...

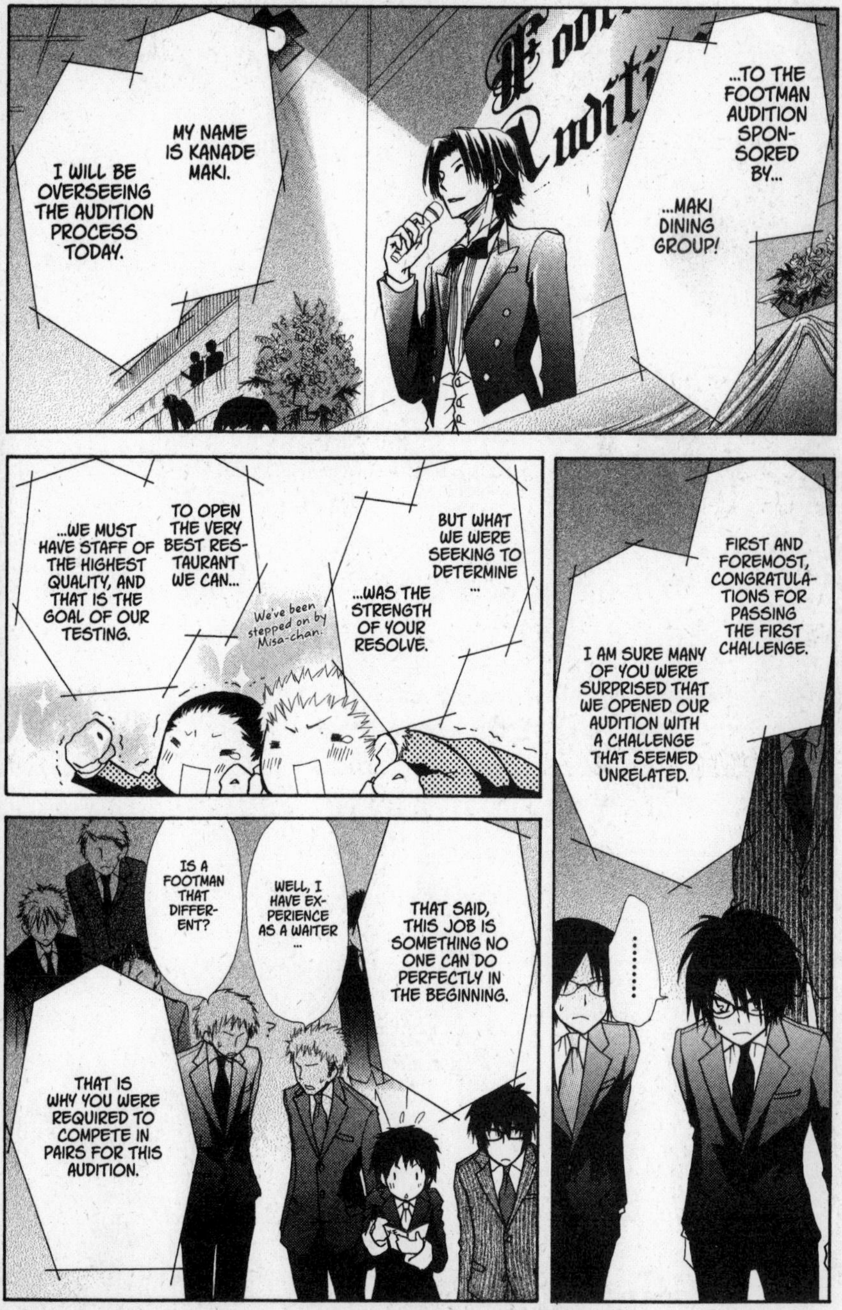
...TO THE FOOTMAN AUDITION SPONSORED BY...
...MAKI DINING GROUP!
MY NAME IS KANADE MAKI.
I WILL BE OVERSEEING THE AUDITION PROCESS TODAY.
FIRST AND FOREMOST, CONGRATULATIONS FOR PASSING THE FIRST CHALLENGE.
I AM SURE MANY OF YOU WERE SURPRISED THAT WE OPENED OUR AUDITION WITH A CHALLENGE THAT SEEMED UNRELATED.
....
BUT WHAT WE WERE SEEKING TO DETERMINE...
...WAS THE STRENGTH OF YOUR RESOLVE.
TO OPEN THE VERY BEST RESTAURANT WE CAN...
...WE MUST HAVE STAFF OF THE HIGHEST QUALITY, AND THAT IS THE GOAL OF OUR TESTING.
We've been stepped on by Misa-chan.
THAT SAID, THIS JOB IS SOMETHING NO ONE CAN DO PERFECTLY IN THE BEGINNING.
WELL, I HAVE EXPERIENCE AS A WAITER...
IS A FOOTMAN THAT DIFFERENT?
THAT IS WHY YOU WERE REQUIRED TO COMPETE IN PAIRS FOR THIS AUDITION.

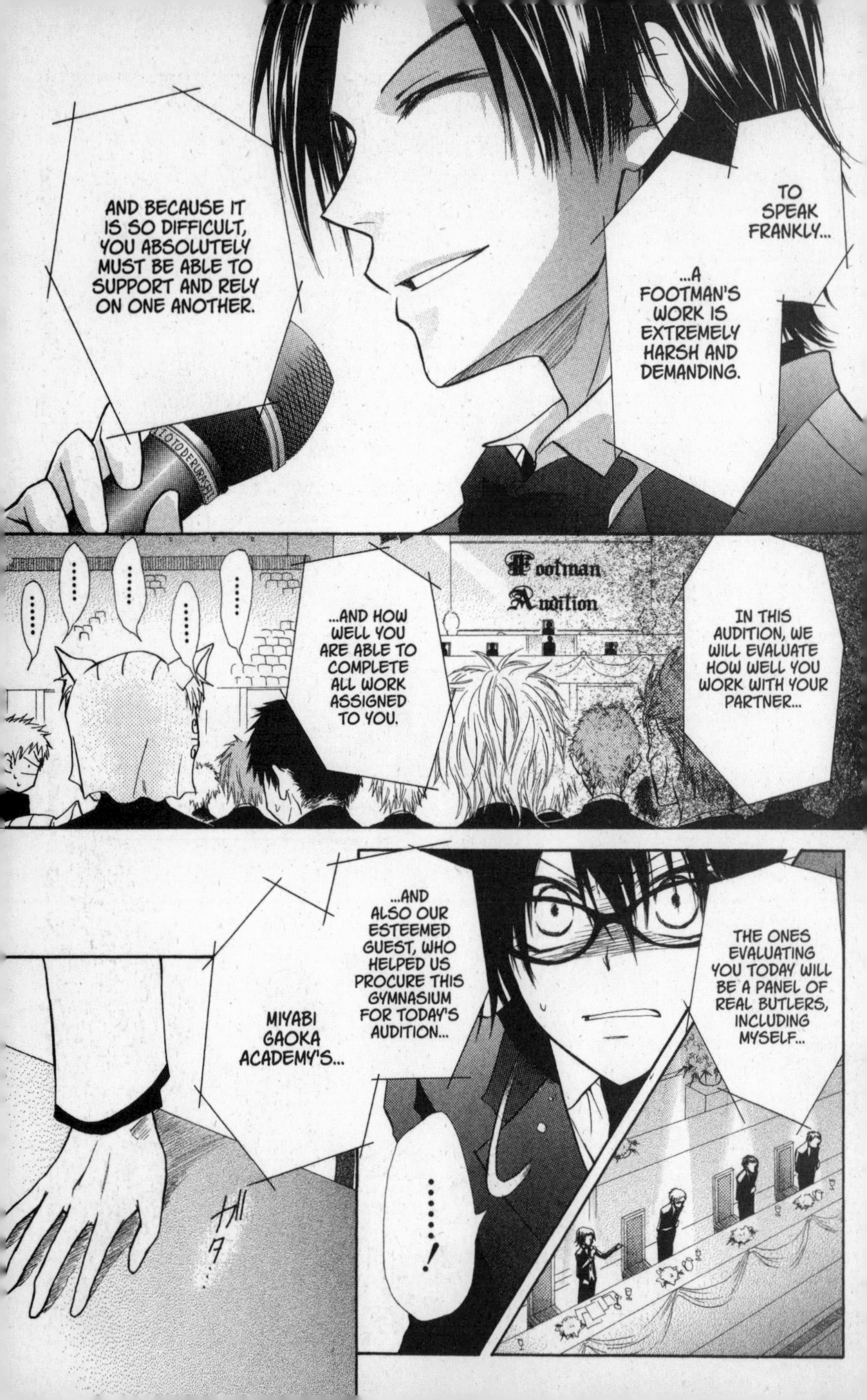

TO SPEAK FRANKLY...
...A FOOTMAN'S WORK IS EXTREMELY HARSH AND DEMANDING.
AND BECAUSE IT IS SO DIFFICULT, YOU ABSOLUTELY MUST BE ABLE TO SUPPORT AND RELY ON ONE ANOTHER.
IN THIS AUDITION, WE WILL EVALUATE HOW WELL YOU WORK WITH YOUR PARTNER...
Footman Audition
...AND HOW WELL YOU ARE ABLE TO COMPLETE ALL WORK ASSIGNED TO YOU.
......
......
......
......
......
THE ONES EVALUATING YOU TODAY WILL BE A PANEL OF REAL BUTLERS, INCLUDING MYSELF...
...AND ALSO OUR ESTEEMED GUEST, WHO HELPED US PROCURE THIS GYMNASIUM FOR TODAY'S AUDITION...
MIYABI GAOKA ACADEMY'S...
......!

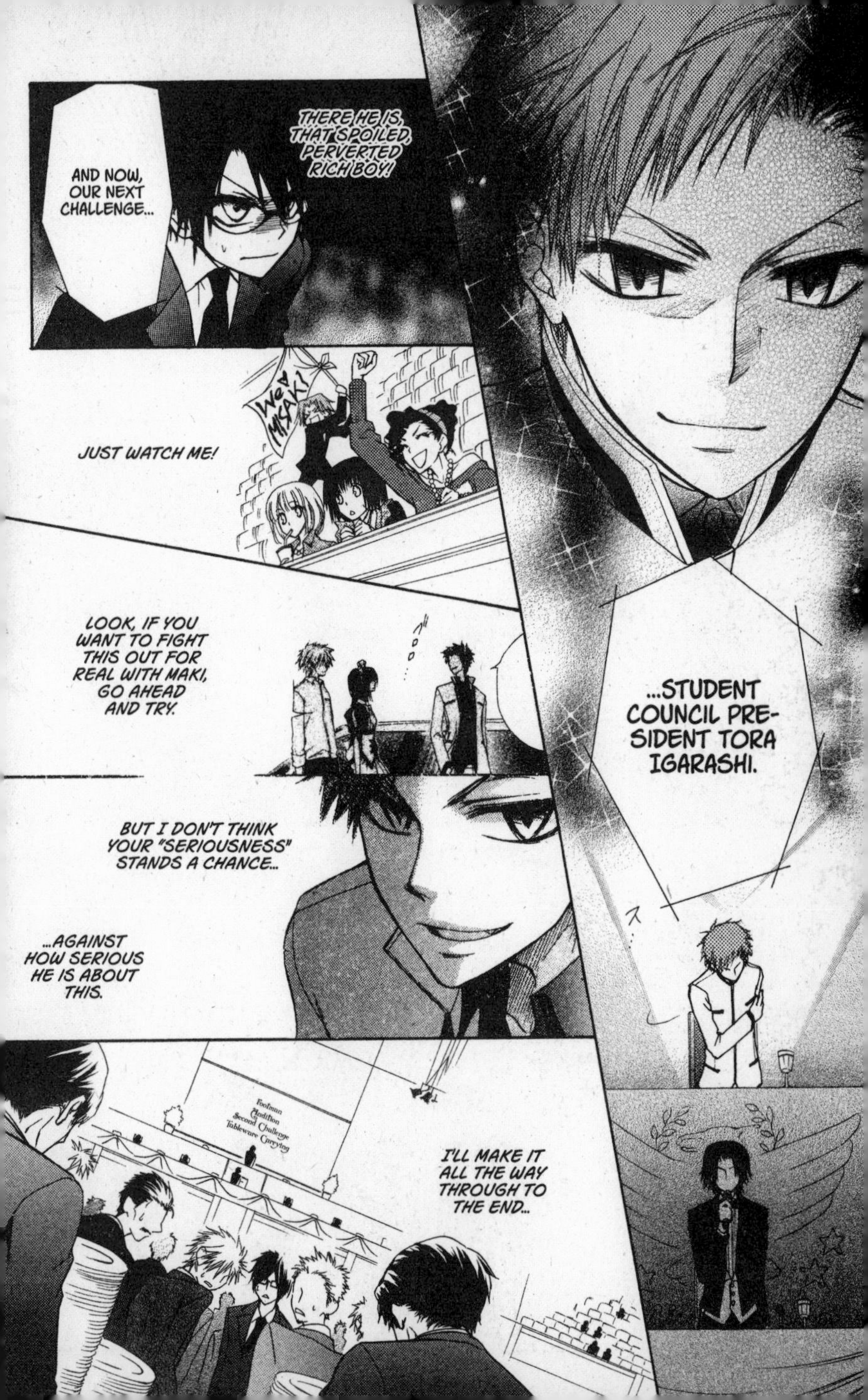
AND NOW, OUR NEXT CHALLENGE...
THERE HE IS, THAT SPOILED, PERVERTED RICH BOY!
...STUDENT COUNCIL PRE-SIDENT TORA IGARASHI.
We ♥ MISAKI
JUST WATCH ME!
LOOK, IF YOU WANT TO FIGHT THIS OUT FOR REAL WITH MAKI, GO AHEAD AND TRY.
BUT I DON'T THINK YOUR "SERIOUSNESS" STANDS A CHANCE...
...AGAINST HOW SERIOUS HE IS ABOUT THIS.
Footman Audition Second Challenge Tableware Carrying
I'LL MAKE IT ALL THE WAY THROUGH TO THE END...

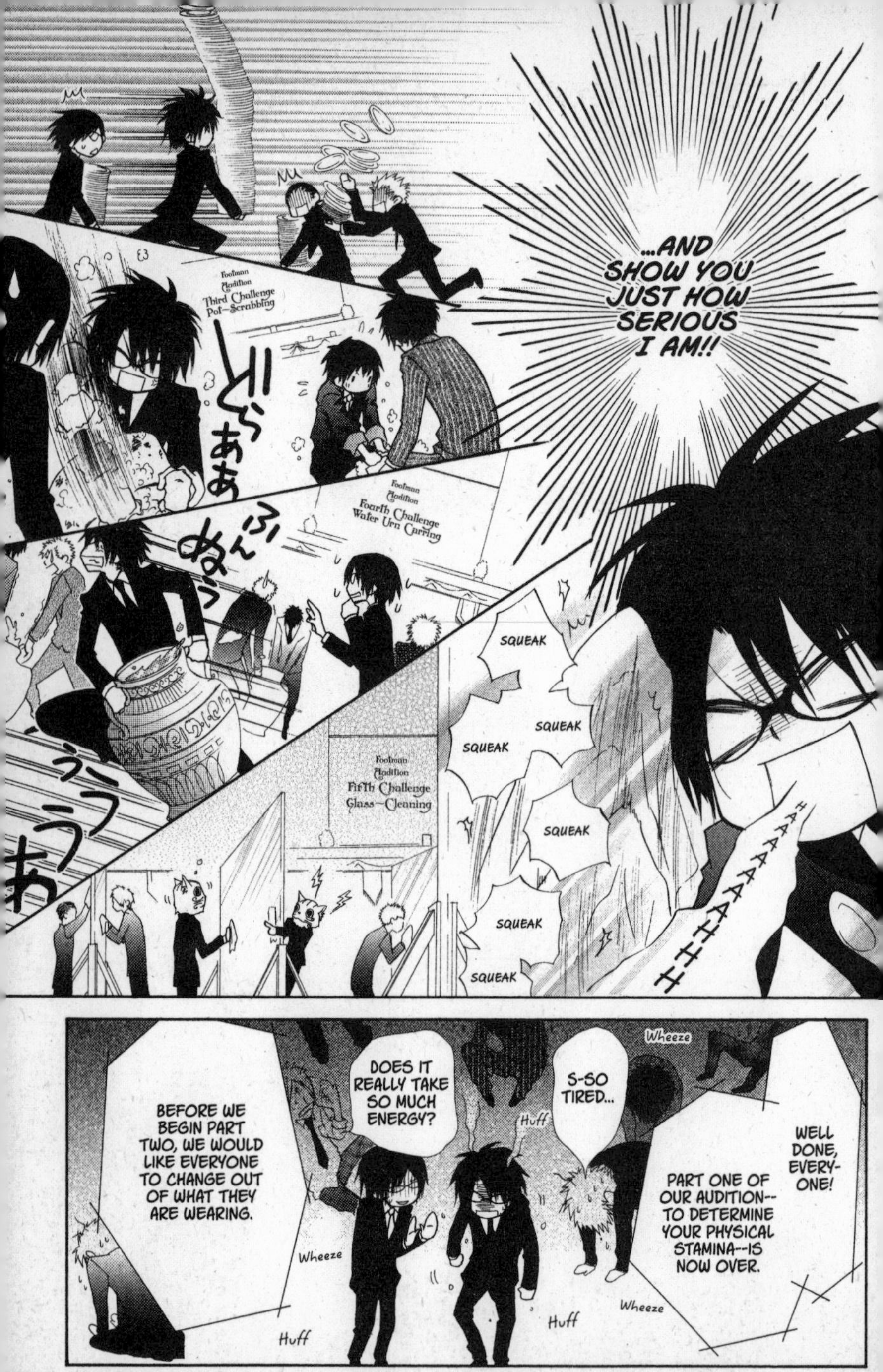
...AND SHOW YOU JUST HOW SERIOUS I AM!!
Footman Audition Third Challenge Pot-Scrubbing
どらああ
Footman Audition Fourth Challenge Water Urn Carring
ふんぬう
ううお
Footman Audition Fifth Challenge Glass~Clenning
SQUEAK
SQUEAK
SQUEAK
SQUEAK
SQUEAK
SQUEAK
HAAAAAAAAAHHHH
WELL DONE, EVERYONE!
PART ONE OF OUR AUDITION--TO DETERMINE YOUR PHYSICAL STAMINA--IS NOW OVER.
Wheeze
Wheeze
S-SO TIRED...
Huff
Huff
DOES IT REALLY TAKE SO MUCH ENERGY?
Wheeze
BEFORE WE BEGIN PART TWO, WE WOULD LIKE EVERYONE TO CHANGE OUT OF WHAT THEY ARE WEARING.
Huff

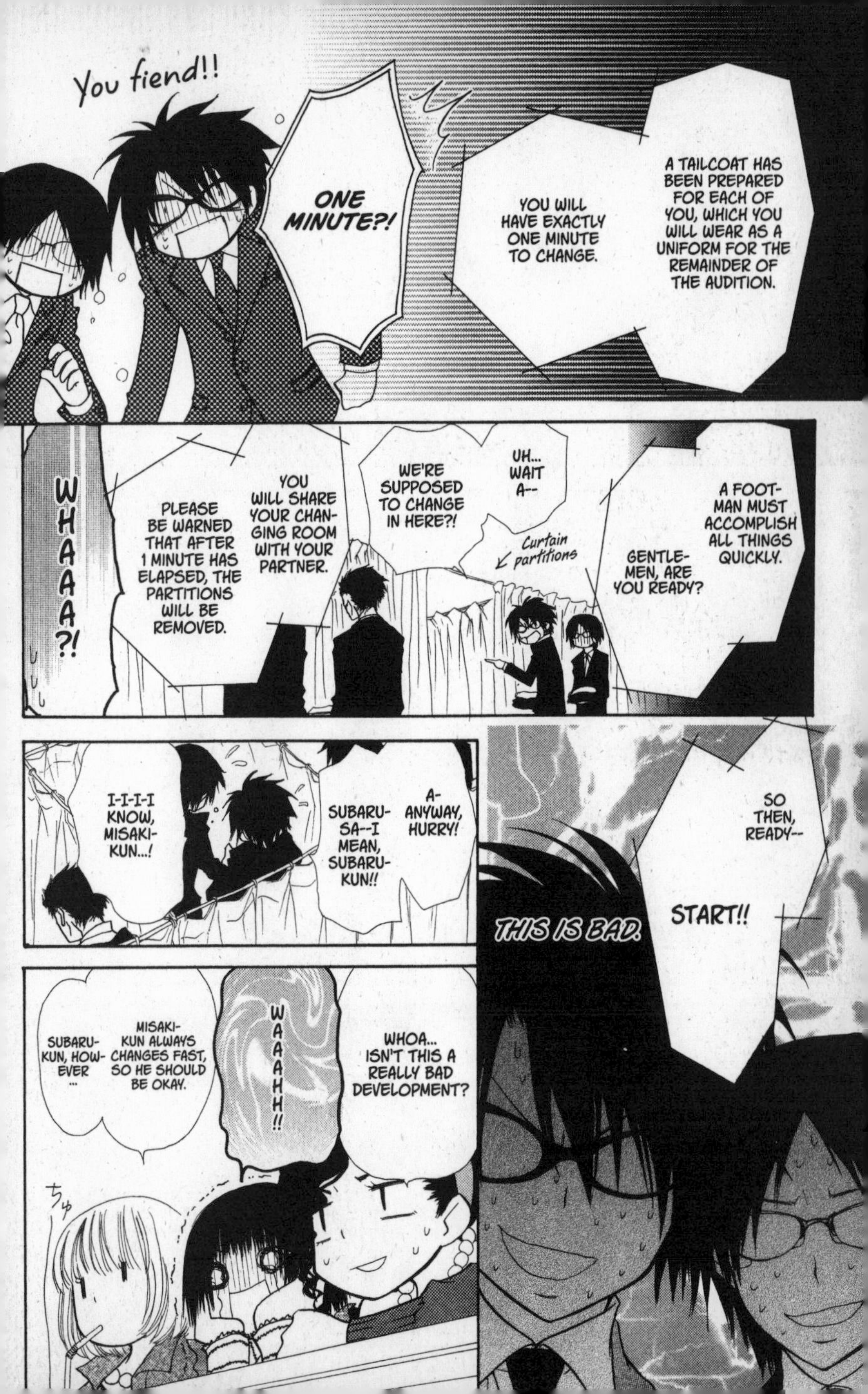
A TAILCOAT HAS BEEN PREPARED FOR EACH OF YOU, WHICH YOU WILL WEAR AS A UNIFORM FOR THE REMAINDER OF THE AUDITION.
YOU WILL HAVE EXACTLY ONE MINUTE TO CHANGE.
ONE MINUTE?!
You fiend!!
A FOOT-MAN MUST ACCOMPLISH ALL THINGS QUICKLY.
GENTLE-MEN, ARE YOU READY?
UH... WAIT A--
Curtain partitions
WE'RE SUPPOSED TO CHANGE IN HERE?!
YOU WILL SHARE YOUR CHAN-GING ROOM WITH YOUR PARTNER.
PLEASE BE WARNED THAT AFTER 1 MINUTE HAS ELAPSED, THE PARTITIONS WILL BE REMOVED.
WHAAAA?!
SO THEN, READY--
START!!
THIS IS BAD.
A-ANYWAY, HURRY!
SUBARU-SA--I MEAN, SUBARU-KUN!!
I-I-I-I KNOW, MISAKI-KUN...!
WHOA... ISN'T THIS A REALLY BAD DEVELOPMENT?
WAAAHH!!
MISAKI-KUN ALWAYS CHANGES FAST, SO HE SHOULD BE OKAY.
SUBARU-KUN, HOW-EVER ...

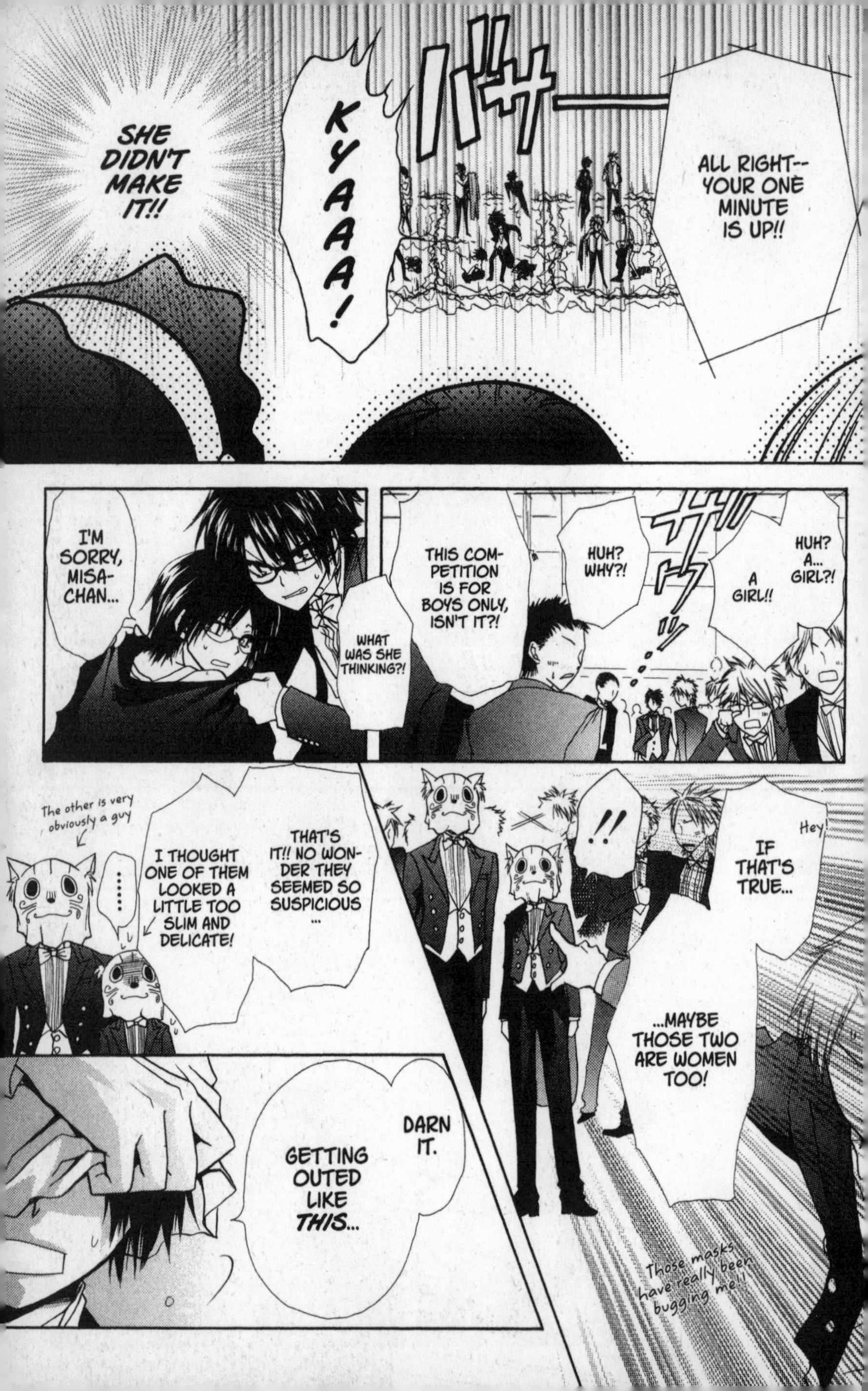
ALL RIGHT-- YOUR ONE MINUTE IS UP!!
バサー
KYAAAA!
SHE DIDN'T MAKE IT!!
HUH? A... GIRL?!
A GIRL!!
HUH? WHY?!
THIS COMPETITION IS FOR BOYS ONLY, ISN'T IT?!
WHAT WAS SHE THINKING?!
I'M SORRY, MISA-CHAN...
Hey!
IF THAT'S TRUE...
!!
...MAYBE THOSE TWO ARE WOMEN TOO!
Those masks have really been bugging me!!
THAT'S IT!! NO WONDER THEY SEEMED SO SUSPICIOUS...
I THOUGHT ONE OF THEM LOOKED A LITTLE TOO SLIM AND DELICATE!
......
The other is very obviously a guy
DARN IT.
GETTING OUTED LIKE THIS...

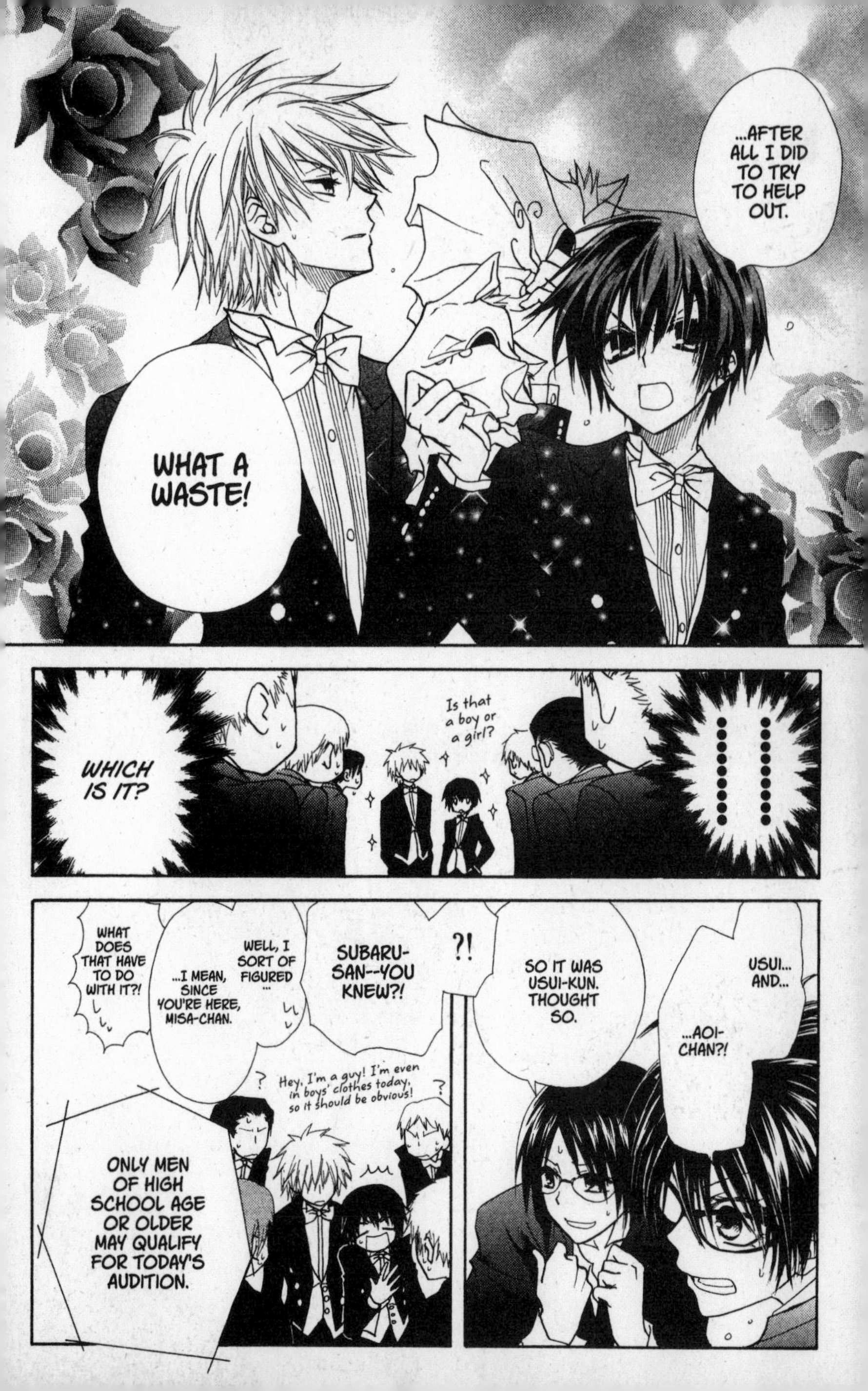
...AFTER ALL I DID TO TRY TO HELP OUT.
WHAT A WASTE!
....
Is that a boy or a girl?
WHICH IS IT?
USUI... AND...
...AOI-CHAN?!
SO IT WAS USUI-KUN. THOUGHT SO.
?!
SUBARU-SAN--YOU KNEW?!
WELL, I SORT OF FIGURED ...
...I MEAN, SINCE YOU'RE HERE, MISA-CHAN.
WHAT DOES THAT HAVE TO DO WITH IT?!
Hey, I'm a guy! I'm even in boys' clothes today, so it should be obvious!
ONLY MEN OF HIGH SCHOOL AGE OR OLDER MAY QUALIFY FOR TODAY'S AUDITION.

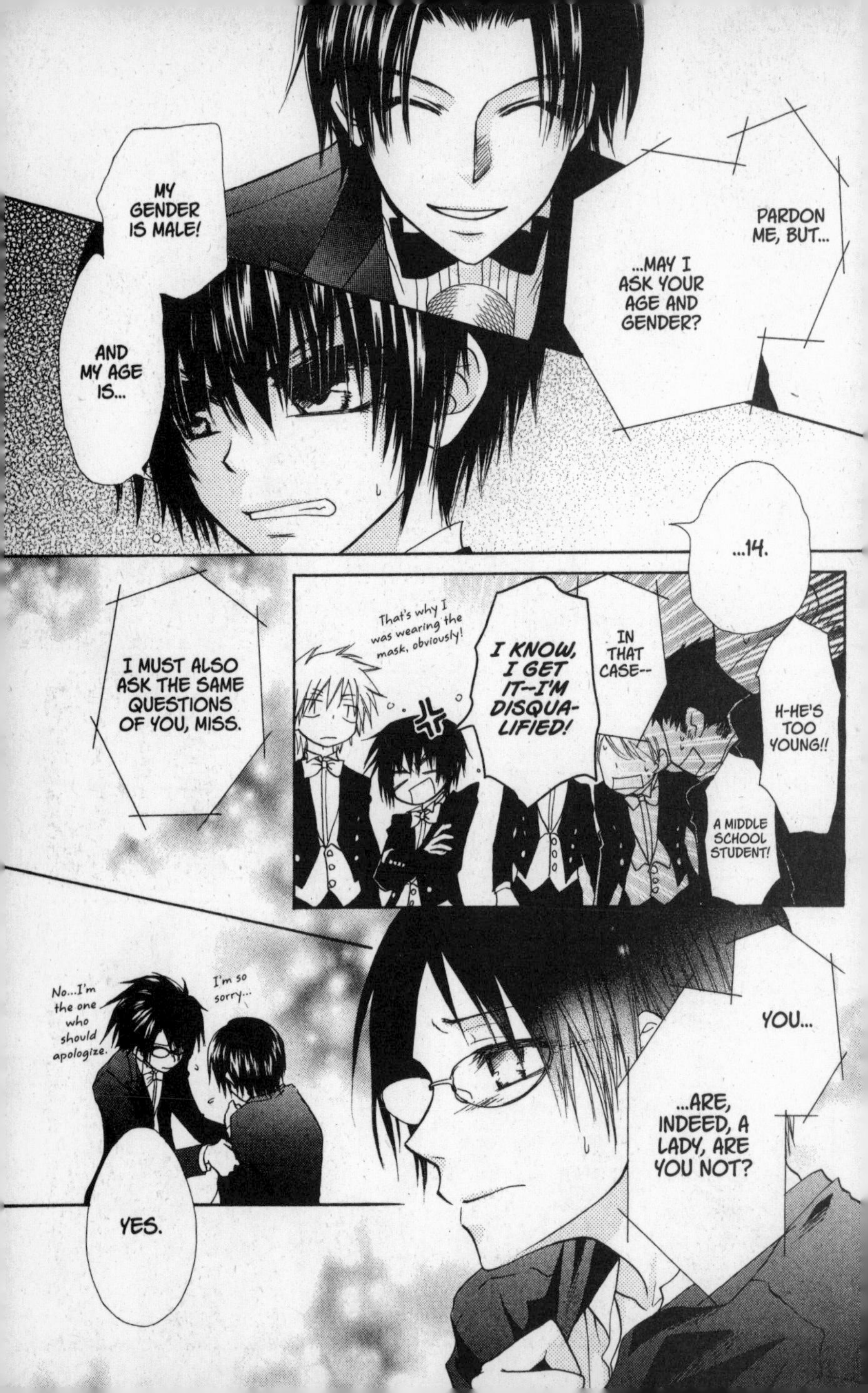
PARDON ME, BUT...
...MAY I ASK YOUR AGE AND GENDER?
MY GENDER IS MALE!
AND MY AGE IS...
...14.
H-HE'S TOO YOUNG!!
A MIDDLE SCHOOL STUDENT!
IN THAT CASE--
I KNOW, I GET IT--I'M DISQUALIFIED!
That's why I was wearing the mask, obviously!
I MUST ALSO ASK THE SAME QUESTIONS OF YOU, MISS.
YOU...
...ARE, INDEED, A LADY, ARE YOU NOT?
YES.
I'm so sorry...
No...I'm the one who should apologize.

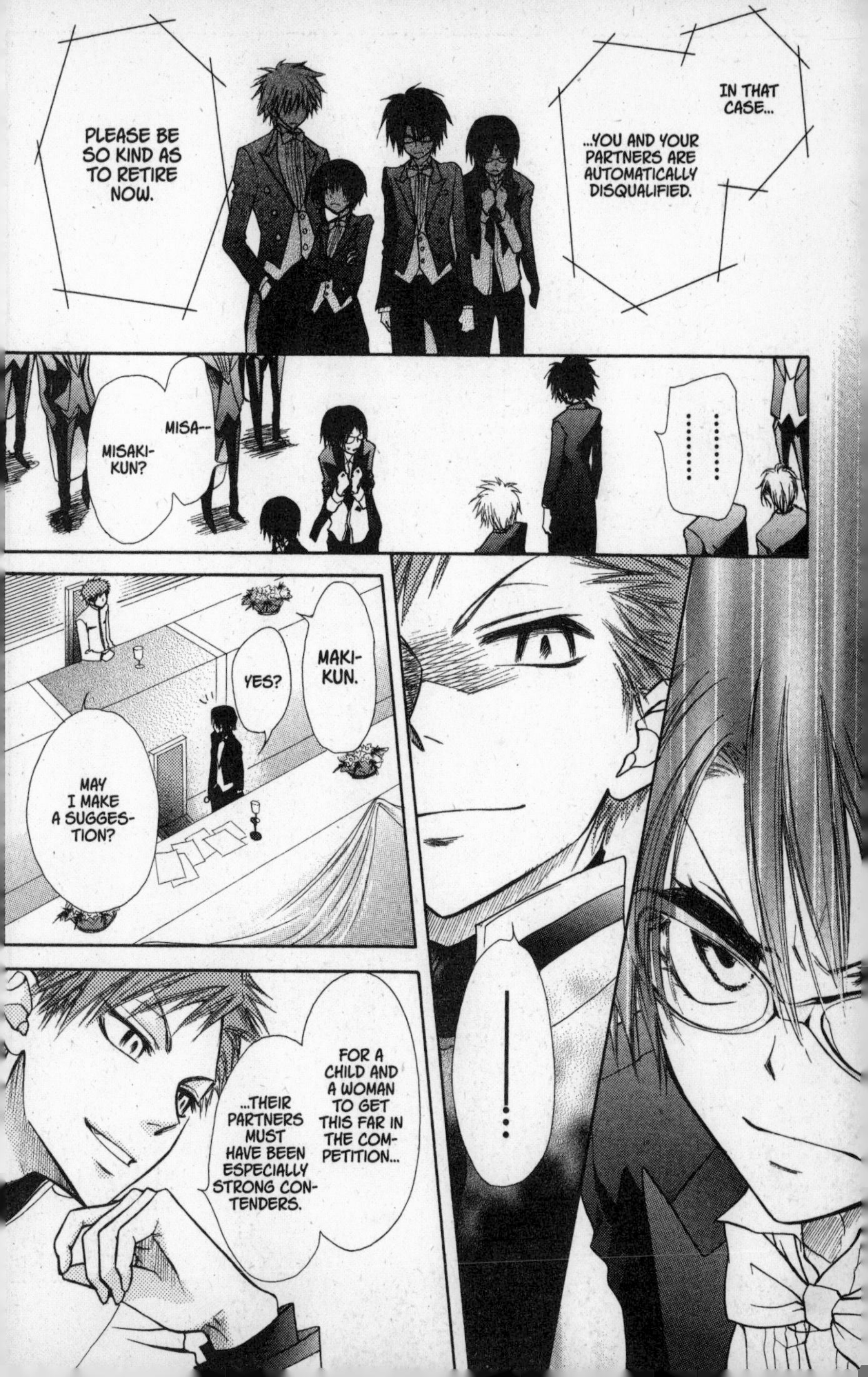
IN THAT CASE...
...YOU AND YOUR PARTNERS ARE AUTOMATICALLY DISQUALIFIED.
PLEASE BE SO KIND AS TO RETIRE NOW.
......
MISA--
MISAKI-KUN?
...!
MAKI-KUN.
YES?
MAY I MAKE A SUGGES-TION?
FOR A CHILD AND A WOMAN TO GET THIS FAR IN THE COM-PETITION...
...THEIR PARTNERS MUST HAVE BEEN ESPECIALLY STRONG CON-TENDERS.

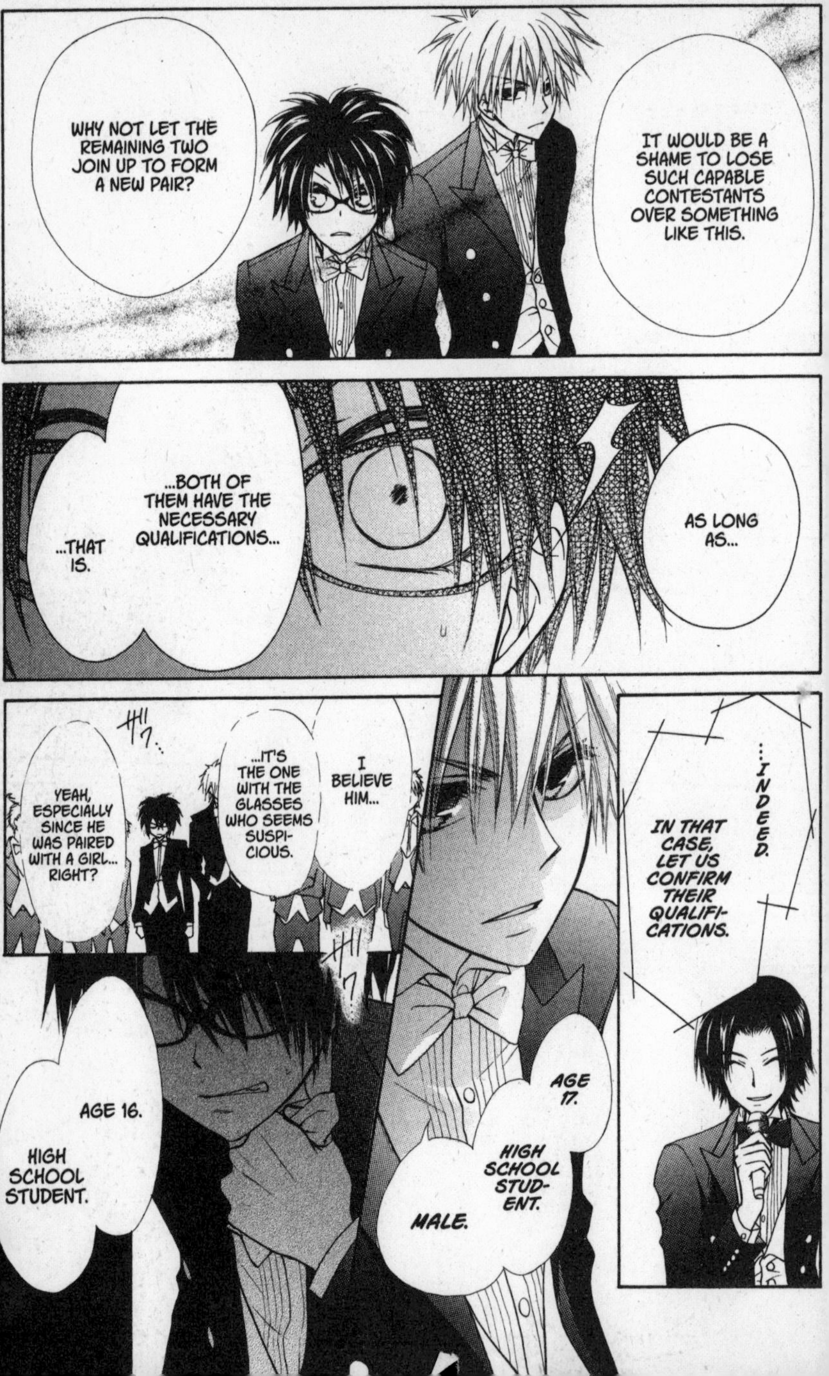
IT WOULD BE A SHAME TO LOSE SUCH CAPABLE CONTESTANTS OVER SOMETHING LIKE THIS.
WHY NOT LET THE REMAINING TWO JOIN UP TO FORM A NEW PAIR?
AS LONG AS...
...BOTH OF THEM HAVE THE NECESSARY QUALIFICATIONS...
...THAT IS.
...INDEED.
IN THAT CASE, LET US CONFIRM THEIR QUALIFICATIONS.
AGE 17.
HIGH SCHOOL STUDENT.
MALE.
I BELIEVE HIM...
...IT'S THE ONE WITH THE GLASSES WHO SEEMS SUSPICIOUS.
YEAH, ESPECIALLY SINCE HE WAS PAIRED WITH A GIRL... RIGHT?
AGE 16.
HIGH SCHOOL STUDENT.

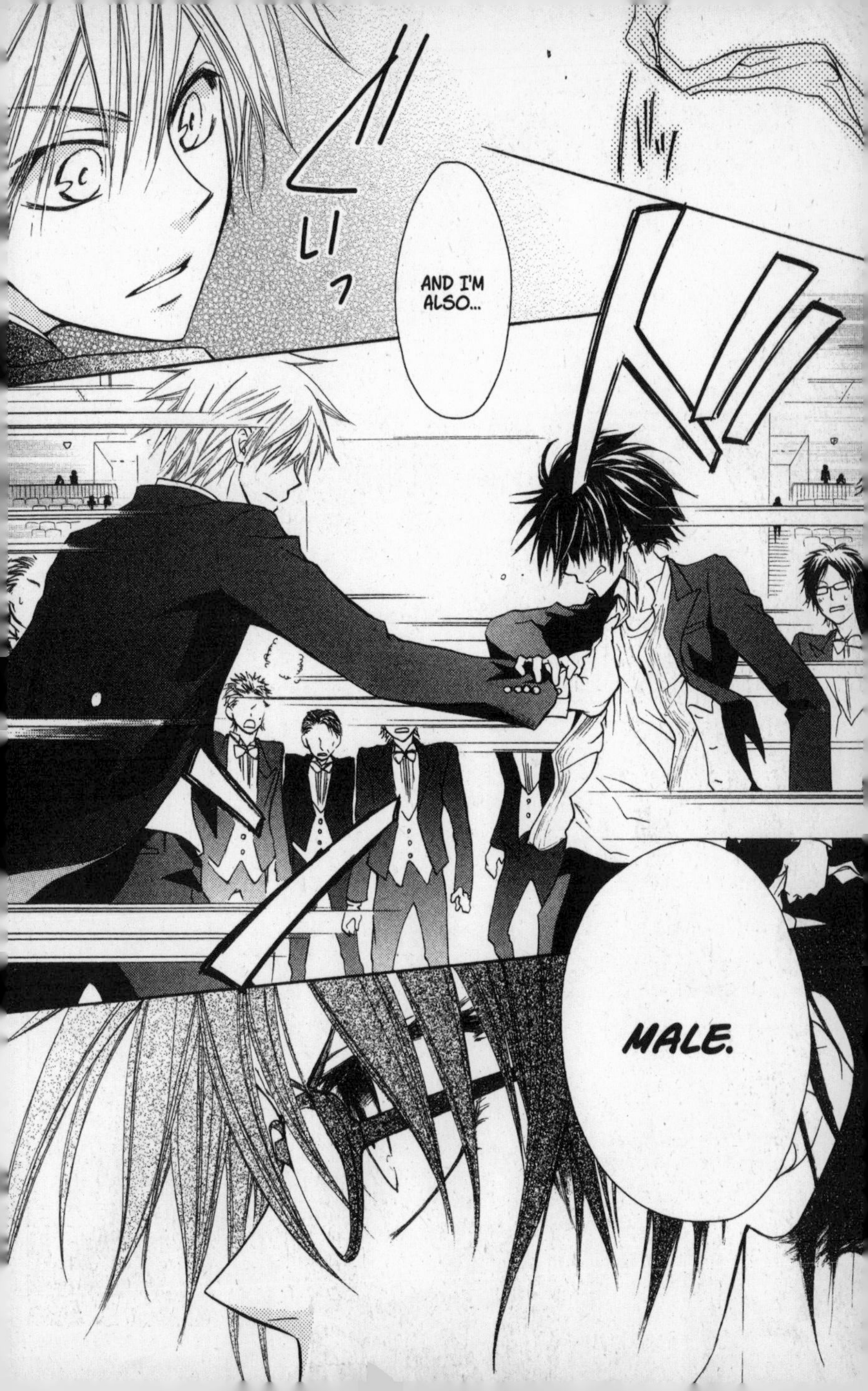
AND I'M ALSO...
MALE.

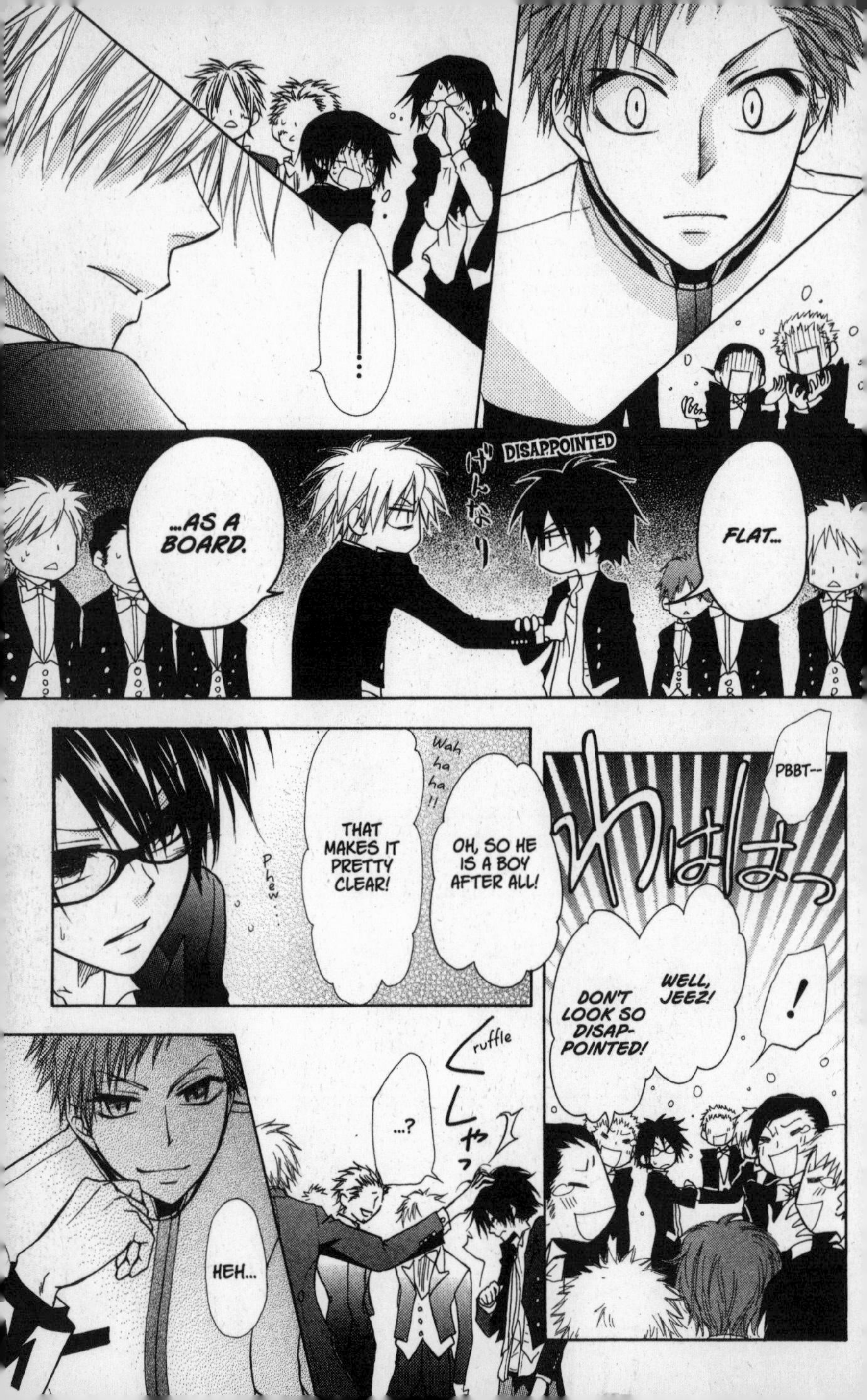
—!...
FLAT...
げんなり
DISAPPOINTED
...AS A BOARD.
PBBT--
わははっ
WELL, JEEZ!
DON'T LOOK SO DISAP-POINTED!
!
OH, SO HE IS A BOY AFTER ALL!
Wah ha ha!!
THAT MAKES IT PRETTY CLEAR!
Phew...
くしゃっ
ruffle
...?
HEH...

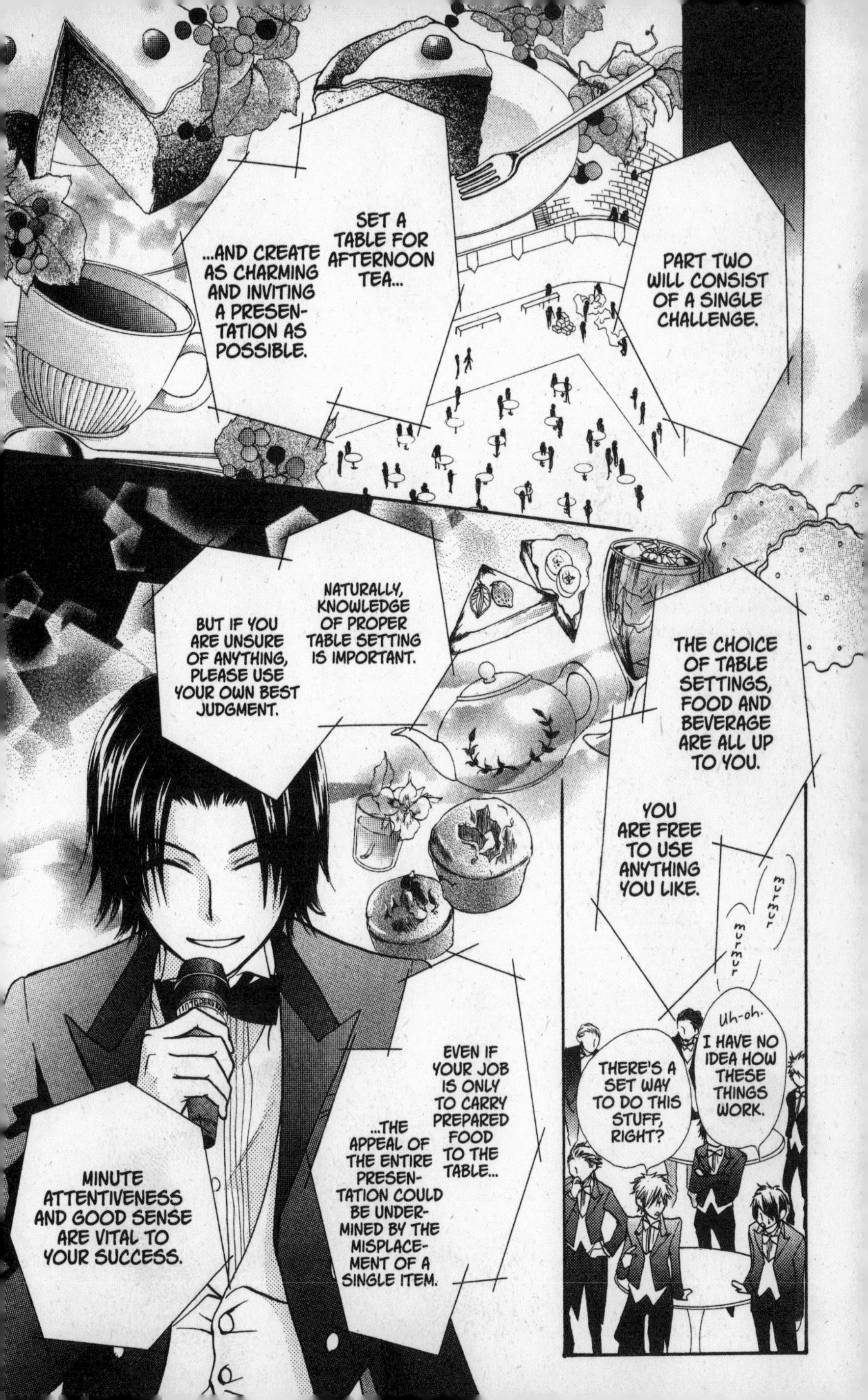
PART TWO WILL CONSIST OF A SINGLE CHALLENGE.
SET A TABLE FOR AFTERNOON TEA...
...AND CREATE AS CHARMING AND INVITING A PRESEN-TATION AS POSSIBLE.
THE CHOICE OF TABLE SETTINGS, FOOD AND BEVERAGE ARE ALL UP TO YOU.
YOU ARE FREE TO USE ANYTHING YOU LIKE.
NATURALLY, KNOWLEDGE OF PROPER TABLE SETTING IS IMPORTANT.
BUT IF YOU ARE UNSURE OF ANYTHING, PLEASE USE YOUR OWN BEST JUDGMENT.
murmur
murmur
Uh-oh.
I HAVE NO IDEA HOW THESE THINGS WORK.
THERE'S A SET WAY TO DO THIS STUFF, RIGHT?
EVEN IF YOUR JOB IS ONLY TO CARRY PREPARED FOOD TO THE TABLE...
...THE APPEAL OF THE ENTIRE PRESEN-TATION COULD BE UNDER-MINED BY THE MISPLACE-MENT OF A SINGLE ITEM.
MINUTE ATTENTIVENESS AND GOOD SENSE ARE VITAL TO YOUR SUCCESS.

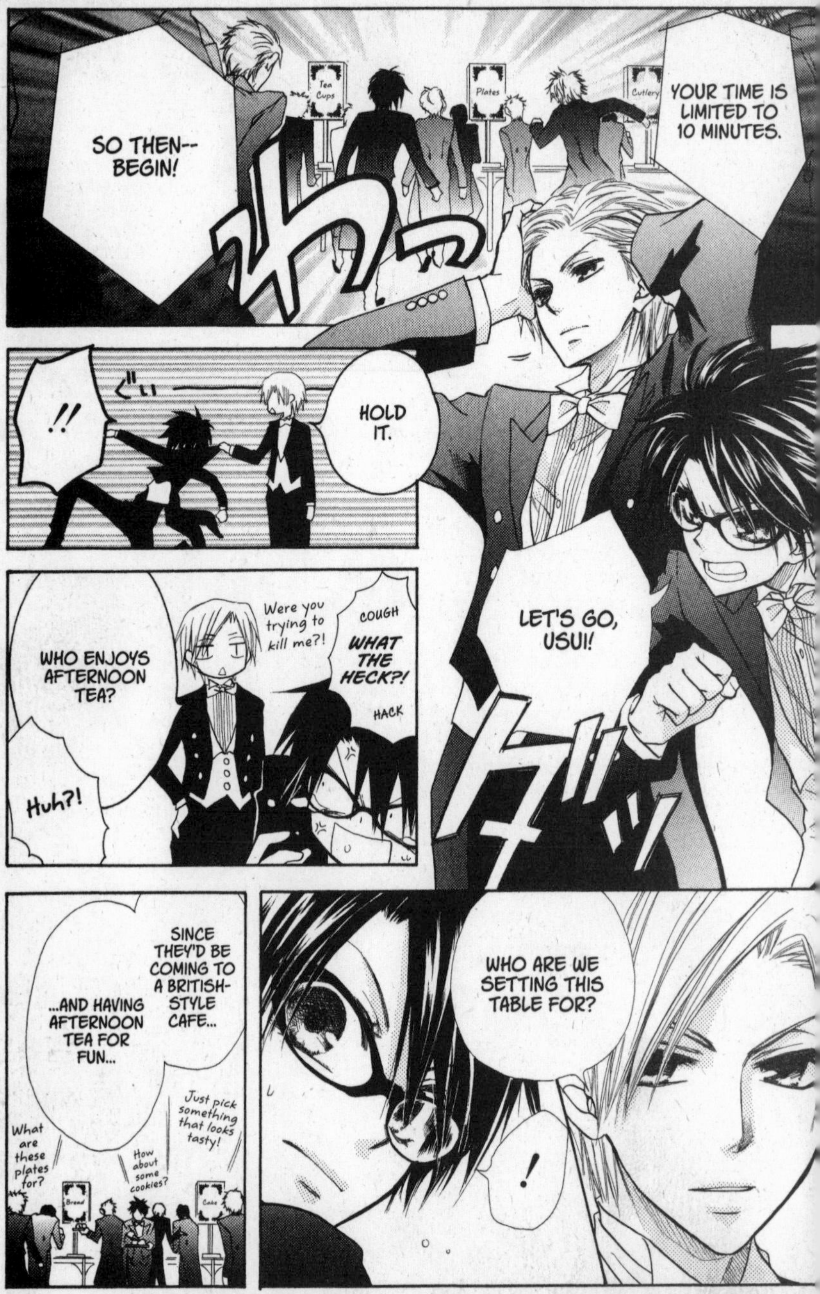
Cutlery
Plates
Tea Cups
YOUR TIME IS LIMITED TO 10 MINUTES.
SO THEN-- BEGIN!
LET'S GO, USUI!
HOLD IT.
!!
COUGH
WHAT THE HECK?!
HACK
Were you trying to kill me?!
WHO ENJOYS AFTERNOON TEA?
Huh?!
WHO ARE WE SETTING THIS TABLE FOR?
!
SINCE THEY'D BE COMING TO A BRITISH-STYLE CAFE...
...AND HAVING AFTERNOON TEA FOR FUN...
Just pick something that looks tasty!
Cake
How about some cookies?
Bread
What are these plates for?

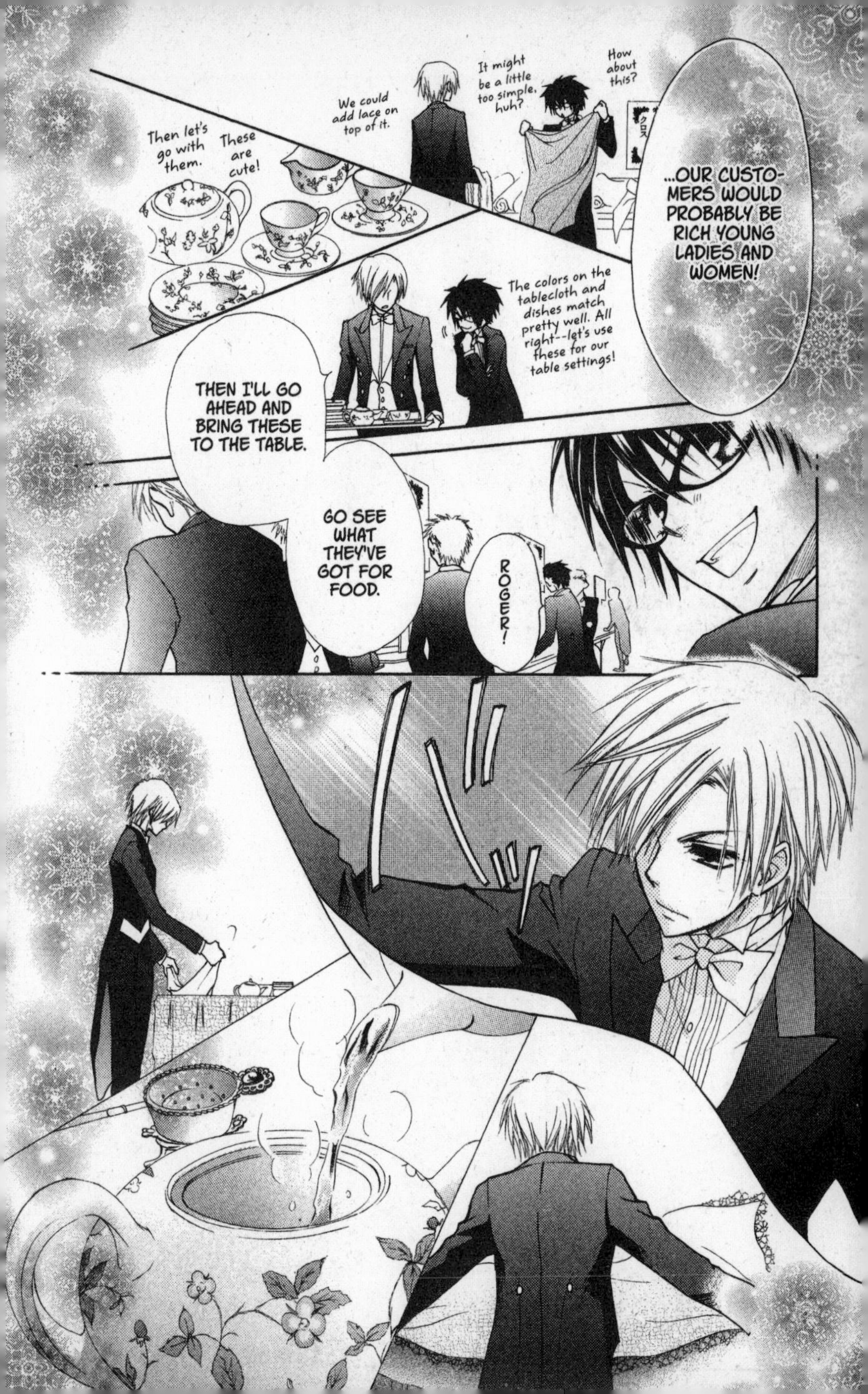
...OUR CUSTOMERS WOULD PROBABLY BE RICH YOUNG LADIES AND WOMEN!
How about this?
It might be a little too simple, huh?
We could add lace on top of it.
These are cute!
Then let's go with them.
The colors on the tablecloth and dishes match pretty well. All right--let's use these for our table settings!
THEN I'LL GO AHEAD AND BRING THESE TO THE TABLE.
GO SEE WHAT THEY'VE GOT FOR FOOD.
ROGER!

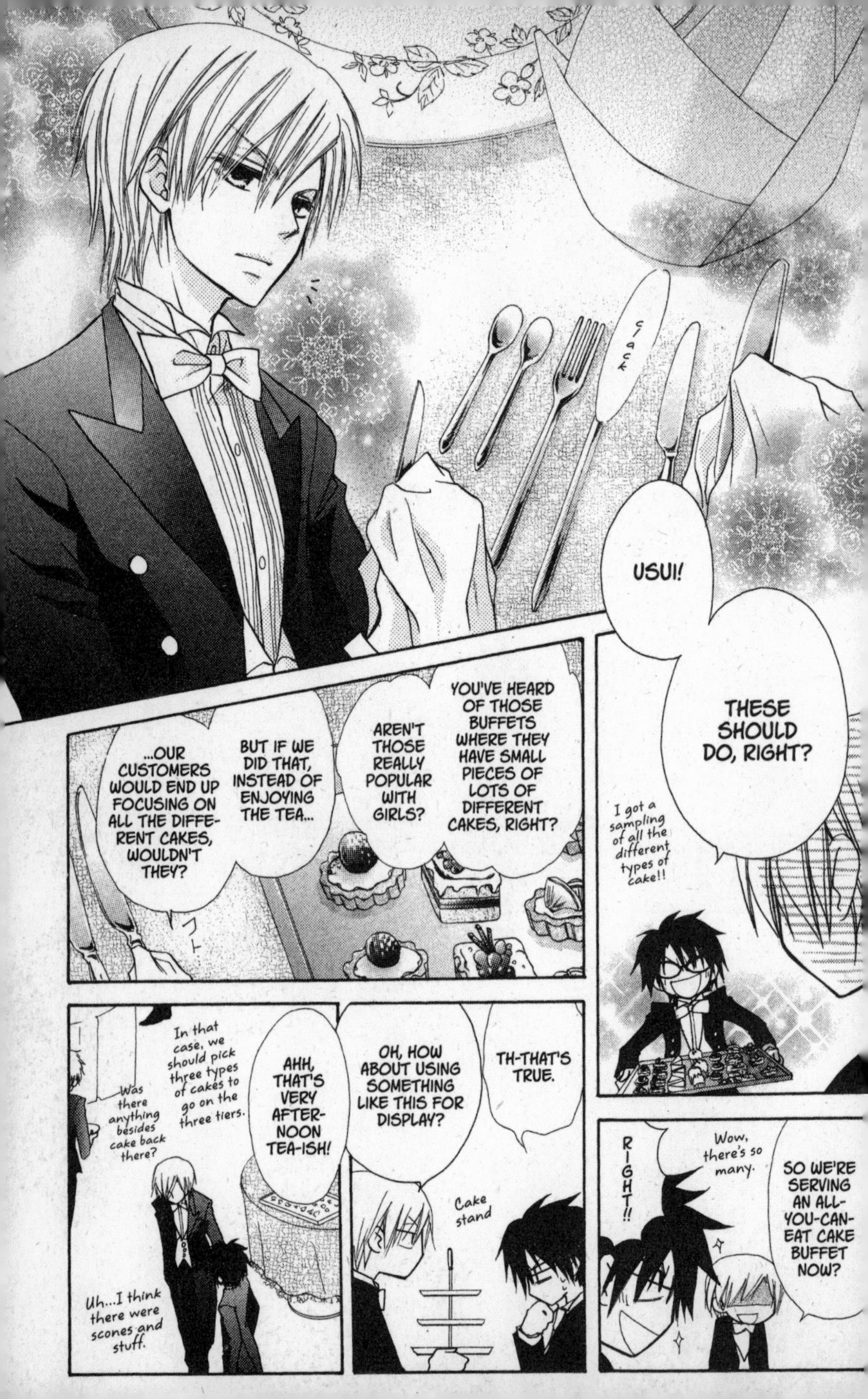
clack
USUI!
THESE SHOULD DO, RIGHT?
I got a sampling of all the different types of cake!!
SO WE'RE SERVING AN ALL-YOU-CAN-EAT CAKE BUFFET NOW?
RIGHT!!
Wow, there's so many.
YOU'VE HEARD OF THOSE BUFFETS WHERE THEY HAVE SMALL PIECES OF LOTS OF DIFFERENT CAKES, RIGHT?
AREN'T THOSE REALLY POPULAR WITH GIRLS?
BUT IF WE DID THAT, INSTEAD OF ENJOYING THE TEA...
...OUR CUSTOMERS WOULD END UP FOCUSING ON ALL THE DIFFERENT CAKES, WOULDN'T THEY?
TH-THAT'S TRUE.
OH, HOW ABOUT USING SOMETHING LIKE THIS FOR DISPLAY?
Cake stand
AHH, THAT'S VERY AFTERNOON TEA-ISH!
In that case, we should pick three types of cakes to go on the three tiers.
Was there anything besides cake back there?
Uh...I think there were scones and stuff.

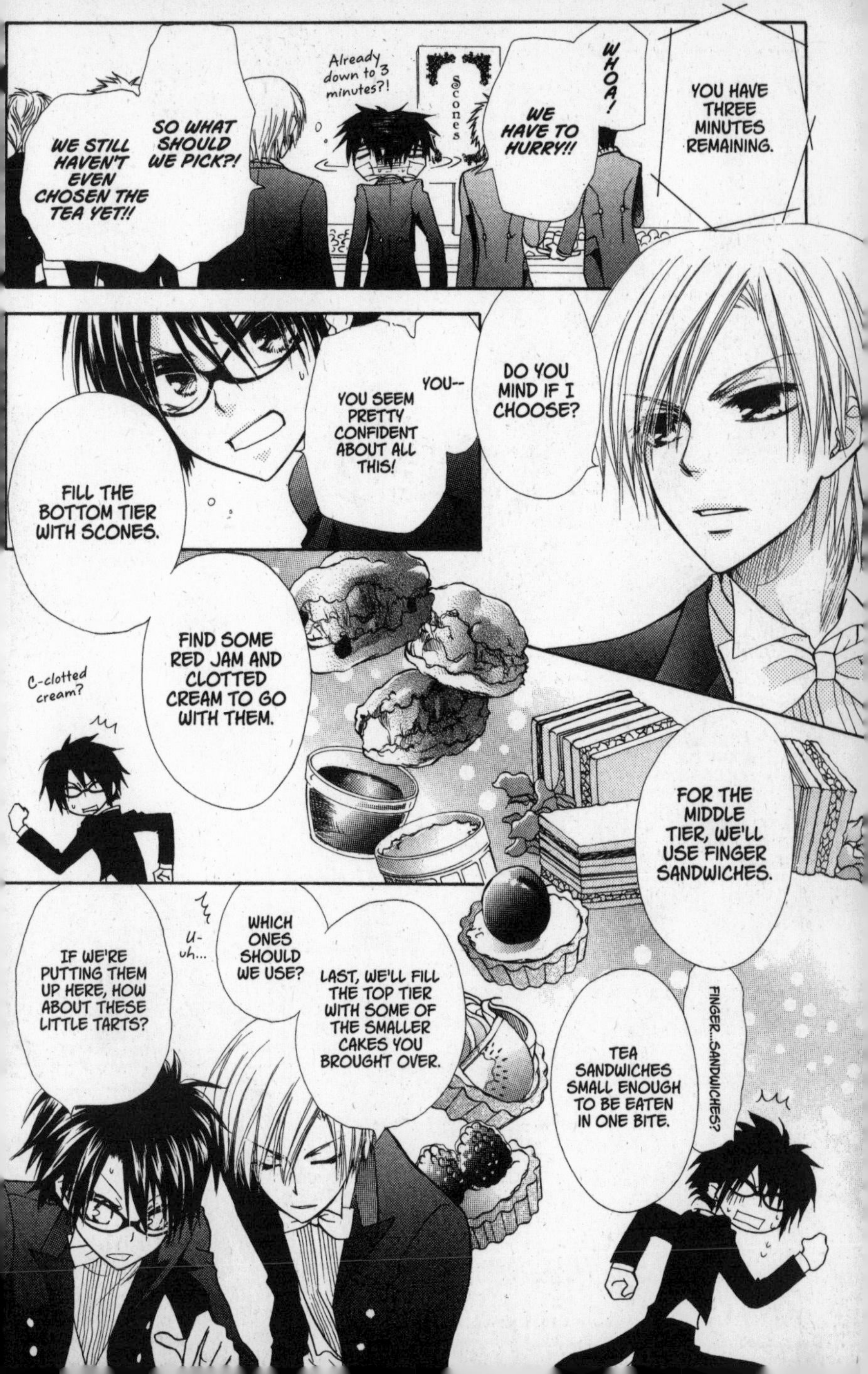
YOU HAVE THREE MINUTES REMAINING.
WHOA!
WE HAVE TO HURRY!!
Scones
Already down to 3 minutes?!
SO WHAT SHOULD WE PICK?!
WE STILL HAVEN'T EVEN CHOSEN THE TEA YET!!
DO YOU MIND IF I CHOOSE?
YOU--
YOU SEEM PRETTY CONFIDENT ABOUT ALL THIS!
FILL THE BOTTOM TIER WITH SCONES.
FIND SOME RED JAM AND CLOTTED CREAM TO GO WITH THEM.
C-clotted cream?
FOR THE MIDDLE TIER, WE'LL USE FINGER SANDWICHES.
FINGER...SANDWICHES?
TEA SANDWICHES SMALL ENOUGH TO BE EATEN IN ONE BITE.
LAST, WE'LL FILL THE TOP TIER WITH SOME OF THE SMALLER CAKES YOU BROUGHT OVER.
WHICH ONES SHOULD WE USE?
U-uh...
IF WE'RE PUTTING THEM UP HERE, HOW ABOUT THESE LITTLE TARTS?

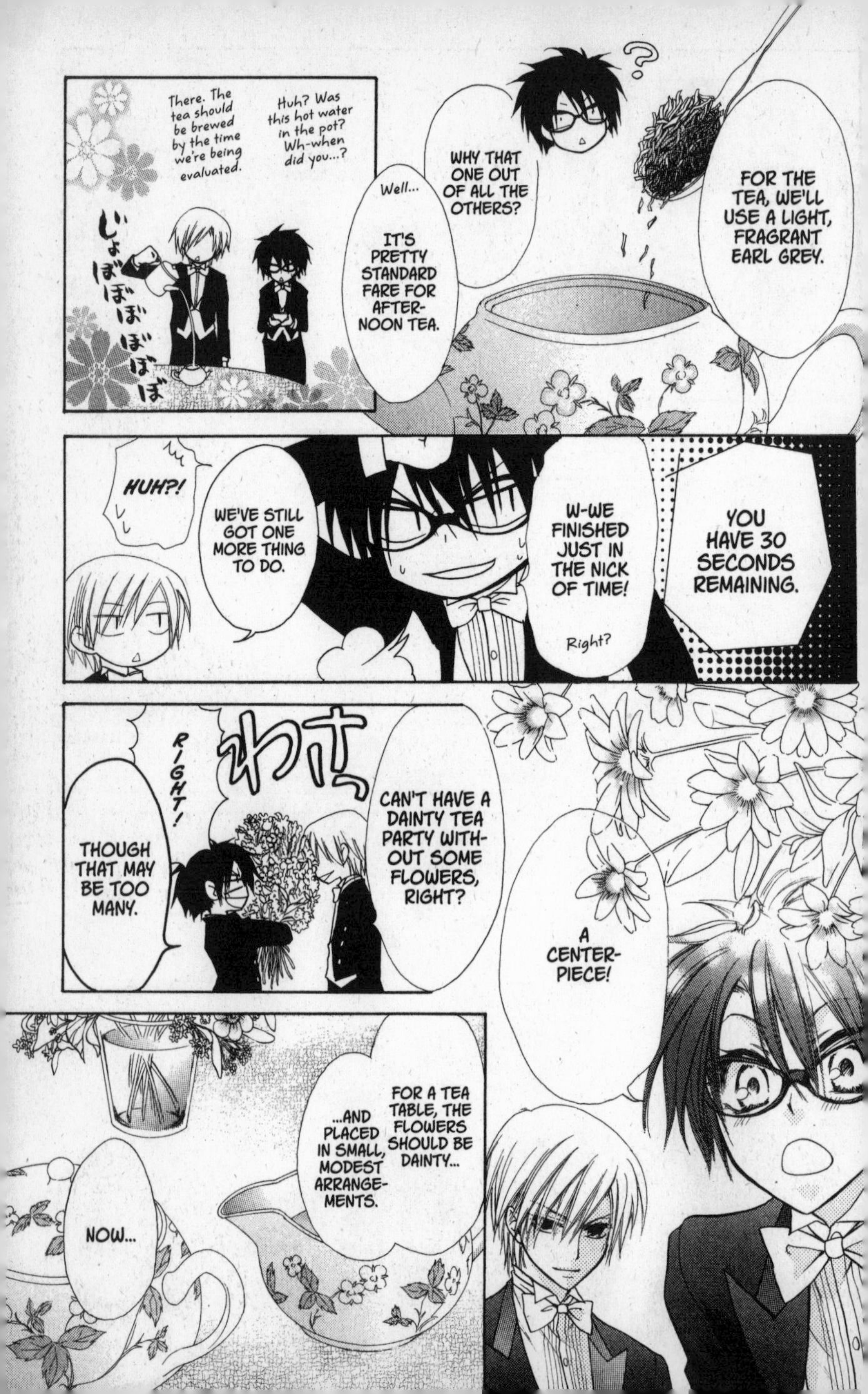
FOR THE TEA, WE'LL USE A LIGHT, FRAGRANT EARL GREY.
WHY THAT ONE OUT OF ALL THE OTHERS?
Well...
IT'S PRETTY STANDARD FARE FOR AFTER-NOON TEA.
Huh? Was this hot water in the pot? Wh-when did you...?
There. The tea should be brewed by the time we're being evaluated.
じょぼぼぼぼぼ
YOU HAVE 30 SECONDS REMAINING.
W-WE FINISHED JUST IN THE NICK OF TIME!
Right?
WE'VE STILL GOT ONE MORE THING TO DO.
HUH?!
A CENTER-PIECE!
CAN'T HAVE A DAINTY TEA PARTY WITH-OUT SOME FLOWERS, RIGHT?
わさっ
RIGHT!
THOUGH THAT MAY BE TOO MANY.
FOR A TEA TABLE, THE FLOWERS SHOULD BE DAINTY...
...AND PLACED IN SMALL, MODEST ARRANGE-MENTS.
NOW...

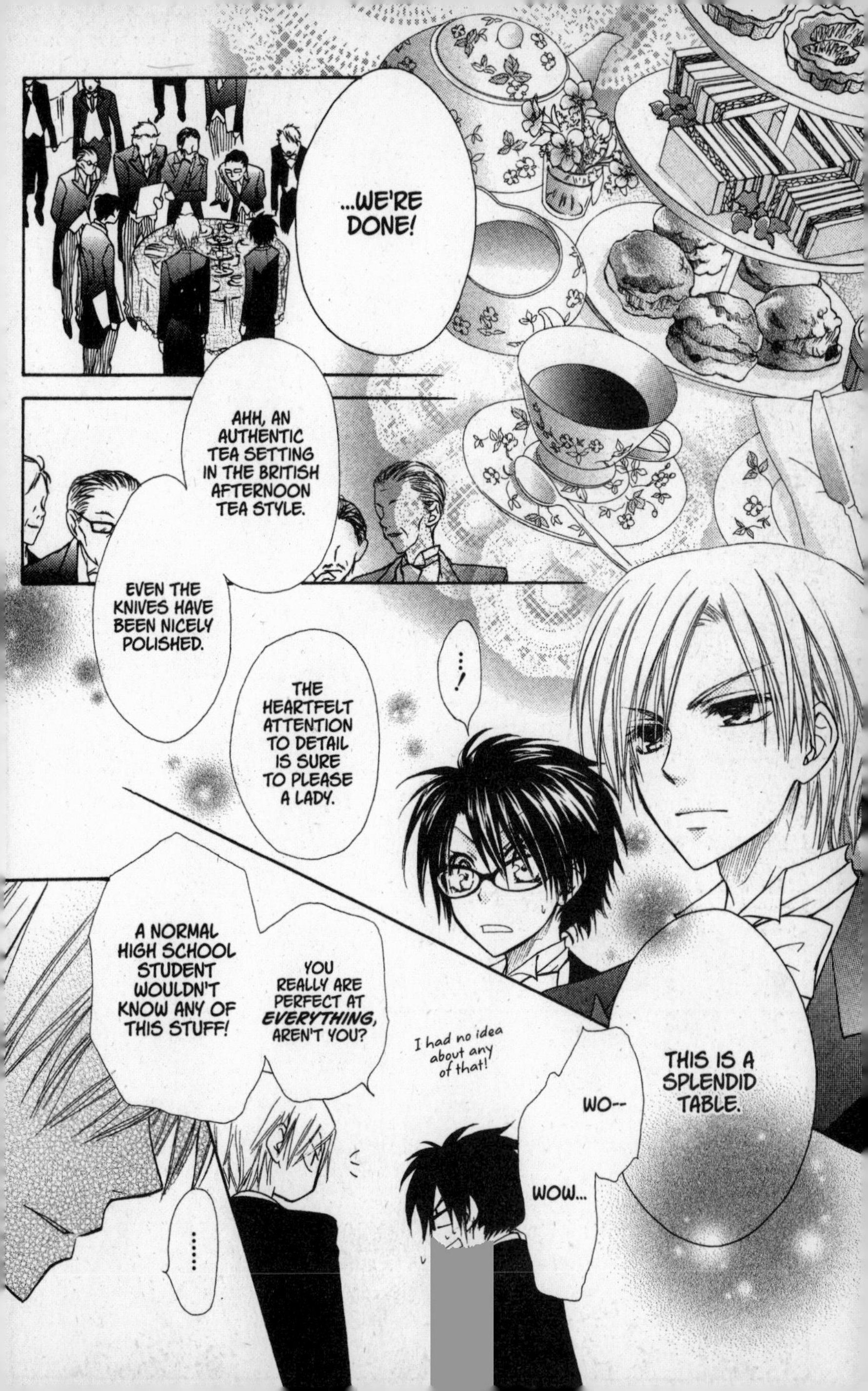
...WE'RE DONE!
AHH, AN AUTHENTIC TEA SETTING IN THE BRITISH AFTERNOON TEA STYLE.
EVEN THE KNIVES HAVE BEEN NICELY POLISHED.
THE HEARTFELT ATTENTION TO DETAIL IS SURE TO PLEASE A LADY.
...!
THIS IS A SPLENDID TABLE.
WO--
WOW...
I had no idea about any of that!
YOU REALLY ARE PERFECT AT *EVERYTHING*, AREN'T YOU?
A NORMAL HIGH SCHOOL STUDENT WOULDN'T KNOW ANY OF THIS STUFF!
......

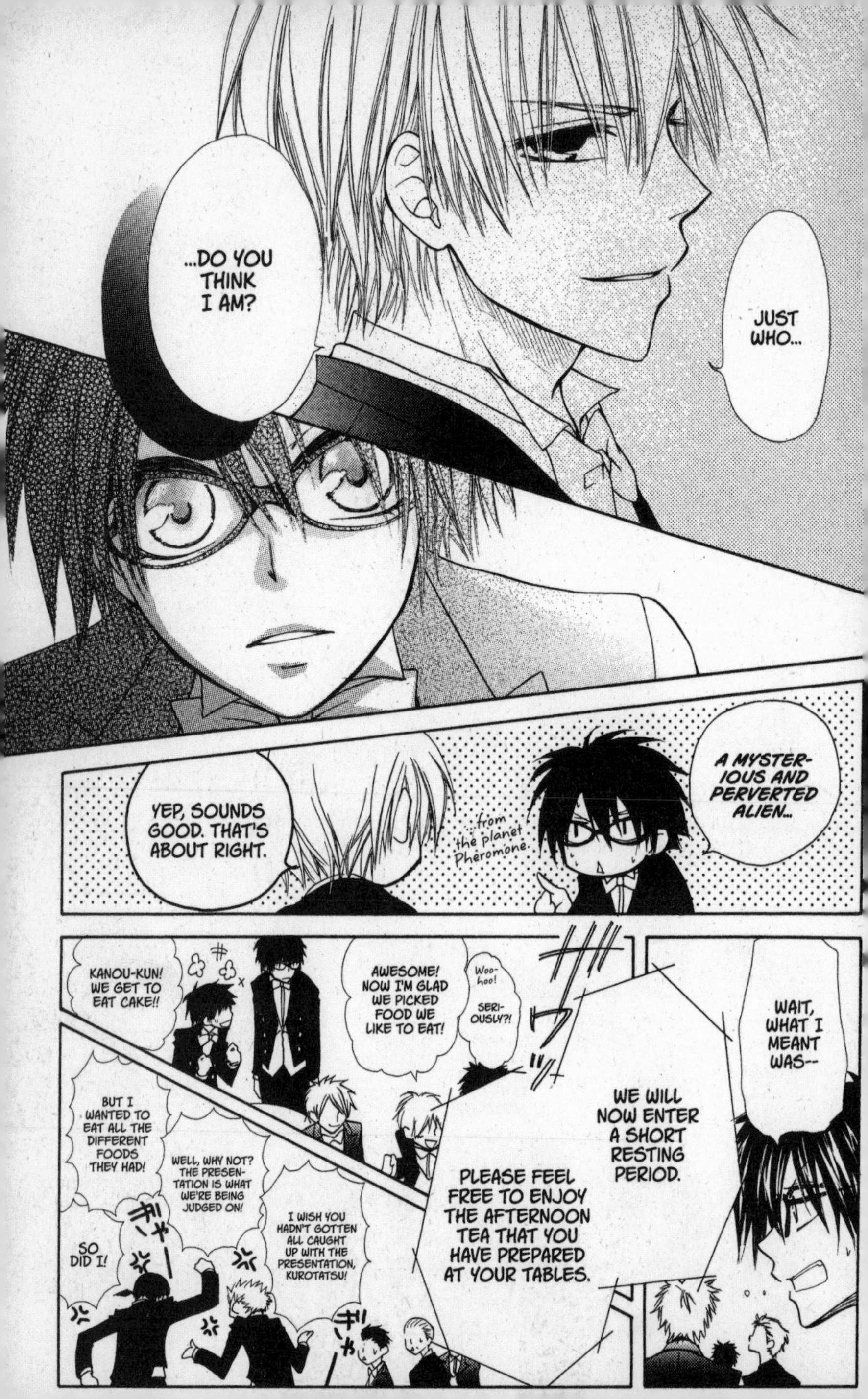
JUST WHO...
...DO YOU THINK I AM?
A MYSTERIOUS AND PERVERTED ALIEN...
...from the planet Pheromone.
YEP, SOUNDS GOOD. THAT'S ABOUT RIGHT.
WAIT, WHAT I MEANT WAS--
WE WILL NOW ENTER A SHORT RESTING PERIOD.
PLEASE FEEL FREE TO ENJOY THE AFTERNOON TEA THAT YOU HAVE PREPARED AT YOUR TABLES.
Woo-hoo!
SERIOUSLY?!
AWESOME! NOW I'M GLAD WE PICKED FOOD WE LIKE TO EAT!
KANOU-KUN! WE GET TO EAT CAKE!!
I WISH YOU HADN'T GOTTEN ALL CAUGHT UP WITH THE PRESENTATION, KUROTATSU!
WELL, WHY NOT? THE PRESENTATION IS WHAT WE'RE BEING JUDGED ON!
BUT I WANTED TO EAT ALL THE DIFFERENT FOODS THEY HAD!
SO DID I!

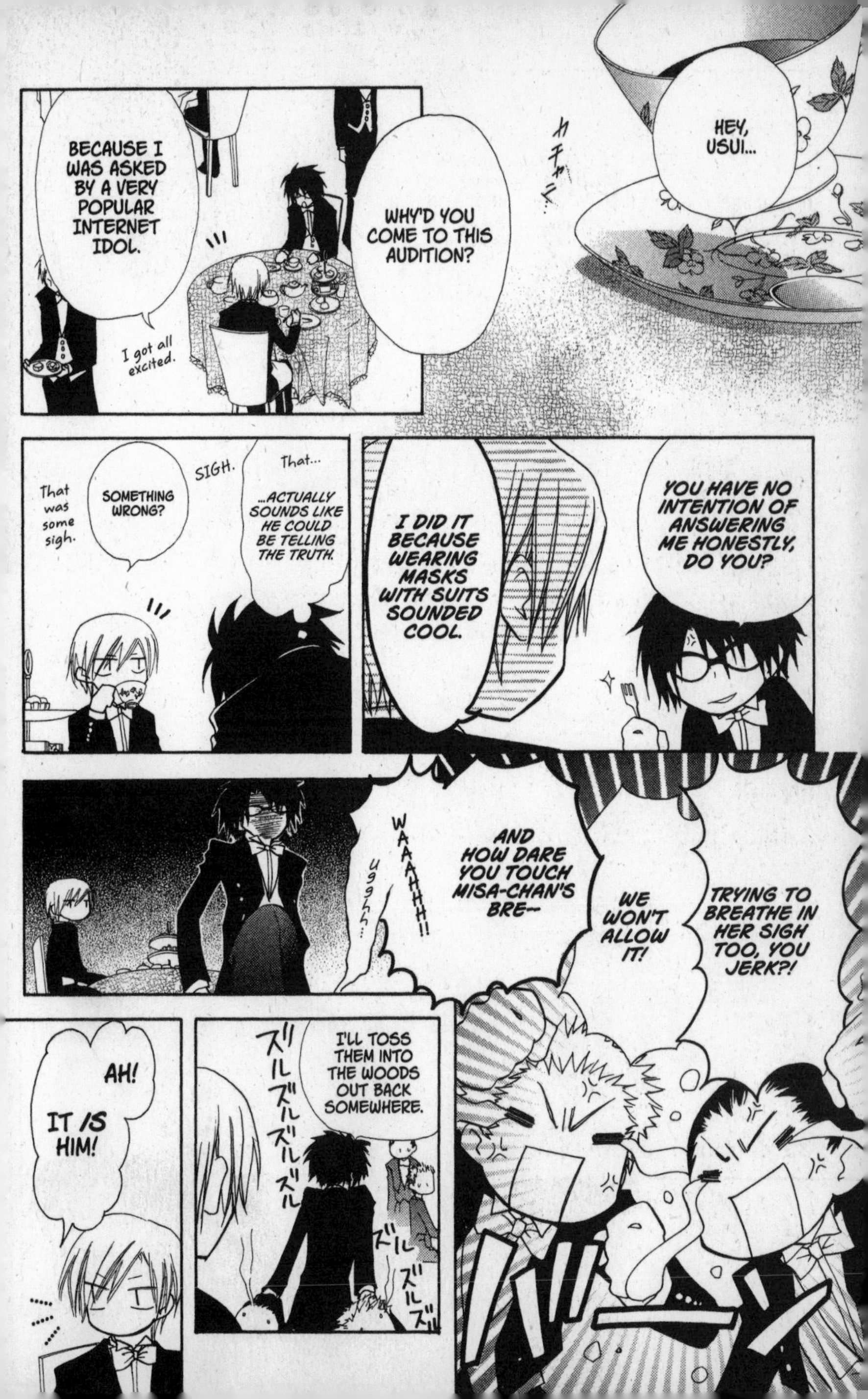
HEY, USUI...
カチャン...
WHY'D YOU COME TO THIS AUDITION?
BECAUSE I WAS ASKED BY A VERY POPULAR INTERNET IDOL.
I got all excited.
YOU HAVE NO INTENTION OF ANSWERING ME HONESTLY, DO YOU?
I DID IT BECAUSE WEARING MASKS WITH SUITS SOUNDED COOL.
That...
...ACTUALLY SOUNDS LIKE HE COULD BE TELLING THE TRUTH.
SIGH.
SOMETHING WRONG?
That was some sigh.
TRYING TO BREATHE IN HER SIGH TOO, YOU JERK?!
WE WON'T ALLOW IT!
AND HOW DARE YOU TOUCH MISA-CHAN'S BRE--
WAAAHHH!!
Ugghh...
I'LL TOSS THEM INTO THE WOODS OUT BACK SOMEWHERE.
ズルズルズルズル
ズルズルズル
AH!
IT IS HIM!
.....

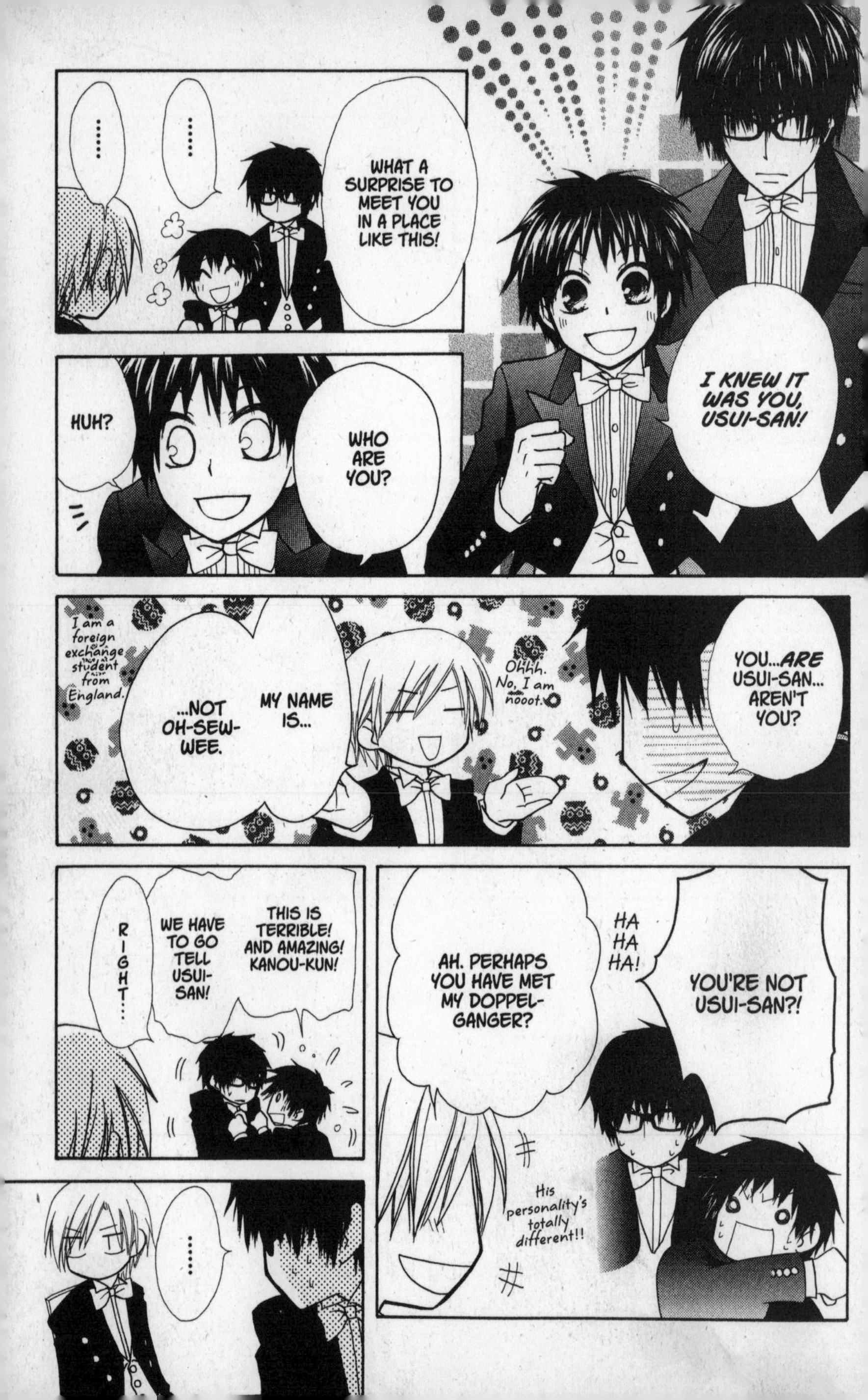
I KNEW IT WAS YOU, USUI-SAN!
WHAT A SURPRISE TO MEET YOU IN A PLACE LIKE THIS!
......
......
WHO ARE YOU?
HUH?
YOU...ARE USUI-SAN... AREN'T YOU?
Ohhh. No, I am nooot.
MY NAME IS...
...NOT OH-SEW-WEE.
I am a foreign exchange student from England.
YOU'RE NOT USUI-SAN?!
HA HA HA!
AH. PERHAPS YOU HAVE MET MY DOPPEL-GANGER?
His personality's totally different!!
THIS IS TERRIBLE! AND AMAZING! KANOU-KUN!
WE HAVE TO GO TELL USUI-SAN!
RIGHT...
......

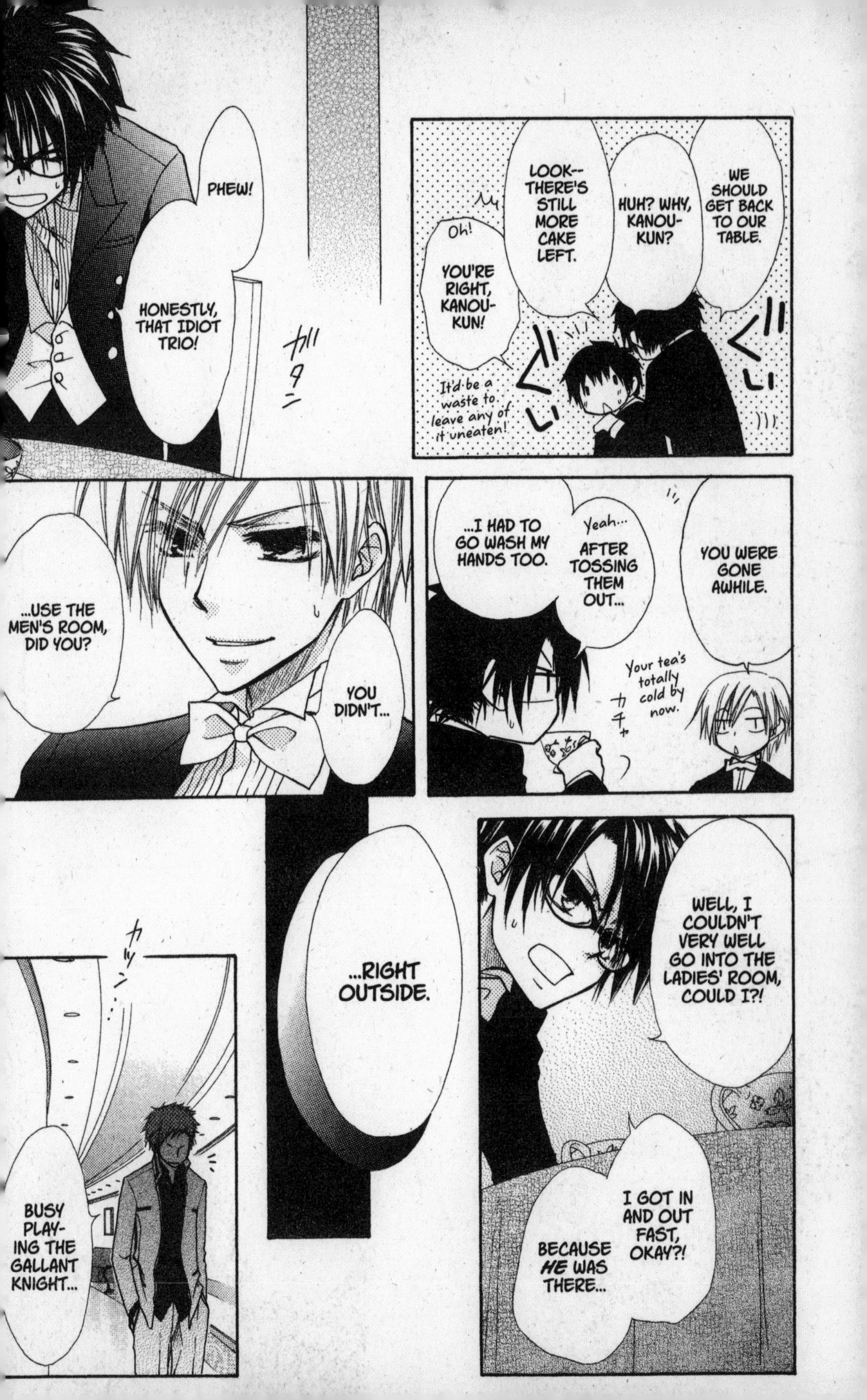
WE SHOULD GET BACK TO OUR TABLE.
HUH? WHY, KANOU-KUN?
LOOK-- THERE'S STILL MORE CAKE LEFT.
Oh! YOU'RE RIGHT, KANOU-KUN!
It'd be a waste to leave any of it uneaten!
PHEW!
HONESTLY, THAT IDIOT TRIO!
YOU WERE GONE AWHILE.
Your tea's totally cold by now.
Yeah... AFTER TOSSING THEM OUT...
...I HAD TO GO WASH MY HANDS TOO.
YOU DIDN'T...
...USE THE MEN'S ROOM, DID YOU?
WELL, I COULDN'T VERY WELL GO INTO THE LADIES' ROOM, COULD I?!
I GOT IN AND OUT FAST, OKAY?!
BECAUSE *HE* WAS THERE...
...RIGHT OUTSIDE.
BUSY PLAYING THE GALLANT KNIGHT...

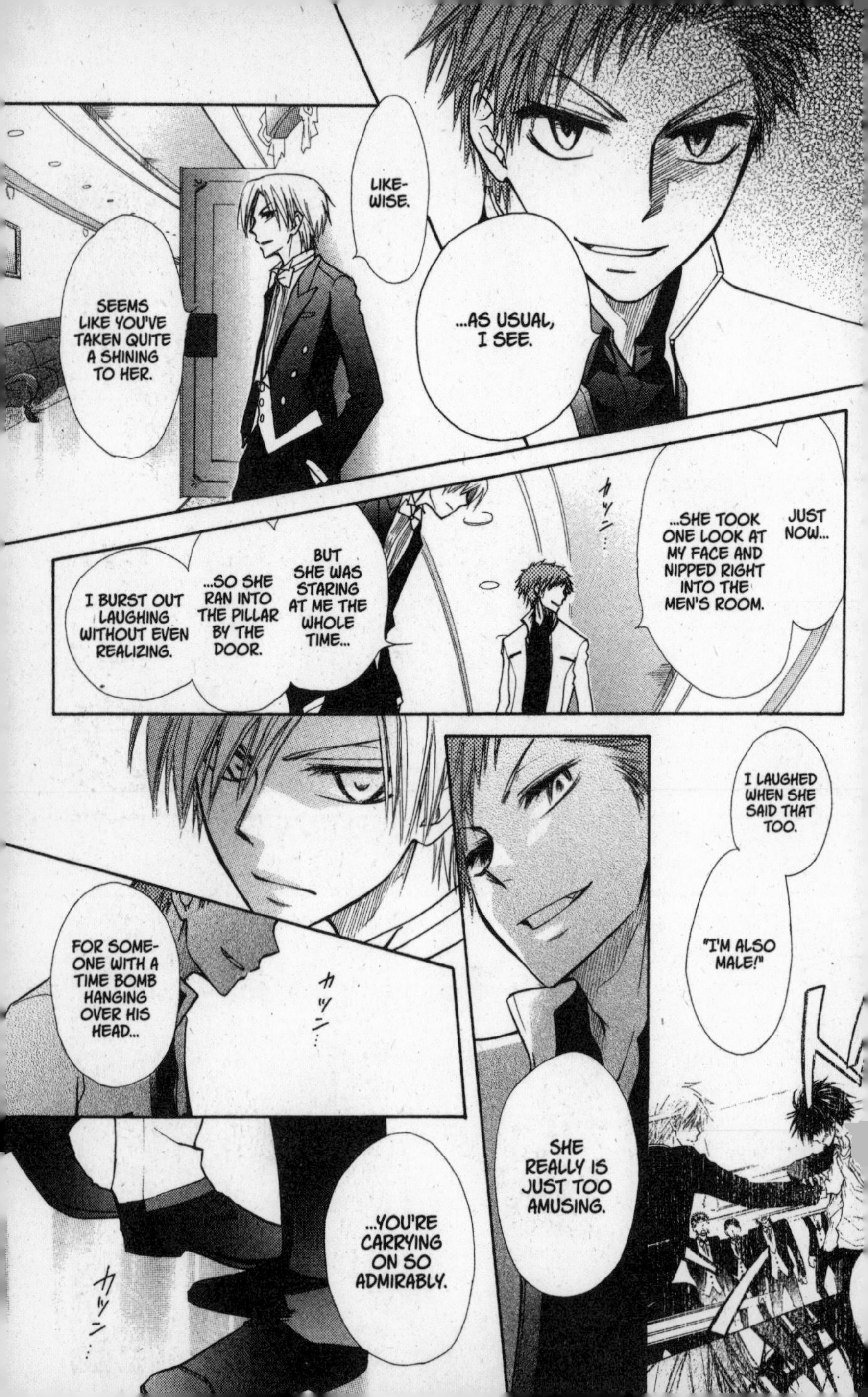
LIKE-WISE.
...AS USUAL, I SEE.
SEEMS LIKE YOU'VE TAKEN QUITE A SHINING TO HER.
JUST NOW...
...SHE TOOK ONE LOOK AT MY FACE AND NIPPED RIGHT INTO THE MEN'S ROOM.
カッン…
BUT SHE WAS STARING AT ME THE WHOLE TIME...
...SO SHE RAN INTO THE PILLAR BY THE DOOR.
I BURST OUT LAUGHING WITHOUT EVEN REALIZING.
I LAUGHED WHEN SHE SAID THAT TOO.
"I'M ALSO MALE!"
SHE REALLY IS JUST TOO AMUSING.
カッン…
FOR SOME-ONE WITH A TIME BOMB HANGING OVER HIS HEAD...
...YOU'RE CARRYING ON SO ADMIRABLY.
カッン…

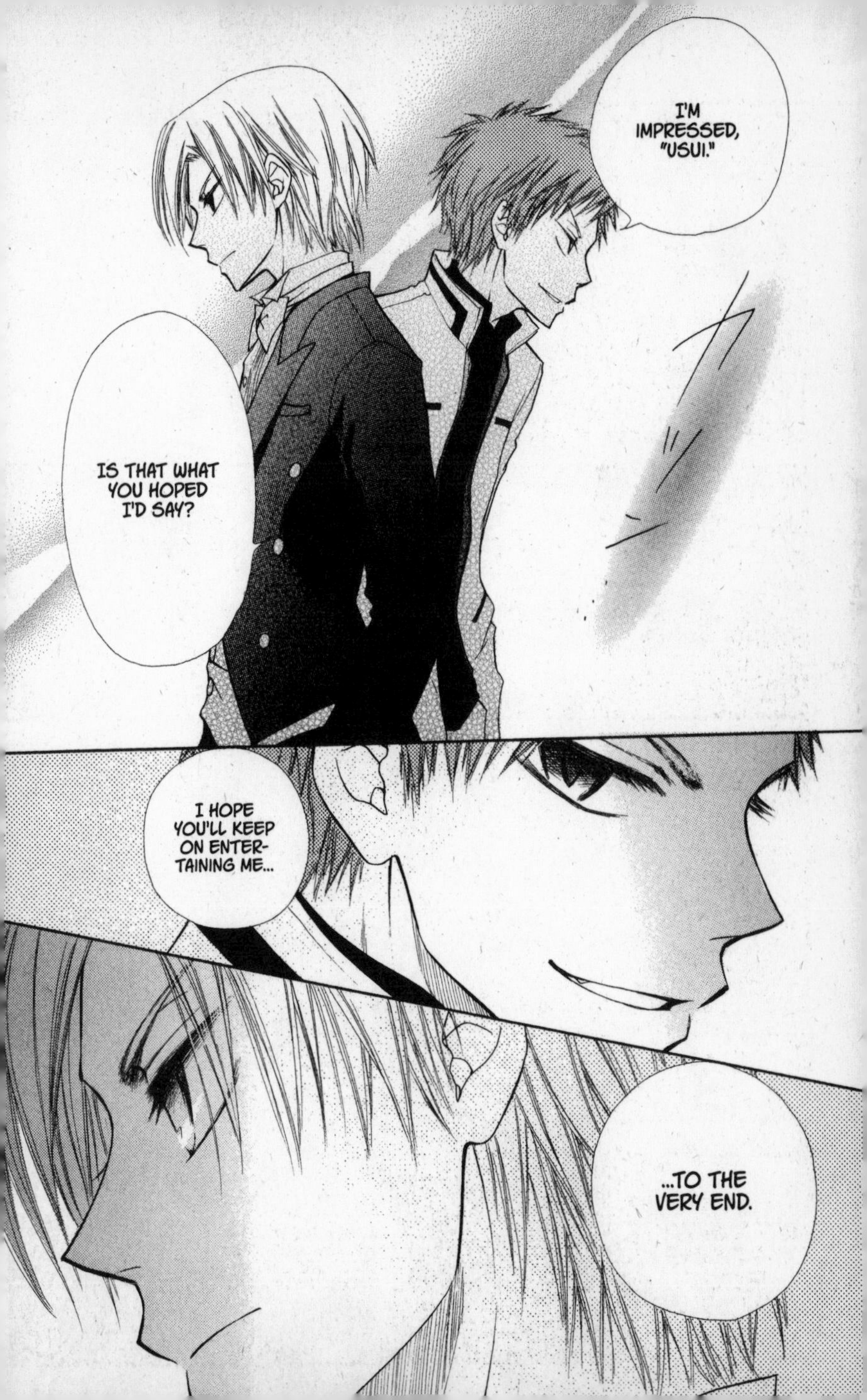
I'M IMPRESSED, "USUI."
IS THAT WHAT YOU HOPED I'D SAY?
I HOPE YOU'LL KEEP ON ENTER-TAINING ME...
...TO THE VERY END.

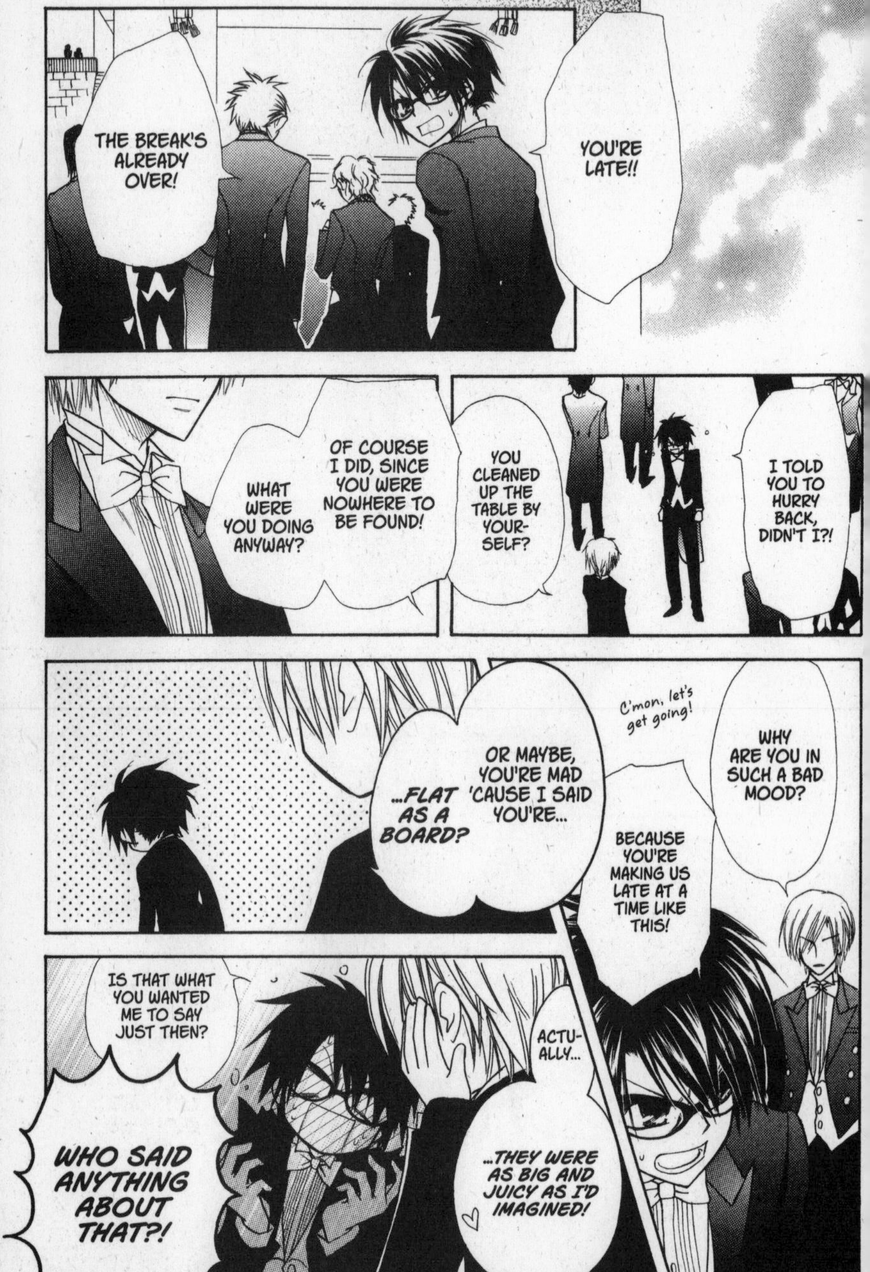
YOU'RE LATE!!
THE BREAK'S ALREADY OVER!
I TOLD YOU TO HURRY BACK, DIDN'T I?!
YOU CLEANED UP THE TABLE BY YOUR-SELF?
OF COURSE I DID, SINCE YOU WERE NOWHERE TO BE FOUND!
WHAT WERE YOU DOING ANYWAY?
WHY ARE YOU IN SUCH A BAD MOOD?
C'mon, let's get going!
BECAUSE YOU'RE MAKING US LATE AT A TIME LIKE THIS!
OR MAYBE, YOU'RE MAD 'CAUSE I SAID YOU'RE...
...FLAT AS A BOARD?
IS THAT WHAT YOU WANTED ME TO SAY JUST THEN?
ACTU-ALLY...
...THEY WERE AS BIG AND JUICY AS I'D IMAGINED!
WHO SAID ANYTHING ABOUT THAT?!

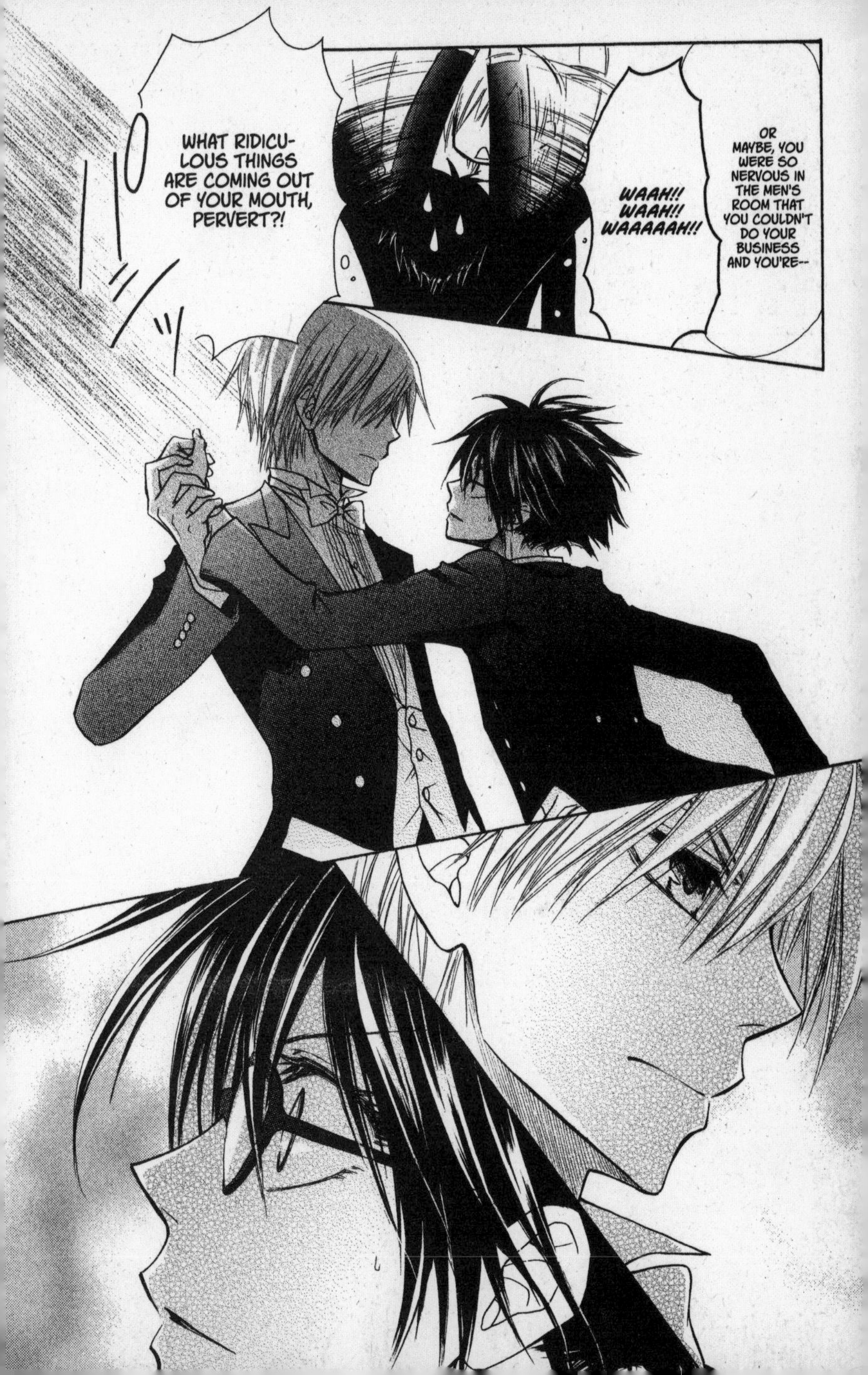
OR MAYBE, YOU WERE SO NERVOUS IN THE MEN'S ROOM THAT YOU COULDN'T DO YOUR BUSINESS AND YOU'RE--
WAAH!! WAAH!! WAAAAAH!!
WHAT RIDICULOUS THINGS ARE COMING OUT OF YOUR MOUTH, PERVERT?!

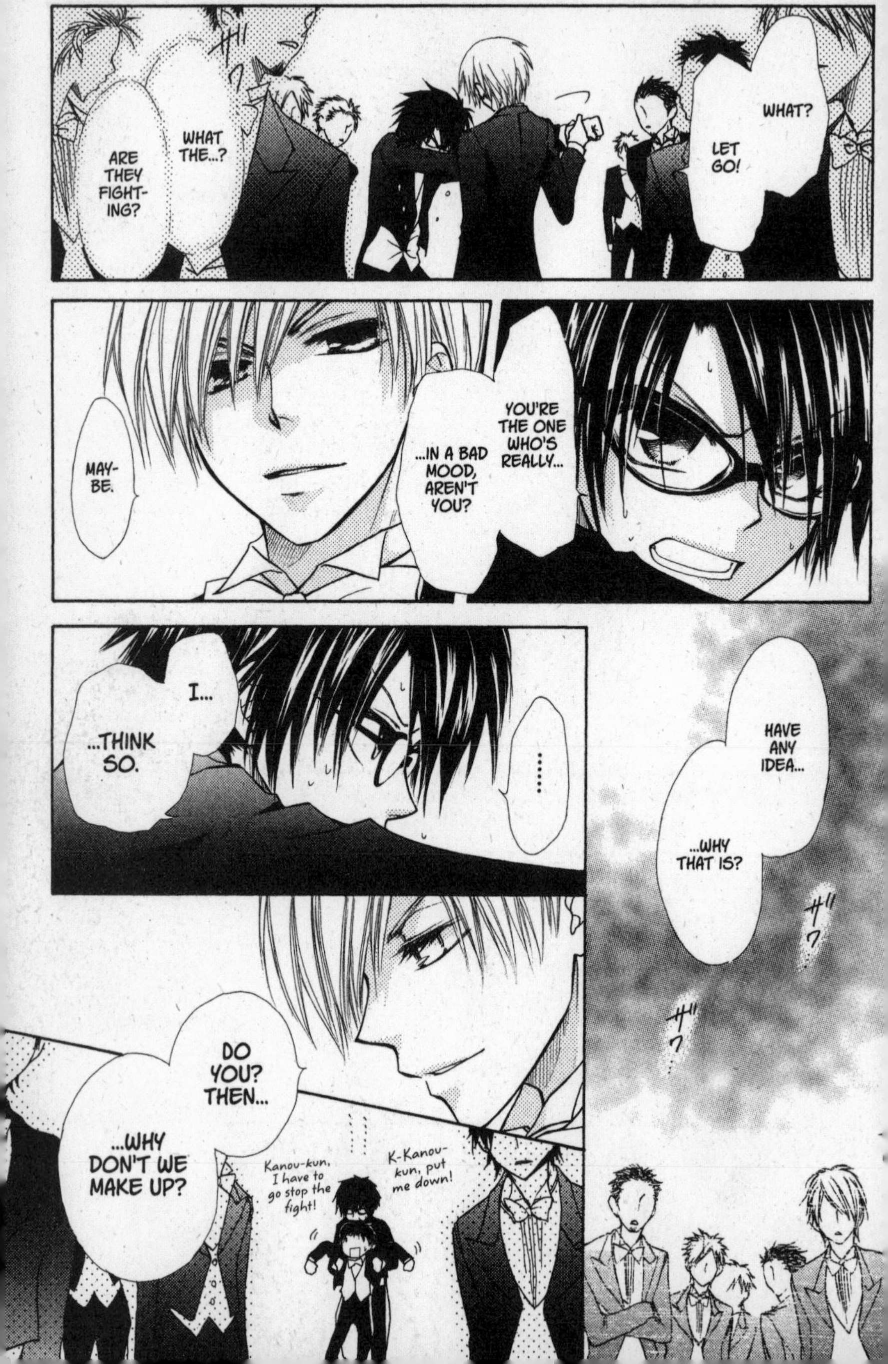
WHAT?
LET GO!
WHAT THE...?
ARE THEY FIGHTING?
YOU'RE THE ONE WHO'S REALLY...
...IN A BAD MOOD, AREN'T YOU?
MAYBE.
HAVE ANY IDEA...
...WHY THAT IS?
......
I...
...THINK SO.
DO YOU? THEN...
...WHY DON'T WE MAKE UP?
K-Kanou-kun, put me down!
Kanou-kun, I have to go stop the fight!

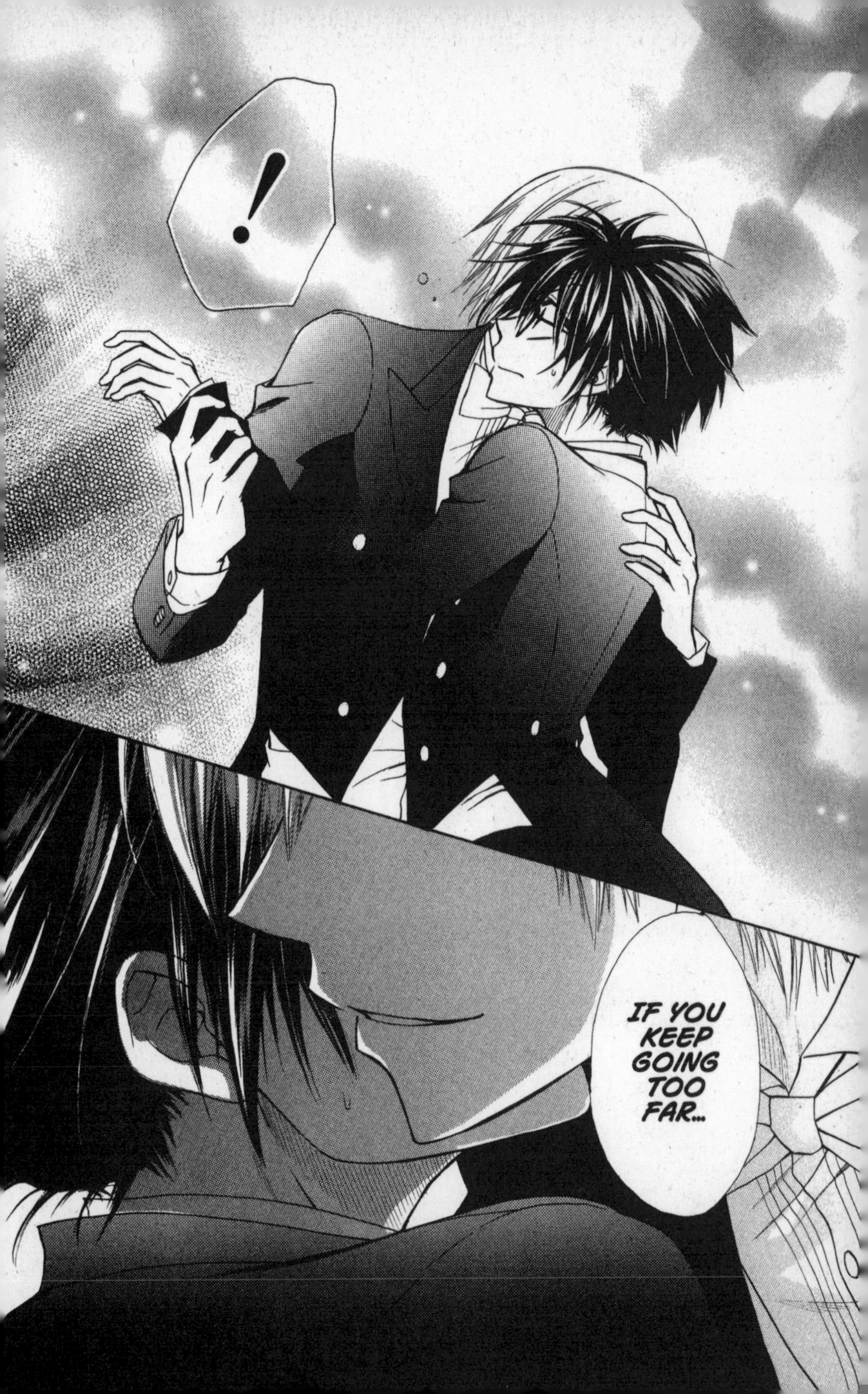
!
IF YOU KEEP GOING TOO FAR...

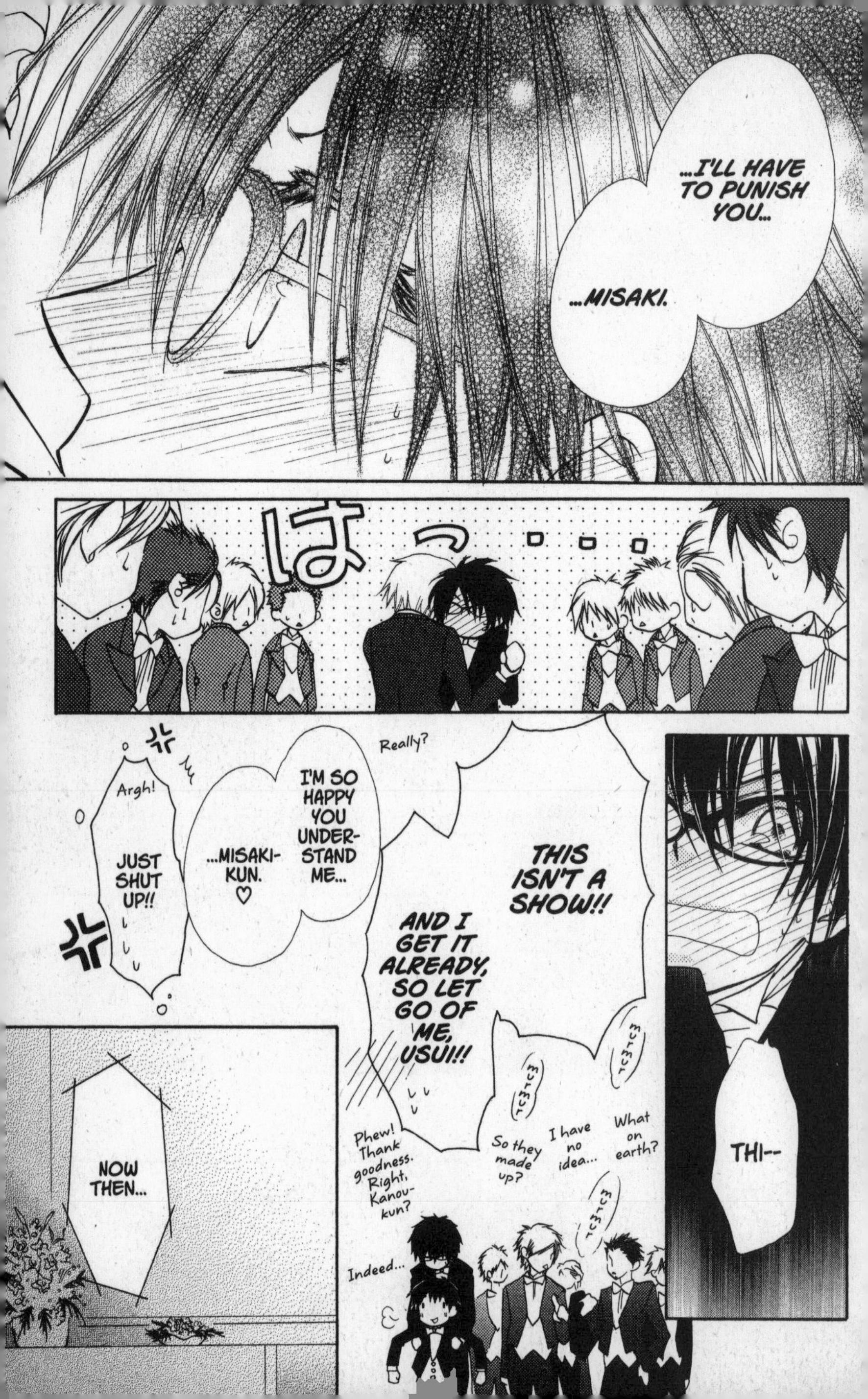
...I'LL HAVE TO PUNISH YOU...
...MISAKI.
はっ
THI--
THIS ISN'T A SHOW!!
AND I GET IT ALREADY, SO LET GO OF ME, USUI!!
Really?
I'M SO HAPPY YOU UNDERSTAND ME...
...MISAKI-KUN. ♡
Argh!
JUST SHUT UP!!
murmur
What on earth?
I have no idea...
So they made up?
murmur
murmur
Phew! Thank goodness. Right, Kanou-kun?
Indeed...
NOW THEN...

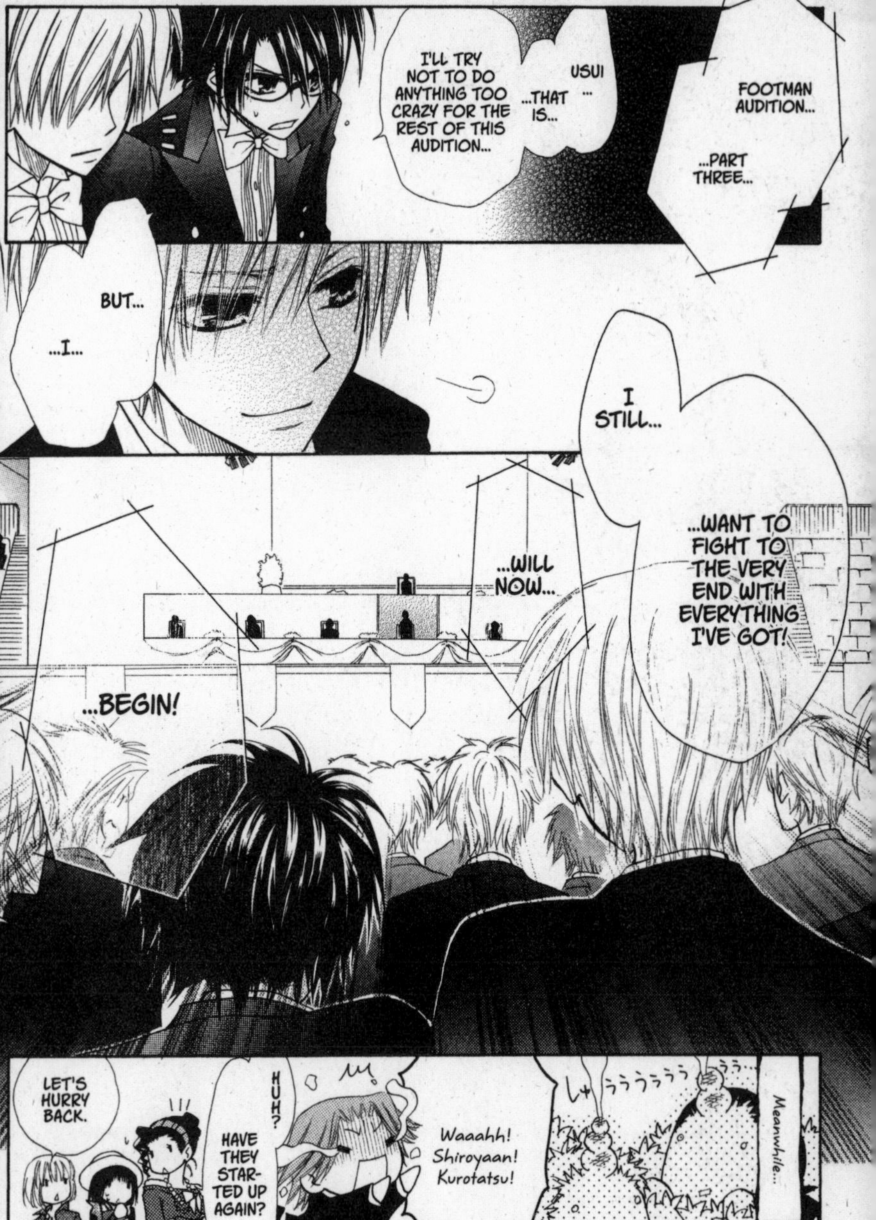
FOOTMAN AUDITION...
...PART THREE...
USUI ...
...THAT IS...
I'LL TRY NOT TO DO ANYTHING TOO CRAZY FOR THE REST OF THIS AUDITION...
BUT...
...I...
I STILL...
...WANT TO FIGHT TO THE VERY END WITH EVERYTHING I'VE GOT!
...WILL NOW...
...BEGIN!
Meanwhile...
しゅううううううう
うう...
Waaahh! Shiroyaan! Kurotatsu!
HUH? HAVE THEY STARTED UP AGAIN?
LET'S HURRY BACK.

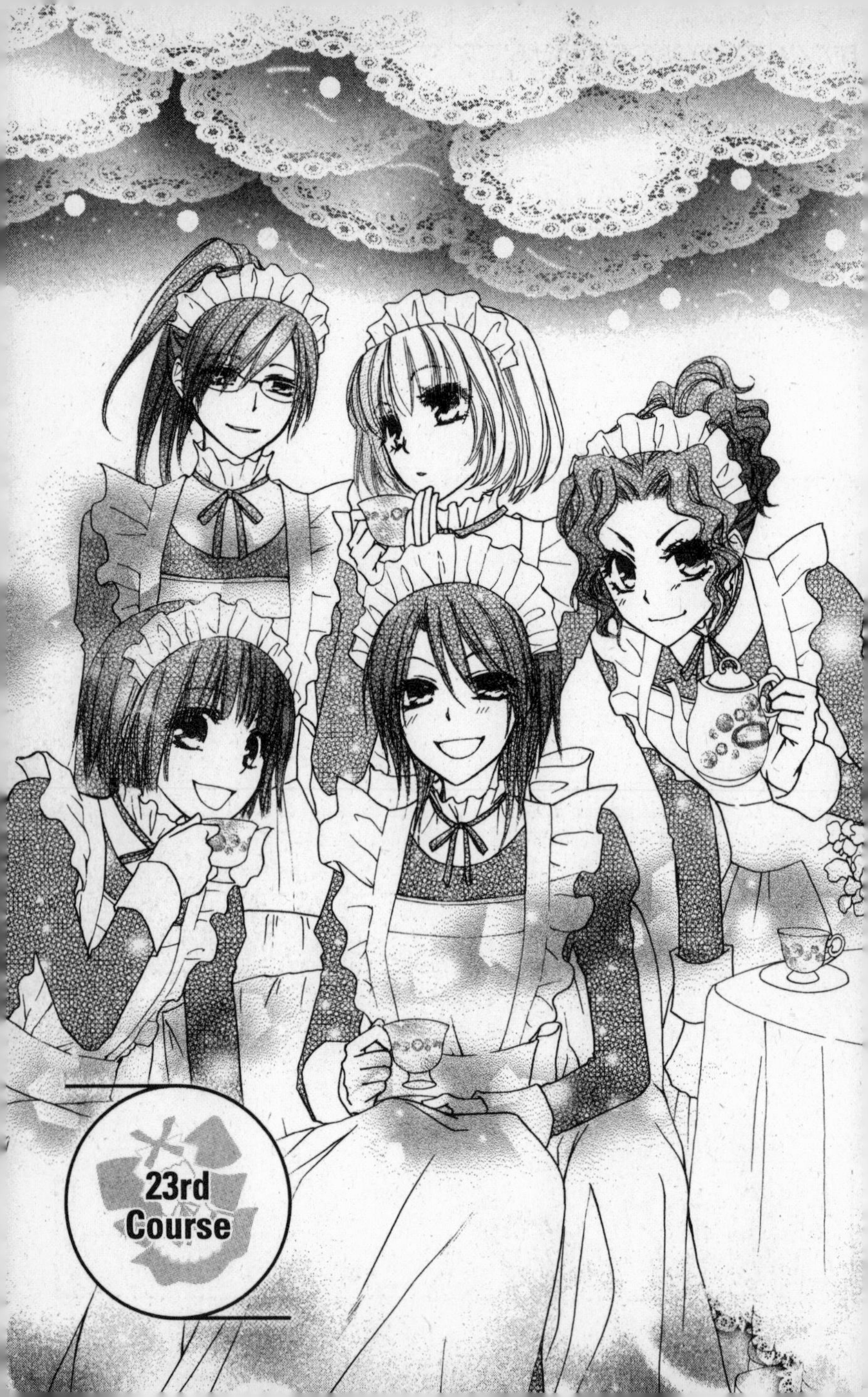
23rd Course

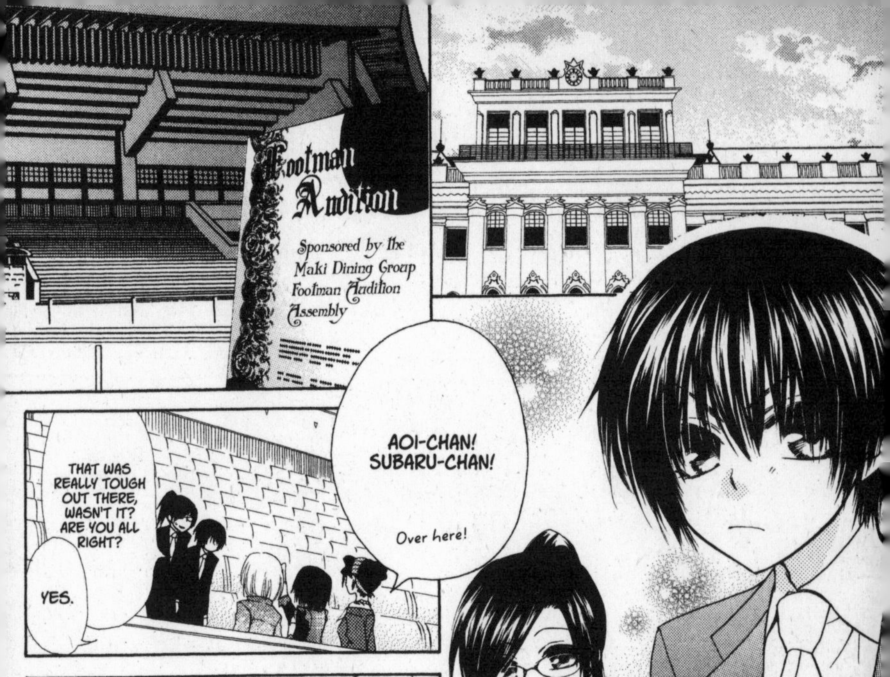
Footman Audition
Sponsored by the Maki Dining Group Footman Audition Assembly
AOI-CHAN! SUBARU-CHAN!
Over here!
THAT WAS REALLY TOUGH OUT THERE, WASN'T IT? ARE YOU ALL RIGHT?
YES.
BUT STILL... AOI-CHAN!
HOW COULD YOU GO AND DO SOMETHING LIKE THIS WITHOUT SAYING A WORD TO ME?
YEAH, YEAH, SPARE ME THE LECTURE!

Extraneous Question Corner

Question 4

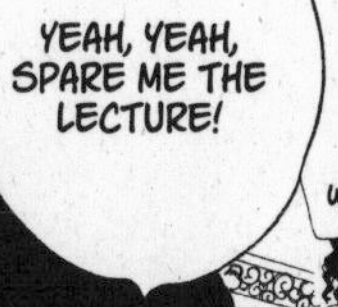

Q: Who's your favorite character?

A: I love every single one of my characters without exception. Misaki is easy to draw, Usui is a pervert, Yukimura ended up becoming **that way** without my even meaning to...but I guess the Idiot Trio are so much fun I love them the most. As a rule, I like idiots. In a way, the whole cast is kind of idiotic...

And it's full of perverts too.

By "that way," do you mean this?! →

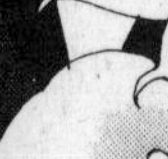

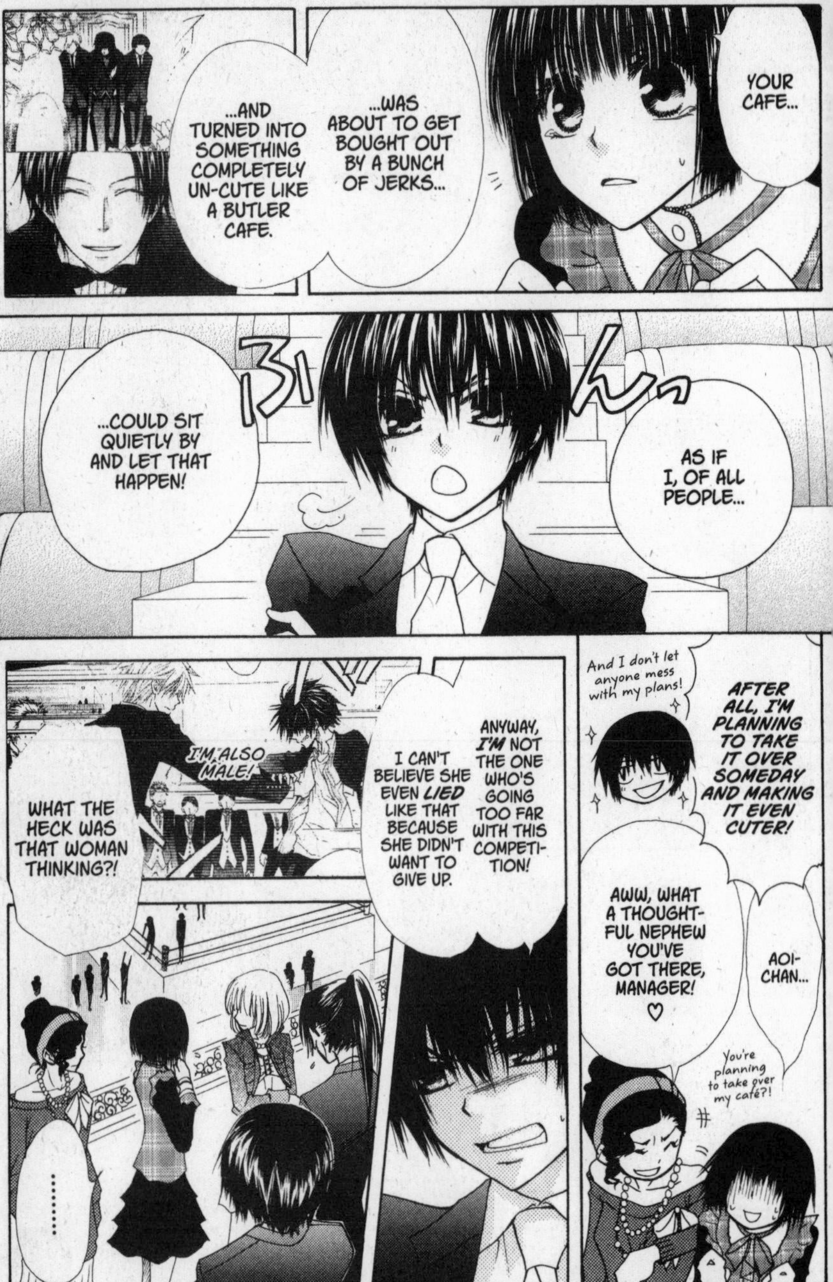

YOUR CAFE...
...WAS ABOUT TO GET BOUGHT OUT BY A BUNCH OF JERKS...
...AND TURNED INTO SOMETHING COMPLETELY UN-CUTE LIKE A BUTLER CAFE.
AS IF I, OF ALL PEOPLE...
ふん
...COULD SIT QUIETLY BY AND LET THAT HAPPEN!
AFTER ALL, I'M PLANNING TO TAKE IT OVER SOMEDAY AND MAKING IT EVEN CUTER!
And I don't let anyone mess with my plans!
AOI-CHAN...
AWW, WHAT A THOUGHTFUL NEPHEW YOU'VE GOT THERE, MANAGER! ♡
You're planning to take over my café?!
ANYWAY, *I'M* NOT THE ONE WHO'S GOING TOO FAR WITH THIS COMPETITION!
I CAN'T BELIEVE SHE EVEN *LIED* LIKE THAT BECAUSE SHE DIDN'T WANT TO GIVE UP.
I'M ALSO MALE!
WHAT THE HECK WAS THAT WOMAN THINKING?!
......

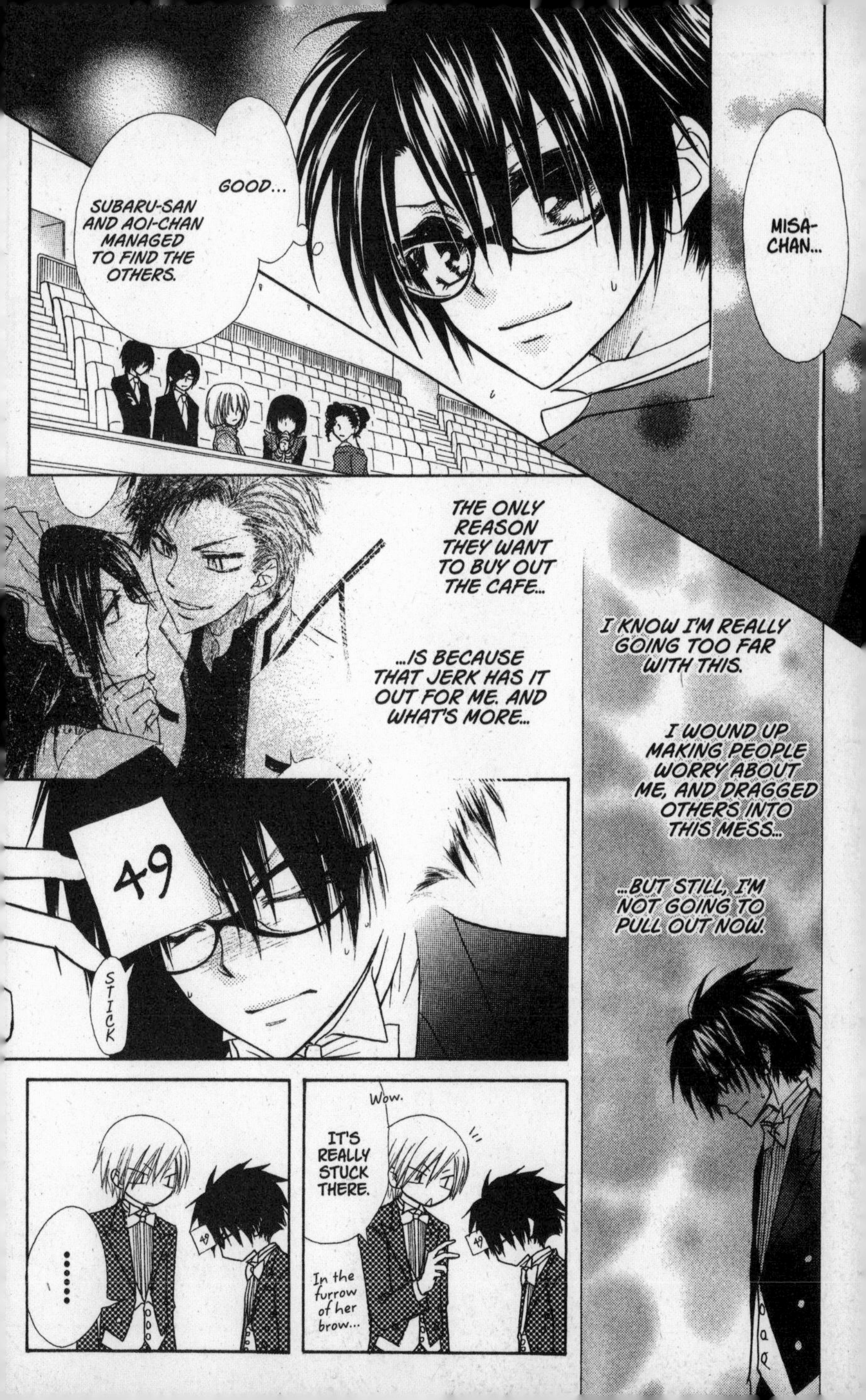

MISA-CHAN...
GOOD...
SUBARU-SAN AND AOI-CHAN MANAGED TO FIND THE OTHERS.
I KNOW I'M REALLY GOING TOO FAR WITH THIS.
I WOUND UP MAKING PEOPLE WORRY ABOUT ME, AND DRAGGED OTHERS INTO THIS MESS...
...BUT STILL, I'M NOT GOING TO PULL OUT NOW.
THE ONLY REASON THEY WANT TO BUY OUT THE CAFE...
...IS BECAUSE THAT JERK HAS IT OUT FOR ME. AND WHAT'S MORE...
49
STICK
Wow.
IT'S REALLY STUCK THERE.
In the furrow of her brow...
......

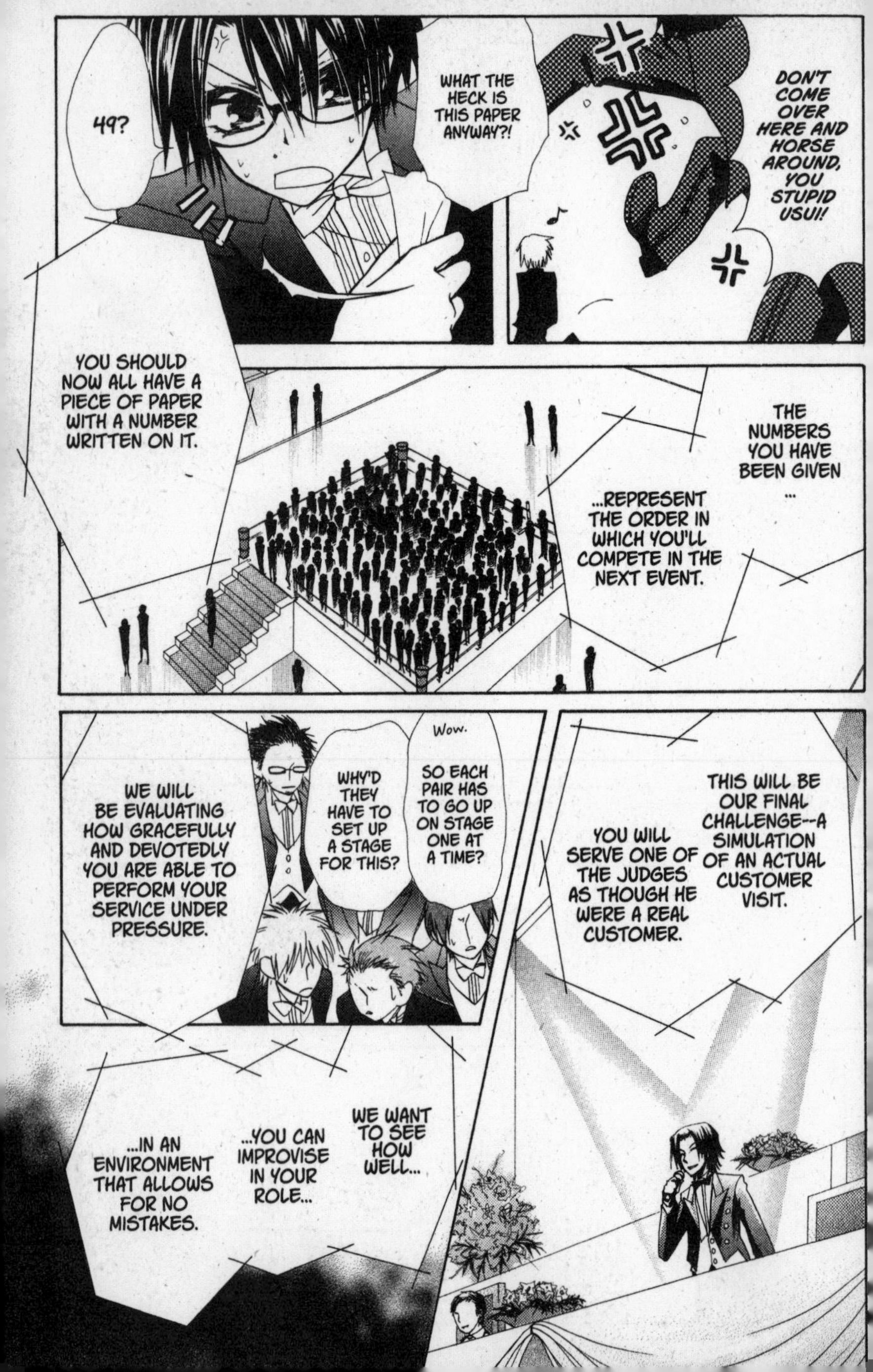
DON'T COME OVER HERE AND HORSE AROUND, YOU STUPID USUI!
WHAT THE HECK IS THIS PAPER ANYWAY?!
49?
YOU SHOULD NOW ALL HAVE A PIECE OF PAPER WITH A NUMBER WRITTEN ON IT.
THE NUMBERS YOU HAVE BEEN GIVEN ...
...REPRESENT THE ORDER IN WHICH YOU'LL COMPETE IN THE NEXT EVENT.
THIS WILL BE OUR FINAL CHALLENGE--A SIMULATION OF AN ACTUAL CUSTOMER VISIT.
YOU WILL SERVE ONE OF THE JUDGES AS THOUGH HE WERE A REAL CUSTOMER.
Wow.
SO EACH PAIR HAS TO GO UP ON STAGE ONE AT A TIME?
WHY'D THEY HAVE TO SET UP A STAGE FOR THIS?
WE WILL BE EVALUATING HOW GRACEFULLY AND DEVOTEDLY YOU ARE ABLE TO PERFORM YOUR SERVICE UNDER PRESSURE.
WE WANT TO SEE HOW WELL...
...YOU CAN IMPROVISE IN YOUR ROLE...
...IN AN ENVIRONMENT THAT ALLOWS FOR NO MISTAKES.

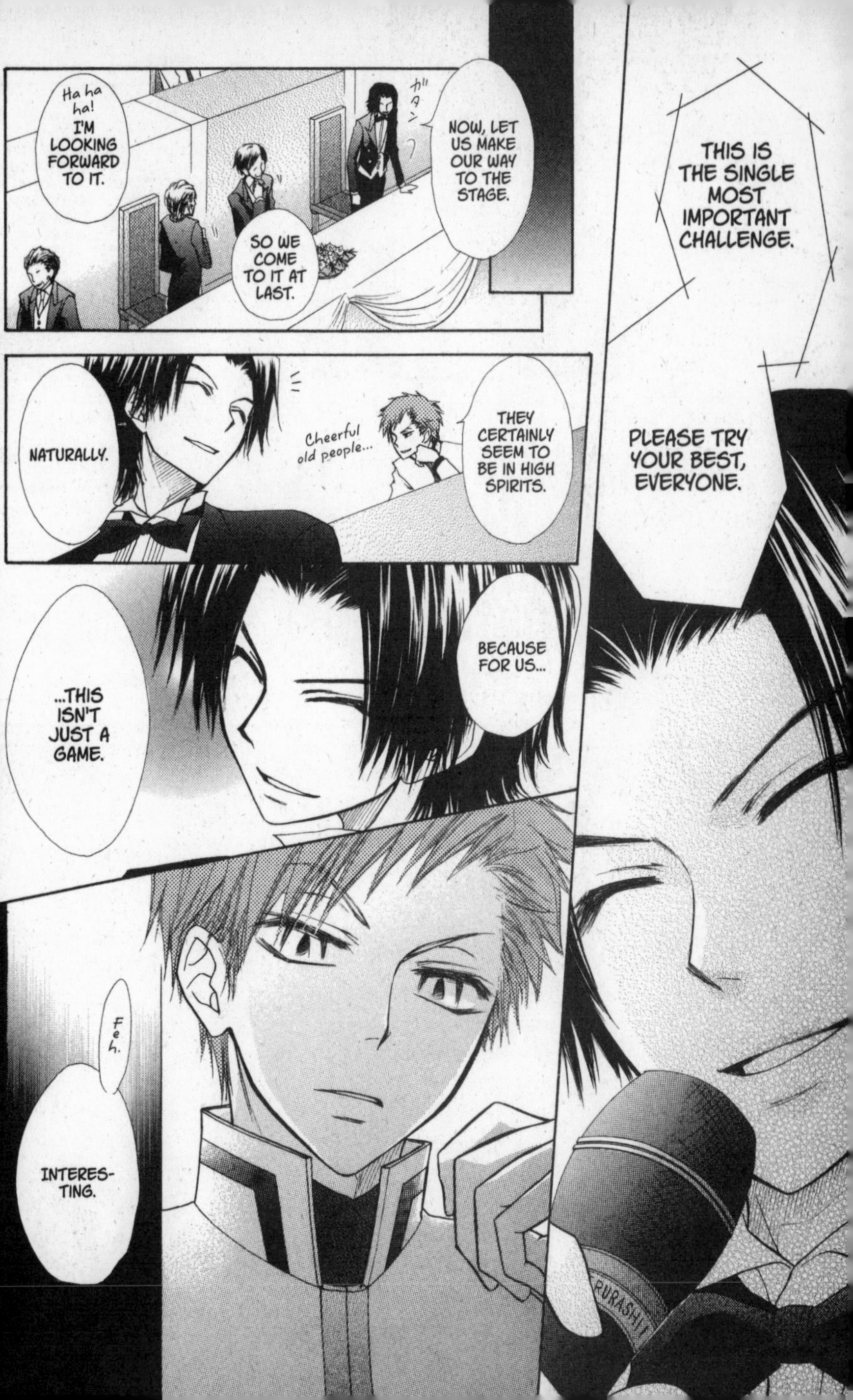
THIS IS THE SINGLE MOST IMPORTANT CHALLENGE.
PLEASE TRY YOUR BEST, EVERYONE.
ガタン
NOW, LET US MAKE OUR WAY TO THE STAGE.
SO WE COME TO IT AT LAST.
Ha ha ha! I'M LOOKING FORWARD TO IT.
THEY CERTAINLY SEEM TO BE IN HIGH SPIRITS.
Cheerful old people...
NATURALLY.
BECAUSE FOR US...
...THIS ISN'T JUST A GAME.
Feh.
INTERESTING.

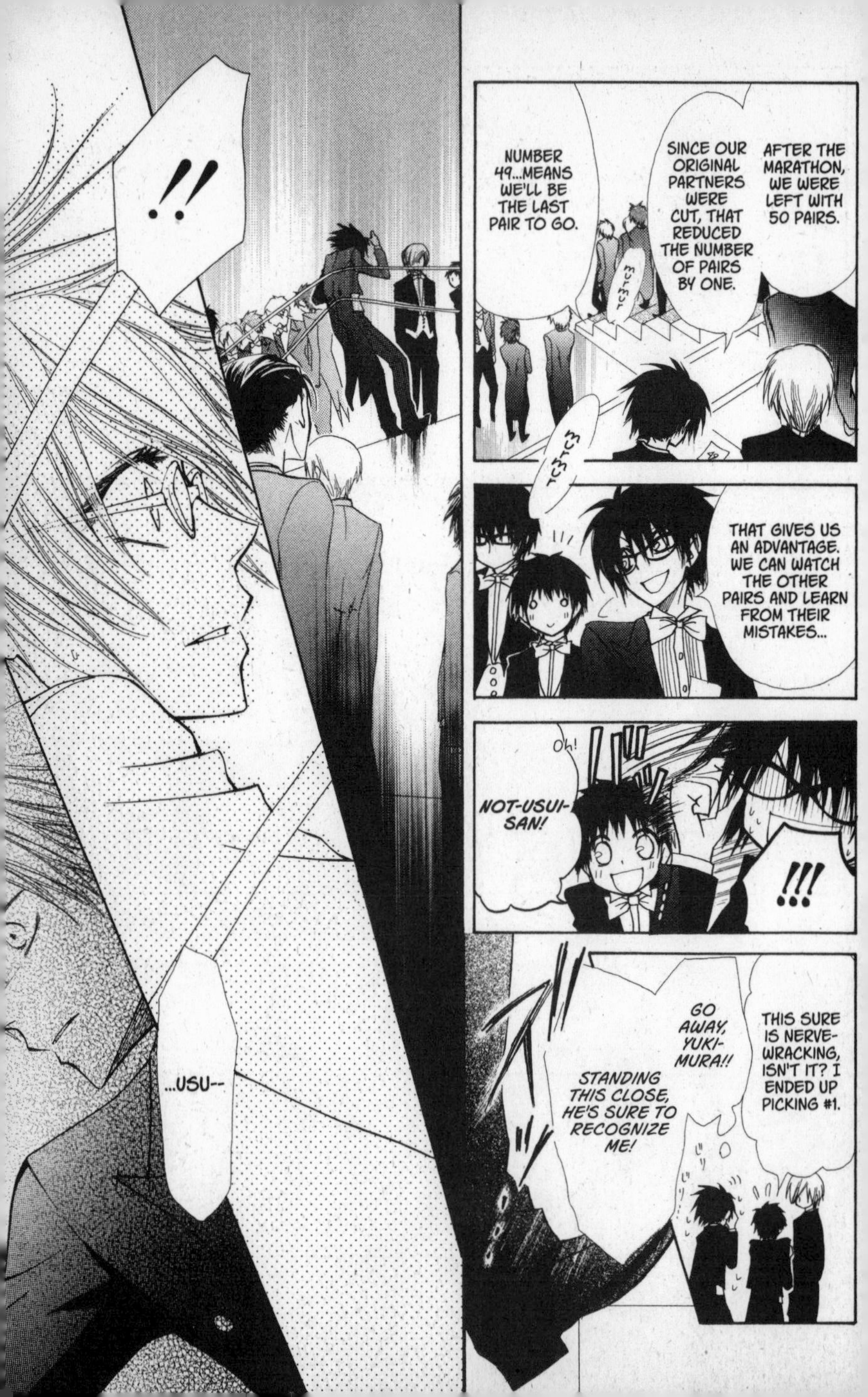
AFTER THE MARATHON, WE WERE LEFT WITH 50 PAIRS.
SINCE OUR ORIGINAL PARTNERS WERE CUT, THAT REDUCED THE NUMBER OF PAIRS BY ONE.
murmur
NUMBER 49...MEANS WE'LL BE THE LAST PAIR TO GO.
murmur
THAT GIVES US AN ADVANTAGE. WE CAN WATCH THE OTHER PAIRS AND LEARN FROM THEIR MISTAKES...
!!!
Oh!
NOT-USUI-SAN!
THIS SURE IS NERVE-WRACKING, ISN'T IT? I ENDED UP PICKING #1.
GO AWAY, YUKI-MURA!!
STANDING THIS CLOSE, HE'S SURE TO RECOGNIZE ME!
!!
...USU--

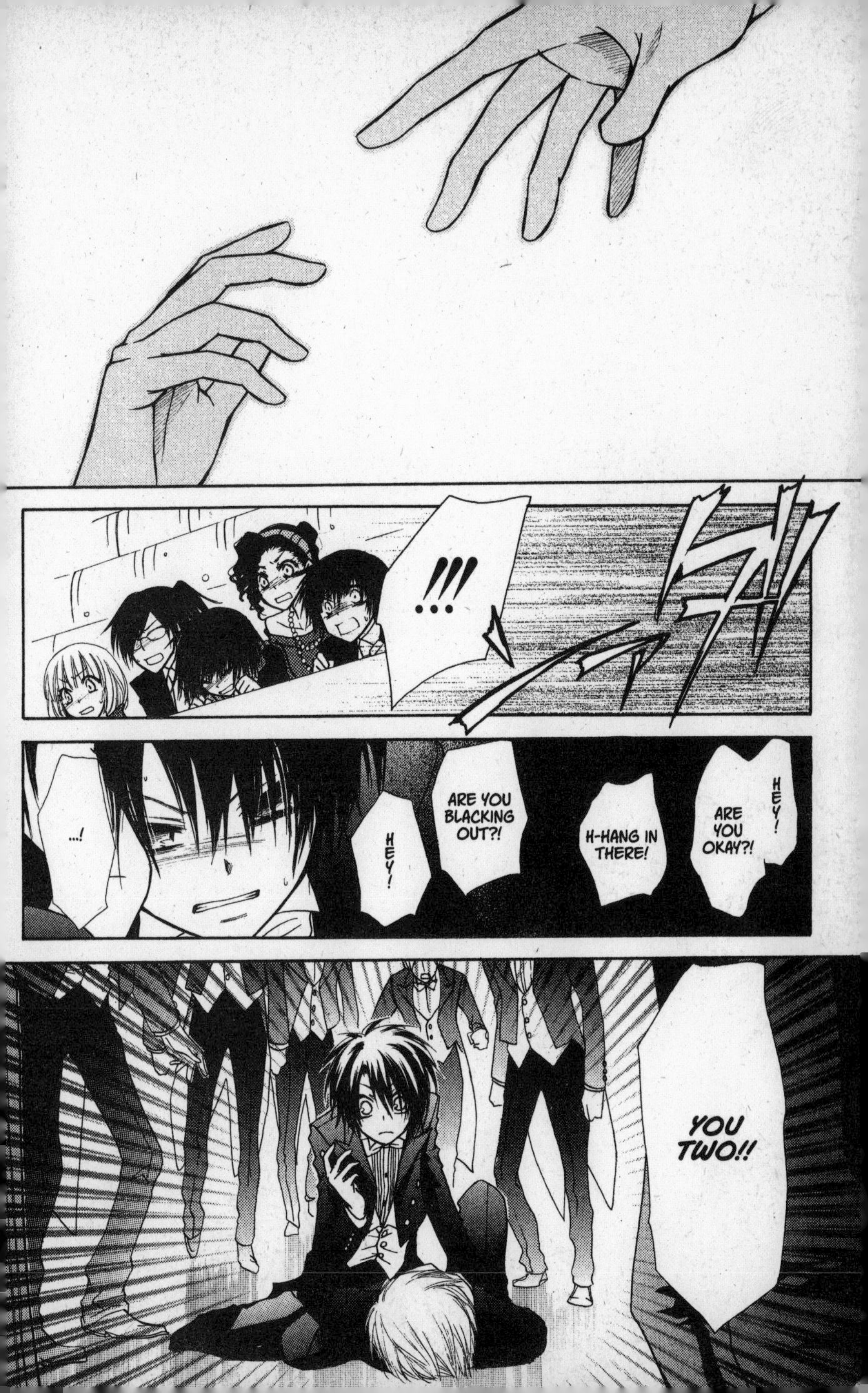

!!!...
HEY! ARE YOU OKAY?!
H-HANG IN THERE!
ARE YOU BLACKING OUT?! HEY!
...!
YOU TWO!!

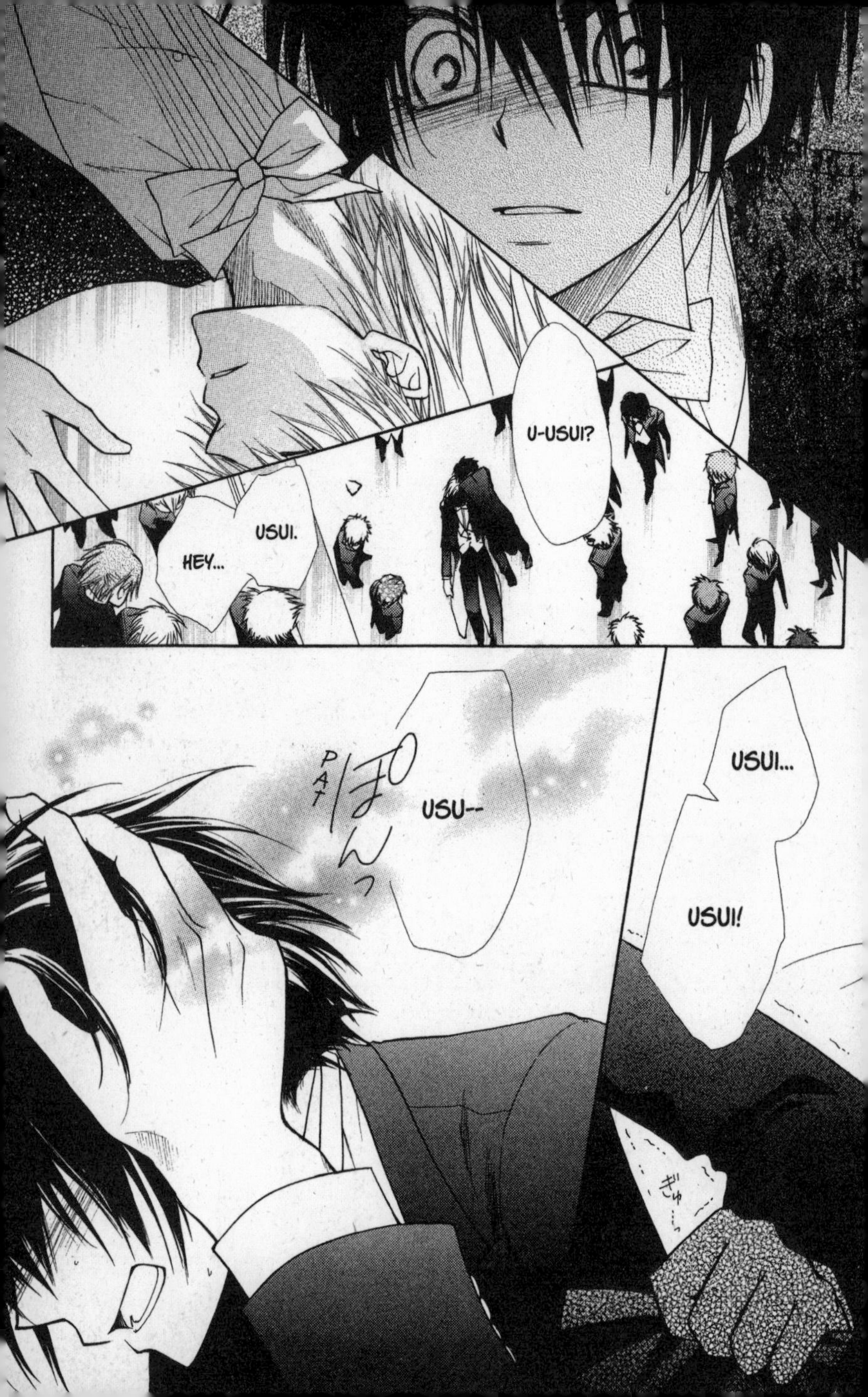
U-USUI?
HEY... USUI.
USUI...
USUI!
ぽんっ
PAT
USU--

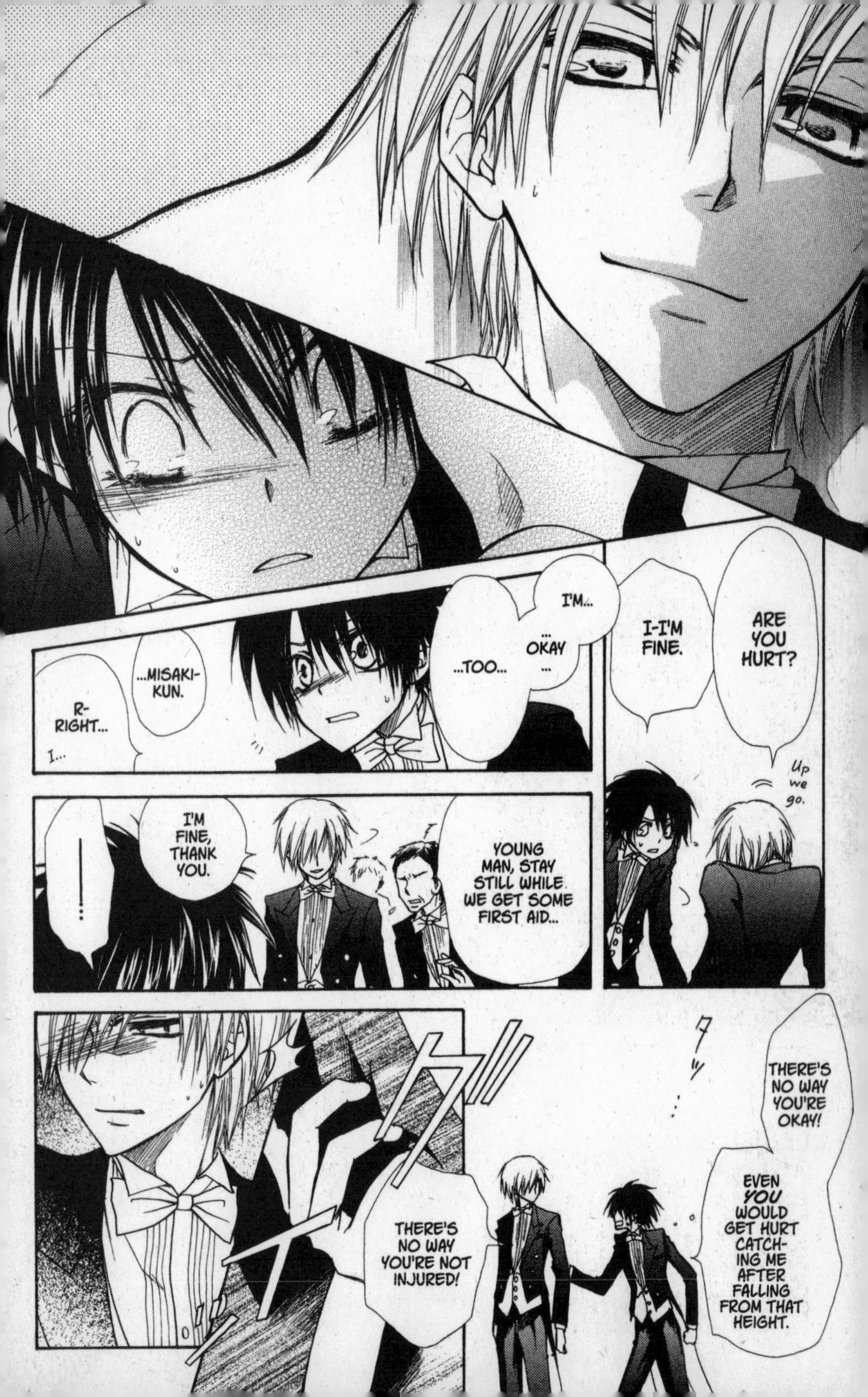
ARE YOU HURT?
I-I'M FINE.
Up we go.
I'M... ...OKAY...
...TOO...
...MISAKI-KUN.
R-RIGHT... I...
YOUNG MAN, STAY STILL WHILE WE GET SOME FIRST AID...
I'M FINE, THANK YOU.
THERE'S NO WAY YOU'RE OKAY!
EVEN YOU WOULD GET HURT CATCHING ME AFTER FALLING FROM THAT HEIGHT.
THERE'S NO WAY YOU'RE NOT INJURED!

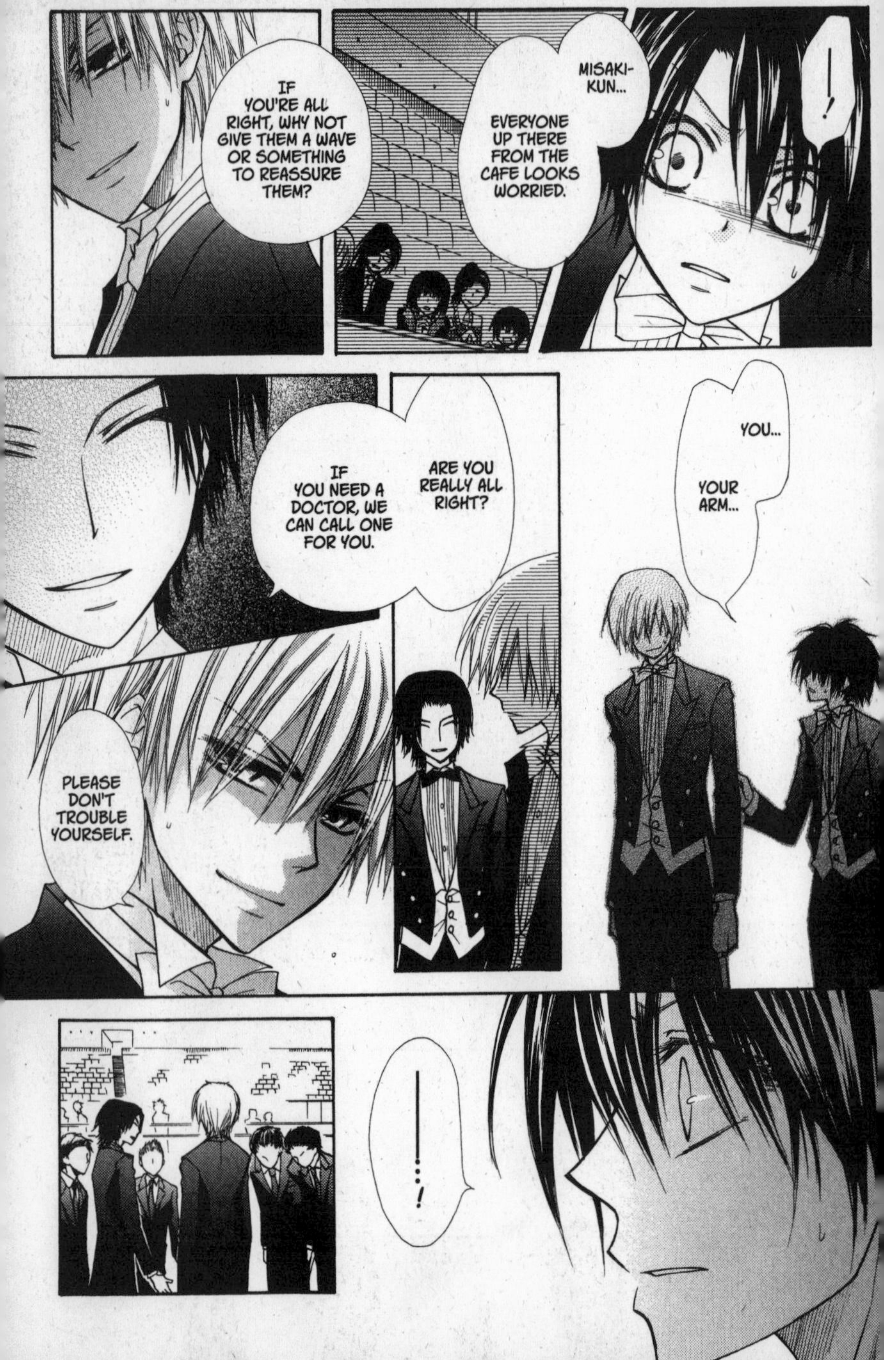
!
MISAKI-KUN...
EVERYONE UP THERE FROM THE CAFE LOOKS WORRIED.
IF YOU'RE ALL RIGHT, WHY NOT GIVE THEM A WAVE OR SOMETHING TO REASSURE THEM?
YOU...
YOUR ARM...
ARE YOU REALLY ALL RIGHT?
IF YOU NEED A DOCTOR, WE CAN CALL ONE FOR YOU.
PLEASE DON'T TROUBLE YOURSELF.
......!

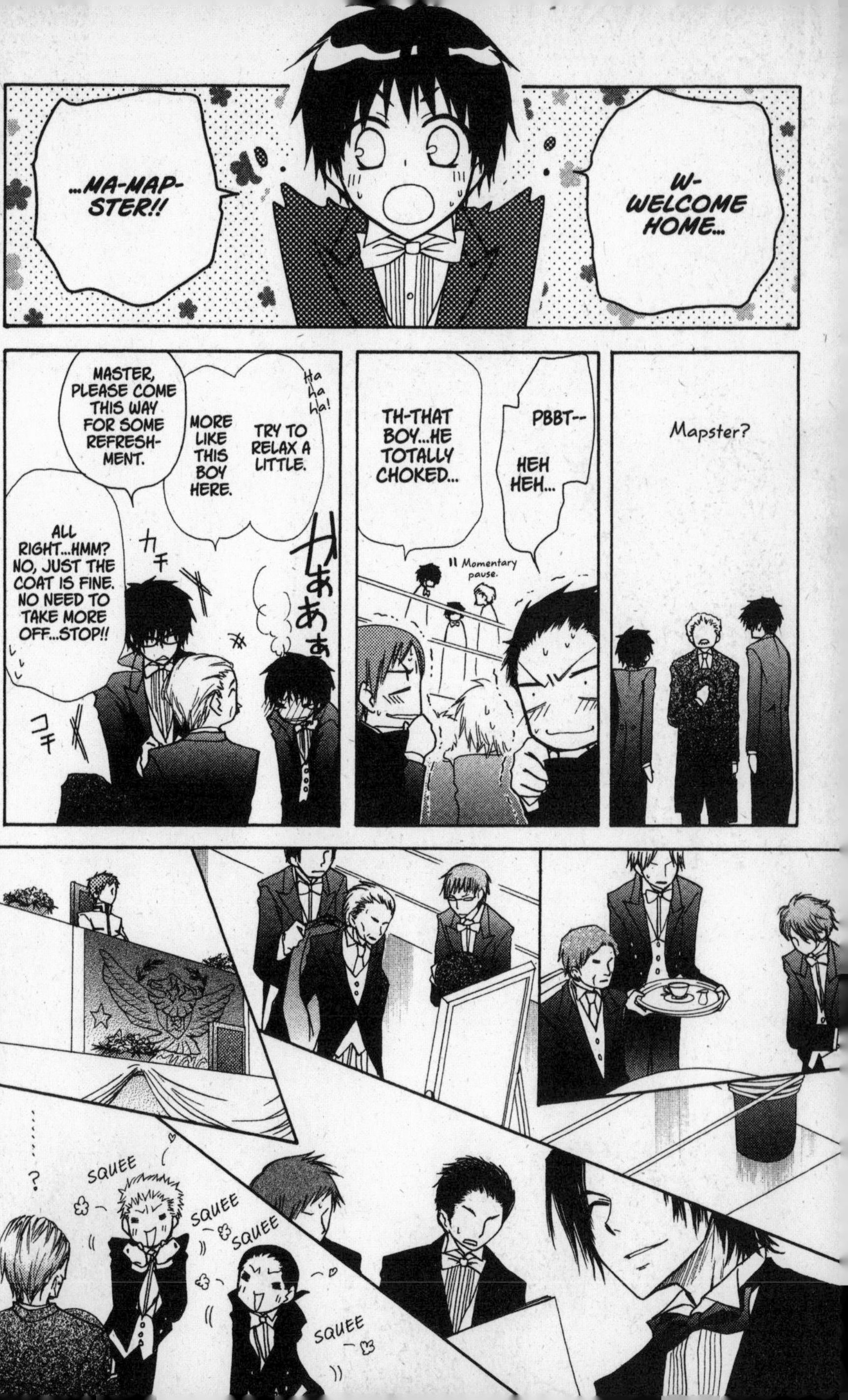
W-
WELCOME HOME...
...MA-MAPSTER!!
Mapster?
PBBT--
HEH HEH...
TH-THAT BOY...HE TOTALLY CHOKED...
Momentary pause.
Ha ha ha!
TRY TO RELAX A LITTLE.
MORE LIKE THIS BOY HERE.
MASTER, PLEASE COME THIS WAY FOR SOME REFRESHMENT.
ALL RIGHT...HMM? NO, JUST THE COAT IS FINE. NO NEED TO TAKE MORE OFF...STOP!!
かあああ
カチ
コチ
SQUEE
SQUEE
SQUEE
SQUEE
......?

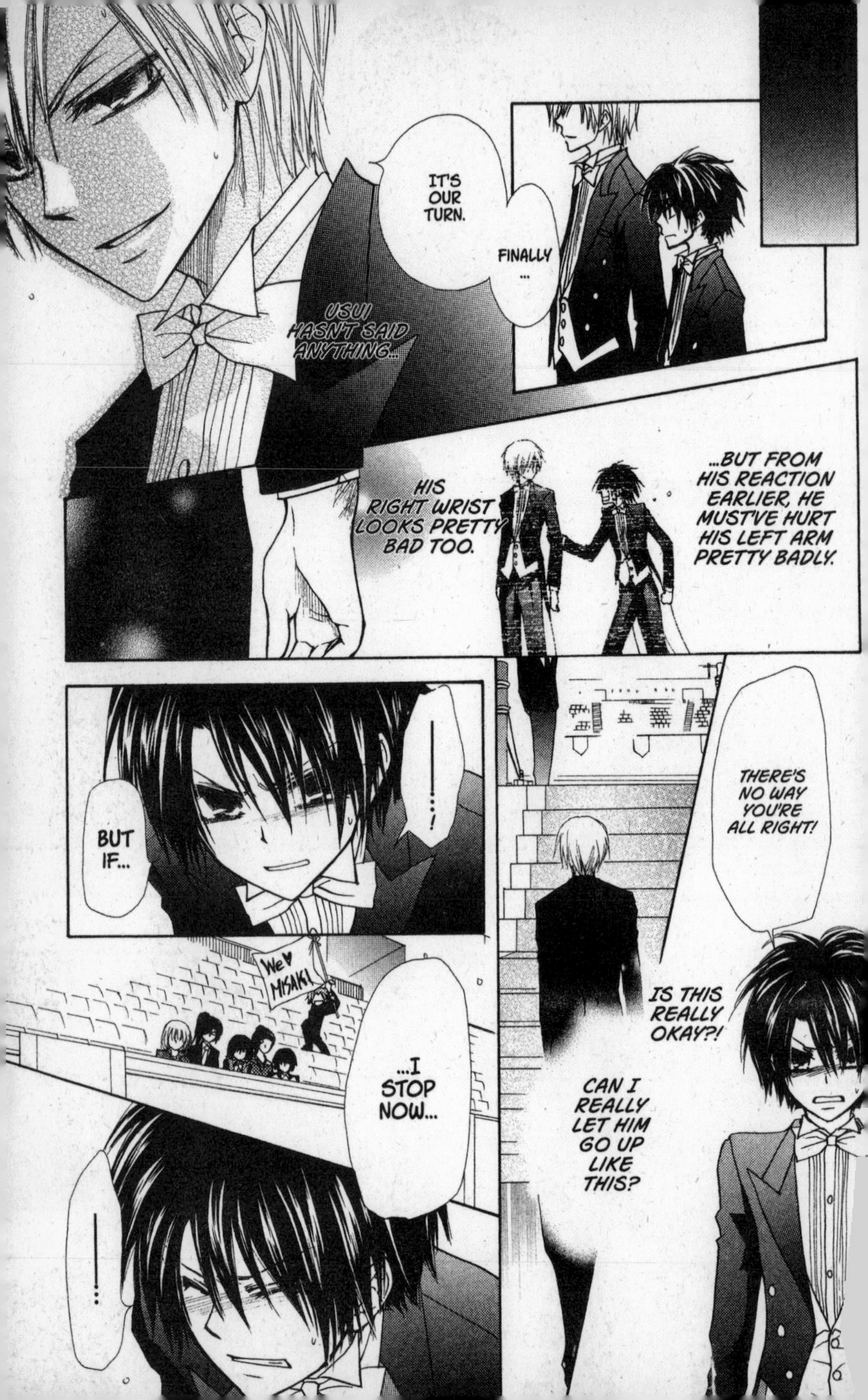
IT'S OUR TURN.
FINALLY...
USUI HASN'T SAID ANYTHING...
...BUT FROM HIS REACTION EARLIER, HE MUST'VE HURT HIS LEFT ARM PRETTY BADLY.
HIS RIGHT WRIST LOOKS PRETTY BAD TOO.
THERE'S NO WAY YOU'RE ALL RIGHT!
IS THIS REALLY OKAY?!
CAN I REALLY LET HIM GO UP LIKE THIS?
......!
BUT IF...
We ♥ MISAKI
...I STOP NOW...
......

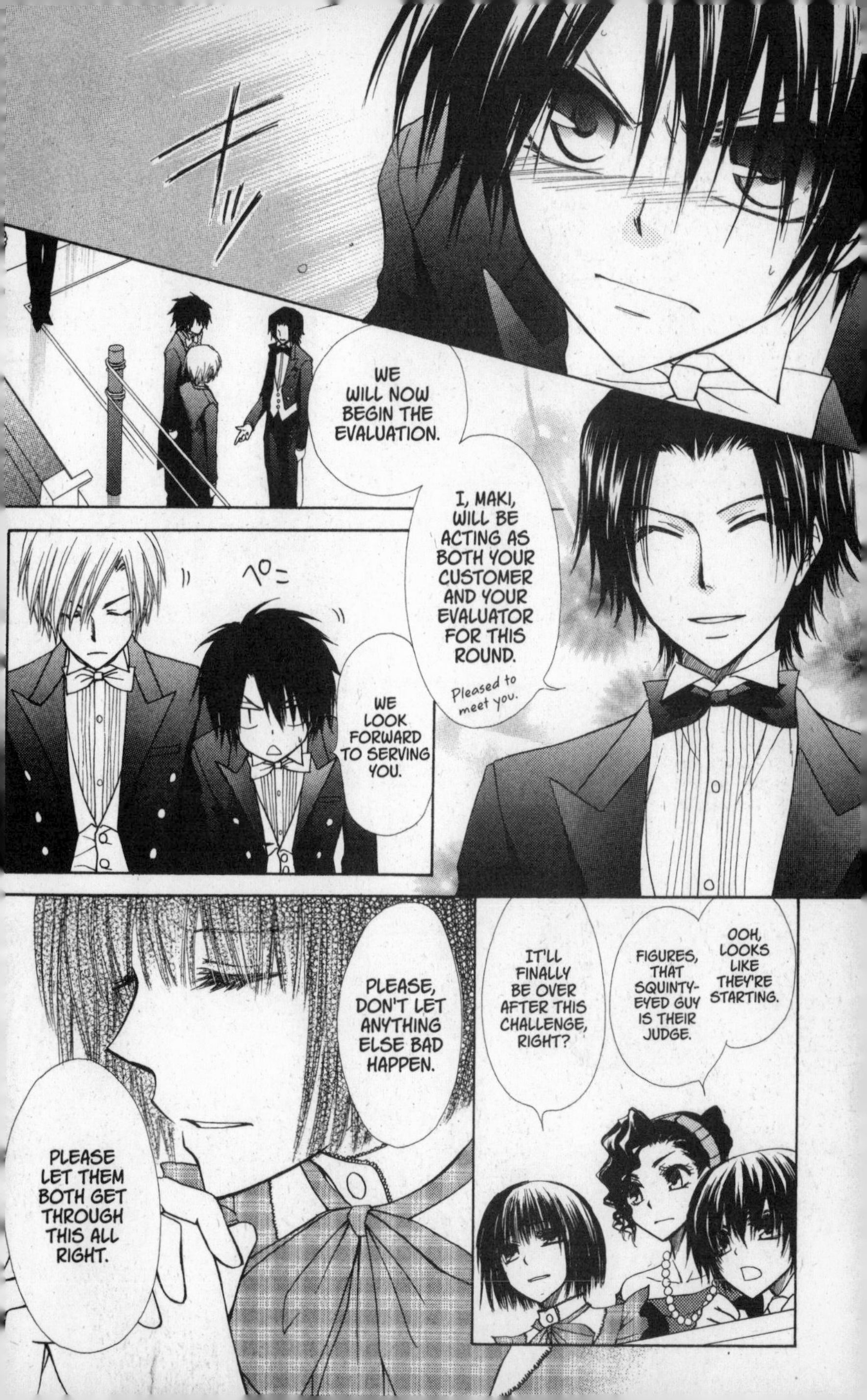
WE WILL NOW BEGIN THE EVALUATION.
I, MAKI, WILL BE ACTING AS BOTH YOUR CUSTOMER AND YOUR EVALUATOR FOR THIS ROUND.
Pleased to meet you.
WE LOOK FORWARD TO SERVING YOU.
OOH, LOOKS LIKE THEY'RE STARTING.
FIGURES, THAT SQUINTY-EYED GUY IS THEIR JUDGE.
IT'LL FINALLY BE OVER AFTER THIS CHALLENGE, RIGHT?
PLEASE, DON'T LET ANYTHING ELSE BAD HAPPEN.
PLEASE LET THEM BOTH GET THROUGH THIS ALL RIGHT.

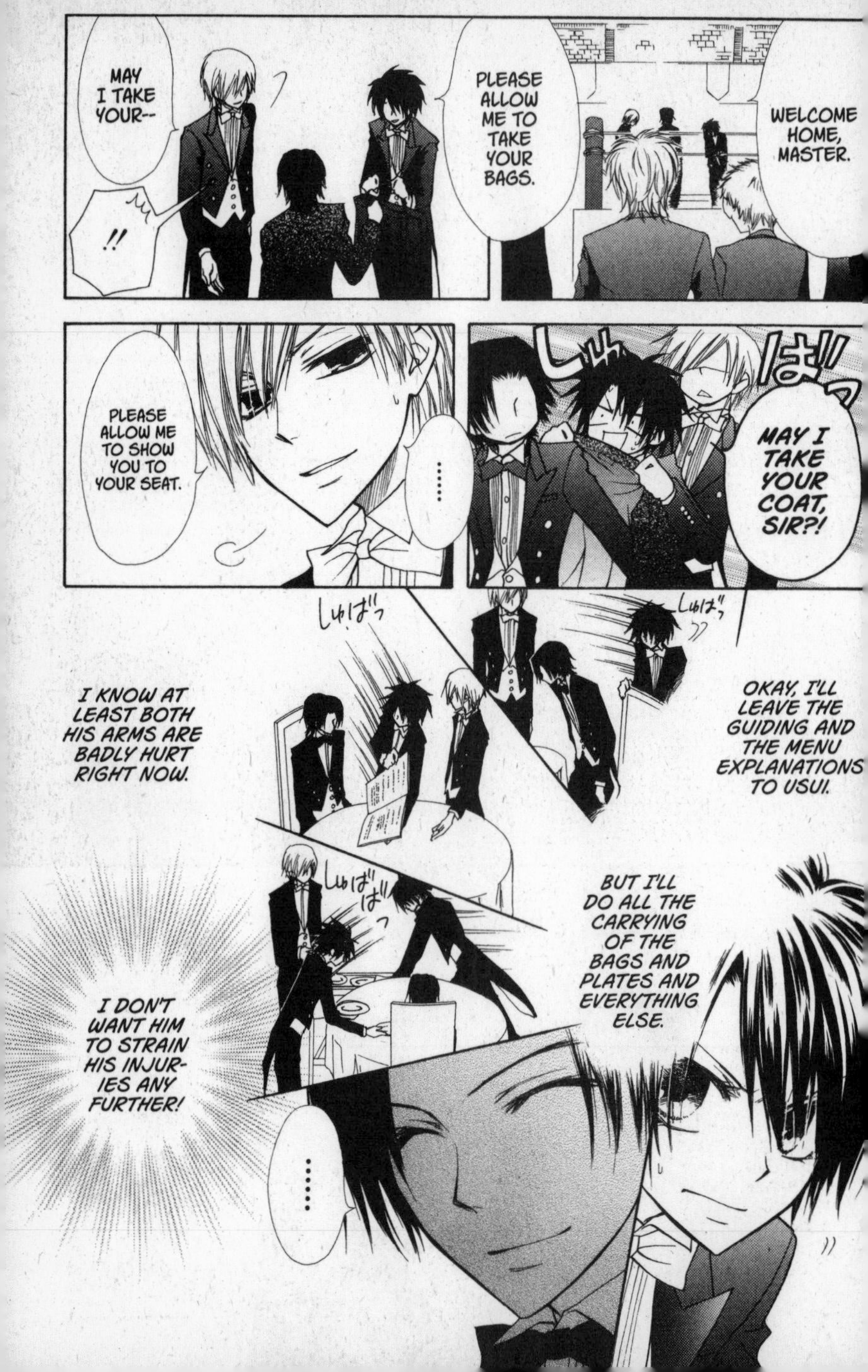

WELCOME HOME, MASTER.
PLEASE ALLOW ME TO TAKE YOUR BAGS.
MAY I TAKE YOUR--
!!
しゅばっ
MAY I TAKE YOUR COAT, SIR?!
......
PLEASE ALLOW ME TO SHOW YOU TO YOUR SEAT.
OKAY, I'LL LEAVE THE GUIDING AND THE MENU EXPLANATIONS TO USUI.
しゅばっ
しゅばっ
I KNOW AT LEAST BOTH HIS ARMS ARE BADLY HURT RIGHT NOW.
BUT I'LL DO ALL THE CARRYING OF THE BAGS AND PLATES AND EVERYTHING ELSE.
しゅばばっ
I DON'T WANT HIM TO STRAIN HIS INJURIES ANY FURTHER!
......

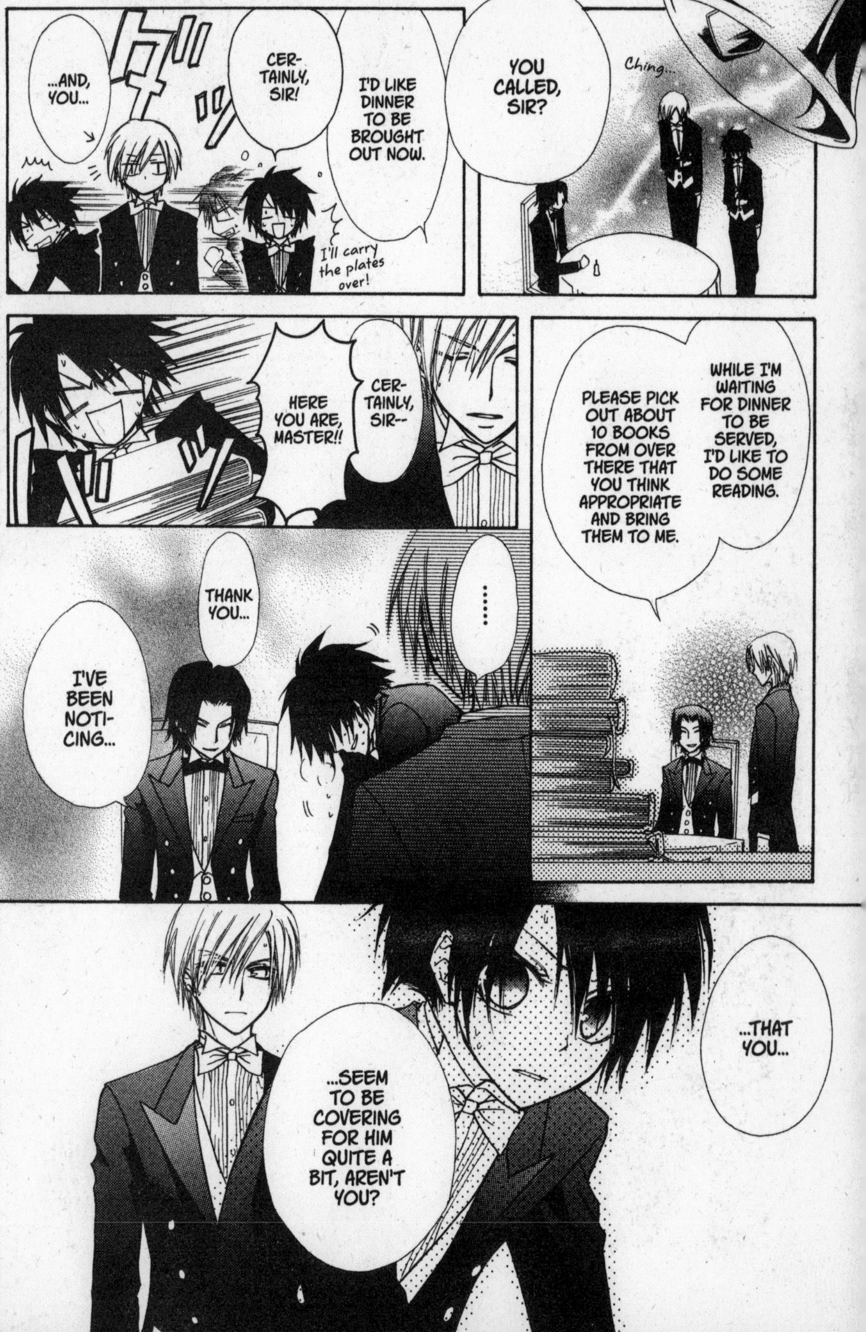
Ching...
YOU CALLED, SIR?
I'D LIKE DINNER TO BE BROUGHT OUT NOW.
CER-TAINLY, SIR!
I'll carry the plates over!
...AND, YOU...
WHILE I'M WAITING FOR DINNER TO BE SERVED, I'D LIKE TO DO SOME READING.
PLEASE PICK OUT ABOUT 10 BOOKS FROM OVER THERE THAT YOU THINK APPROPRIATE AND BRING THEM TO ME.
CER-TAINLY, SIR--
HERE YOU ARE, MASTER!!
......
THANK YOU...
I'VE BEEN NOTI-CING...
...THAT YOU...
...SEEM TO BE COVERING FOR HIM QUITE A BIT, AREN'T YOU?

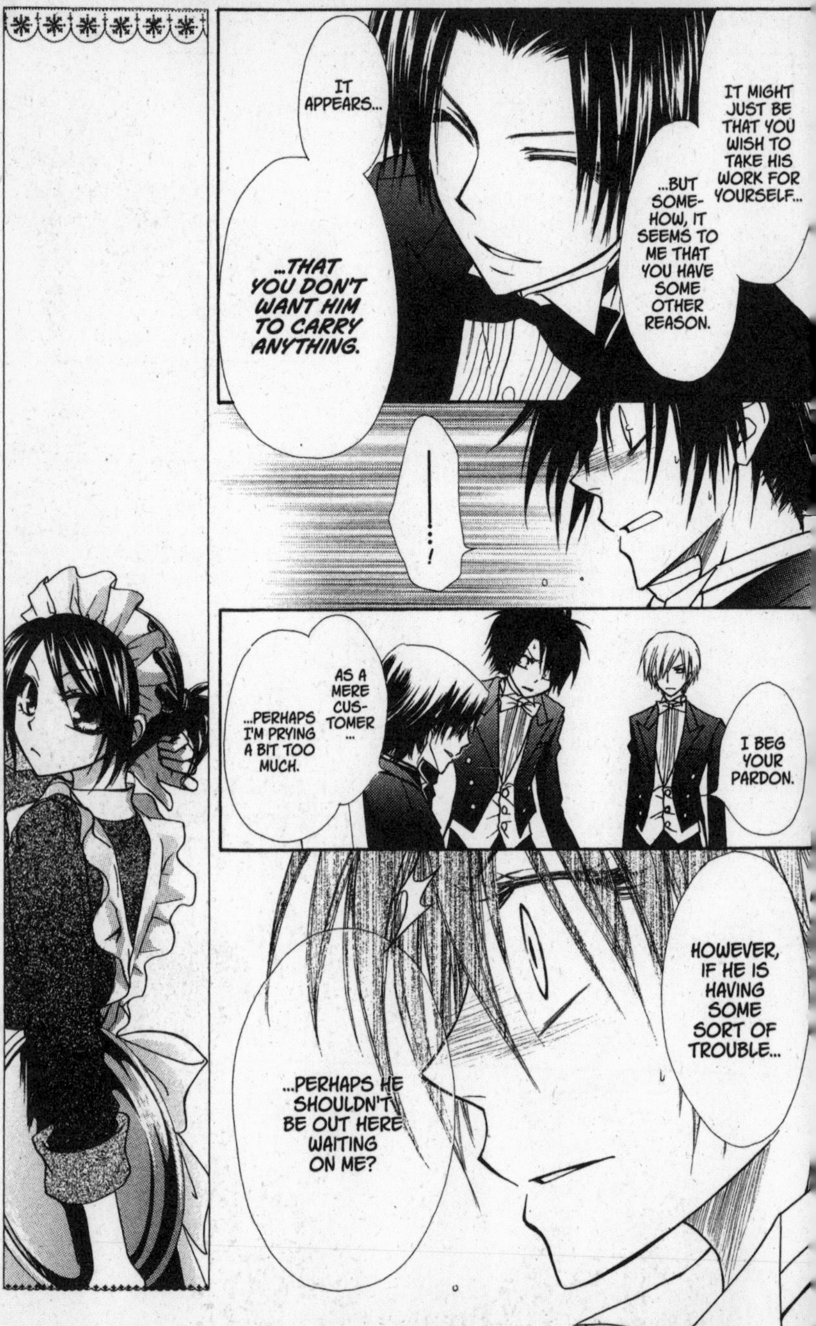
IT MIGHT JUST BE THAT YOU WISH TO TAKE HIS WORK FOR YOURSELF...
...BUT SOME-HOW, IT SEEMS TO ME THAT YOU HAVE SOME OTHER REASON.
IT APPEARS...
...THAT YOU DON'T WANT HIM TO CARRY ANYTHING.
...!
I BEG YOUR PARDON.
AS A MERE CUS-TOMER...
...PERHAPS I'M PRYING A BIT TOO MUCH.
HOWEVER, IF HE IS HAVING SOME SORT OF TROUBLE...
...PERHAPS HE SHOULDN'T BE OUT HERE WAITING ON ME?

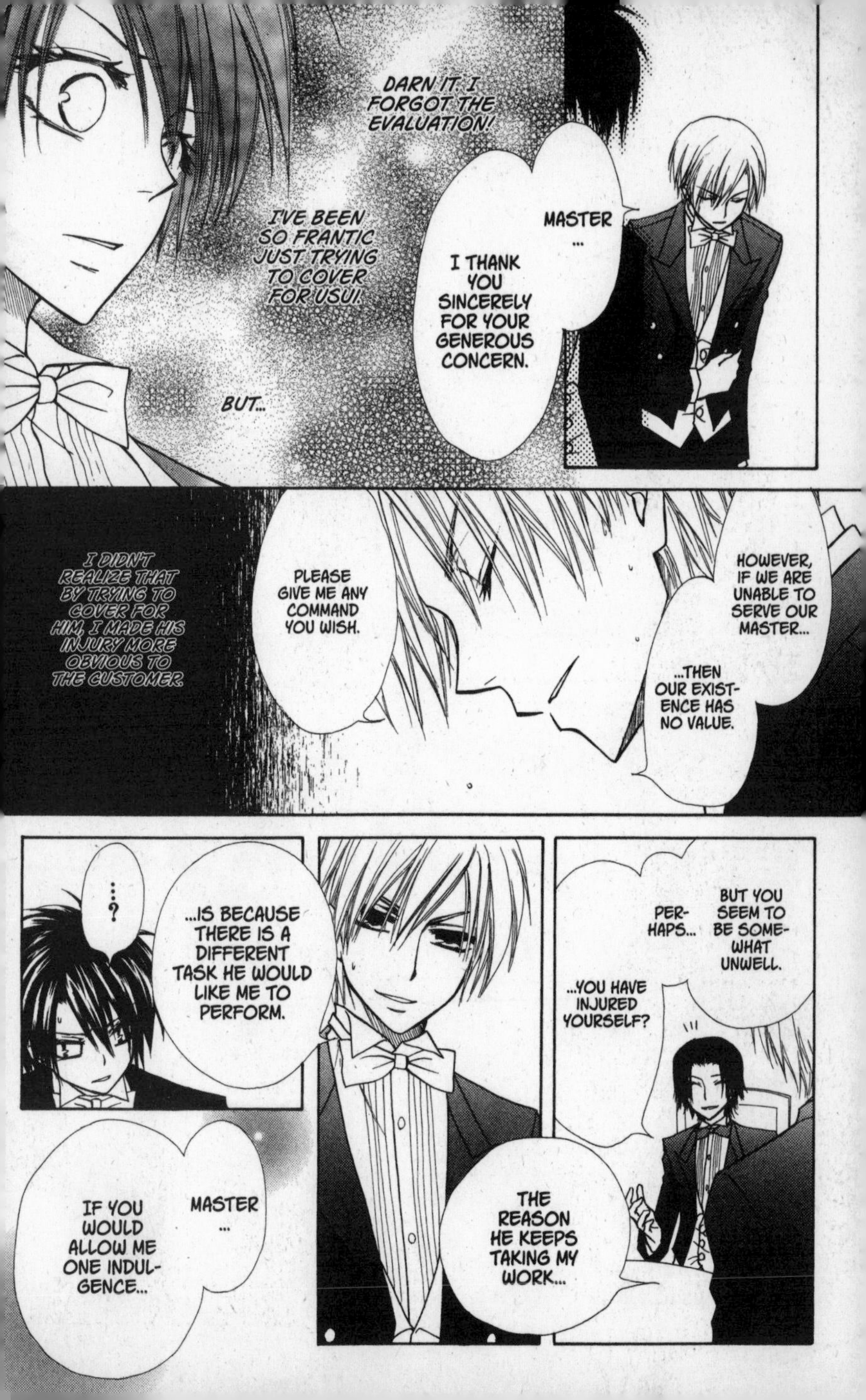
MASTER ...
I THANK YOU SINCERELY FOR YOUR GENEROUS CONCERN.
DARN IT. I FORGOT THE EVALUATION!
I'VE BEEN SO FRANTIC JUST TRYING TO COVER FOR USUI.
BUT...
HOWEVER, IF WE ARE UNABLE TO SERVE OUR MASTER...
...THEN OUR EXISTENCE HAS NO VALUE.
PLEASE GIVE ME ANY COMMAND YOU WISH.
I DIDN'T REALIZE THAT BY TRYING TO COVER FOR HIM, I MADE HIS INJURY MORE OBVIOUS TO THE CUSTOMER.
BUT YOU SEEM TO BE SOME-WHAT UNWELL.
PER-HAPS...
...YOU HAVE INJURED YOURSELF?
THE REASON HE KEEPS TAKING MY WORK...
...IS BECAUSE THERE IS A DIFFERENT TASK HE WOULD LIKE ME TO PERFORM.
...?
MASTER ...
IF YOU WOULD ALLOW ME ONE INDUL-GENCE...

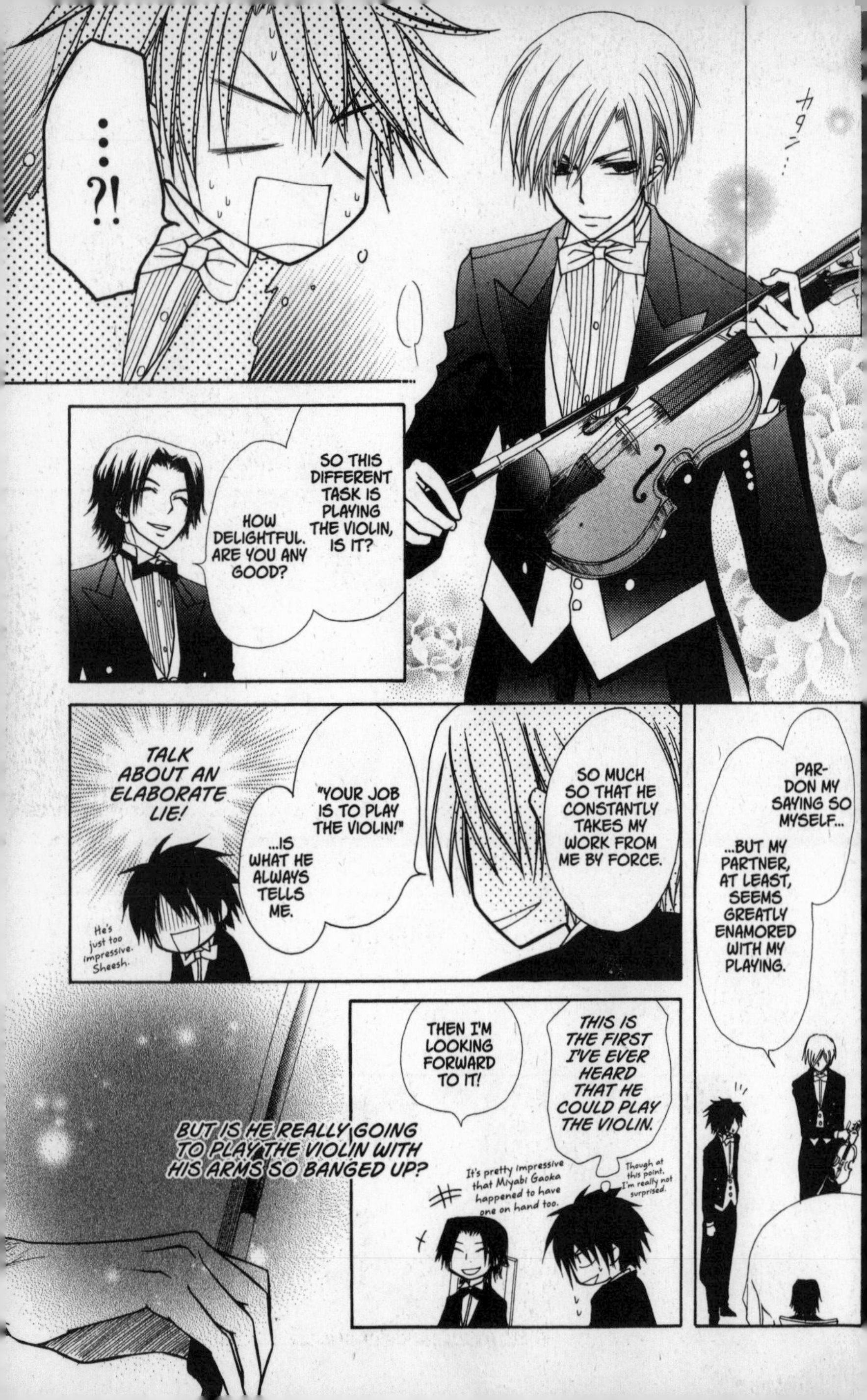
カタン…
…?!
SO THIS DIFFERENT TASK IS PLAYING THE VIOLIN, IS IT?
HOW DELIGHTFUL. ARE YOU ANY GOOD?
PARDON MY SAYING SO MYSELF...
...BUT MY PARTNER, AT LEAST, SEEMS GREATLY ENAMORED WITH MY PLAYING.
SO MUCH SO THAT HE CONSTANTLY TAKES MY WORK FROM ME BY FORCE.
"YOUR JOB IS TO PLAY THE VIOLIN!"
...IS WHAT HE ALWAYS TELLS ME.
TALK ABOUT AN ELABORATE LIE!
He's just too impressive. Sheesh.
THIS IS THE FIRST I'VE EVER HEARD THAT HE COULD PLAY THE VIOLIN.
THEN I'M LOOKING FORWARD TO IT!
Though at this point, I'm really not surprised.
It's pretty impressive that Miyabi Gaoka happened to have one on hand too.
BUT IS HE REALLY GOING TO PLAY THE VIOLIN WITH HIS ARMS SO BANGED UP?

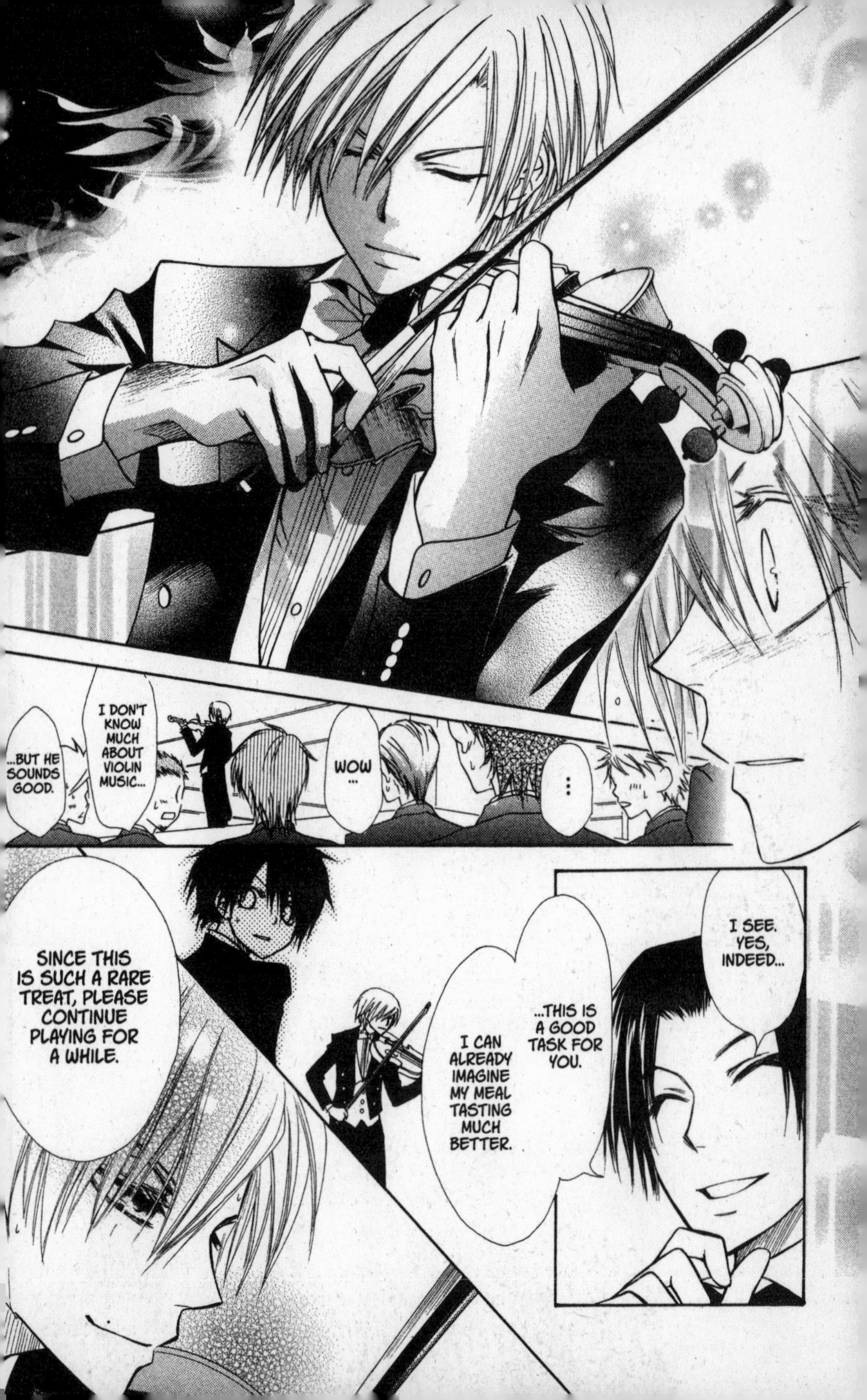
...
WOW ...
I DON'T KNOW MUCH ABOUT VIOLIN MUSIC...
...BUT HE SOUNDS GOOD.
I SEE. YES, INDEED...
...THIS IS A GOOD TASK FOR YOU.
I CAN ALREADY IMAGINE MY MEAL TASTING MUCH BETTER.
SINCE THIS IS SUCH A RARE TREAT, PLEASE CONTINUE PLAYING FOR A WHILE.

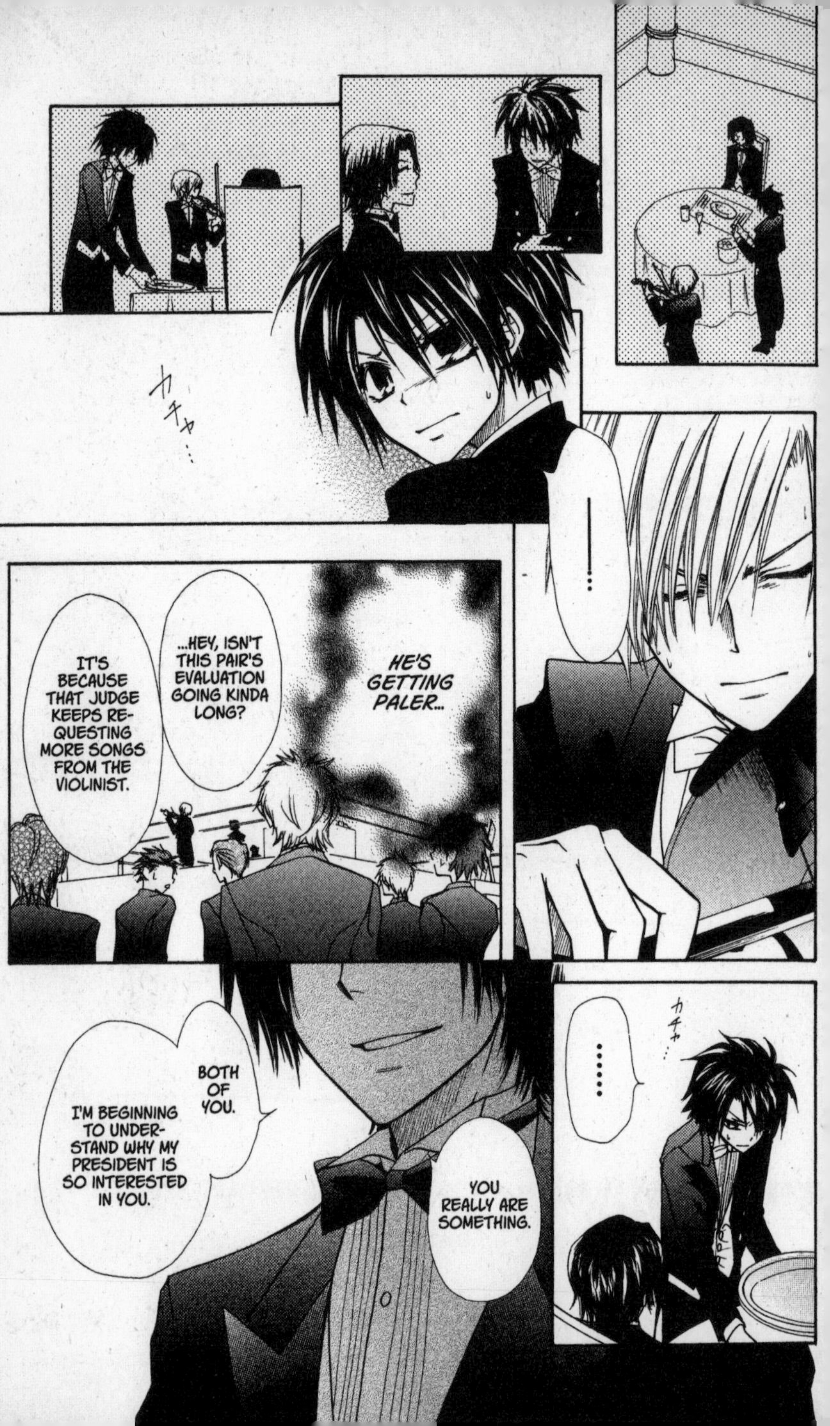

カチャ…
……!
HE'S GETTING PALER...
...HEY, ISN'T THIS PAIR'S EVALUATION GOING KINDA LONG?
IT'S BECAUSE THAT JUDGE KEEPS RE-QUESTING MORE SONGS FROM THE VIOLINIST.
……
カチャ…
BOTH OF YOU.
I'M BEGINNING TO UNDER-STAND WHY MY PRESIDENT IS SO INTERESTED IN YOU.
YOU REALLY ARE SOMETHING.

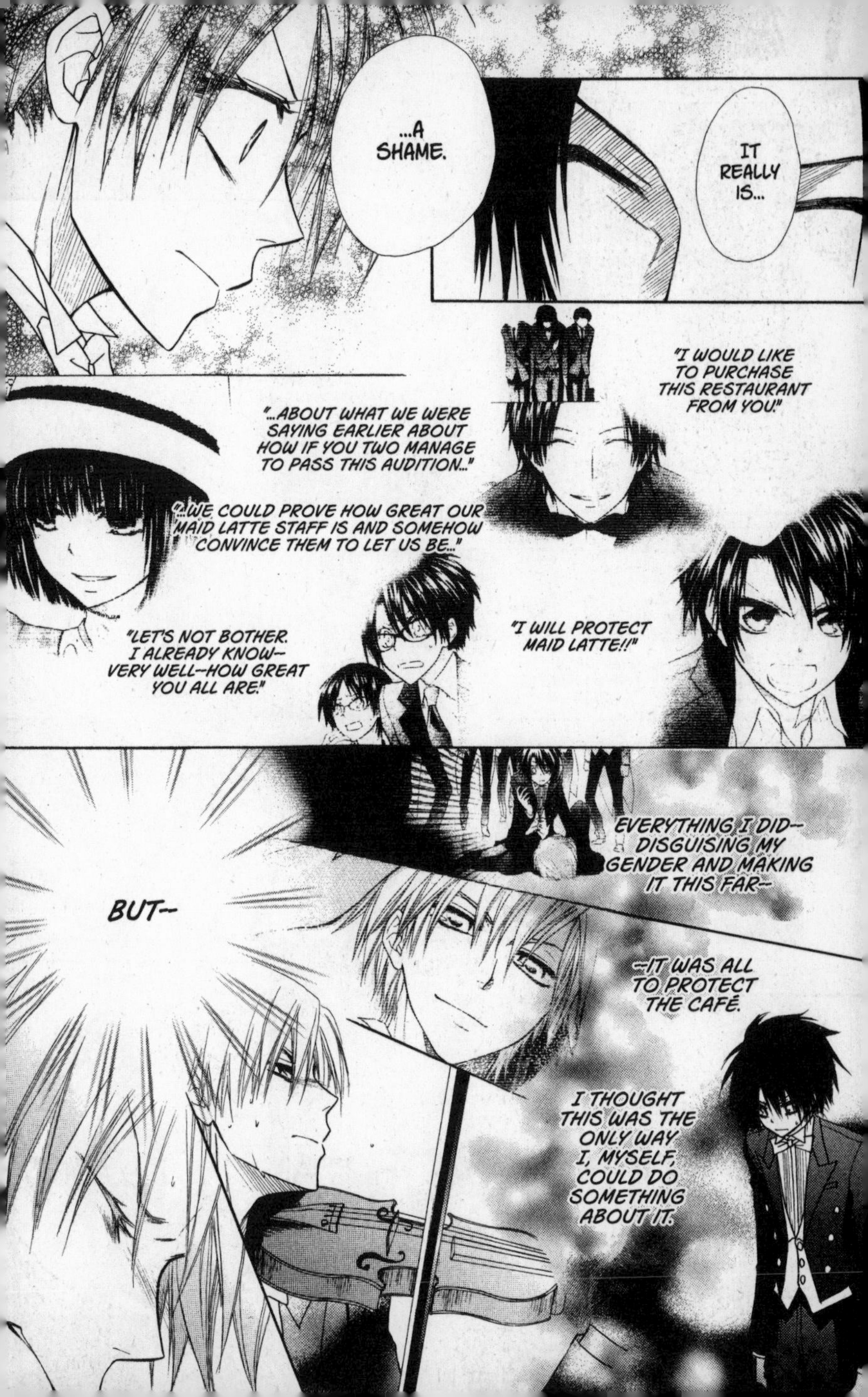
IT REALLY IS...
...A SHAME.
"I WOULD LIKE TO PURCHASE THIS RESTAURANT FROM YOU!"
"...ABOUT WHAT WE WERE SAYING EARLIER ABOUT HOW IF YOU TWO MANAGE TO PASS THIS AUDITION..."
"...WE COULD PROVE HOW GREAT OUR MAID LATTE STAFF IS AND SOMEHOW CONVINCE THEM TO LET US BE..."
"I WILL PROTECT MAID LATTE!!"
"LET'S NOT BOTHER. I ALREADY KNOW--VERY WELL--HOW GREAT YOU ALL ARE."
EVERYTHING I DID--DISGUISING MY GENDER AND MAKING IT THIS FAR--
--IT WAS ALL TO PROTECT THE CAFÉ.
I THOUGHT THIS WAS THE ONLY WAY I, MYSELF, COULD DO SOMETHING ABOUT IT.
BUT--

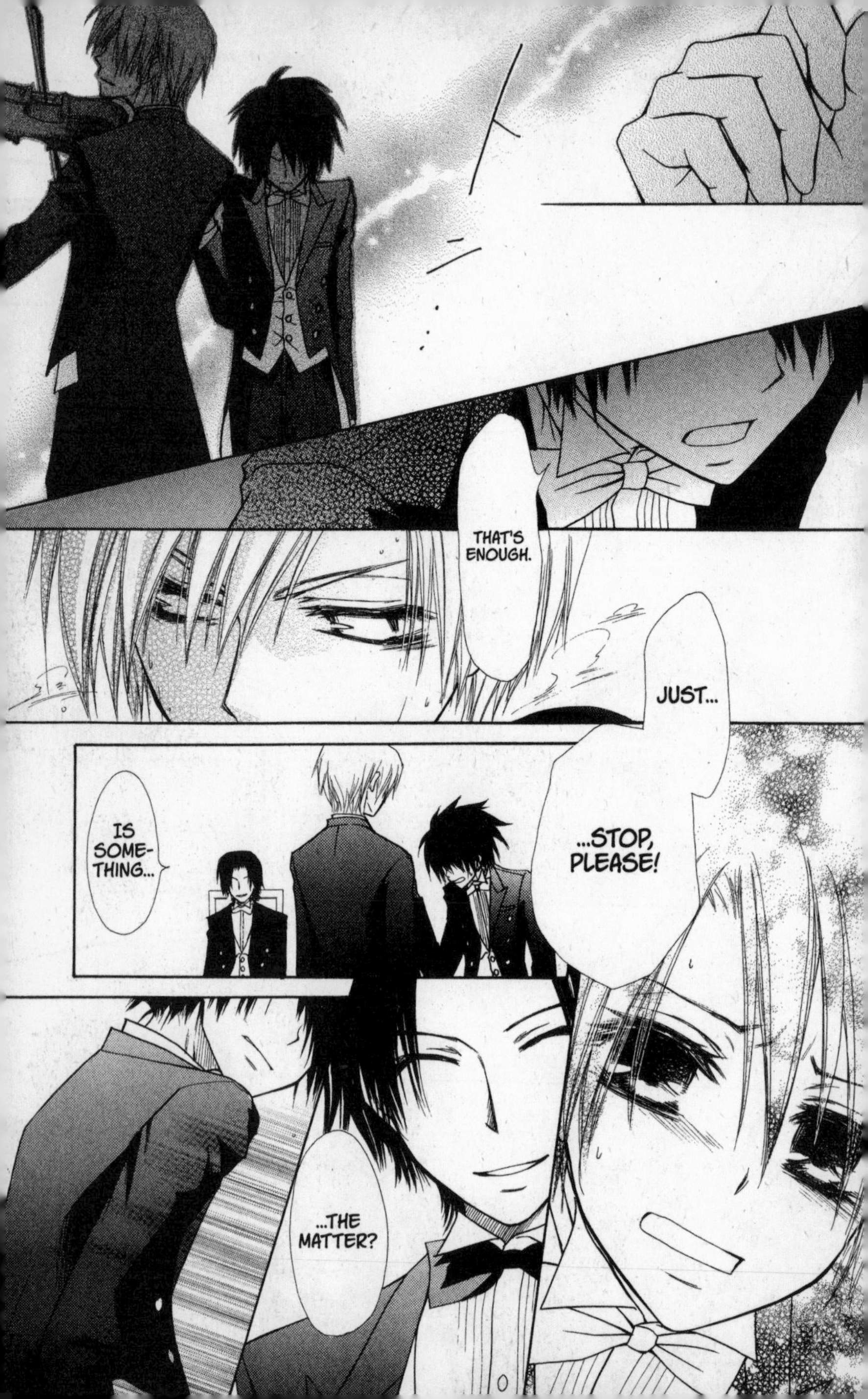
THAT'S ENOUGH.
JUST...
...STOP, PLEASE!
IS SOMETHING...
...THE MATTER?

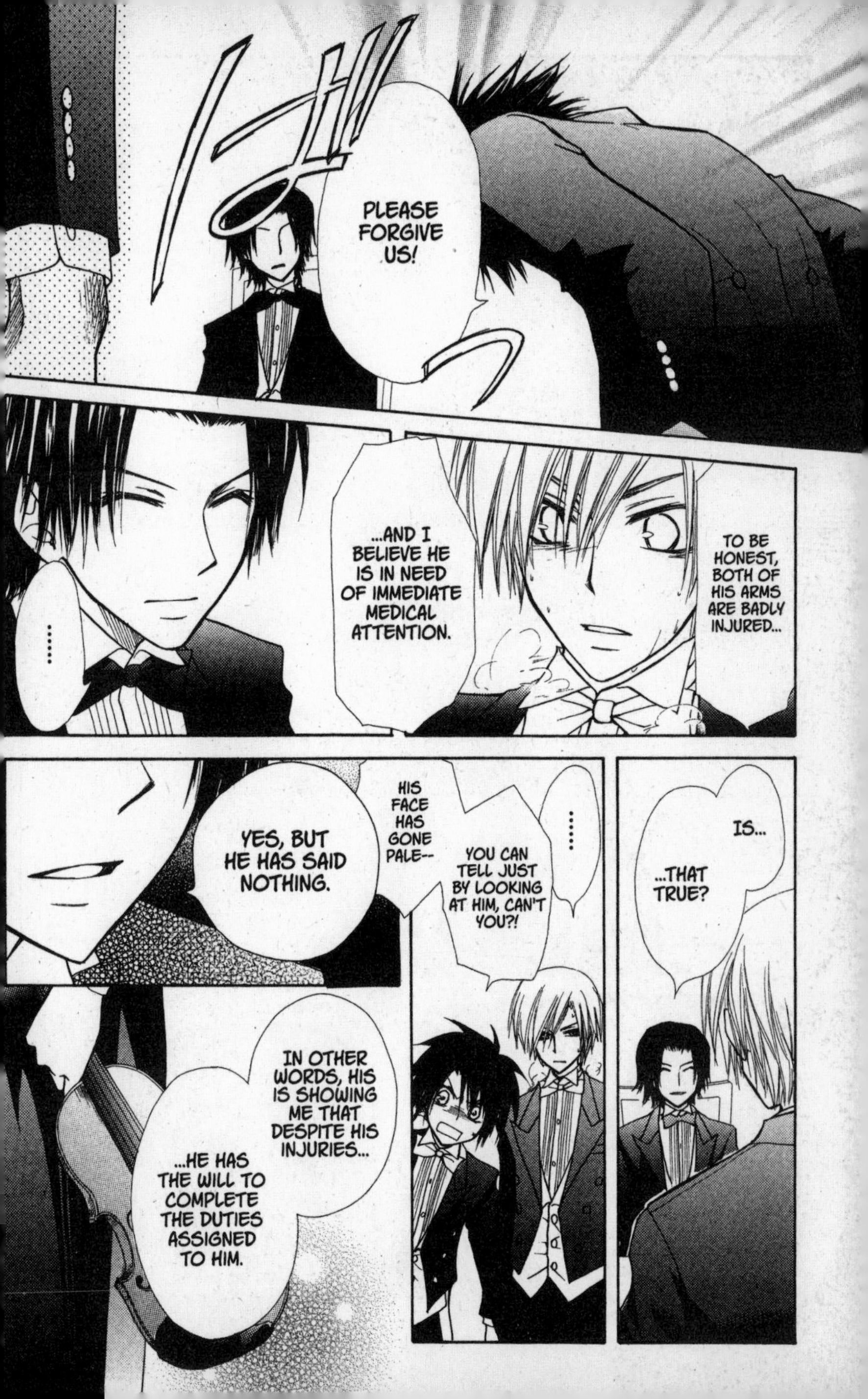
PLEASE FORGIVE US!
TO BE HONEST, BOTH OF HIS ARMS ARE BADLY INJURED...
...AND I BELIEVE HE IS IN NEED OF IMMEDIATE MEDICAL ATTENTION.
......
IS...
...THAT TRUE?
......
YOU CAN TELL JUST BY LOOKING AT HIM, CAN'T YOU?!
HIS FACE HAS GONE PALE--
YES, BUT HE HAS SAID NOTHING.
IN OTHER WORDS, HIS IS SHOWING ME THAT DESPITE HIS INJURIES...
...HE HAS THE WILL TO COMPLETE THE DUTIES ASSIGNED TO HIM.

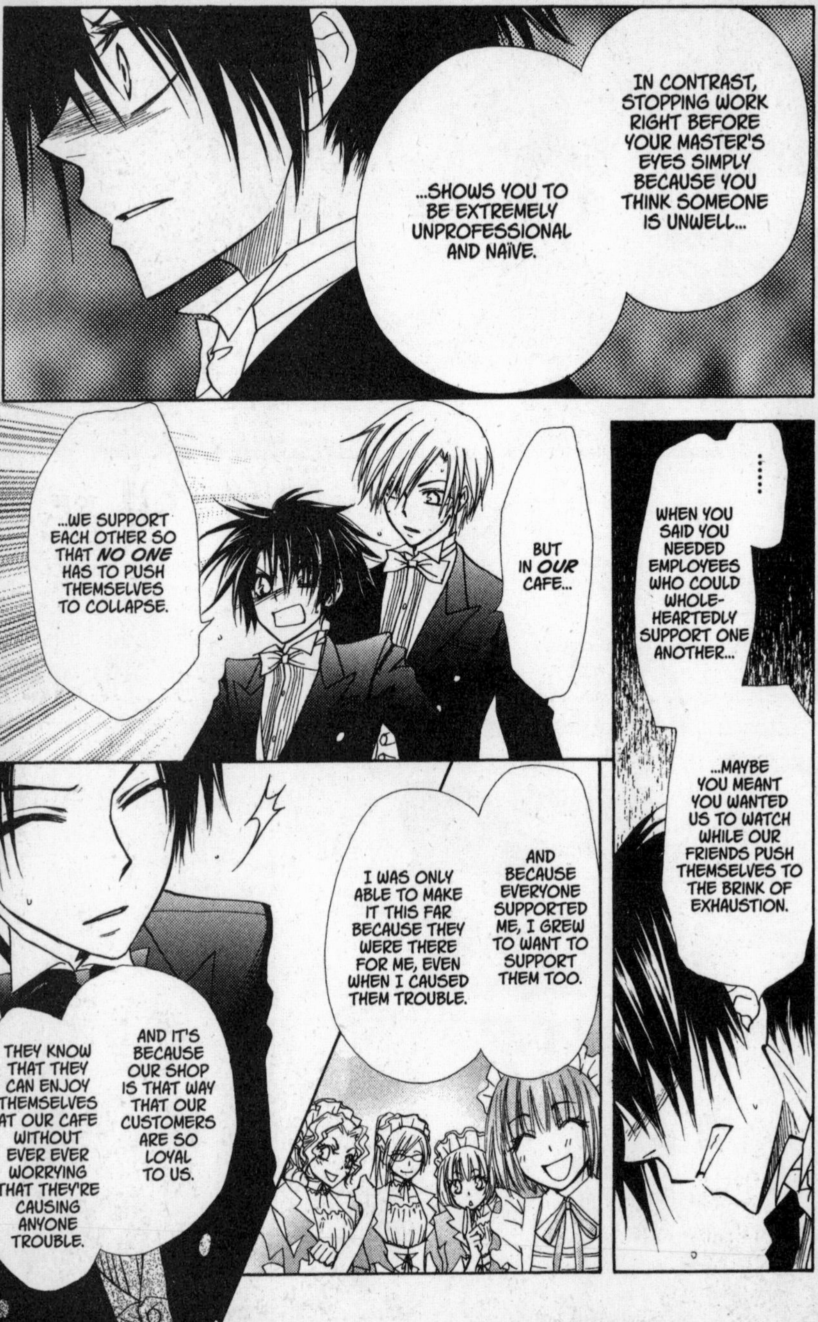
IN CONTRAST, STOPPING WORK RIGHT BEFORE YOUR MASTER'S EYES SIMPLY BECAUSE YOU THINK SOMEONE IS UNWELL...
...SHOWS YOU TO BE EXTREMELY UNPROFESSIONAL AND NAÏVE.
......
WHEN YOU SAID YOU NEEDED EMPLOYEES WHO COULD WHOLE-HEARTEDLY SUPPORT ONE ANOTHER...
...MAYBE YOU MEANT YOU WANTED US TO WATCH WHILE OUR FRIENDS PUSH THEMSELVES TO THE BRINK OF EXHAUSTION.
BUT IN *OUR* CAFE...
...WE SUPPORT EACH OTHER SO THAT *NO ONE* HAS TO PUSH THEMSELVES TO COLLAPSE.
AND BECAUSE EVERYONE SUPPORTED ME, I GREW TO WANT TO SUPPORT THEM TOO.
I WAS ONLY ABLE TO MAKE IT THIS FAR BECAUSE THEY WERE THERE FOR ME, EVEN WHEN I CAUSED THEM TROUBLE.
AND IT'S BECAUSE OUR SHOP IS THAT WAY THAT OUR CUSTOMERS ARE SO LOYAL TO US.
THEY KNOW THAT THEY CAN ENJOY THEMSELVES AT OUR CAFE WITHOUT EVER EVER WORRYING THAT THEY'RE CAUSING ANYONE TROUBLE.

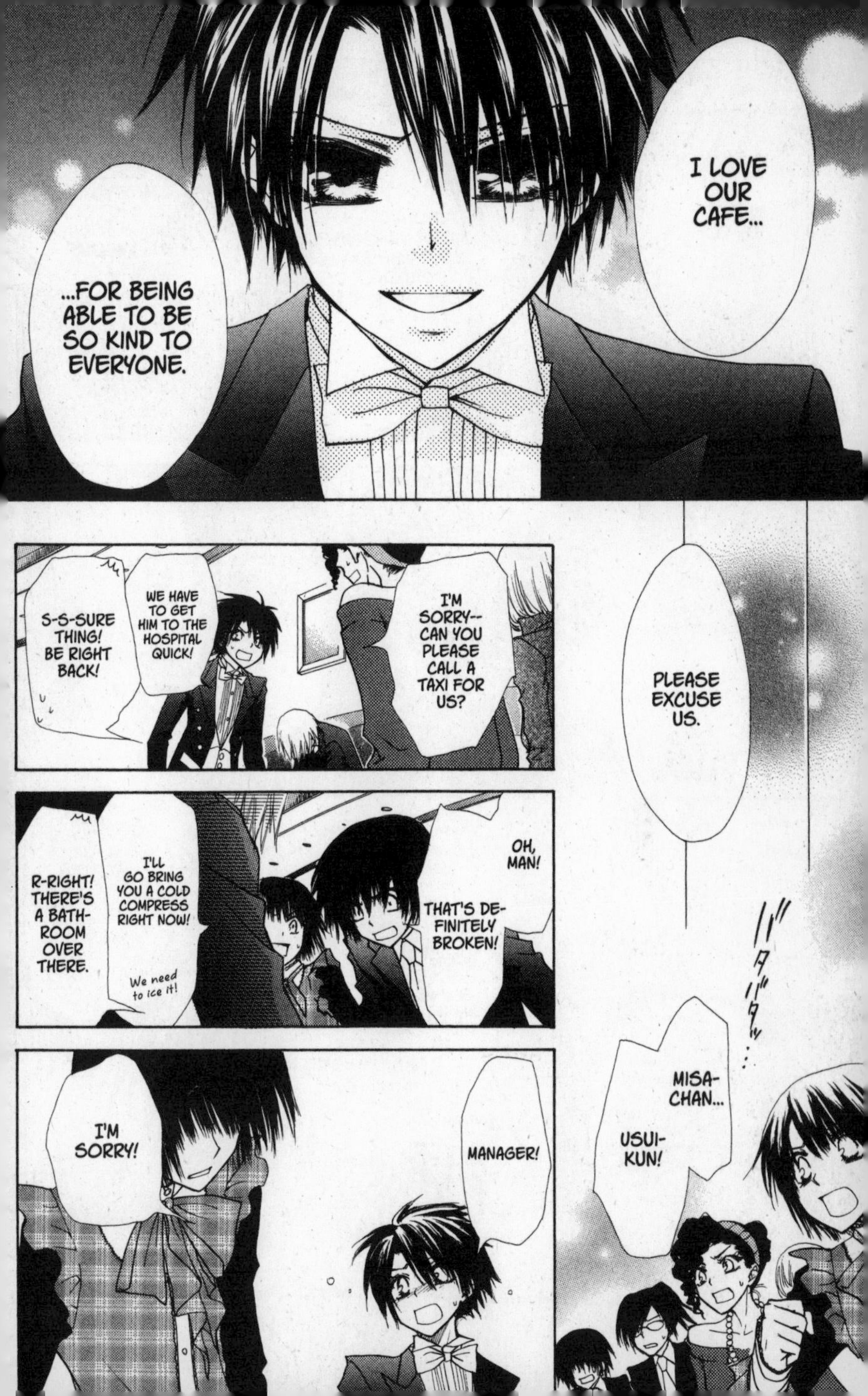
I LOVE OUR CAFE...
...FOR BEING ABLE TO BE SO KIND TO EVERYONE.
PLEASE EXCUSE US.
バタバタ…
MISA-CHAN...
USUI-KUN!
I'M SORRY-- CAN YOU PLEASE CALL A TAXI FOR US?
WE HAVE TO GET HIM TO THE HOSPITAL QUICK!
S-S-SURE THING! BE RIGHT BACK!
OH, MAN!
THAT'S DEFINITELY BROKEN!
I'LL GO BRING YOU A COLD COMPRESS RIGHT NOW!
We need to ice it!
R-RIGHT! THERE'S A BATHROOM OVER THERE.
MANAGER!
I'M SORRY!

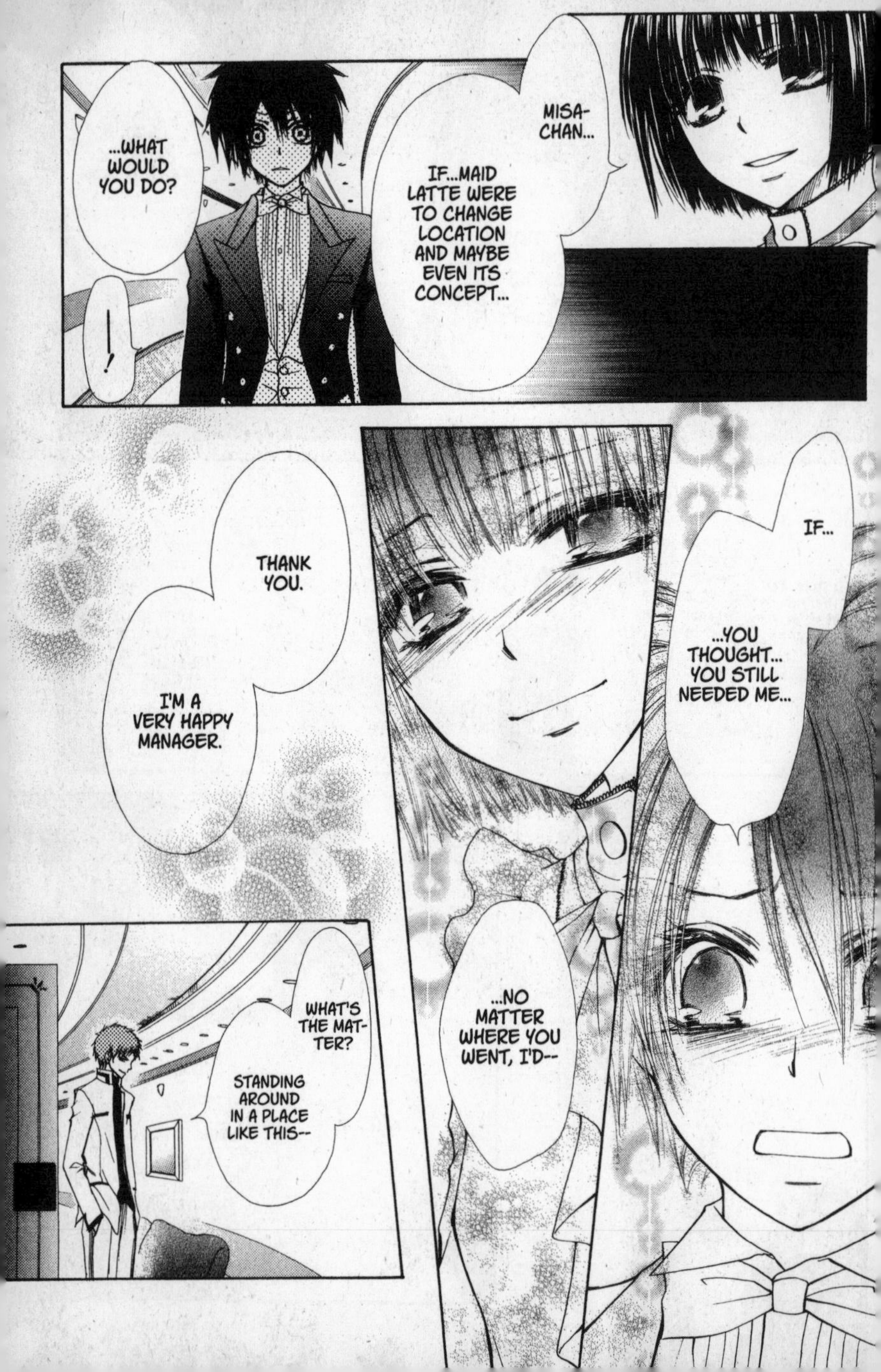
MISA-CHAN...
IF...MAID LATTE WERE TO CHANGE LOCATION AND MAYBE EVEN ITS CONCEPT...
...WHAT WOULD YOU DO?
!
IF...
...YOU THOUGHT... YOU STILL NEEDED ME...
...NO MATTER WHERE YOU WENT, I'D--
THANK YOU.
I'M A VERY HAPPY MANAGER.
WHAT'S THE MATTER?
STANDING AROUND IN A PLACE LIKE THIS--

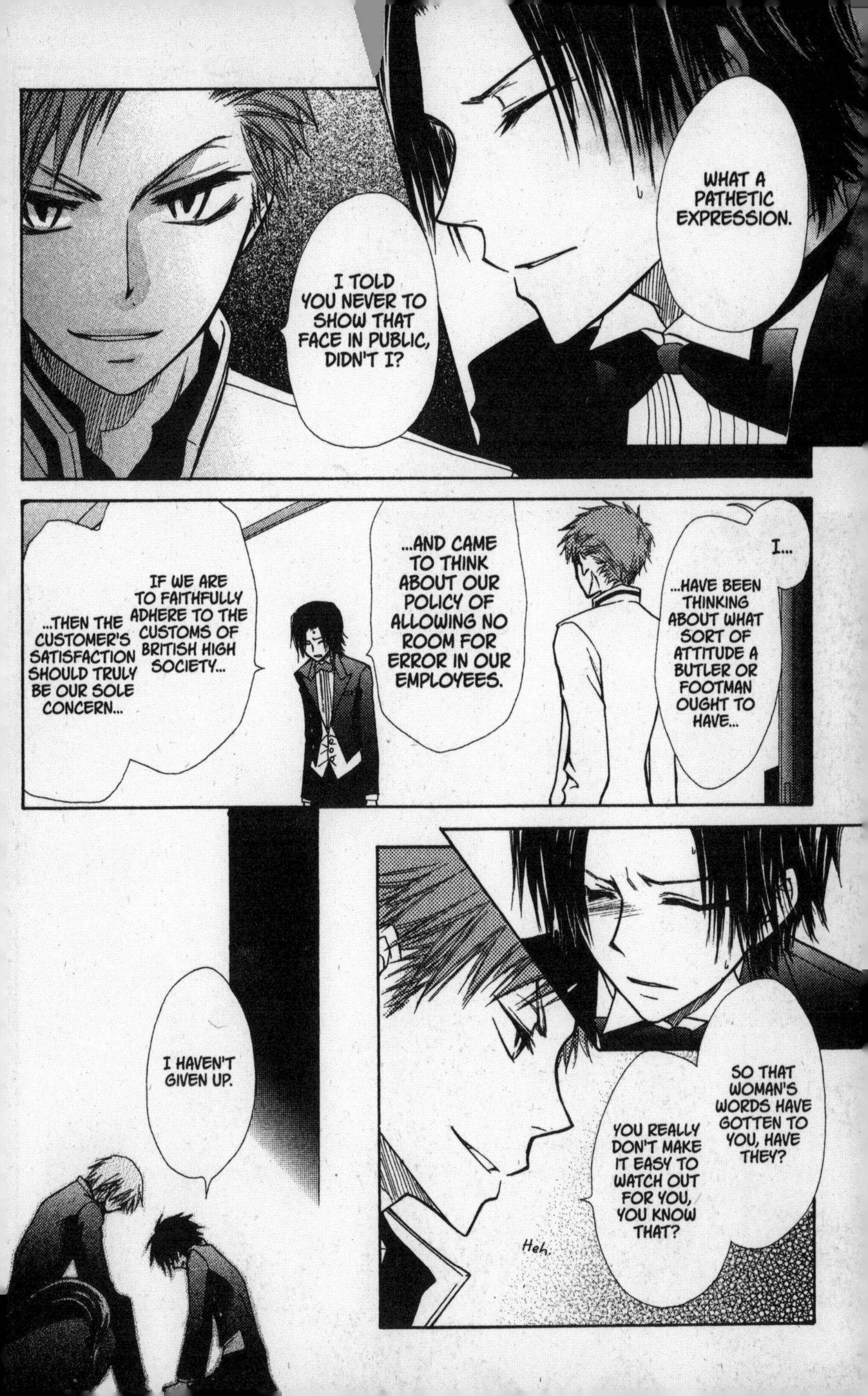
WHAT A PATHETIC EXPRESSION.
I TOLD YOU NEVER TO SHOW THAT FACE IN PUBLIC, DIDN'T I?
I...
...HAVE BEEN THINKING ABOUT WHAT SORT OF ATTITUDE A BUTLER OR FOOTMAN OUGHT TO HAVE...
...AND CAME TO THINK ABOUT OUR POLICY OF ALLOWING NO ROOM FOR ERROR IN OUR EMPLOYEES.
IF WE ARE TO FAITHFULLY ADHERE TO THE CUSTOMS OF BRITISH HIGH SOCIETY...
...THEN THE CUSTOMER'S SATISFACTION SHOULD TRULY BE OUR SOLE CONCERN...
SO THAT WOMAN'S WORDS HAVE GOTTEN TO YOU, HAVE THEY?
YOU REALLY DON'T MAKE IT EASY TO WATCH OUT FOR YOU, YOU KNOW THAT?
Heh.
I HAVEN'T GIVEN UP.

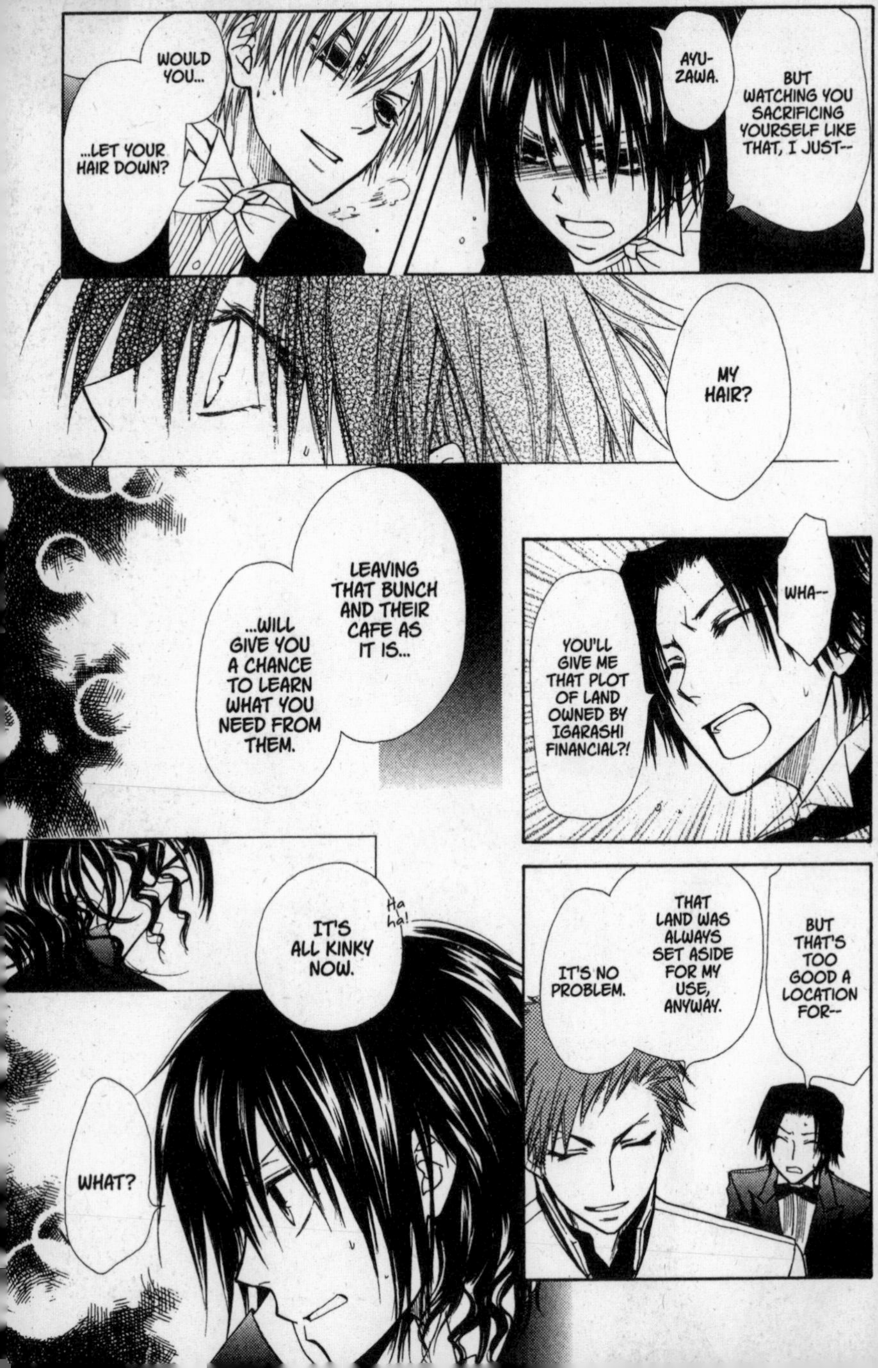
AYU-ZAWA.
BUT WATCHING YOU SACRIFICING YOURSELF LIKE THAT, I JUST--
WOULD YOU...
...LET YOUR HAIR DOWN?
MY HAIR?
WHA--
YOU'LL GIVE ME THAT PLOT OF LAND OWNED BY IGARASHI FINANCIAL?!
LEAVING THAT BUNCH AND THEIR CAFE AS IT IS...
...WILL GIVE YOU A CHANCE TO LEARN WHAT YOU NEED FROM THEM.
BUT THAT'S TOO GOOD A LOCATION FOR--
THAT LAND WAS ALWAYS SET ASIDE FOR MY USE, ANYWAY.
IT'S NO PROBLEM.
Ha ha!
IT'S ALL KINKY NOW.
WHAT?

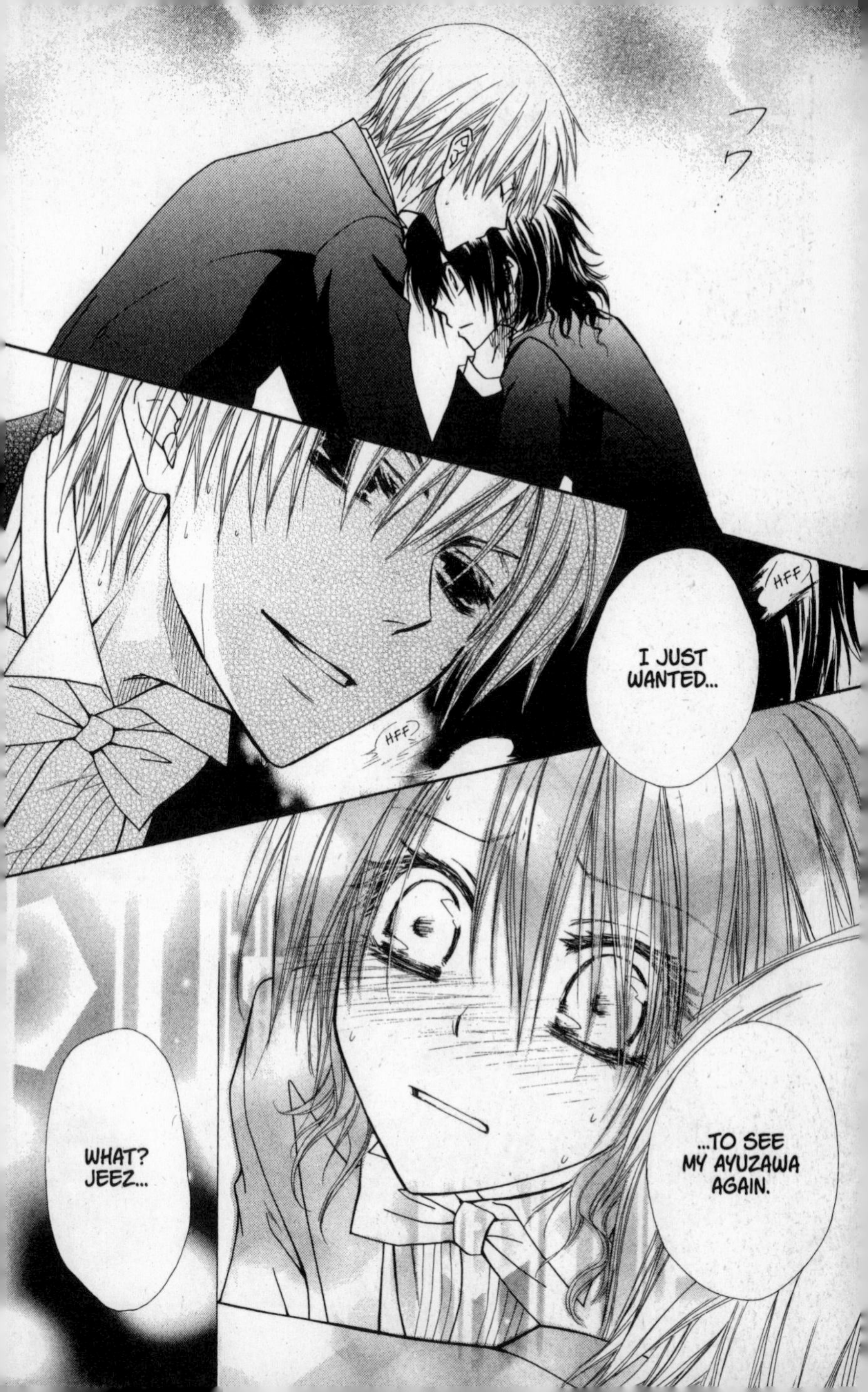

フワ
HFF
I JUST WANTED...
HFF
...TO SEE MY AYUZAWA AGAIN.
WHAT? JEEZ...

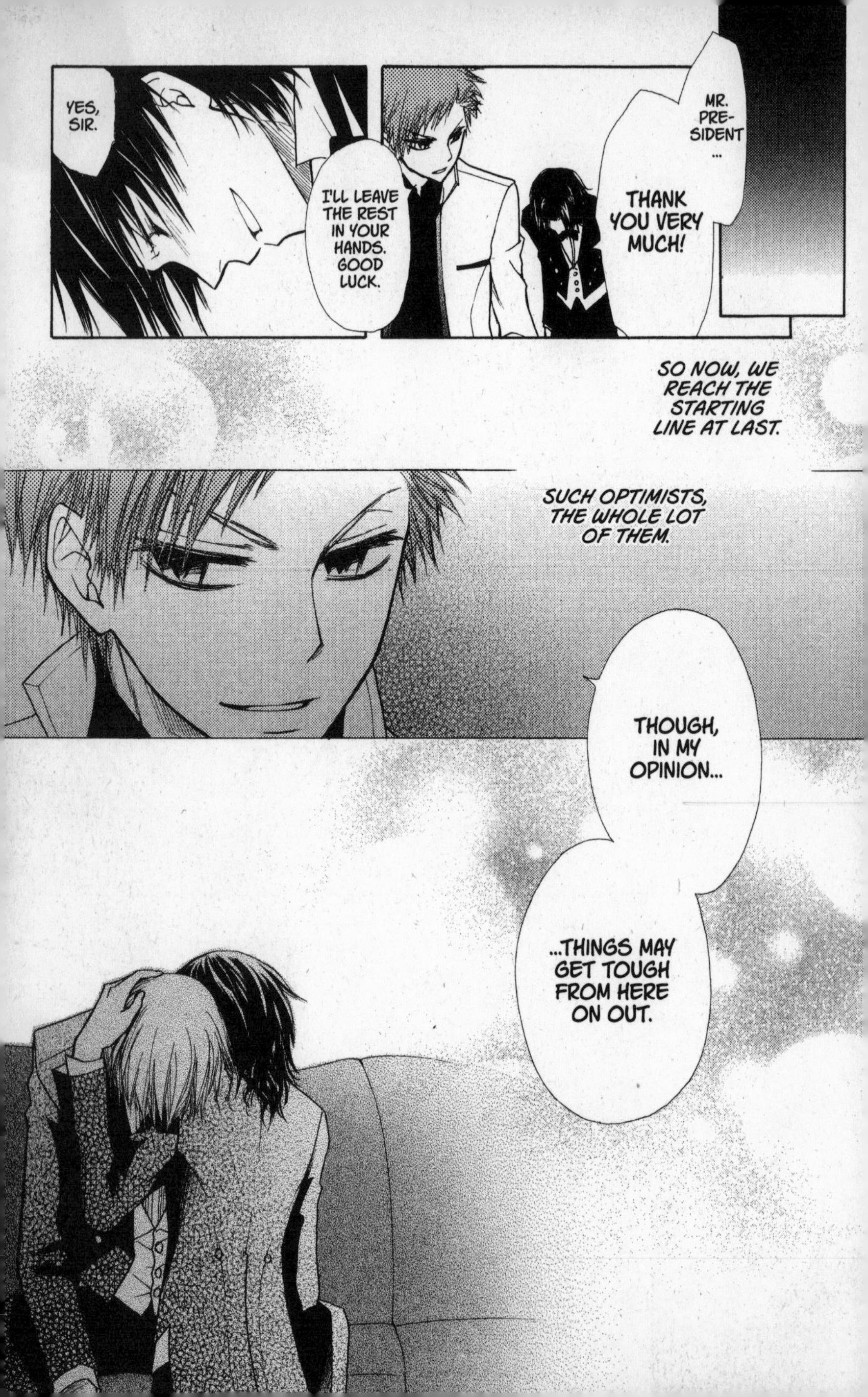
MR. PRE-SIDENT ... THANK YOU VERY MUCH!
I'LL LEAVE THE REST IN YOUR HANDS. GOOD LUCK.
YES, SIR.
SO NOW, WE REACH THE STARTING LINE AT LAST.
SUCH OPTIMISTS, THE WHOLE LOT OF THEM.
THOUGH, IN MY OPINION...
...THINGS MAY GET TOUGH FROM HERE ON OUT.

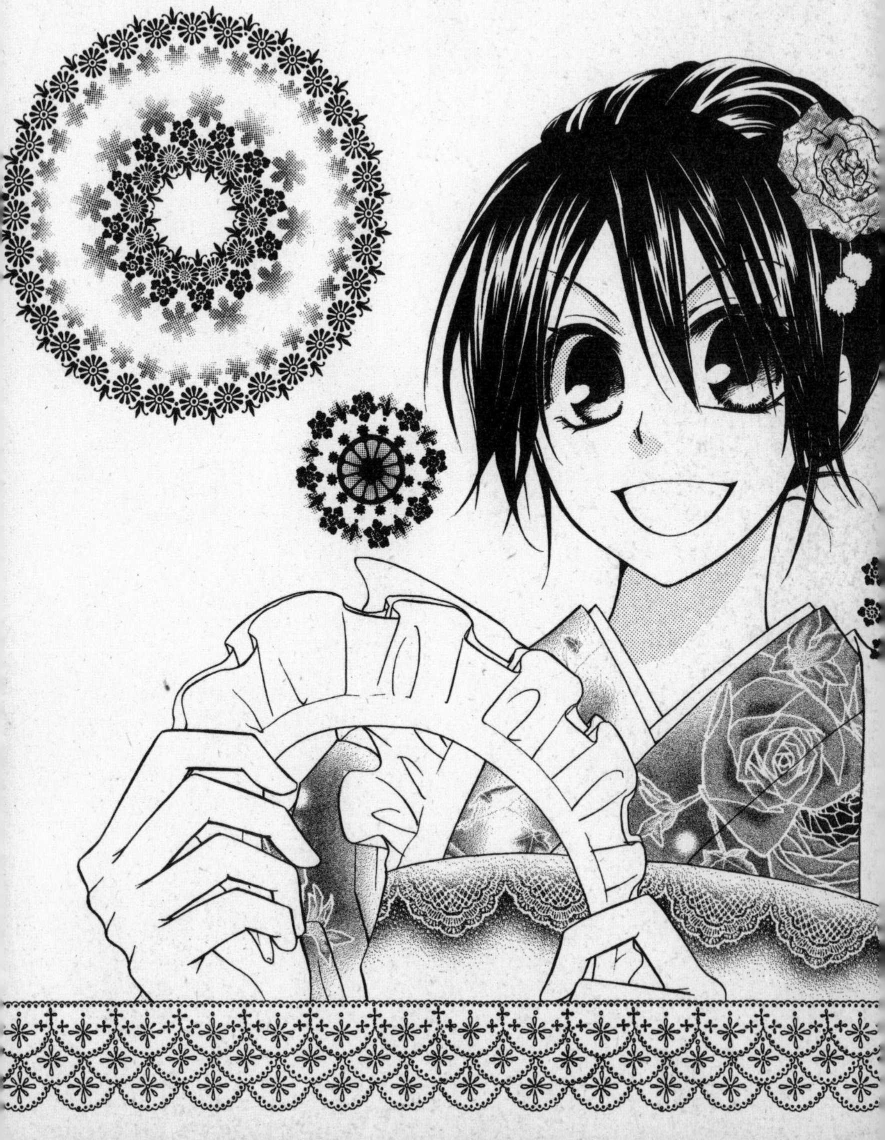

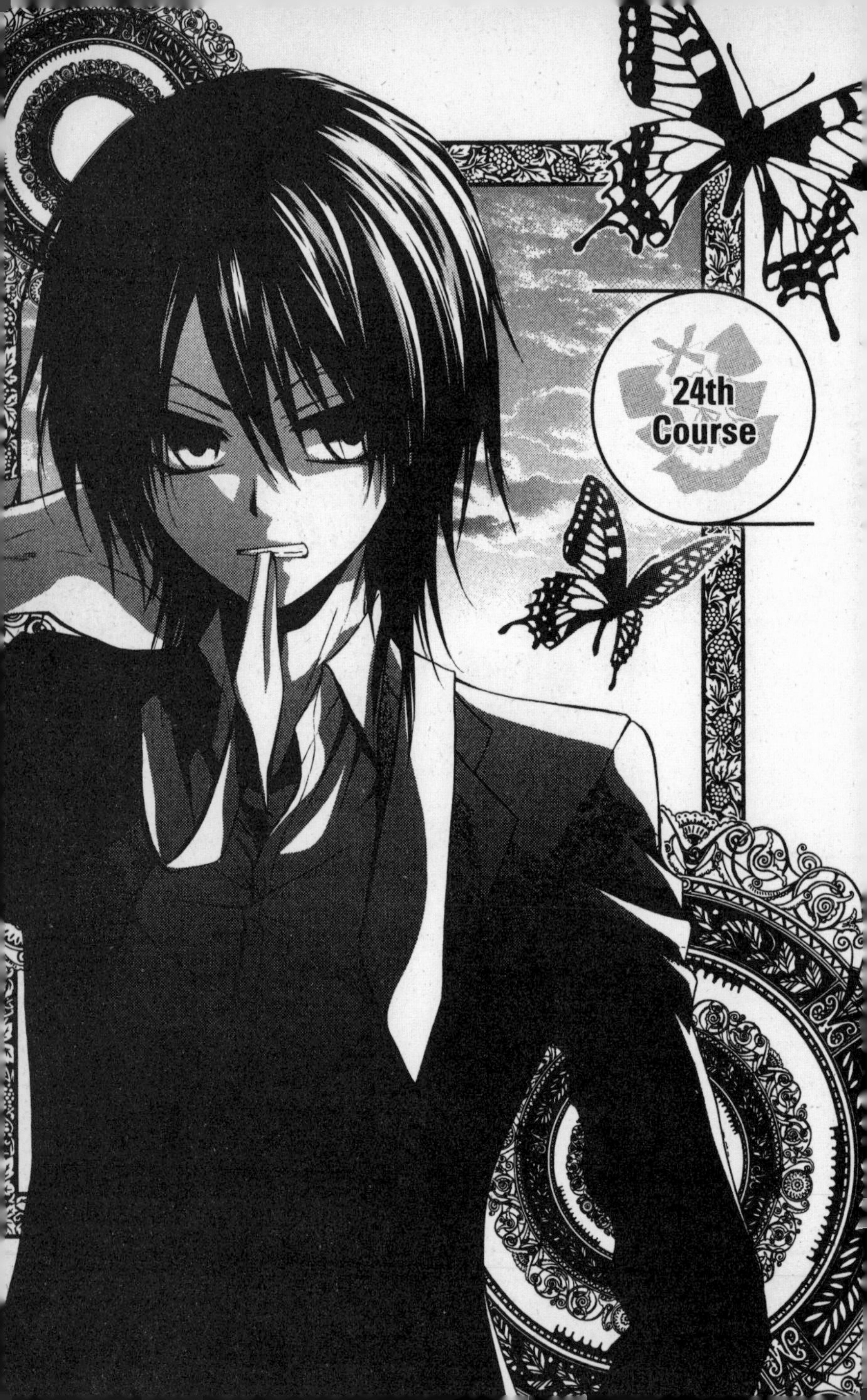
24th
Course

ぱぁあぁあぁあ
IS IT JUST ME, OR DOES THE IDIOT TRIO LOOK EVEN CREEPIER TODAY THAN THEY USUALLY DO?
ぱぁあぁあぁあ
THOUGH SHE'S GOT THE EXACT SAME EXPRESSION!!
IT'S HARDLY SURPRI-SING, AOI-CHAN.
AFTER ALL, MAID LATTE HAS JUST OVERCOME ITS BIGGEST CRISIS YET.
YEAH, ABOUT THAT-- CAN YOU EXPLAIN JUST WHAT HAPPENED?

Until we meet again at book's end...

Extraneous Question Corner

Question 5

Q: I really want one of those character key chains. Are you selling them anywhere?

A: Unfortunately not. You could make them yourself though. In fact, please make some of the Idiot Trio. Then attach them to your cell phone and say, "Ugh, the Idiot Trio always gets in my way!" Or say, "These things are so nasty!" while handling them violently. That's a great way to show them your love.

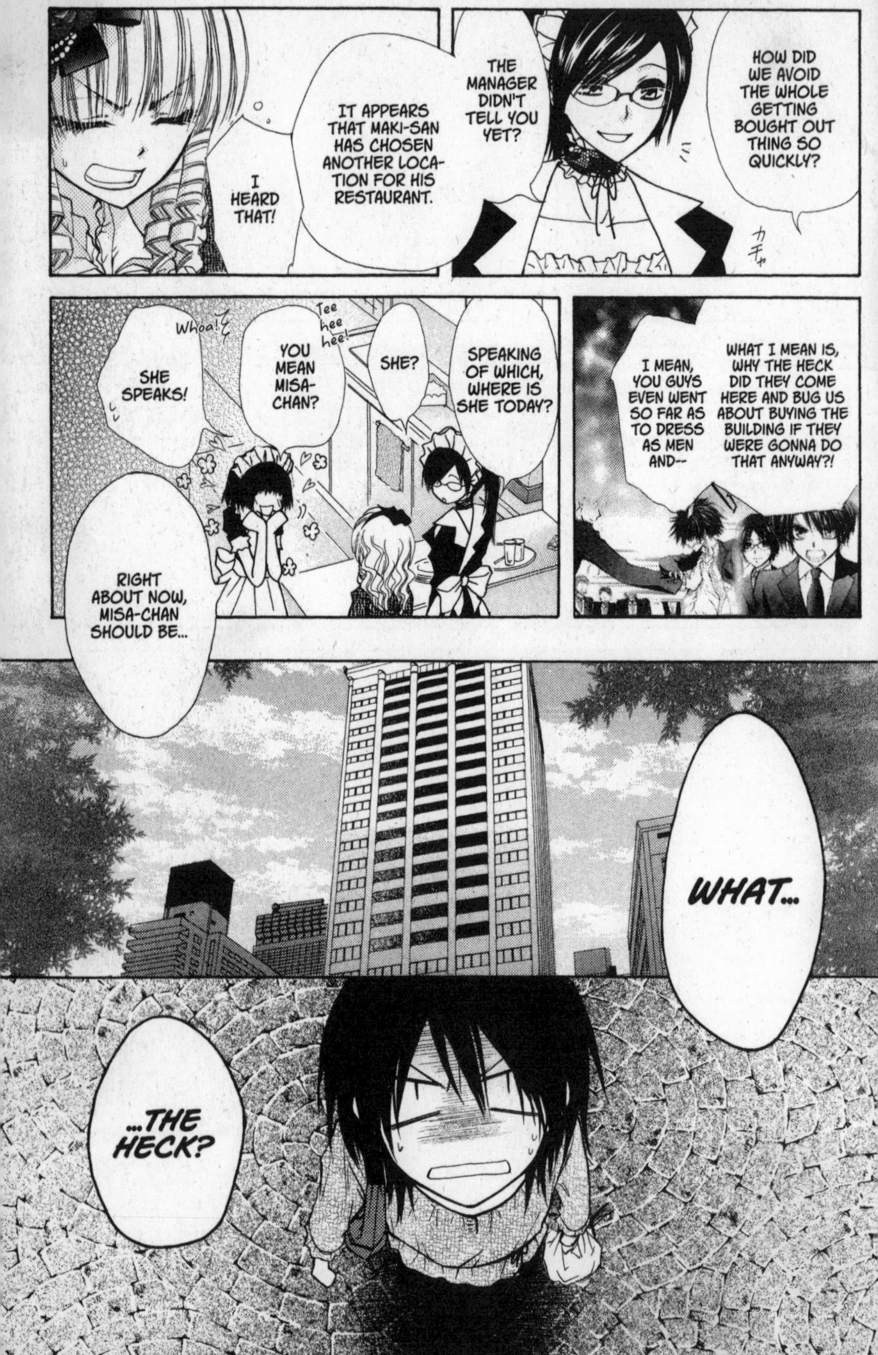
HOW DID WE AVOID THE WHOLE GETTING BOUGHT OUT THING SO QUICKLY?
カチャ
THE MANAGER DIDN'T TELL YOU YET?
IT APPEARS THAT MAKI-SAN HAS CHOSEN ANOTHER LOCA-TION FOR HIS RESTAURANT.
I HEARD THAT!
WHAT I MEAN IS, WHY THE HECK DID THEY COME HERE AND BUG US ABOUT BUYING THE BUILDING IF THEY WERE GONNA DO THAT ANYWAY?!
I MEAN, YOU GUYS EVEN WENT SO FAR AS TO DRESS AS MEN AND--
SPEAKING OF WHICH, WHERE IS SHE TODAY?
SHE?
Tee hee hee!
YOU MEAN MISA-CHAN?
Whoa!
SHE SPEAKS!
RIGHT ABOUT NOW, MISA-CHAN SHOULD BE...
WHAT...
...THE HECK?

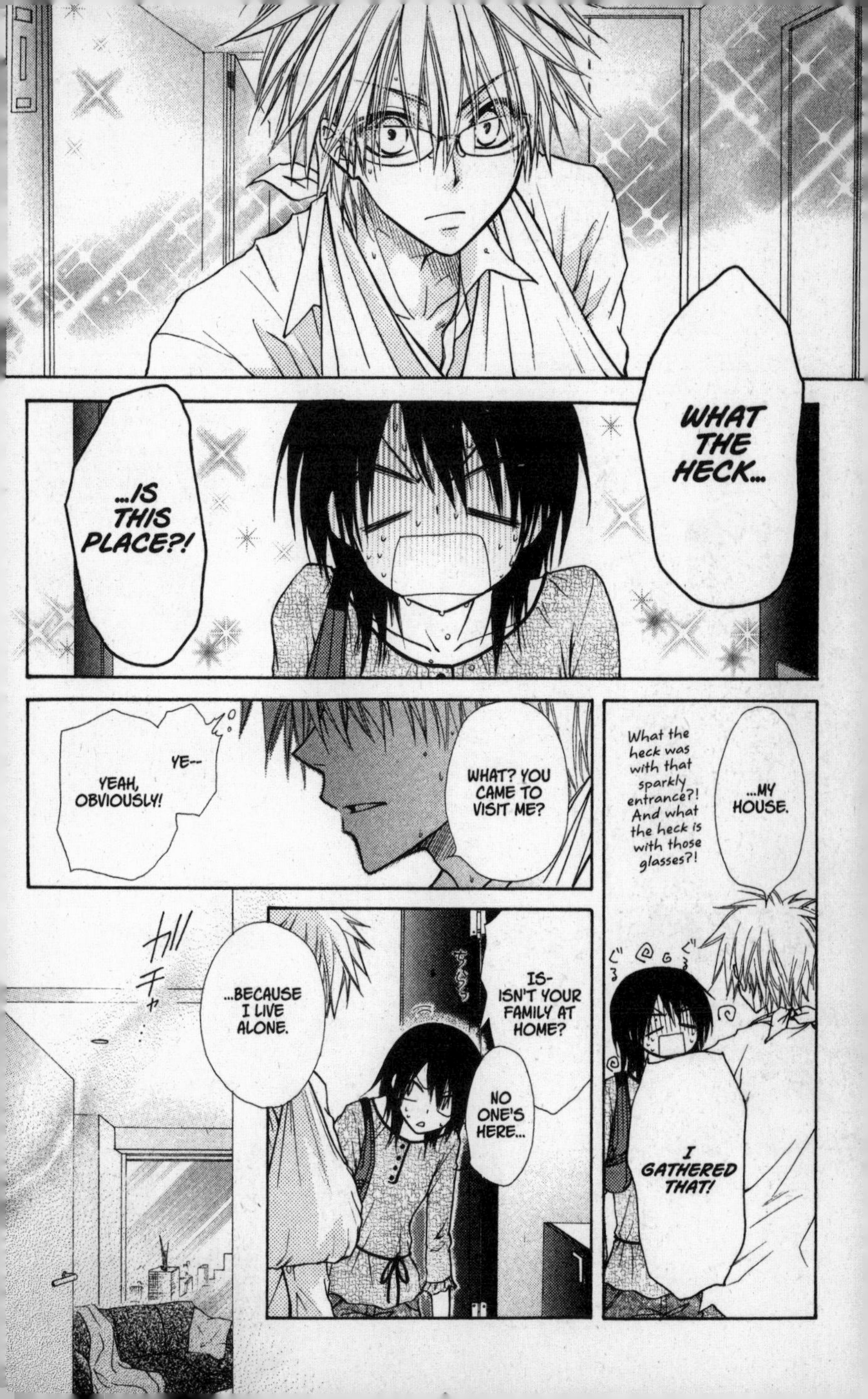
WHAT THE HECK...
...IS THIS PLACE?!
...MY HOUSE.
What the heck was with that sparkly entrance?! And what the heck is with those glasses?!
I GATHERED THAT!
WHAT? YOU CAME TO VISIT ME?
YE-- YEAH, OBVIOUSLY!
IS- ISN'T YOUR FAMILY AT HOME?
NO ONE'S HERE...
...BECAUSE I LIVE ALONE.

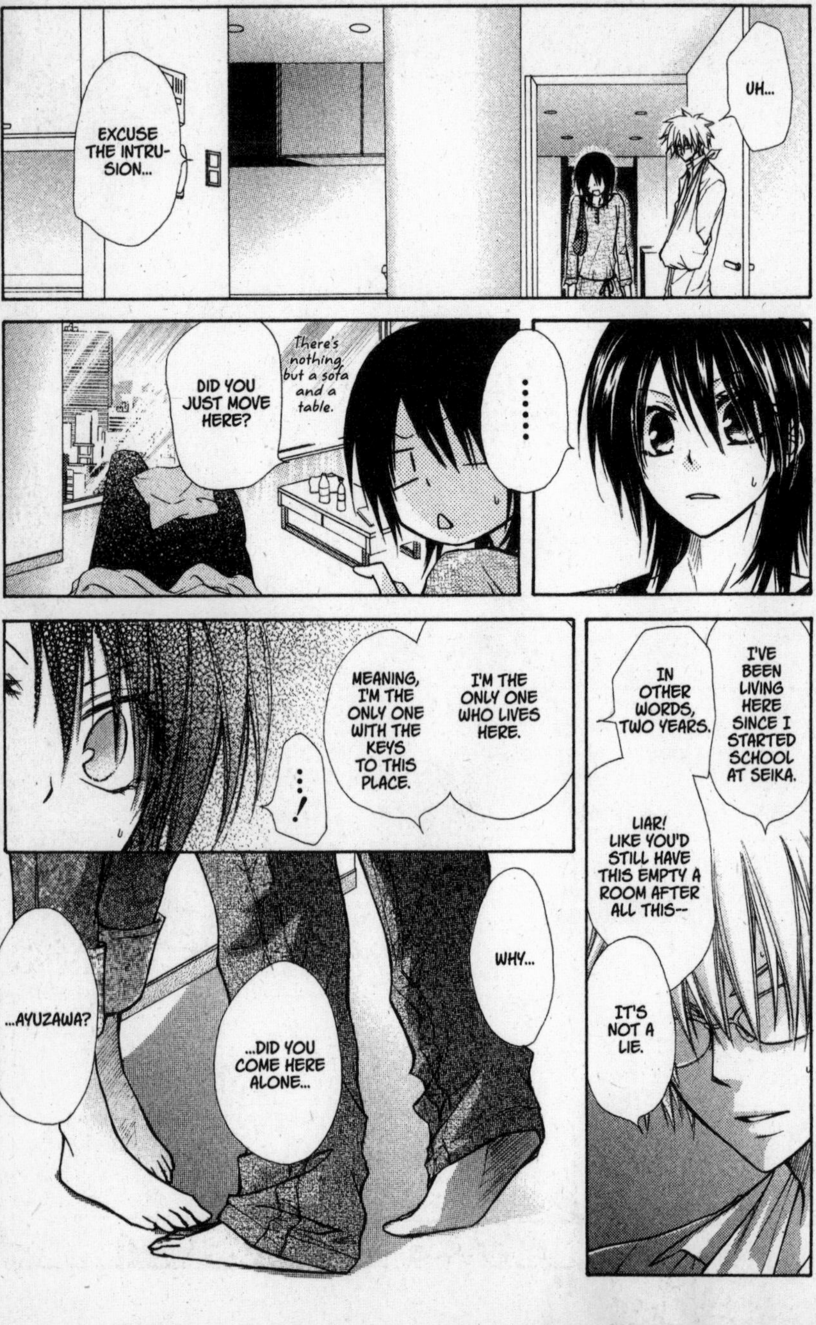
UH...
EXCUSE THE INTRUSION...
......
There's nothing but a sofa and a table.
DID YOU JUST MOVE HERE?
I'VE BEEN LIVING HERE SINCE I STARTED SCHOOL AT SEIKA.
IN OTHER WORDS, TWO YEARS.
LIAR! LIKE YOU'D STILL HAVE THIS EMPTY A ROOM AFTER ALL THIS--
IT'S NOT A LIE.
I'M THE ONLY ONE WHO LIVES HERE.
MEANING, I'M THE ONLY ONE WITH THE KEYS TO THIS PLACE.
...!
WHY...
...DID YOU COME HERE ALONE...
...AYUZAWA?

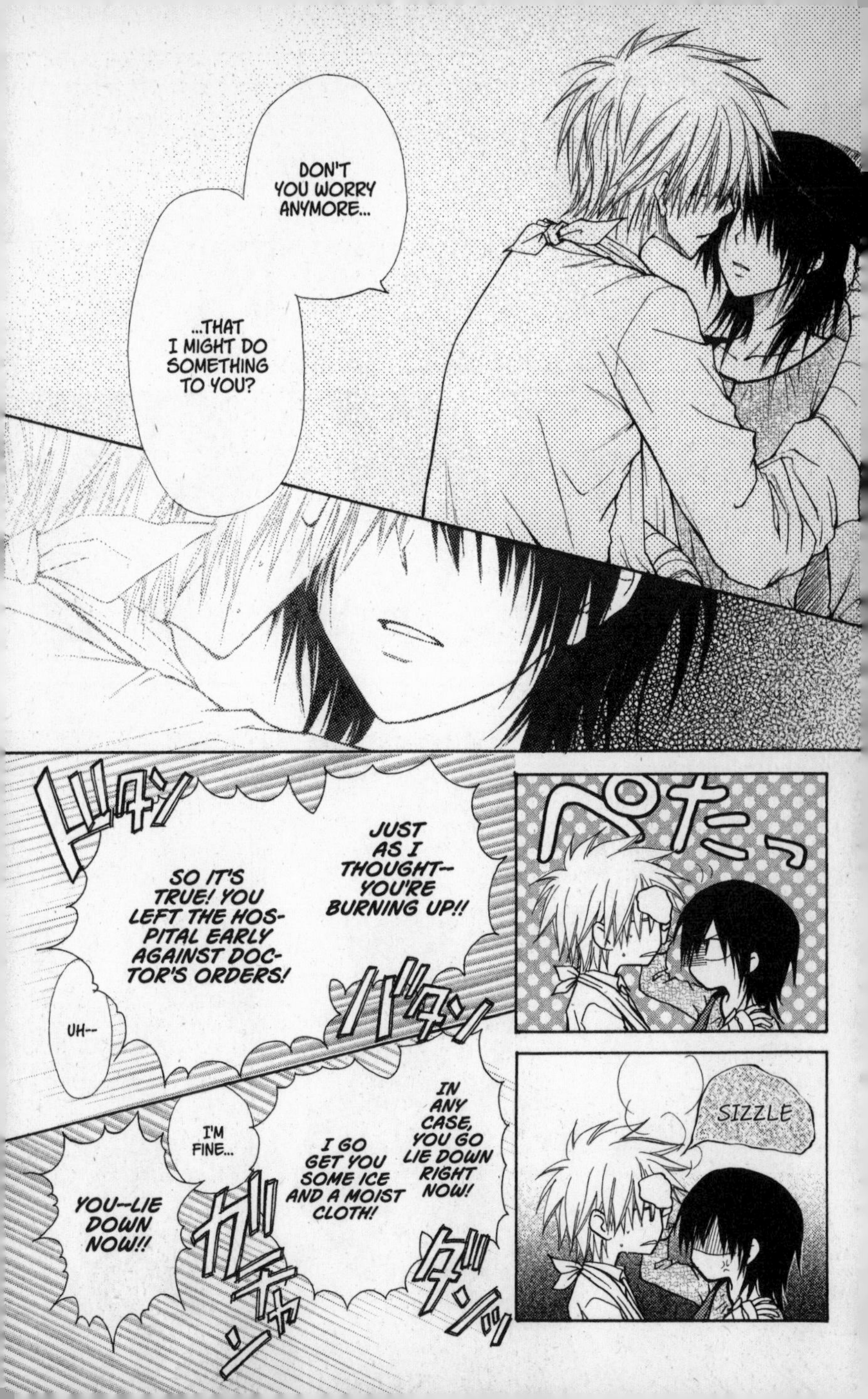
DON'T YOU WORRY ANYMORE...
...THAT I MIGHT DO SOMETHING TO YOU?
ペたーっ
SIZZLE
JUST AS I THOUGHT-- YOU'RE BURNING UP!!
SO IT'S TRUE! YOU LEFT THE HOS-PITAL EARLY AGAINST DOC-TOR'S ORDERS!
ドッタン
UH--
バタン
IN ANY CASE, YOU GO LIE DOWN RIGHT NOW!
I GO GET YOU SOME ICE AND A MOIST CLOTH!
I'M FINE...
YOU--LIE DOWN NOW!!
ダッ
ガチャン

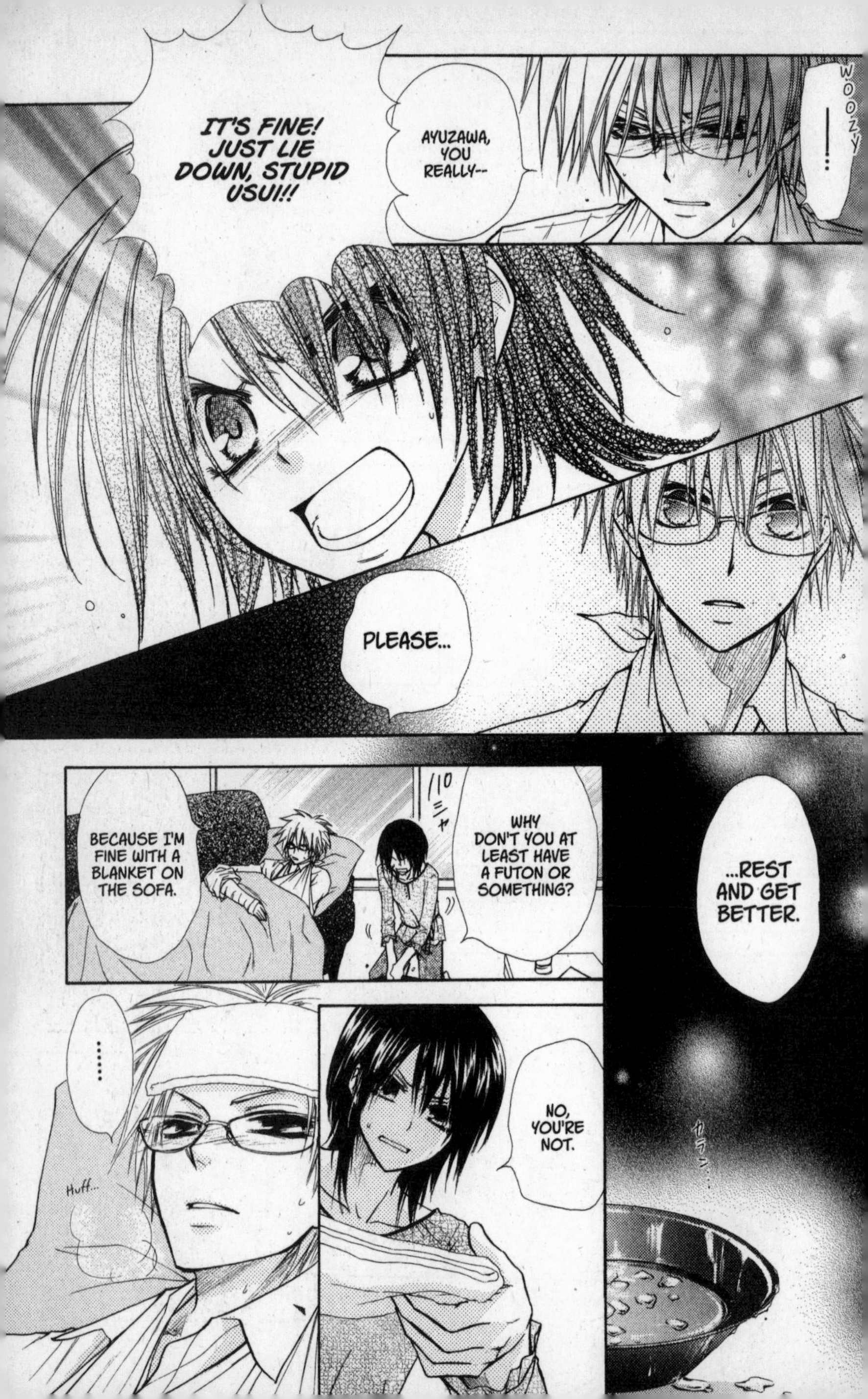
WOOZY
!...
AYUZAWA, YOU REALLY--
IT'S FINE! JUST LIE DOWN, STUPID USUI!!
PLEASE...
...REST AND GET BETTER.
WHY DON'T YOU AT LEAST HAVE A FUTON OR SOMETHING?
BECAUSE I'M FINE WITH A BLANKET ON THE SOFA.
NO, YOU'RE NOT.
......
Huff...

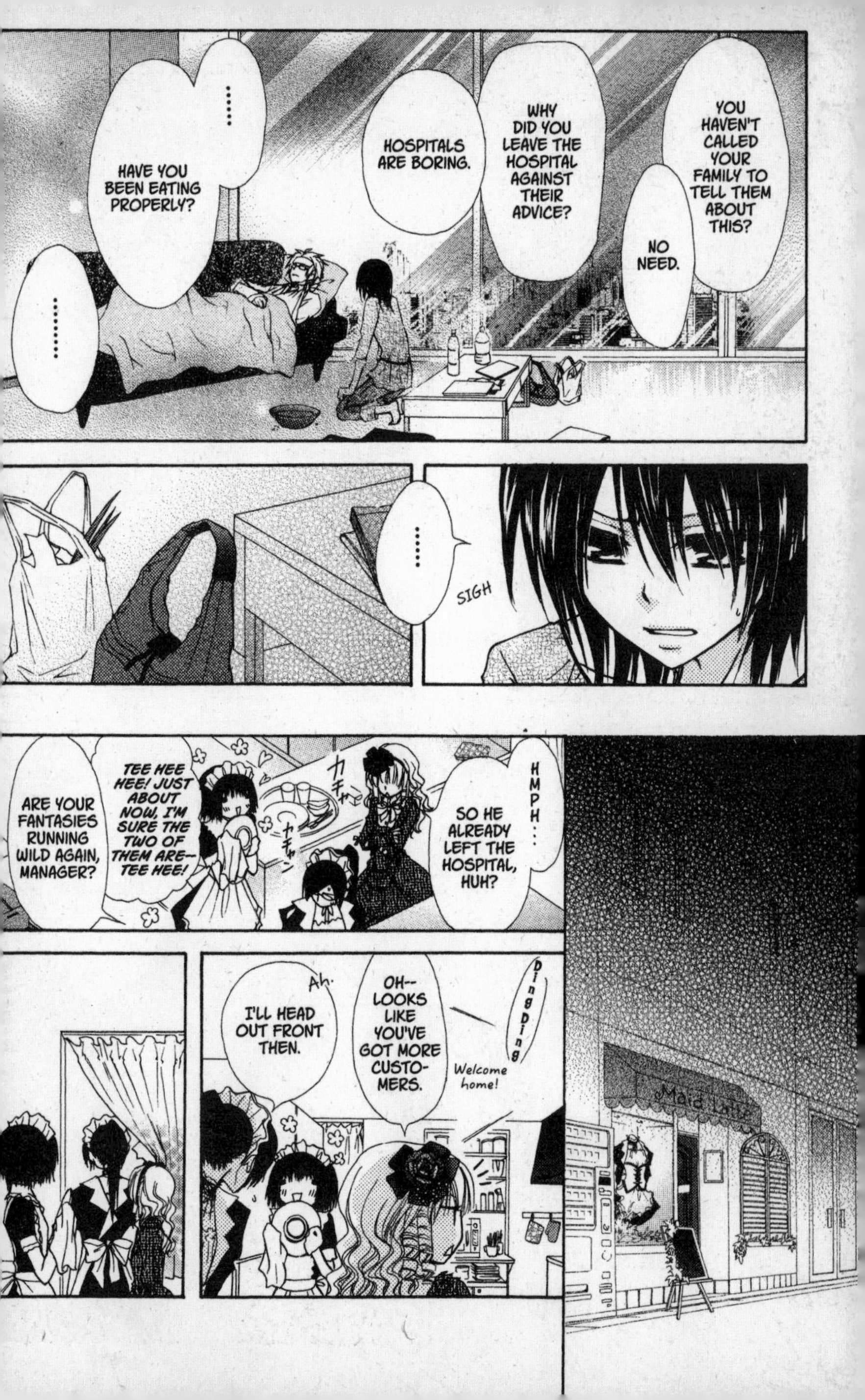
YOU HAVEN'T CALLED YOUR FAMILY TO TELL THEM ABOUT THIS?
NO NEED.
WHY DID YOU LEAVE THE HOSPITAL AGAINST THEIR ADVICE?
HOSPITALS ARE BORING.
......
HAVE YOU BEEN EATING PROPERLY?
....
......
SIGH
Maid Latte
HMPH...
SO HE ALREADY LEFT THE HOSPITAL, HUH?
TEE HEE HEE! JUST ABOUT NOW, I'M SURE THE TWO OF THEM ARE-- TEE HEE!
ARE YOUR FANTASIES RUNNING WILD AGAIN, MANAGER?
Ding Ding
Welcome home!
OH-- LOOKS LIKE YOU'VE GOT MORE CUSTOMERS.
Ah.
I'LL HEAD OUT FRONT THEN.

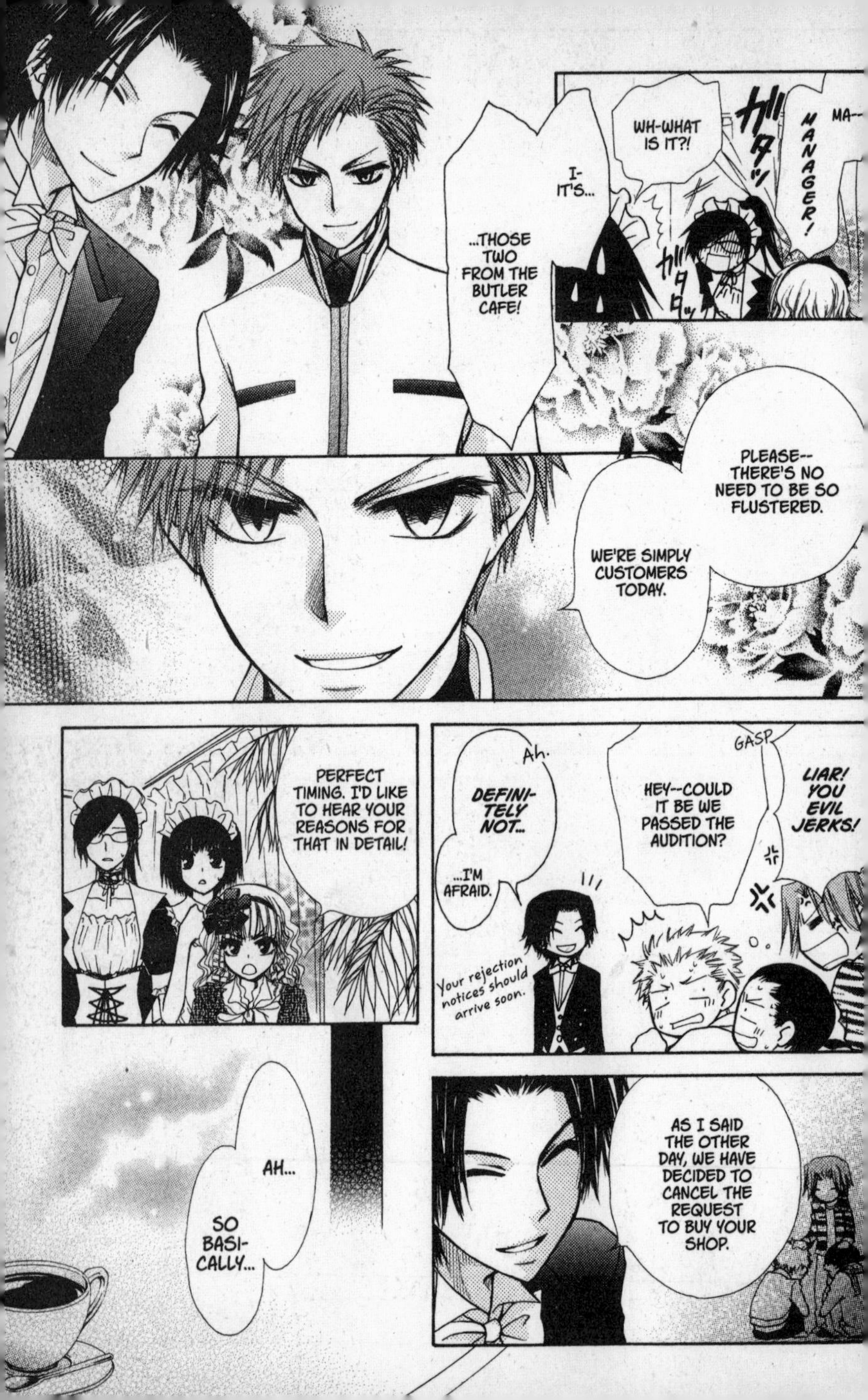
MA-- MANAGER!
ガタッ
WH-WHAT IS IT?!
I- IT'S...
...THOSE TWO FROM THE BUTLER CAFE!
PLEASE-- THERE'S NO NEED TO BE SO FLUSTERED.
WE'RE SIMPLY CUSTOMERS TODAY.
LIAR! YOU EVIL JERKS!
GASP
HEY--COULD IT BE WE PASSED THE AUDITION?
Ah.
DEFINI-TELY NOT...
...I'M AFRAID.
Your rejection notices should arrive soon.
PERFECT TIMING. I'D LIKE TO HEAR YOUR REASONS FOR THAT IN DETAIL!
AS I SAID THE OTHER DAY, WE HAVE DECIDED TO CANCEL THE REQUEST TO BUY YOUR SHOP.
AH...
SO BASI-CALLY...

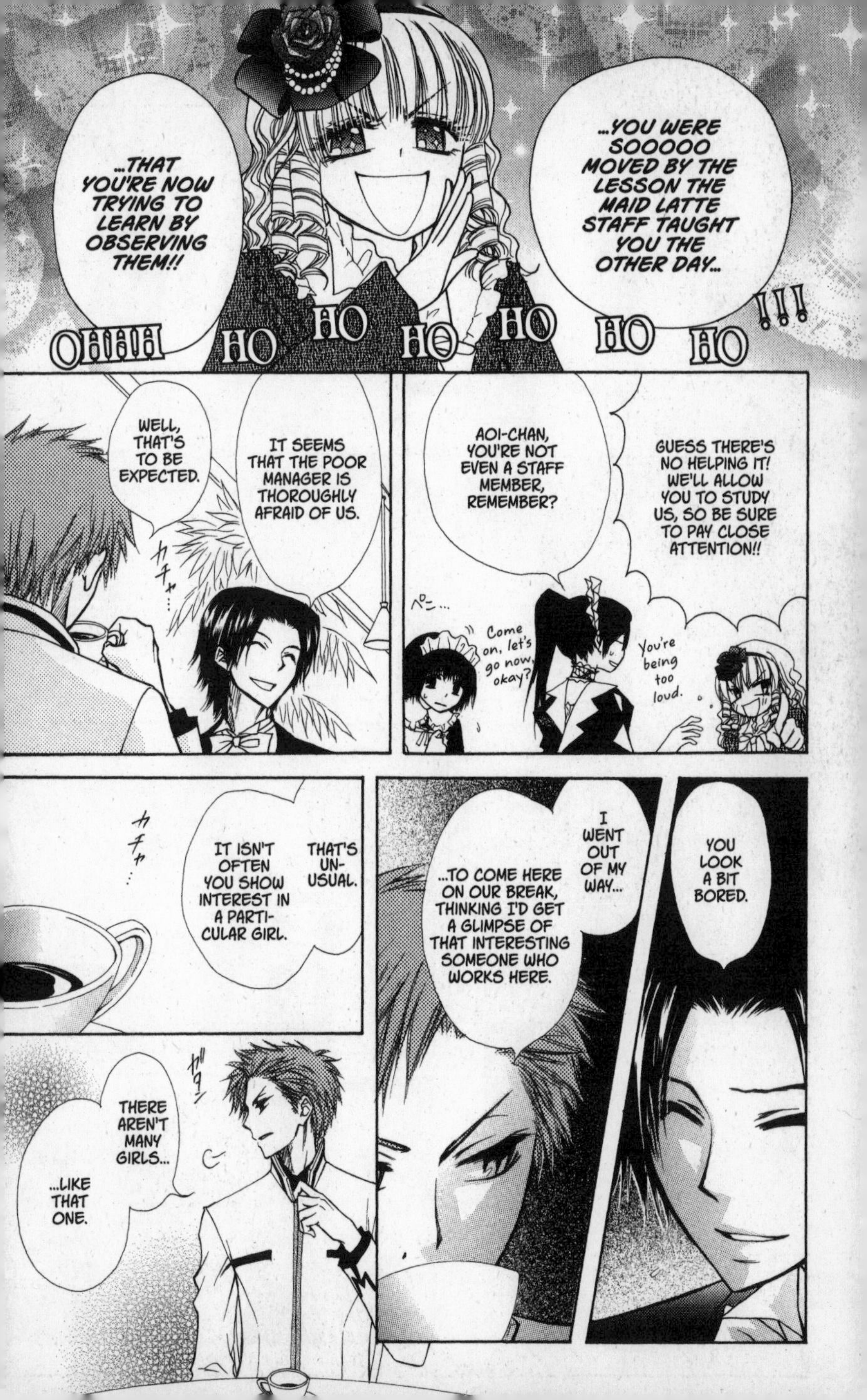
...YOU WERE SOOOOO MOVED BY THE LESSON THE MAID LATTE STAFF TAUGHT YOU THE OTHER DAY...
...THAT YOU'RE NOW TRYING TO LEARN BY OBSERVING THEM!!
OHHH HO HO HO HO HO HO!!!
GUESS THERE'S NO HELPING IT! WE'LL ALLOW YOU TO STUDY US, SO BE SURE TO PAY CLOSE ATTENTION!!
You're being too loud.
AOI-CHAN, YOU'RE NOT EVEN A STAFF MEMBER, REMEMBER?
Come on, let's go now, okay?
ペこ…
IT SEEMS THAT THE POOR MANAGER IS THOROUGHLY AFRAID OF US.
WELL, THAT'S TO BE EXPECTED.
カチャ…
YOU LOOK A BIT BORED.
I WENT OUT OF MY WAY...
...TO COME HERE ON OUR BREAK, THINKING I'D GET A GLIMPSE OF THAT INTERESTING SOMEONE WHO WORKS HERE.
THAT'S UNUSUAL.
IT ISN'T OFTEN YOU SHOW INTEREST IN A PARTICULAR GIRL.
カチャ…
ガタ
THERE AREN'T MANY GIRLS...
...LIKE THAT ONE.

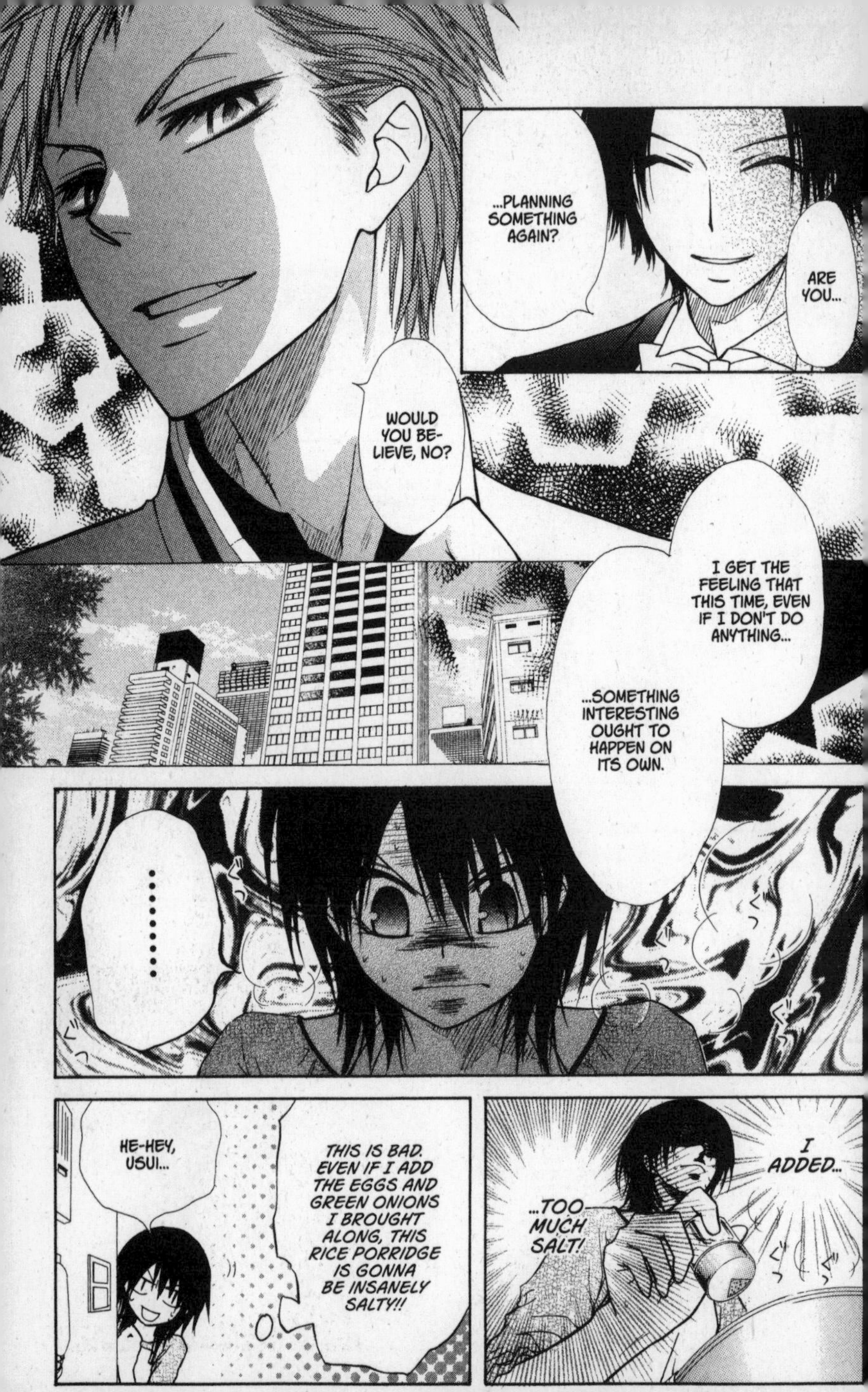
ARE YOU...
...PLANNING SOMETHING AGAIN?
WOULD YOU BE-LIEVE, NO?
I GET THE FEELING THAT THIS TIME, EVEN IF I DON'T DO ANYTHING...
...SOMETHING INTERESTING OUGHT TO HAPPEN ON ITS OWN.
......
I ADDED...
...TOO MUCH SALT!
THIS IS BAD. EVEN IF I ADD THE EGGS AND GREEN ONIONS I BROUGHT ALONG, THIS RICE PORRIDGE IS GONNA BE INSANELY SALTY!!
HE-HEY, USUI...

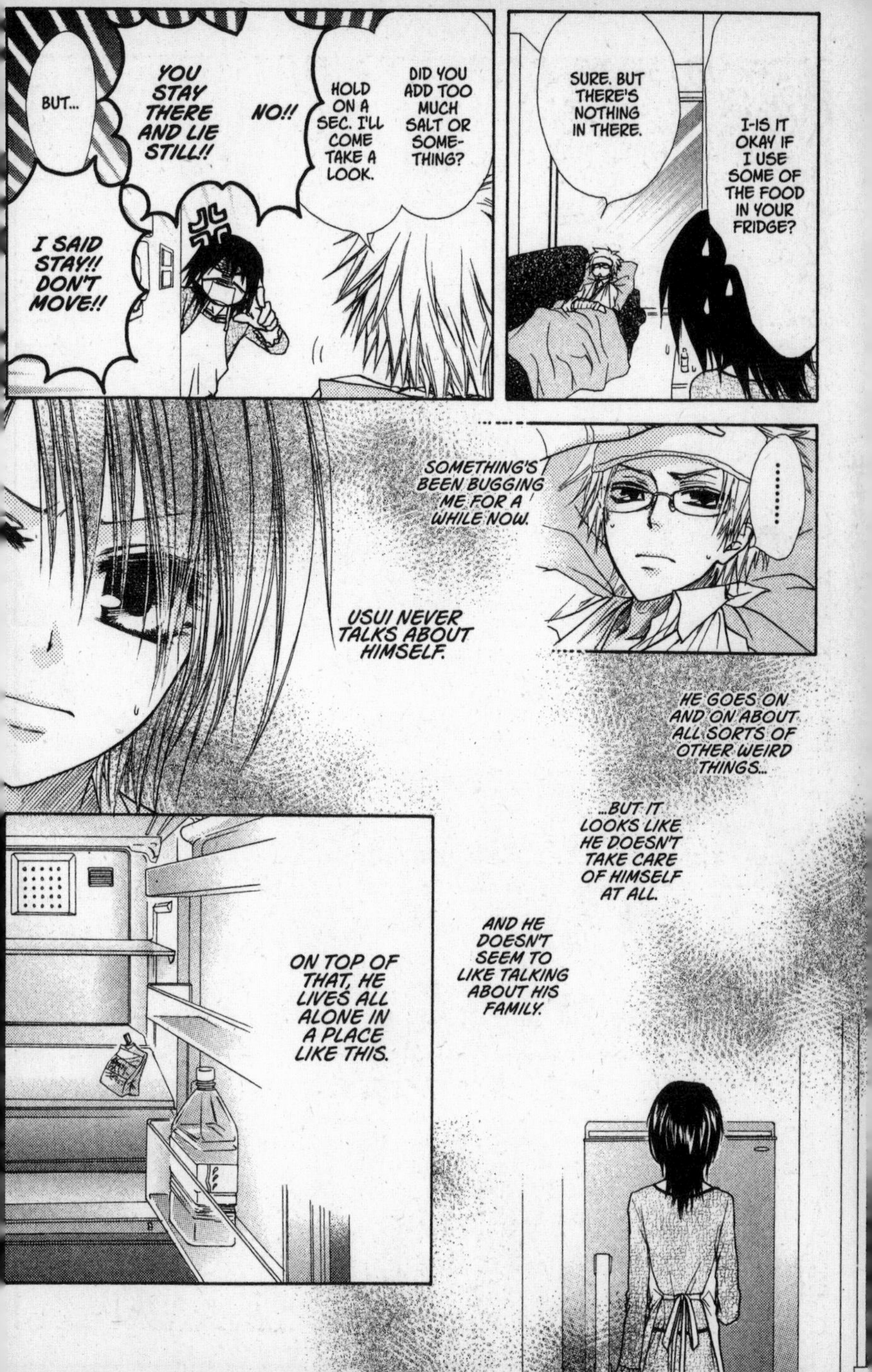
I-IS IT OKAY IF I USE SOME OF THE FOOD IN YOUR FRIDGE?
SURE. BUT THERE'S NOTHING IN THERE.
DID YOU ADD TOO MUCH SALT OR SOME-THING?
HOLD ON A SEC. I'LL COME TAKE A LOOK.
NO!!
YOU STAY THERE AND LIE STILL!!
BUT...
I SAID STAY!! DON'T MOVE!!
......
SOMETHING'S BEEN BUGGING ME FOR A WHILE NOW.
USUI NEVER TALKS ABOUT HIMSELF.
HE GOES ON AND ON ABOUT ALL SORTS OF OTHER WEIRD THINGS...
...BUT IT LOOKS LIKE HE DOESN'T TAKE CARE OF HIMSELF AT ALL.
AND HE DOESN'T SEEM TO LIKE TALKING ABOUT HIS FAMILY.
ON TOP OF THAT, HE LIVES ALL ALONE IN A PLACE LIKE THIS.

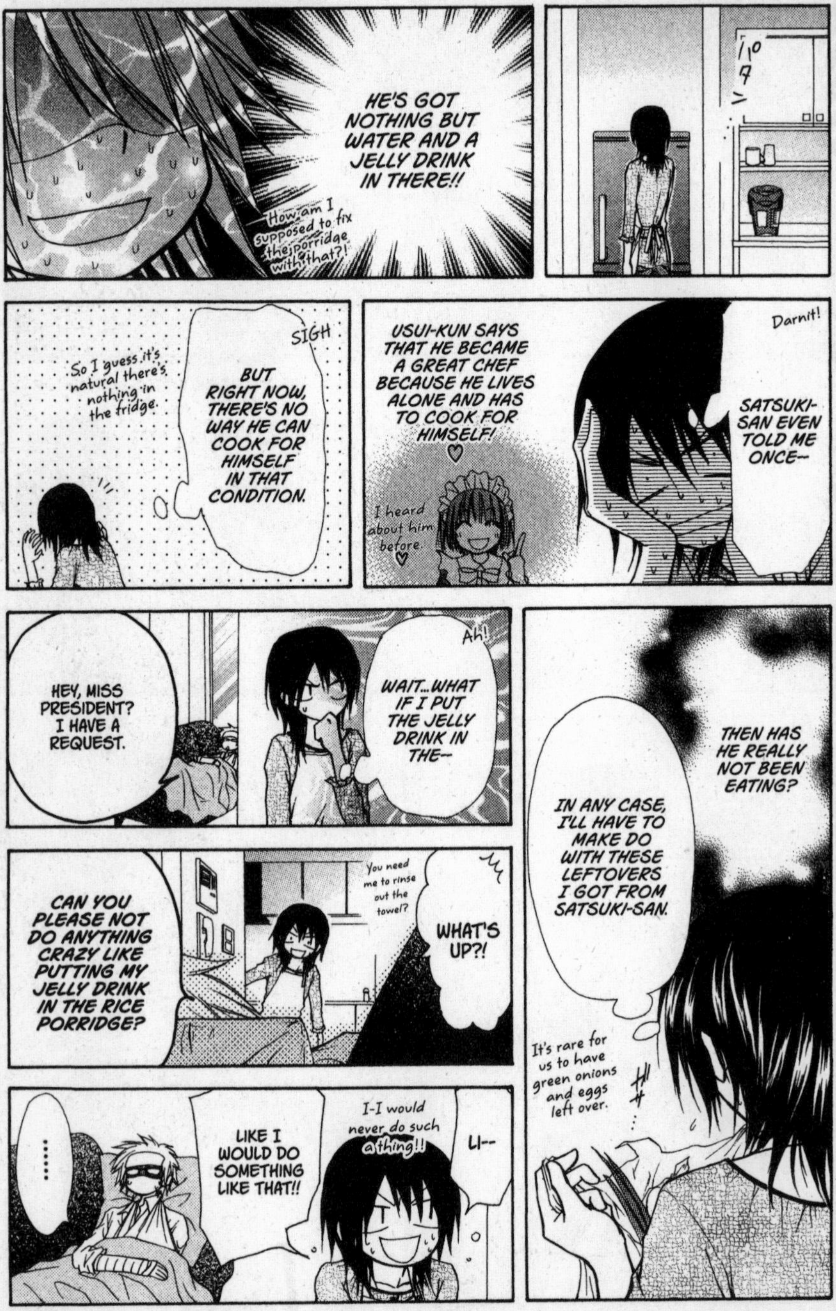
HE'S GOT NOTHING BUT WATER AND A JELLY DRINK IN THERE!!
How am I supposed to fix the porridge with that?!
Darnit!
SATSUKI-SAN EVEN TOLD ME ONCE--
USUI-KUN SAYS THAT HE BECAME A GREAT CHEF BECAUSE HE LIVES ALONE AND HAS TO COOK FOR HIMSELF!
I heard about him before.
SIGH
BUT RIGHT NOW, THERE'S NO WAY HE CAN COOK FOR HIMSELF IN THAT CONDITION.
So I guess it's natural there's nothing in the fridge.
THEN HAS HE REALLY NOT BEEN EATING?
IN ANY CASE, I'LL HAVE TO MAKE DO WITH THESE LEFTOVERS I GOT FROM SATSUKI-SAN.
It's rare for us to have green onions and eggs left over.
Ah!
WAIT...WHAT IF I PUT THE JELLY DRINK IN THE--
HEY, MISS PRESIDENT? I HAVE A REQUEST.
WHAT'S UP?!
You need me to rinse out the towel?
CAN YOU PLEASE NOT DO ANYTHING CRAZY LIKE PUTTING MY JELLY DRINK IN THE RICE PORRIDGE?
LI--
I-I would never do such a thing!!
LIKE I WOULD DO SOMETHING LIKE THAT!!
......

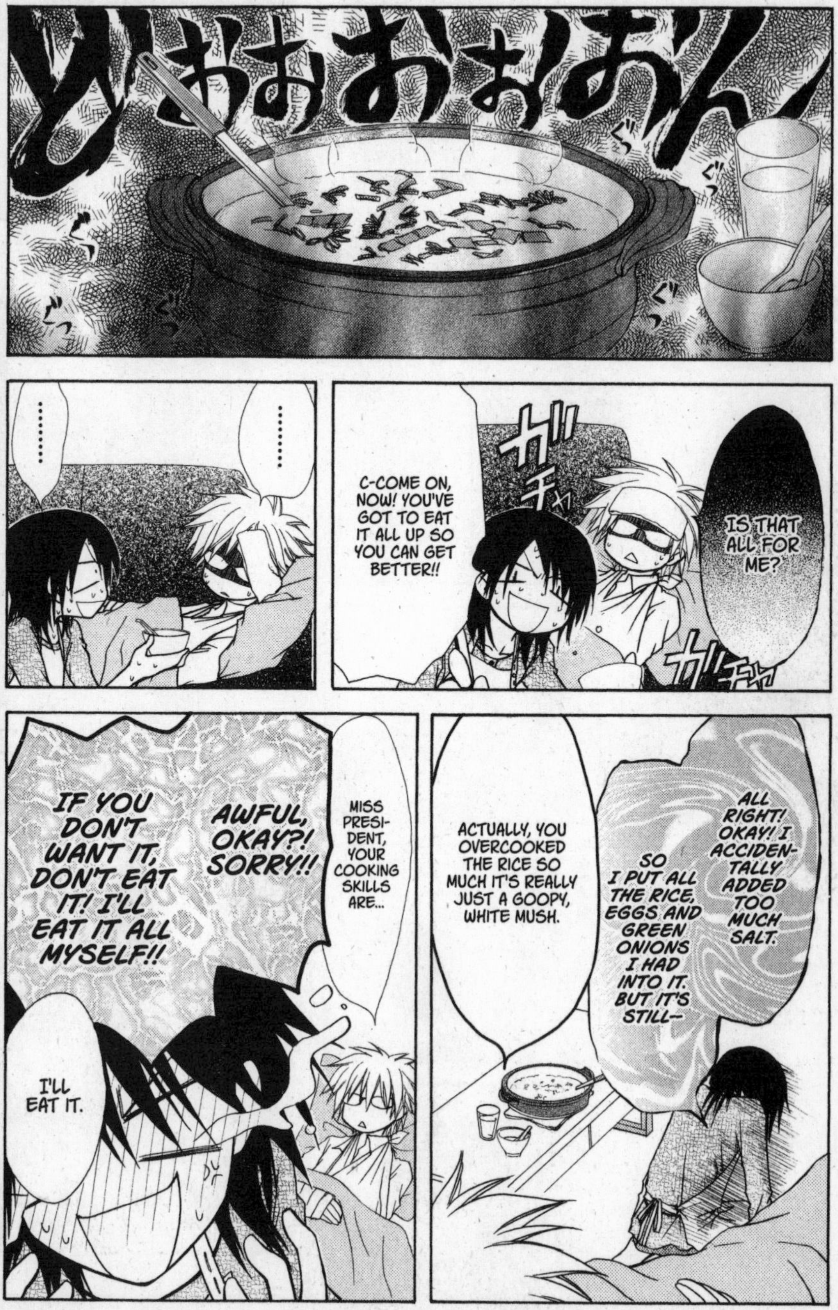
IS THAT ALL FOR ME?
C-COME ON, NOW! YOU'VE GOT TO EAT IT ALL UP SO YOU CAN GET BETTER!!
......
......
ALL RIGHT! OKAY! I ACCIDENTALLY ADDED TOO MUCH SALT.
SO I PUT ALL THE RICE, EGGS AND GREEN ONIONS I HAD INTO IT. BUT IT'S STILL—
ACTUALLY, YOU OVERCOOKED THE RICE SO MUCH IT'S REALLY JUST A GOOPY, WHITE MUSH.
MISS PRESIDENT, YOUR COOKING SKILLS ARE...
AWFUL, OKAY?! SORRY!!
IF YOU DON'T WANT IT, DON'T EAT IT! I'LL EAT IT ALL MYSELF!!
I'LL EAT IT.

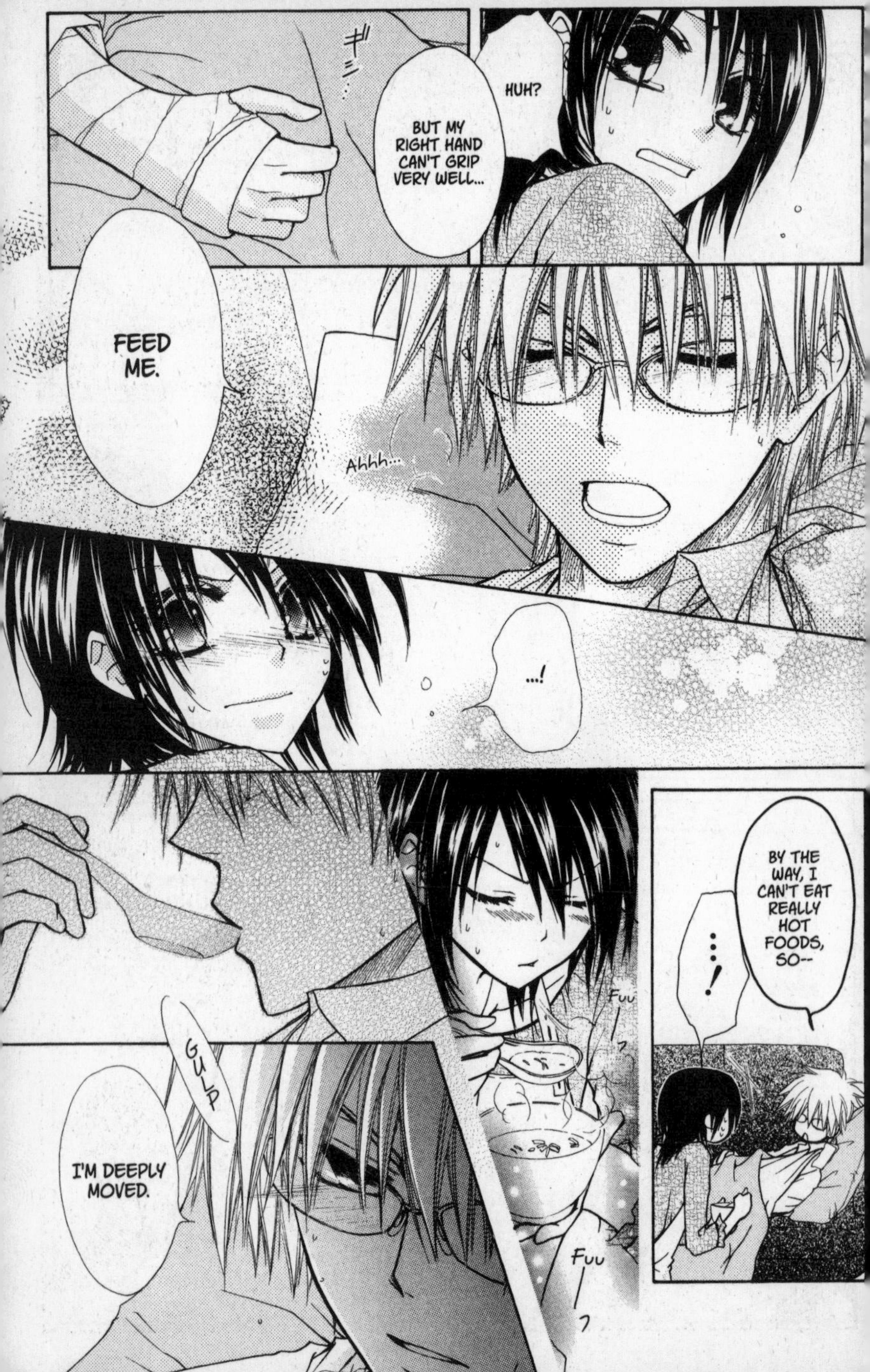
HUH?
BUT MY RIGHT HAND CAN'T GRIP VERY WELL...
FEED ME.
Ahhh...
...!
BY THE WAY, I CAN'T EAT REALLY HOT FOODS, SO--
...!
Fuu
GULP
I'M DEEPLY MOVED.
Fuu

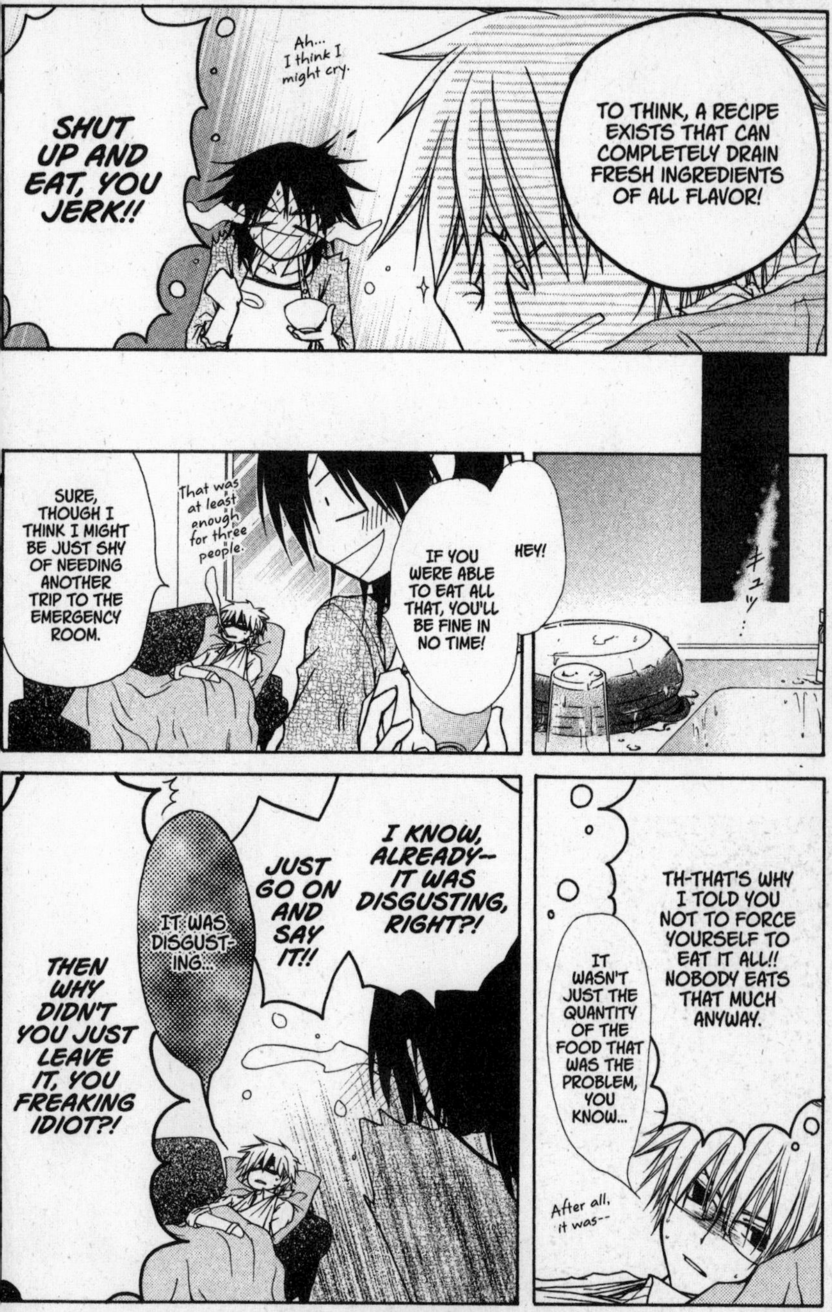

TO THINK, A RECIPE EXISTS THAT CAN COMPLETELY DRAIN FRESH INGREDIENTS OF ALL FLAVOR!
Ah... I think I might cry.
SHUT UP AND EAT, YOU JERK!!
キュッ…
HEY!
IF YOU WERE ABLE TO EAT ALL THAT, YOU'LL BE FINE IN NO TIME!
That was at least enough for three people.
SURE, THOUGH I THINK I MIGHT BE JUST SHY OF NEEDING ANOTHER TRIP TO THE EMERGENCY ROOM.
TH-THAT'S WHY I TOLD YOU NOT TO FORCE YOURSELF TO EAT IT ALL!! NOBODY EATS THAT MUCH ANYWAY.
IT WASN'T JUST THE QUANTITY OF THE FOOD THAT WAS THE PROBLEM, YOU KNOW...
After all, it was--
I KNOW, ALREADY-- IT WAS DISGUSTING, RIGHT?!
JUST GO ON AND SAY IT!!
IT WAS DISGUST-ING...
THEN WHY DIDN'T YOU JUST LEAVE IT, YOU FREAKING IDIOT?!

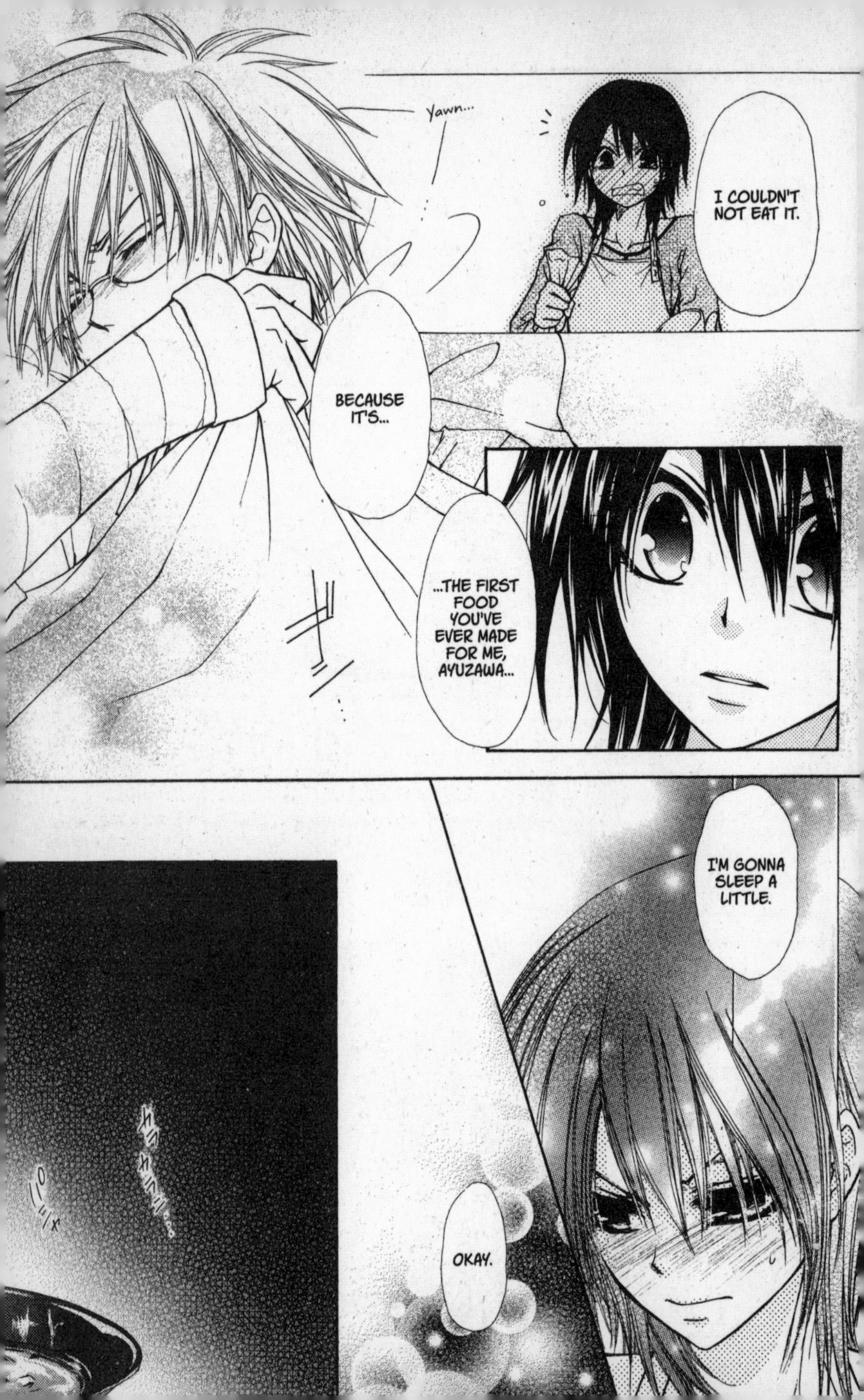
I COULDN'T NOT EAT IT.
BECAUSE IT'S...
...THE FIRST FOOD YOU'VE EVER MADE FOR ME, AYUZAWA...
Yawn...
I'M GONNA SLEEP A LITTLE.
OKAY.

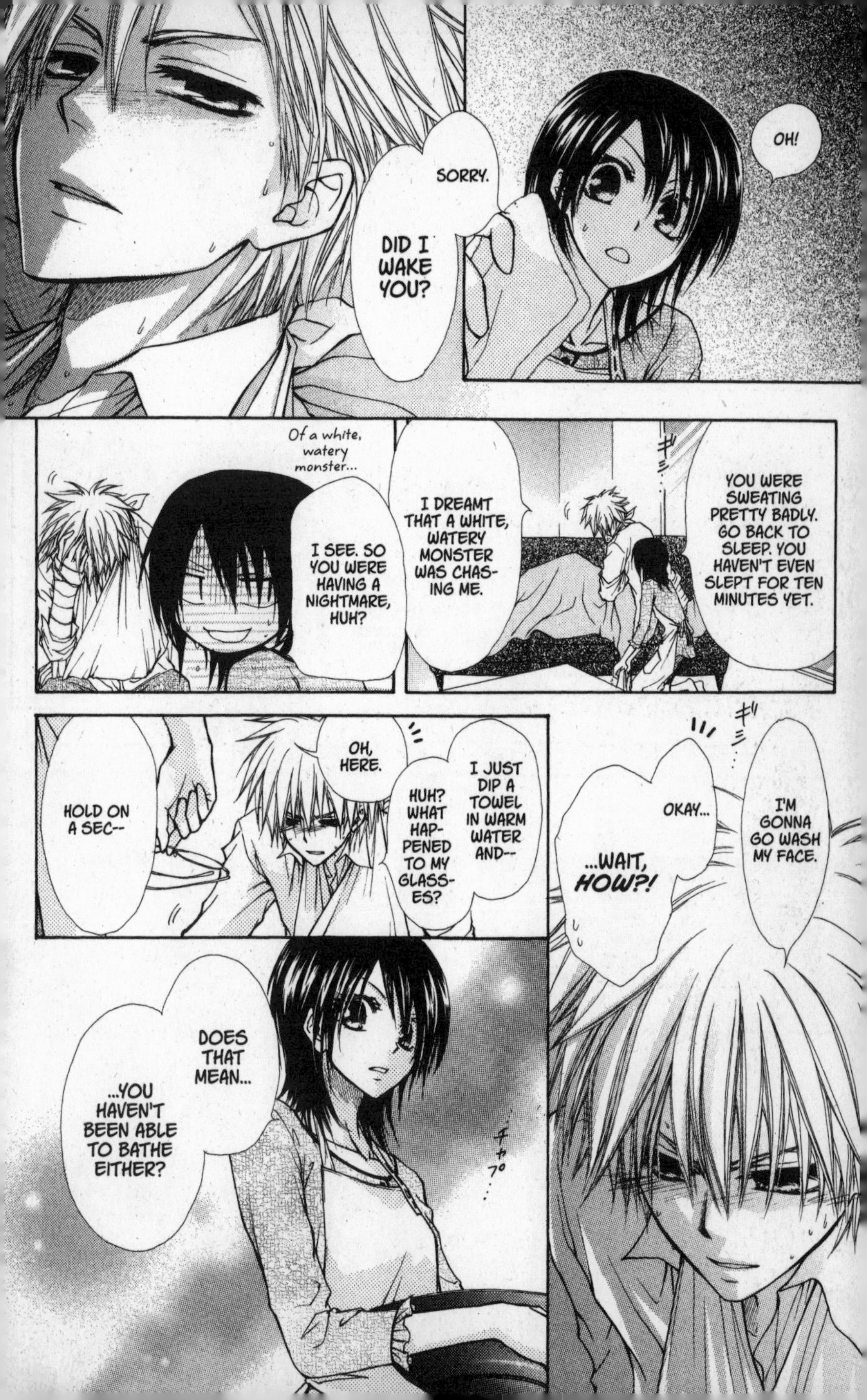
OH!
SORRY.
DID I WAKE YOU?
YOU WERE SWEATING PRETTY BADLY. GO BACK TO SLEEP. YOU HAVEN'T EVEN SLEPT FOR TEN MINUTES YET.
I DREAMT THAT A WHITE, WATERY MONSTER WAS CHASING ME.
I SEE. SO YOU WERE HAVING A NIGHTMARE, HUH?
Of a white, watery monster...
I'M GONNA GO WASH MY FACE.
OKAY...
...WAIT, HOW?!
I JUST DIP A TOWEL IN WARM WATER AND--
HUH? WHAT HAPPENED TO MY GLASSES?
OH, HERE.
HOLD ON A SEC--
DOES THAT MEAN...
...YOU HAVEN'T BEEN ABLE TO BATHE EITHER?

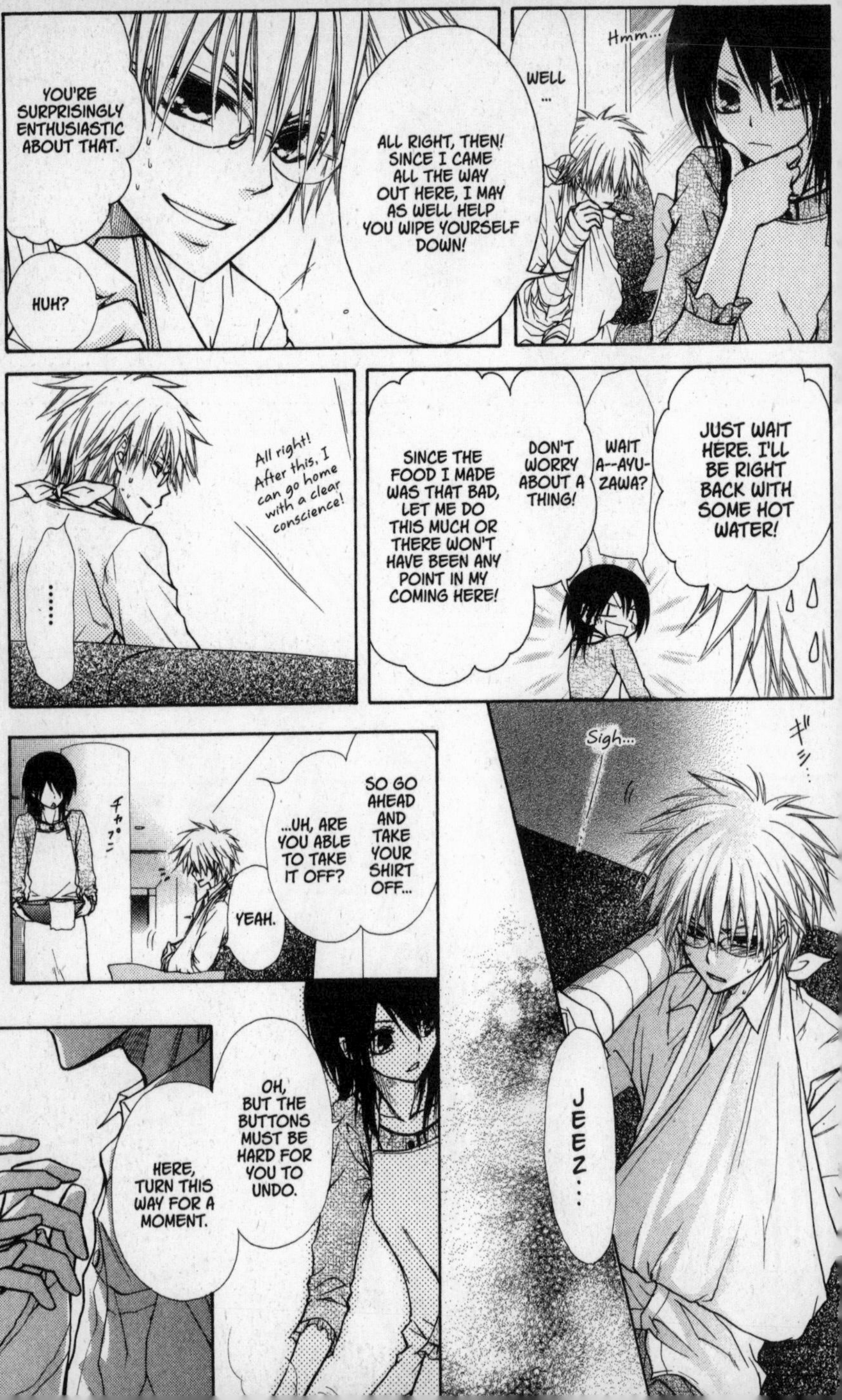
Hmm...
WELL ...
ALL RIGHT, THEN! SINCE I CAME ALL THE WAY OUT HERE, I MAY AS WELL HELP YOU WIPE YOURSELF DOWN!
YOU'RE SURPRISINGLY ENTHUSIASTIC ABOUT THAT.
HUH?
JUST WAIT HERE. I'LL BE RIGHT BACK WITH SOME HOT WATER!
WAIT A--AYU-ZAWA?
DON'T WORRY ABOUT A THING!
SINCE THE FOOD I MADE WAS THAT BAD, LET ME DO THIS MUCH OR THERE WON'T HAVE BEEN ANY POINT IN MY COMING HERE!
All right! After this, I can go home with a clear conscience!
......
ギシ...
Sigh...
JEEZ...
SO GO AHEAD AND TAKE YOUR SHIRT OFF...
...UH, ARE YOU ABLE TO TAKE IT OFF?
YEAH.
チャプ
OH, BUT THE BUTTONS MUST BE HARD FOR YOU TO UNDO.
HERE, TURN THIS WAY FOR A MOMENT.

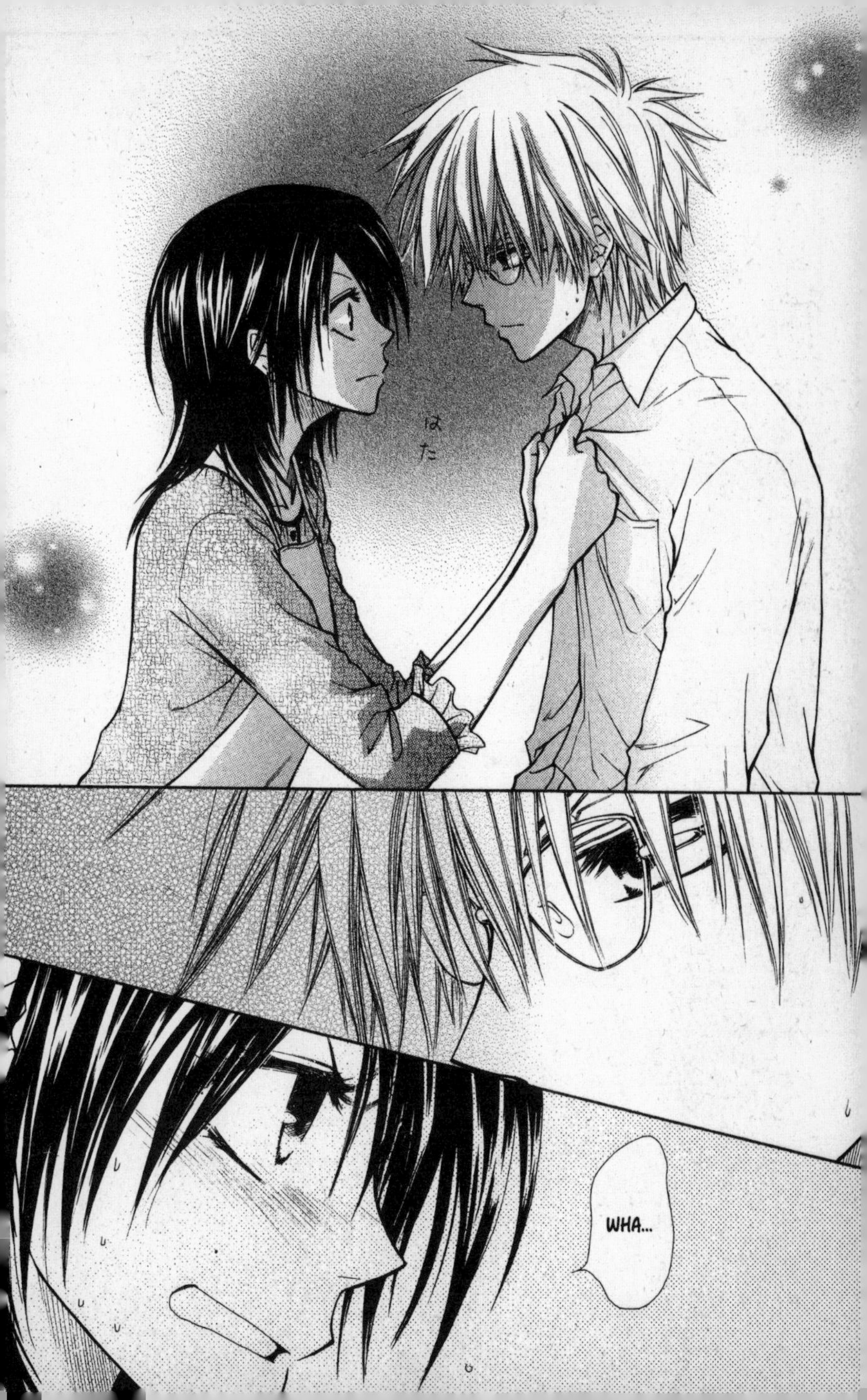
はた
WHA...

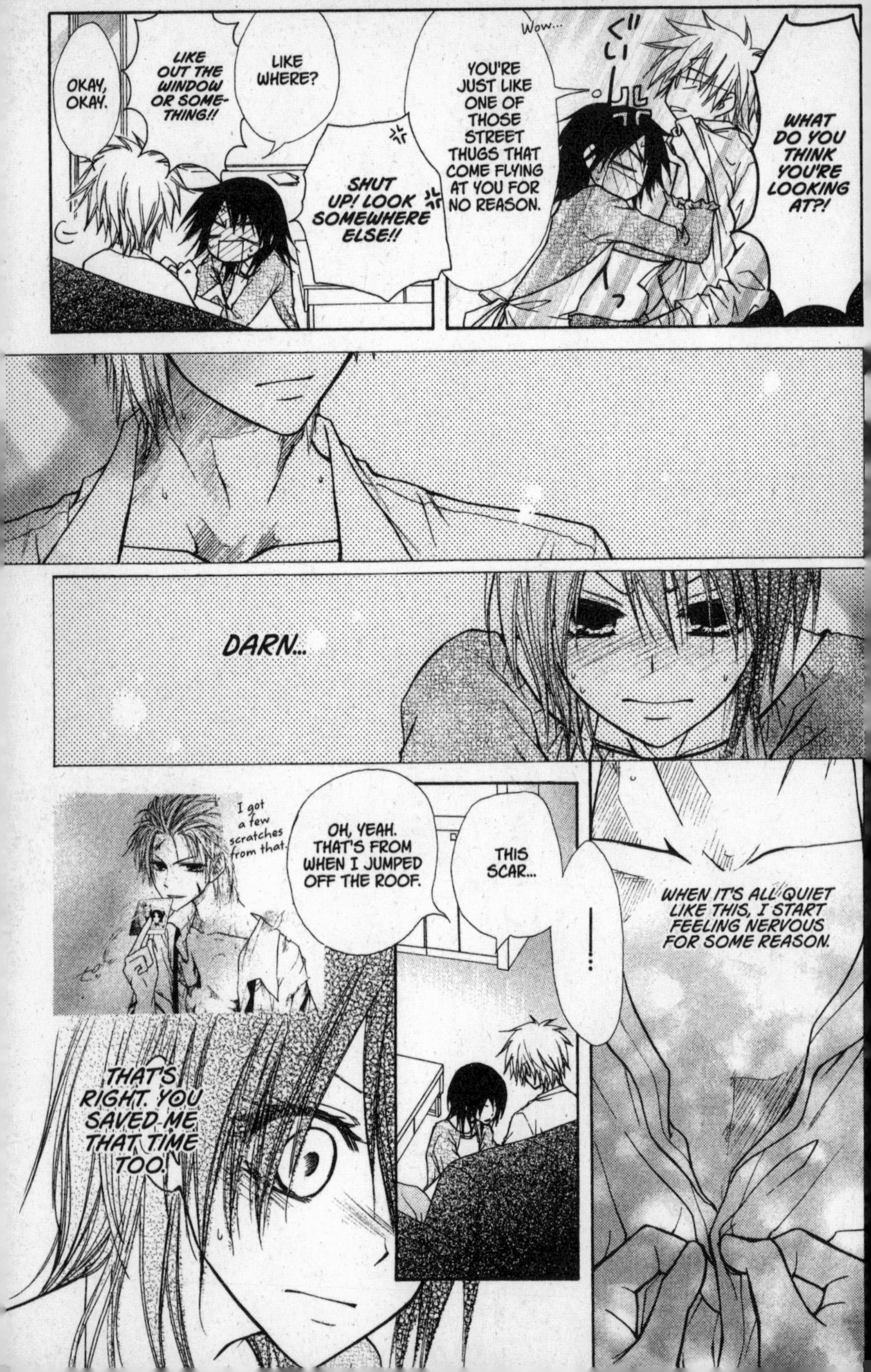
WHAT DO YOU THINK YOU'RE LOOKING AT?!
YOU'RE JUST LIKE ONE OF THOSE STREET THUGS THAT COME FLYING AT YOU FOR NO REASON.
Wow...
SHUT UP! LOOK SOMEWHERE ELSE!!
LIKE WHERE?
LIKE OUT THE WINDOW OR SOMETHING!!
OKAY, OKAY.
DARN...
WHEN IT'S ALL QUIET LIKE THIS, I START FEELING NERVOUS FOR SOME REASON.
!...
THIS SCAR...
OH, YEAH. THAT'S FROM WHEN I JUMPED OFF THE ROOF.
I got a few scratches from that.
THAT'S RIGHT. YOU SAVED ME THAT TIME TOO!

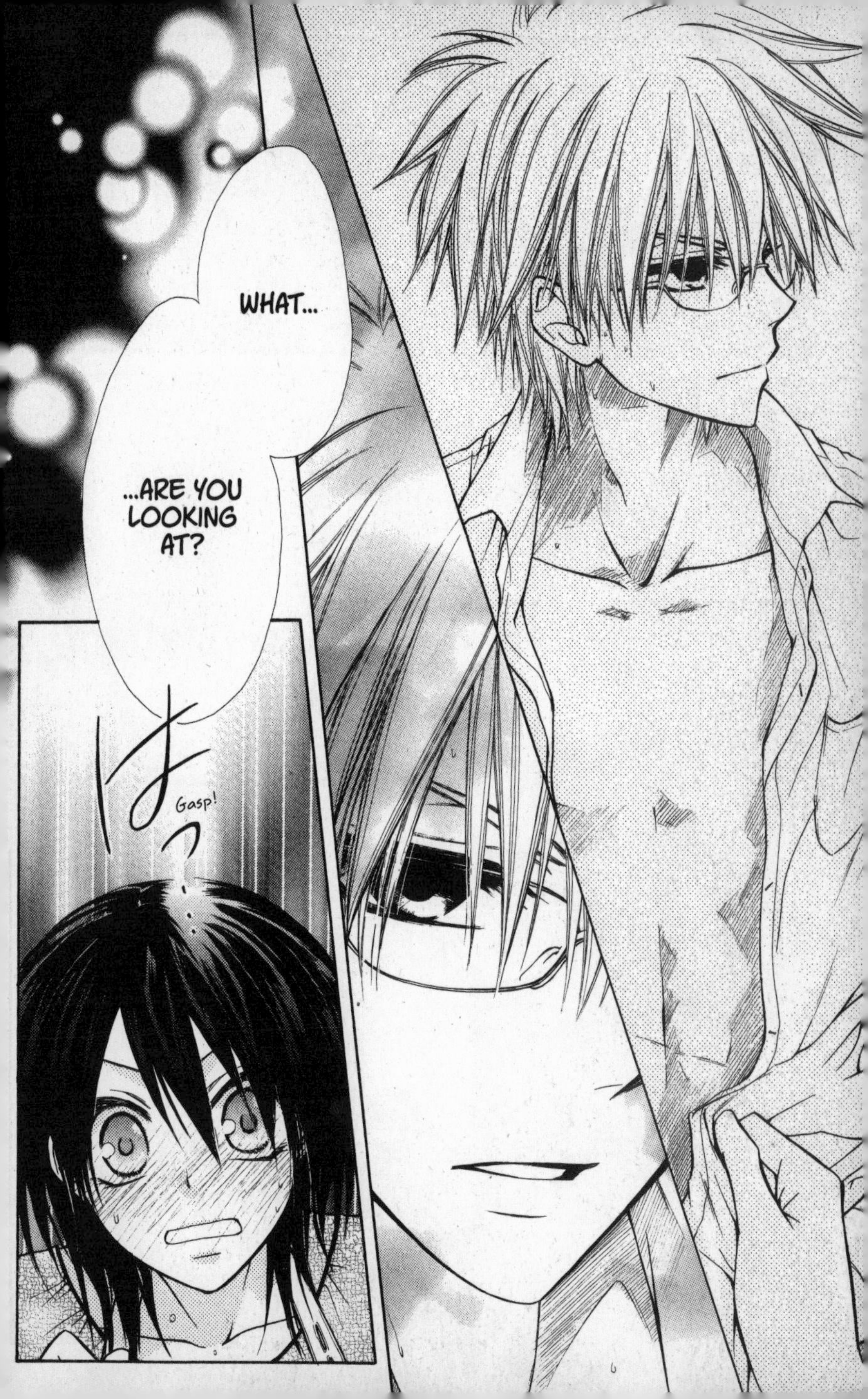
WHAT...
...ARE YOU LOOKING AT?
は
Gasp!

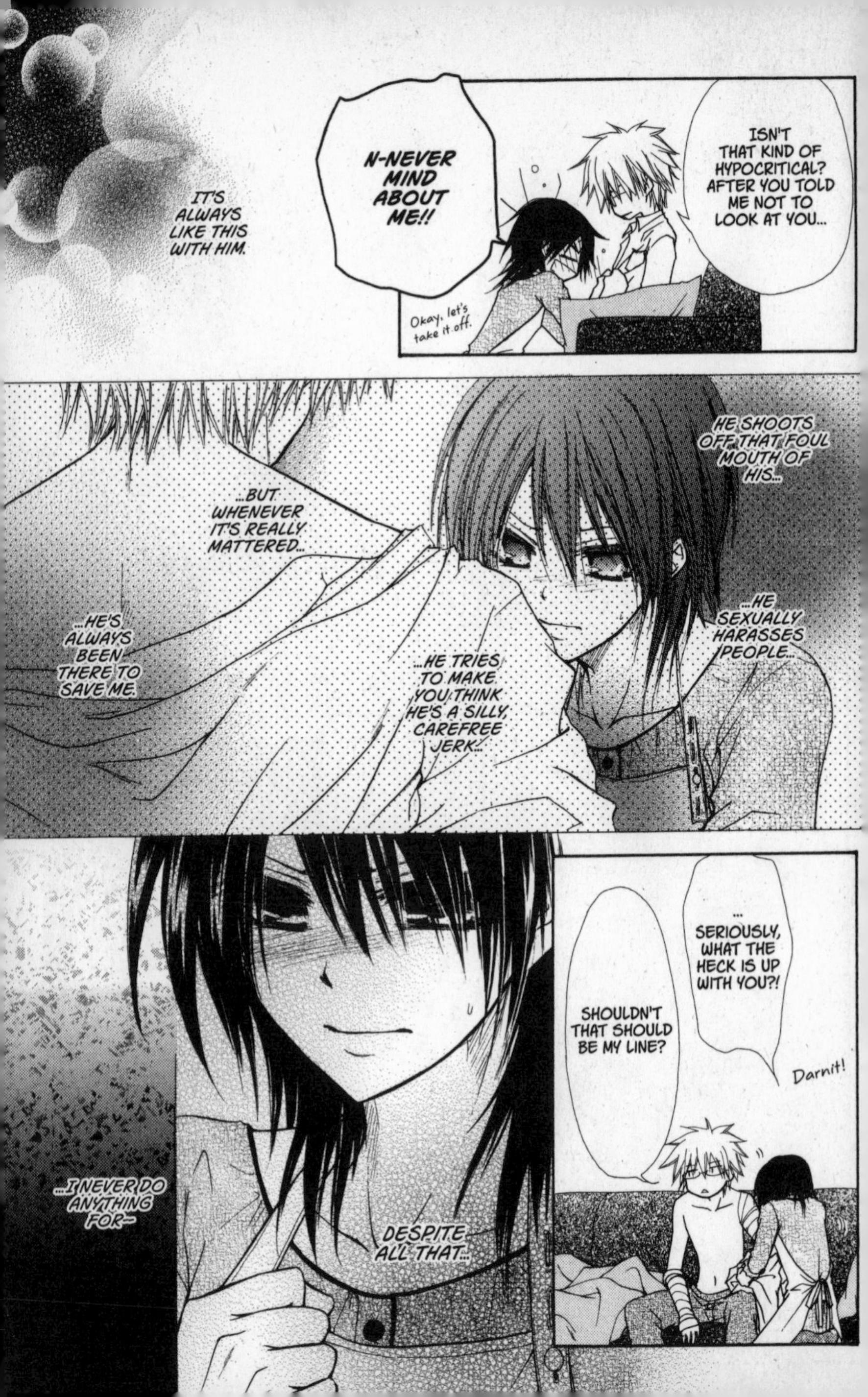

ISN'T THAT KIND OF HYPOCRITICAL? AFTER YOU TOLD ME NOT TO LOOK AT YOU...
N-NEVER MIND ABOUT ME!!
Okay, let's take it off.
IT'S ALWAYS LIKE THIS WITH HIM.
HE SHOOTS OFF THAT FOUL MOUTH OF HIS...
...HE SEXUALLY HARASSES PEOPLE...
...HE TRIES TO MAKE YOU THINK HE'S A SILLY, CAREFREE JERK...
...BUT WHENEVER IT'S REALLY MATTERED...
...HE'S ALWAYS BEEN THERE TO SAVE ME.
... SERIOUSLY, WHAT THE HECK IS UP WITH YOU?!
Darnit!
SHOULDN'T THAT SHOULD BE MY LINE?
DESPITE ALL THAT...
...I NEVER DO ANYTHING FOR–

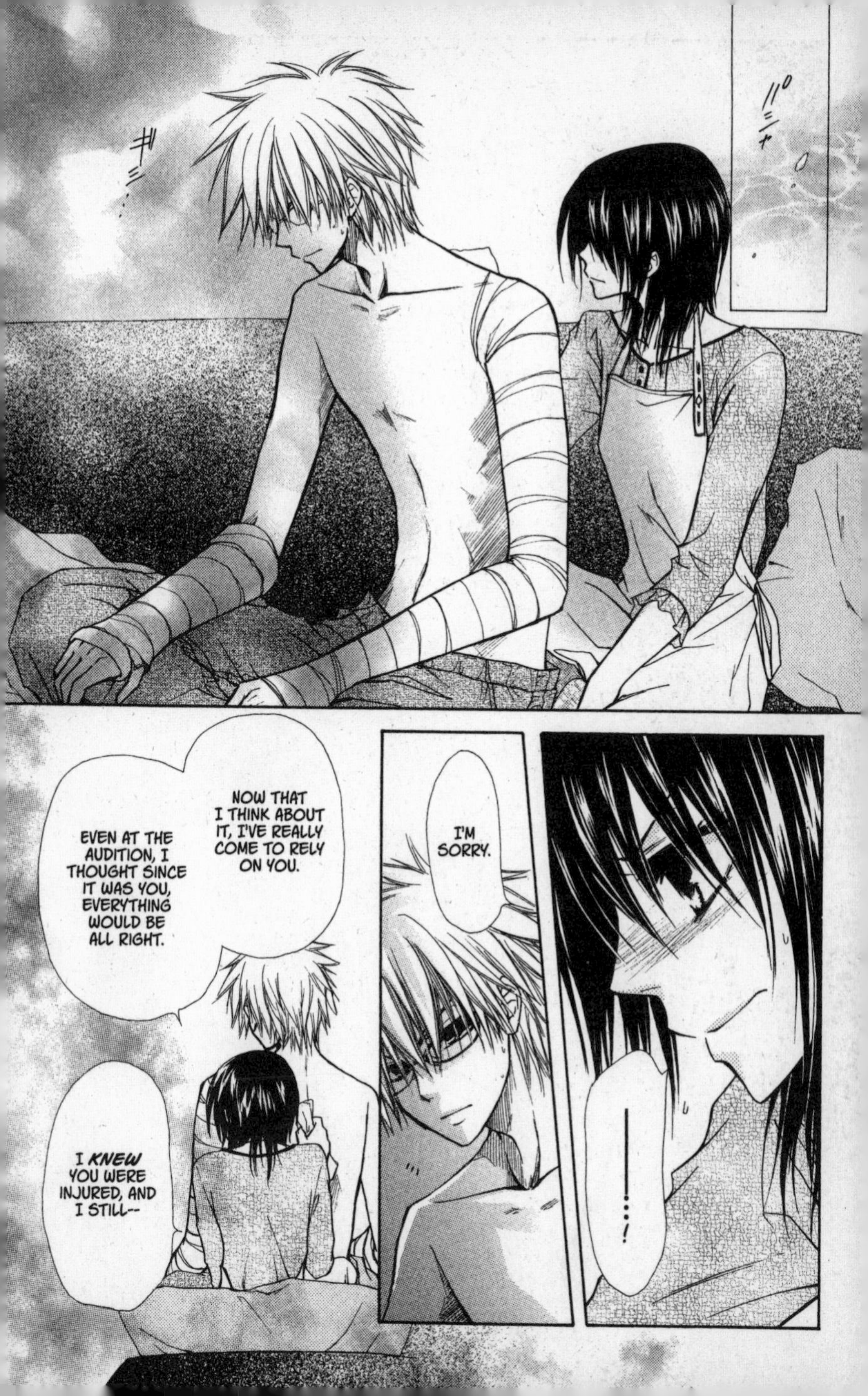
......!
I'M SORRY.
NOW THAT I THINK ABOUT IT, I'VE REALLY COME TO RELY ON YOU.
EVEN AT THE AUDITION, I THOUGHT SINCE IT WAS YOU, EVERYTHING WOULD BE ALL RIGHT.
I *KNEW* YOU WERE INJURED, AND I STILL--

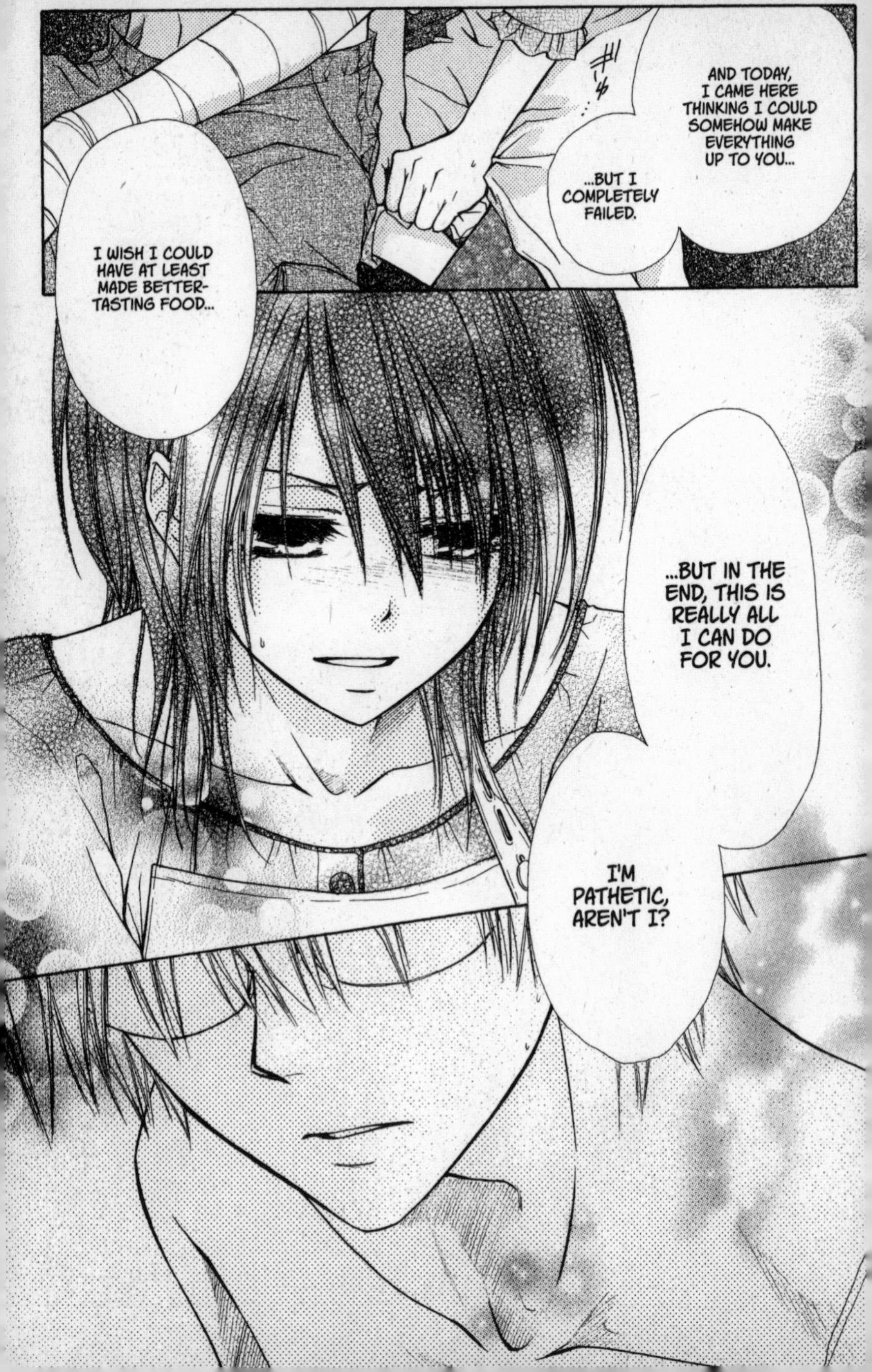
AND TODAY, I CAME HERE THINKING I COULD SOMEHOW MAKE EVERYTHING UP TO YOU...
...BUT I COMPLETELY FAILED.
I WISH I COULD HAVE AT LEAST MADE BETTER-TASTING FOOD...
...BUT IN THE END, THIS IS REALLY ALL I CAN DO FOR YOU.
I'M PATHETIC, AREN'T I?

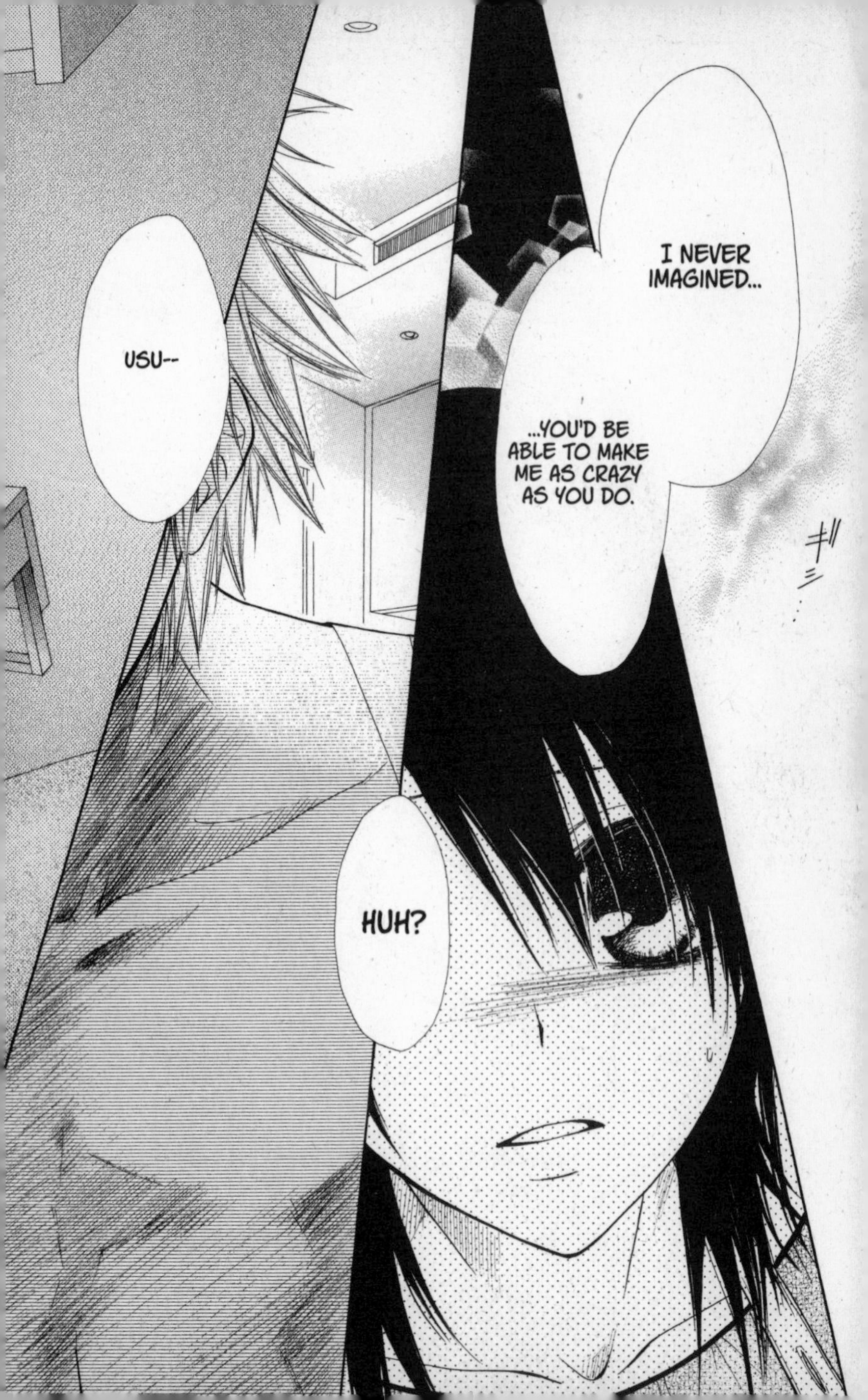
I NEVER IMAGINED...
...YOU'D BE ABLE TO MAKE ME AS CRAZY AS YOU DO.
ギリ
USU--
HUH?

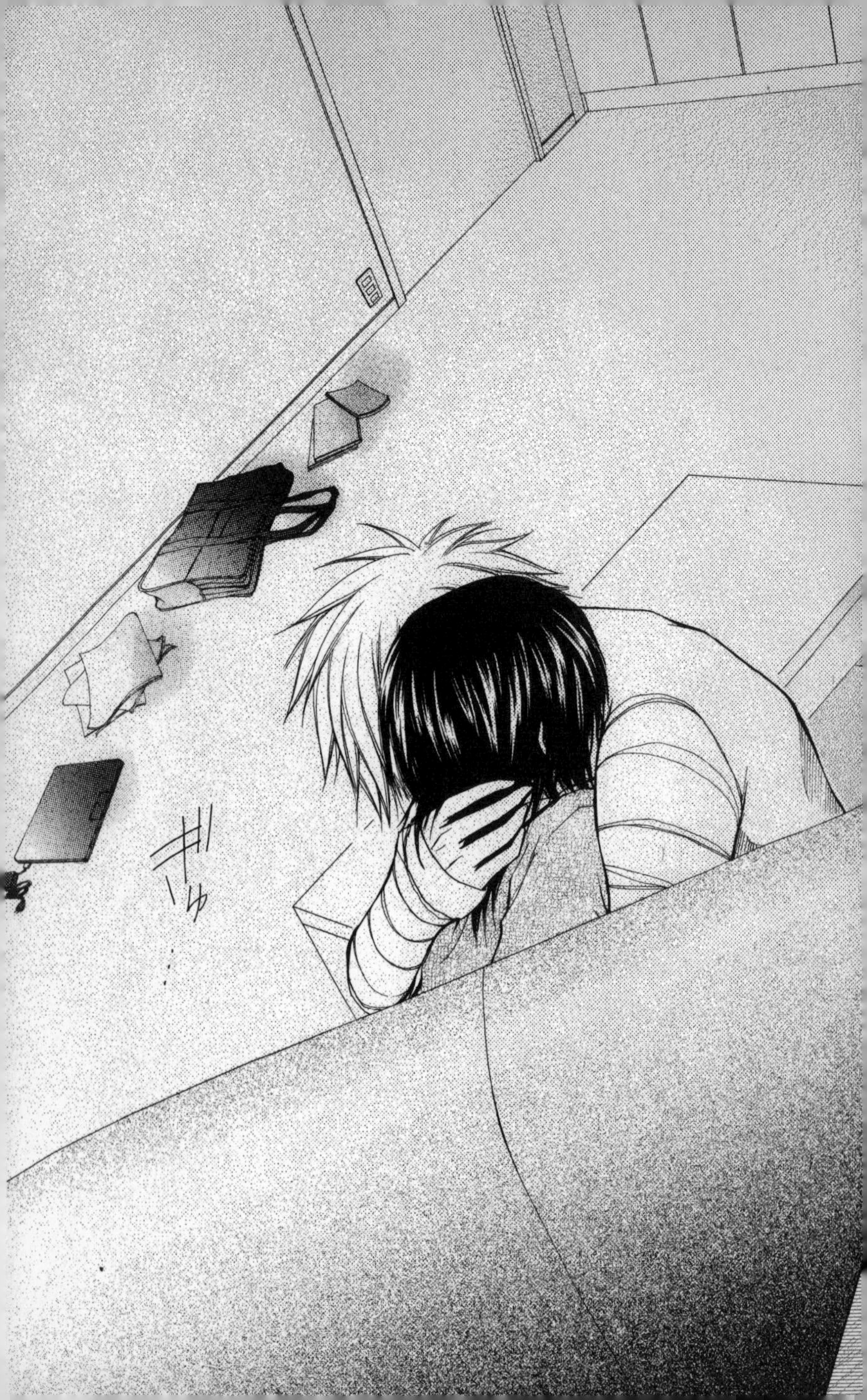
ぎゅ

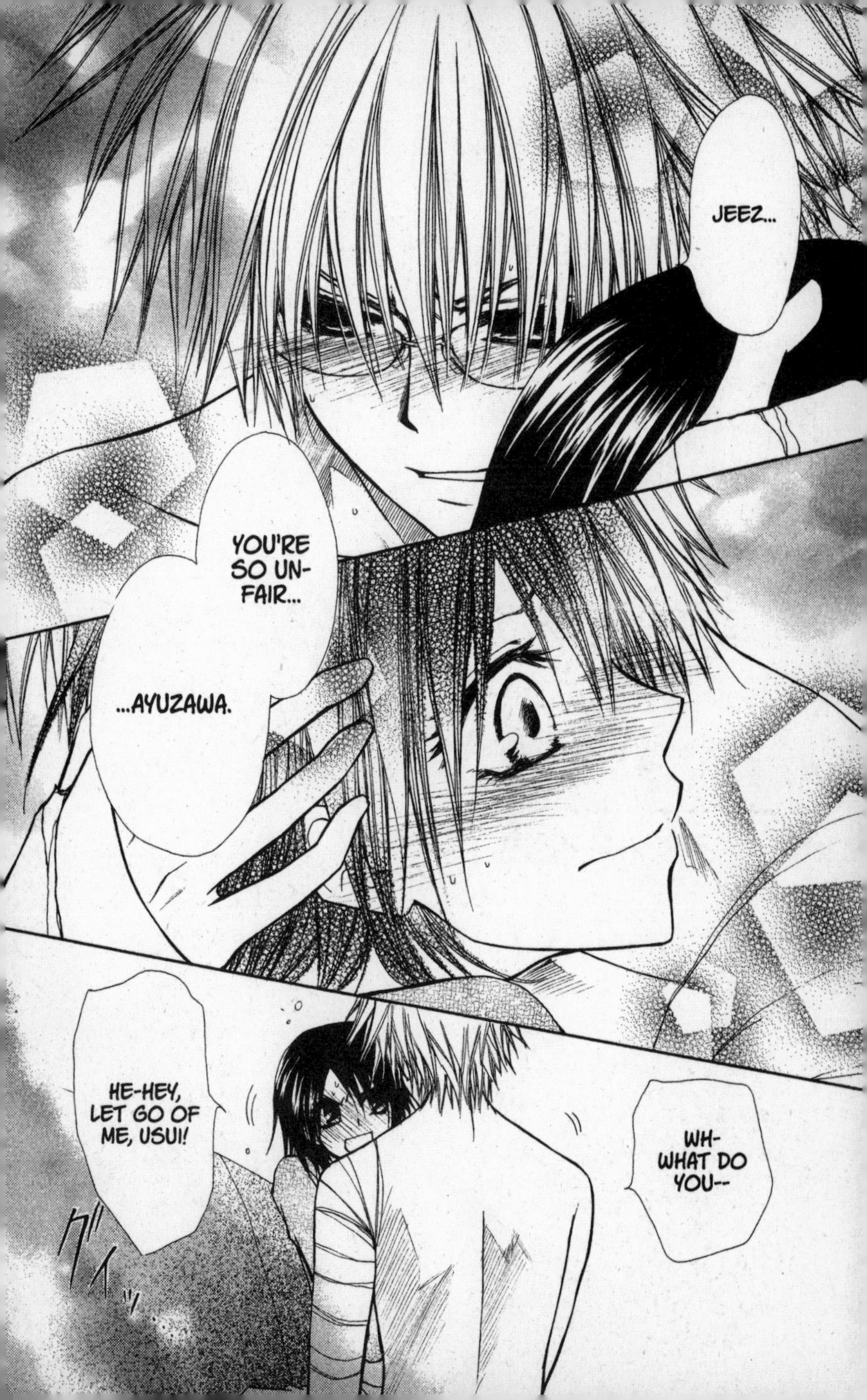
JEEZ...
YOU'RE SO UN-FAIR...
...AYUZAWA.
WH- WHAT DO YOU--
HE-HEY, LET GO OF ME, USUI!
グイッ

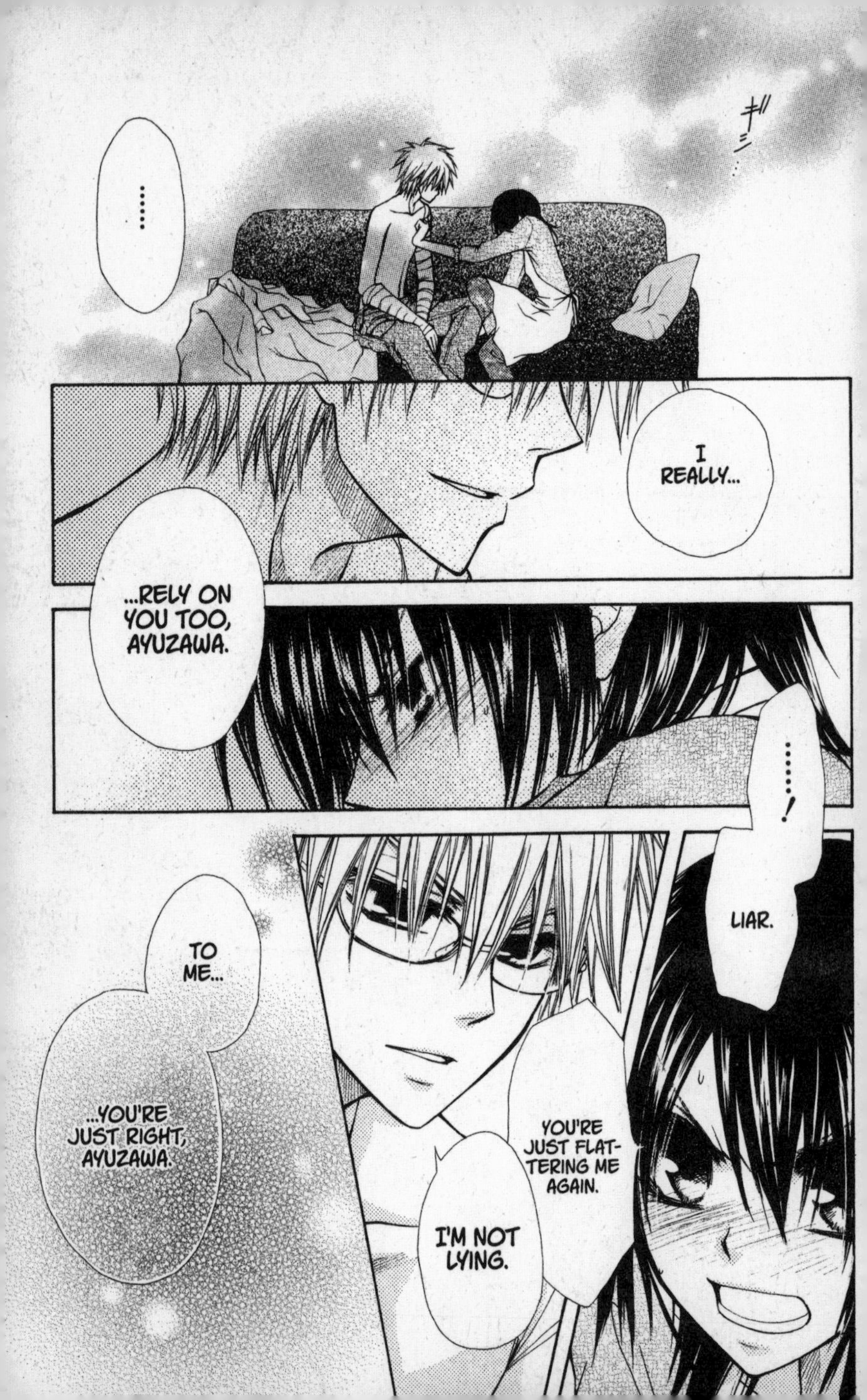
......
I REALLY...
...RELY ON YOU TOO, AYUZAWA.
......!
LIAR.
YOU'RE JUST FLAT-TERING ME AGAIN.
I'M NOT LYING.
TO ME...
...YOU'RE JUST RIGHT, AYUZAWA.

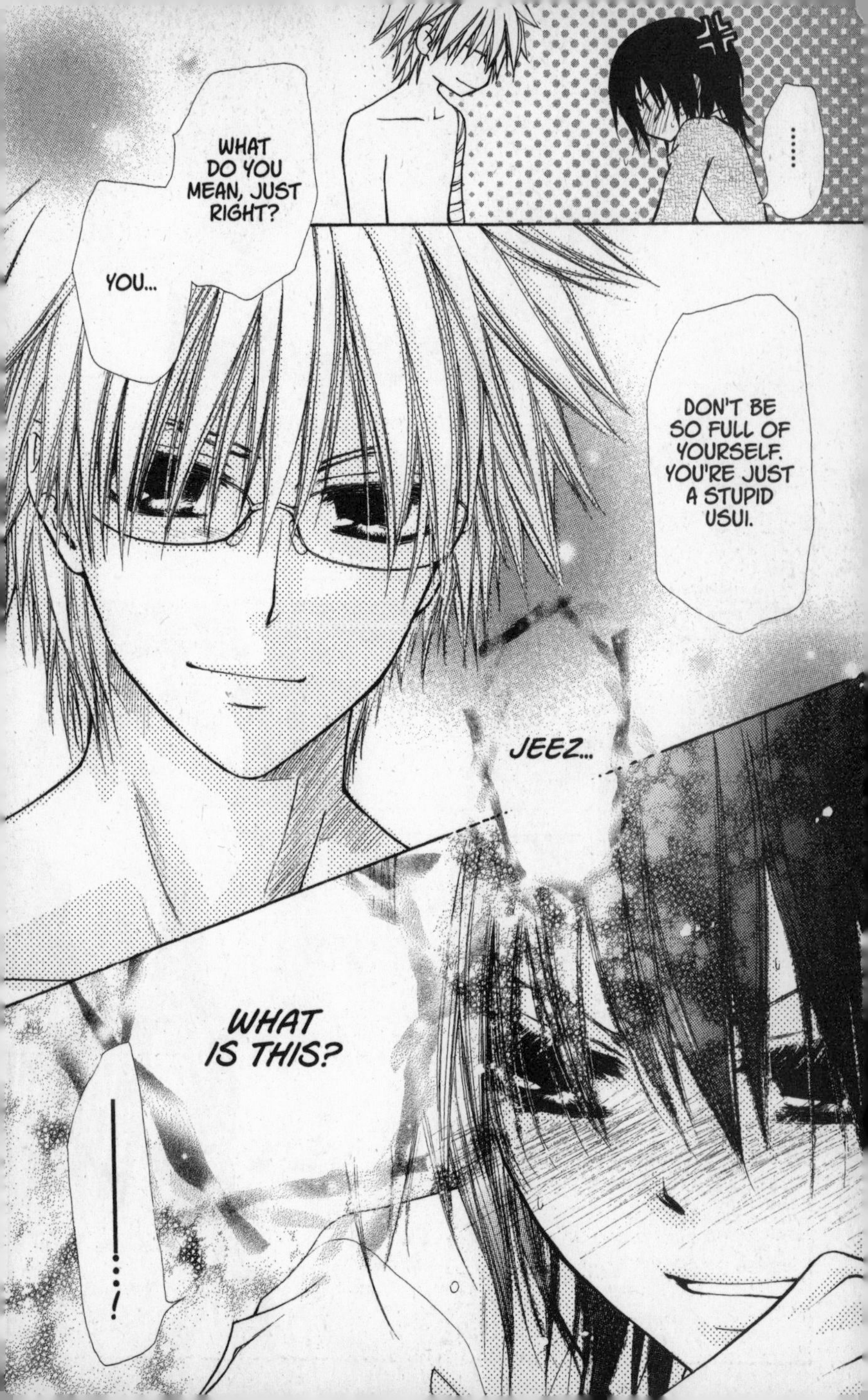
......
WHAT DO YOU MEAN, JUST RIGHT?
YOU...
DON'T BE SO FULL OF YOURSELF. YOU'RE JUST A STUPID USUI.
JEEZ...
WHAT IS THIS?
......!

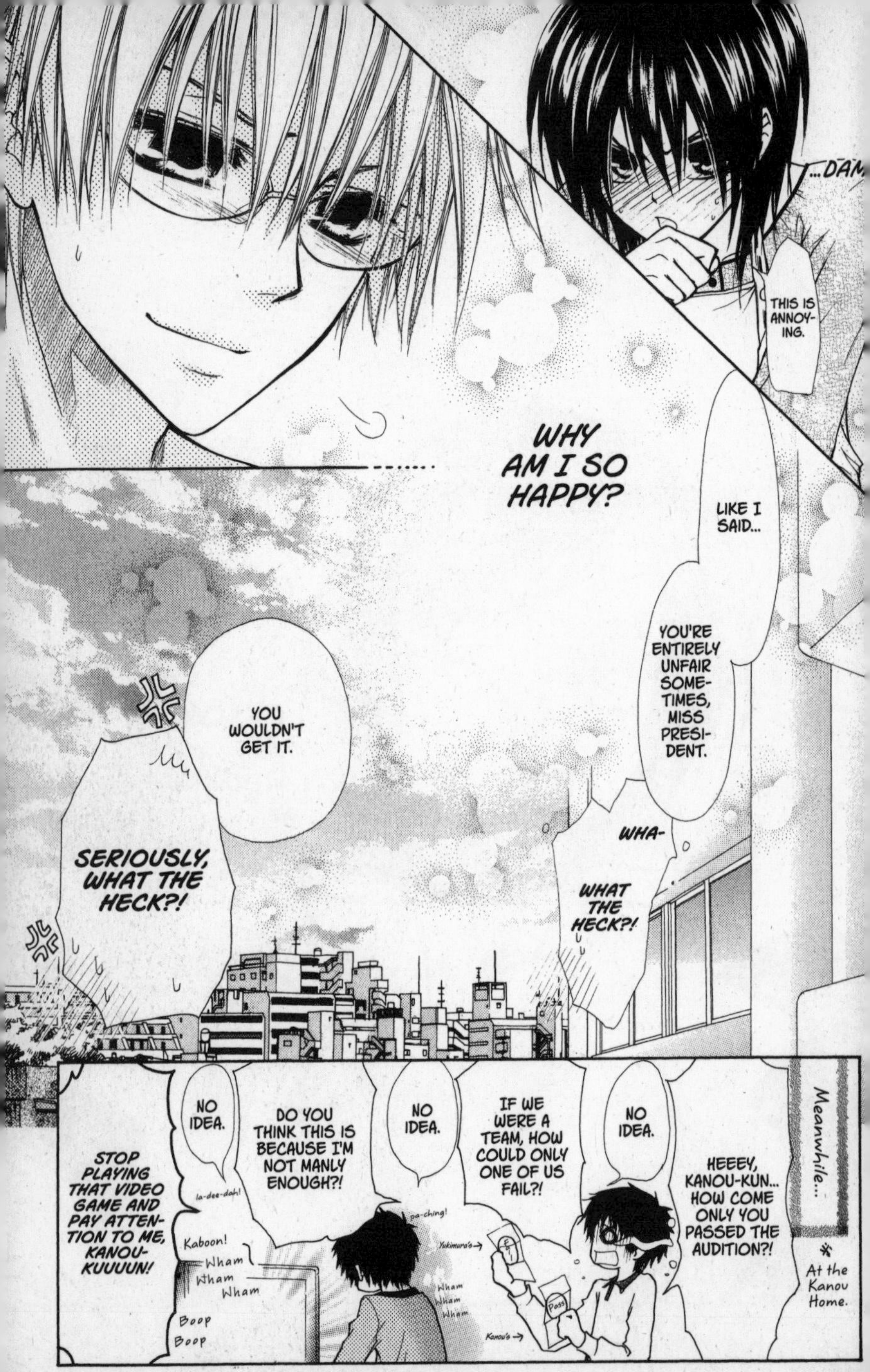

...DAM
THIS IS ANNOY-ING.
WHY AM I SO HAPPY?
LIKE I SAID...
YOU'RE ENTIRELY UNFAIR SOME-TIMES, MISS PRESI-DENT.
WHA-
WHAT THE HECK?!
YOU WOULDN'T GET IT.
SERIOUSLY, WHAT THE HECK?!
Meanwhile...
※ At the Kanou Home.
HEEEY, KANOU-KUN... HOW COME ONLY YOU PASSED THE AUDITION?!
NO IDEA.
Yukimura's
Pass
Kanou's
IF WE WERE A TEAM, HOW COULD ONLY ONE OF US FAIL?!
NO IDEA.
pa-ching!
Wham Wham Wham
DO YOU THINK THIS IS BECAUSE I'M NOT MANLY ENOUGH?!
NO IDEA.
la-dee-dah!
STOP PLAYING THAT VIDEO GAME AND PAY ATTEN-TION TO ME, KANOU-KUUUUN!
Kaboon!
Wham Wham Wham
Boop Boop

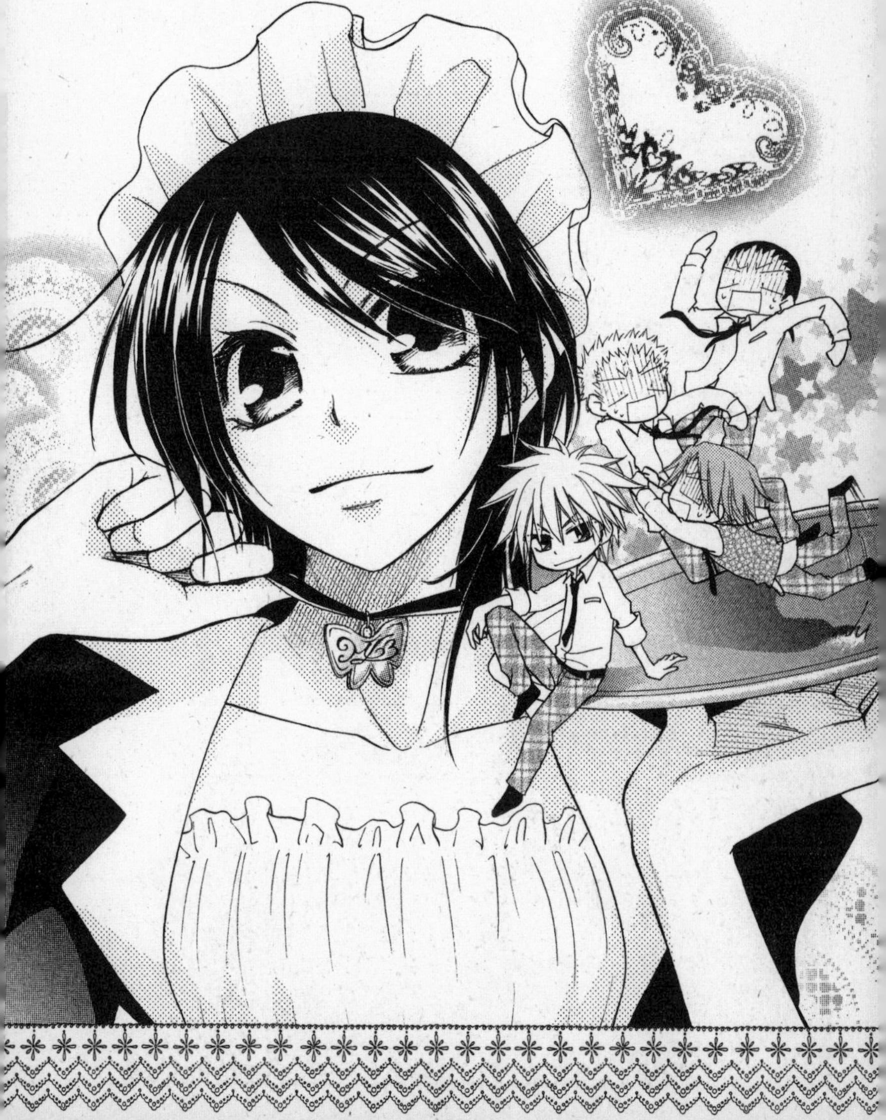

closing time...

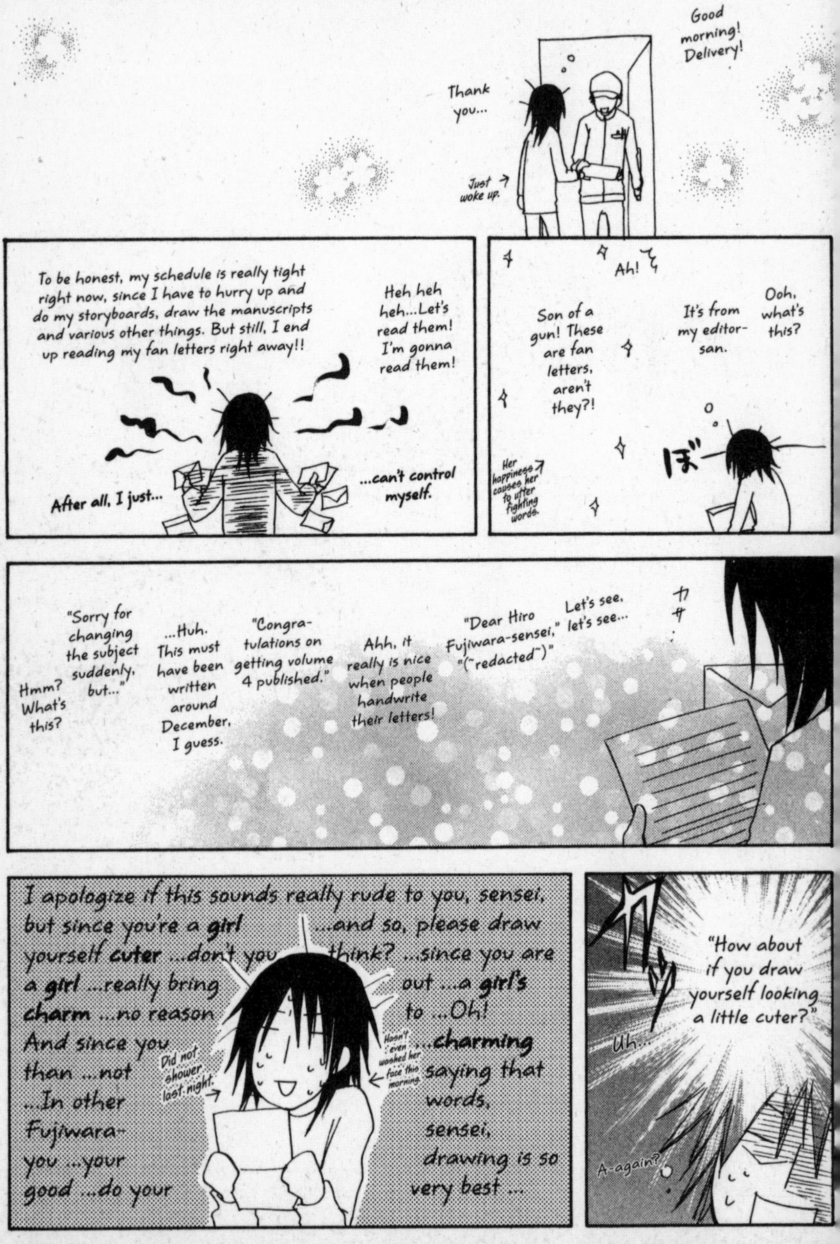
Good morning! Delivery!
Thank you...
Just woke up.
Ah!
Ooh, what's this?
It's from my editor-san.
Son of a gun! These are fan letters, aren't they?!
ぼ
Her happiness causes her to utter fighting words.
Heh heh heh...Let's read them! I'm gonna read them!
To be honest, my schedule is really tight right now, since I have to hurry up and do my storyboards, draw the manuscripts and various other things. But still, I end up reading my fan letters right away!!
After all, I just...
...can't control myself.
カサ
Let's see, let's see...
"Dear Hiro Fujiwara-sensei," "(~redacted~)"
Ahh, it really is nice when people handwrite their letters!
"Congratulations on getting volume 4 published."
...Huh. This must have been written around December, I guess.
"Sorry for changing the subject suddenly, but..."
Hmm? What's this?
"How about if you draw yourself looking a little cuter?"
Uh...
A-again?
I apologize if this sounds really rude to you, sensei,
but since you're a **girl** ...and so, please draw
yourself **cuter** ...don't you think? ...since you are
a **girl** ...really bring out ...a **girl's**
charm ...no reason to ...Oh!
And since you ...**charming**
than ...not saying that
...In other words,
Fujiwara- sensei,
you ...your drawing is so
good ...do your very best ...
Did not shower last night.
Hasn't even washed her face this morning.

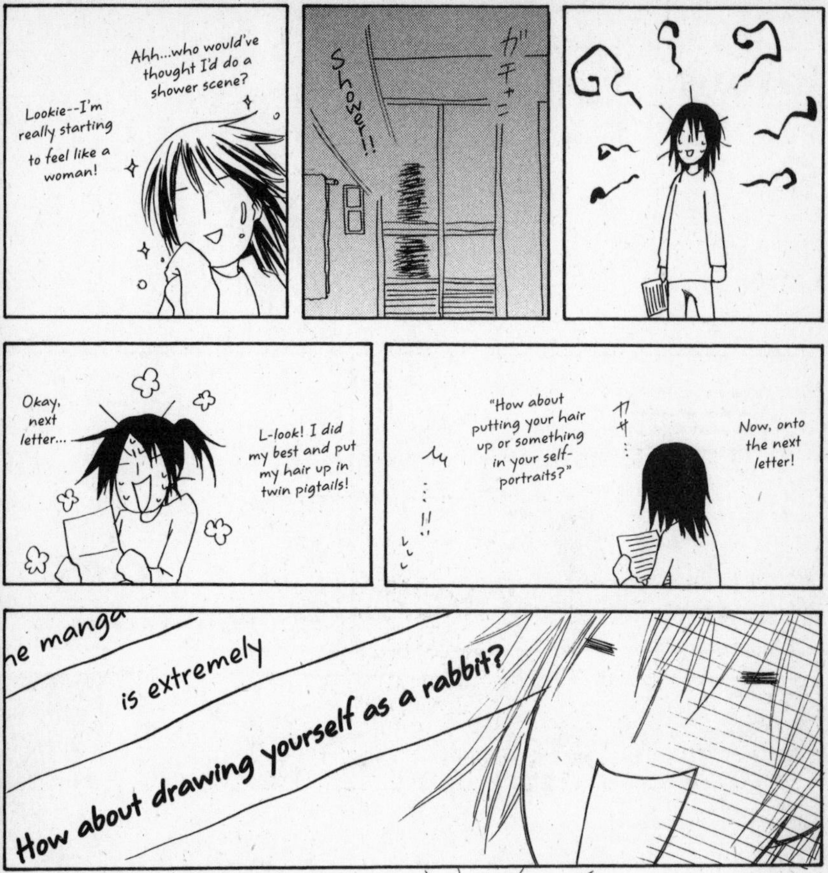
ガチャ
Shower!!
Ahh...who would've thought I'd do a shower scene?
Lookie--I'm really starting to feel like a woman!
Now, onto the next letter!
カサ...
"How about putting your hair up or something in your self-portraits?"
ム
...!!
L-look! I did my best and put my hair up in twin pigtails!
Okay, next letter...
he manga
is extremely
How about drawing yourself as a rabbit?

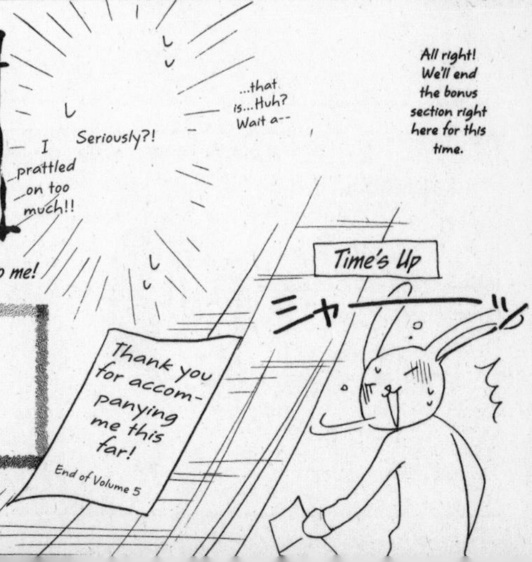
All right! We'll end the bonus section right here for this time.
...that is...Huh? Wait a--
Seriously?!
I prattled on too much!!
Time's Up
ミャー
Thank you for accompanying me this far!
End of Volume 5

Special Thanks!

- Namino-san
- Yuki Fujitsuka-san
- My Mom
- Eri Mizukami-chan
- My Editor

... and you!

Please send questions, thoughts, jokes, anything to me!

Hiro Fujiwara
c/o TOKYOPOP Inc.
5900 Wilshire Blvd.
Suite 2000
Los Angeles, CA 90036

Cafe
Maid
Latte

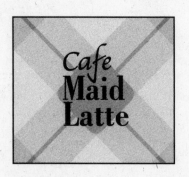

IN THE NEXT VOLUME OF MAID SAMA!

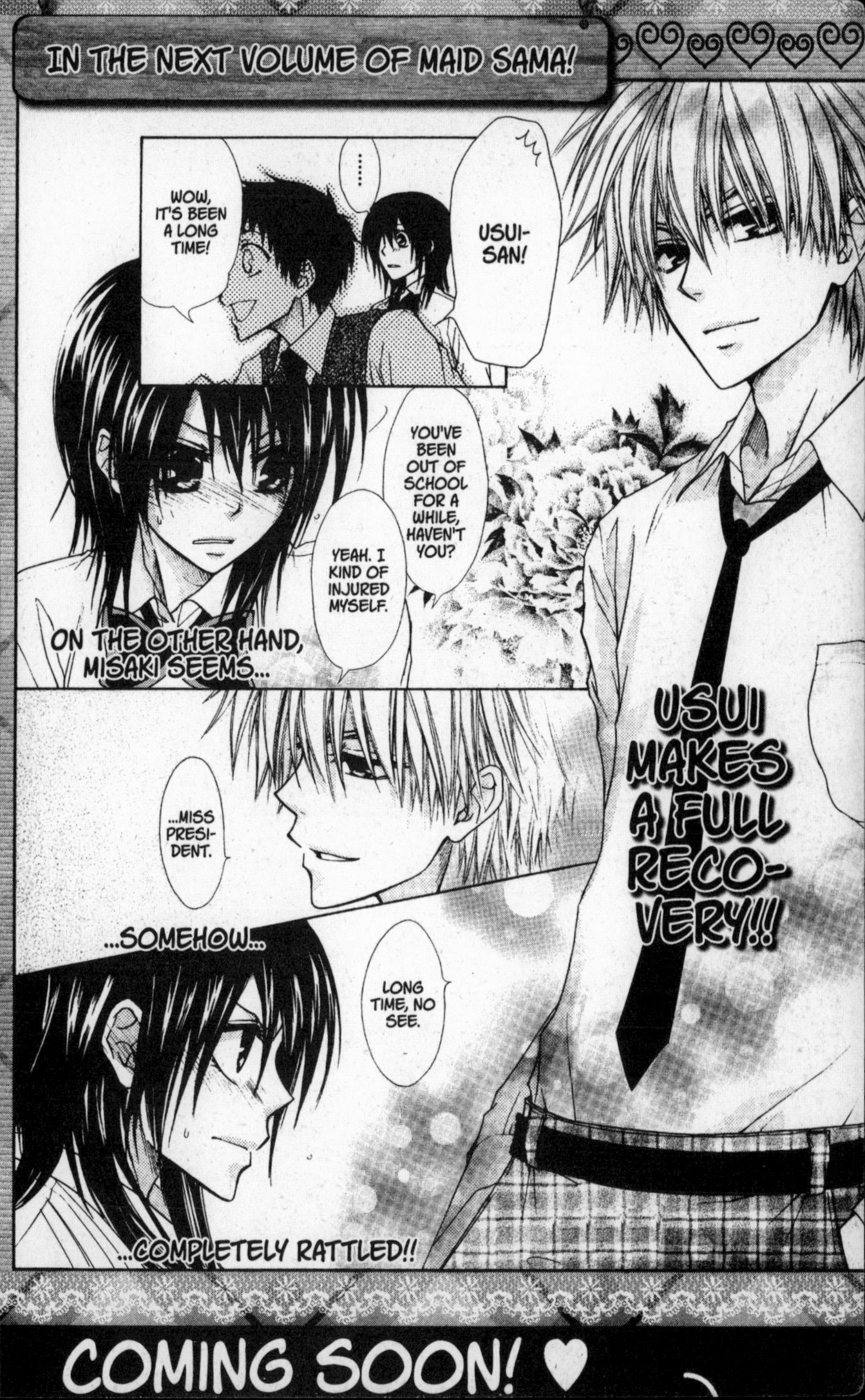
USUI MAKES A FULL RECOVERY!!
USUI-SAN!
......
WOW, IT'S BEEN A LONG TIME!
YOU'VE BEEN OUT OF SCHOOL FOR A WHILE, HAVEN'T YOU?
YEAH. I KIND OF INJURED MYSELF.
ON THE OTHER HAND, MISAKI SEEMS...
...MISS PRESIDENT.
...SOMEHOW...
LONG TIME, NO SEE.
...COMPLETELY RATTLED!!

COMING SOON! ♥

Welcome home, Master!

MAID SAMA! IS A BIG HIT!

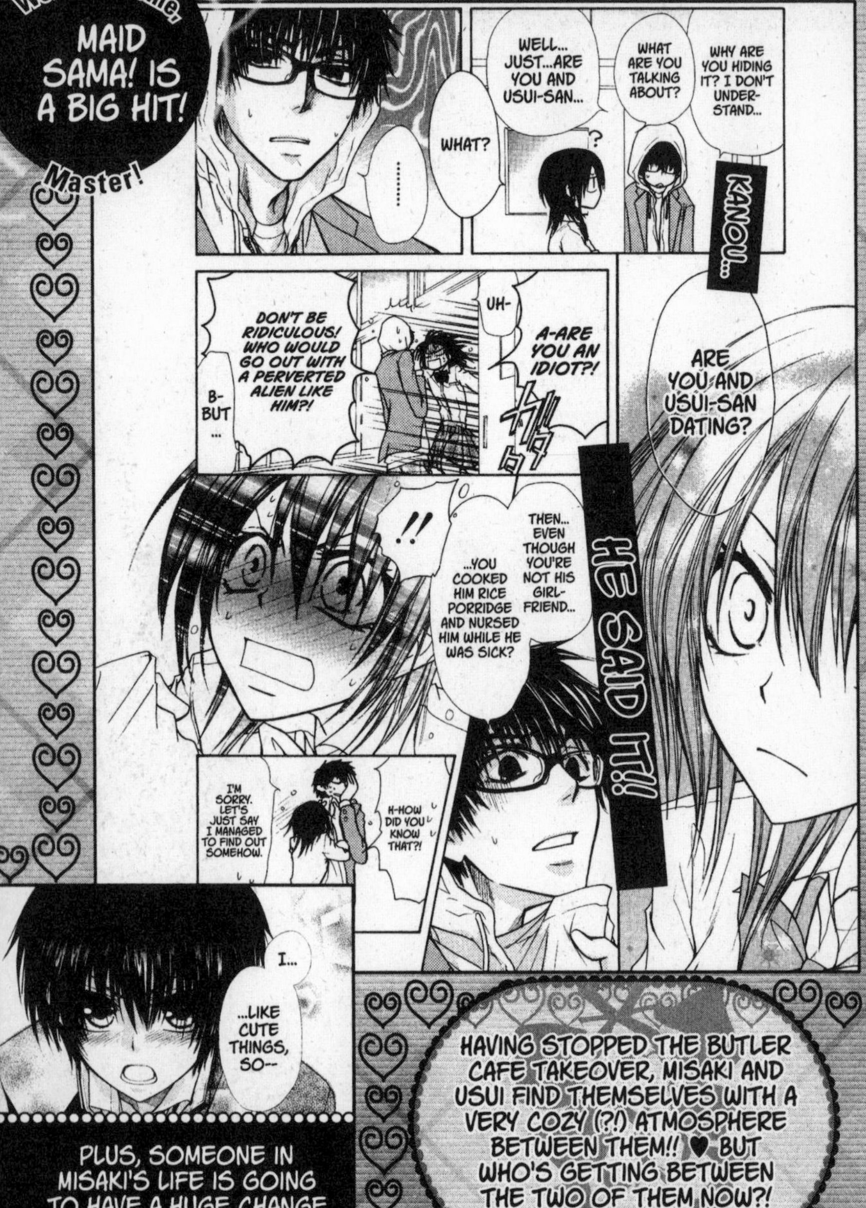

WHY ARE YOU HIDING IT? I DON'T UNDER-STAND...
WHAT ARE YOU TALKING ABOUT?
WELL... JUST...ARE YOU AND USUI-SAN...
?
WHAT?
......
KANOU...
ARE YOU AND USUI-SAN DATING?
HE SAID IT!!
UH-
A-ARE YOU AN IDIOT?!
B-BUT ...
DON'T BE RIDICULOUS! WHO WOULD GO OUT WITH A PERVERTED ALIEN LIKE HIM?!
!!
THEN... EVEN THOUGH YOU'RE NOT HIS GIRL-FRIEND...
...YOU COOKED HIM RICE PORRIDGE AND NURSED HIM WHILE HE WAS SICK?
H-HOW DID YOU KNOW THAT?!
I'M SORRY. LET'S JUST SAY I MANAGED TO FIND OUT SOMEHOW.
I...
...LIKE CUTE THINGS, SO--

HAVING STOPPED THE BUTLER CAFE TAKEOVER, MISAKI AND USUI FIND THEMSELVES WITH A VERY COZY (?!) ATMOSPHERE BETWEEN THEM!! ♥ BUT WHO'S GETTING BETWEEN THE TWO OF THEM NOW?!

PLUS, SOMEONE IN MISAKI'S LIFE IS GOING TO HAVE A HUGE CHANGE IN HIS RELATIONSHIPS!

MAID SAMA! VOLUME 6

Today at Maid Latte, it's
♡ *Miko Day* ♡

TOKYOPOP Insider

Stu Levy, May 2010

Hi everyone! Most of you don't know me but please allow me to introduce myself. While my parents named me Stuart Joel Levy, I really just go by "Stu". Ever since I was a child, people would tease me about being a food, calling me "Beef Stu" and the like. Even in Japanese, I get variations (although I'm 「スチュウ」 "Su-chu" whereas "stew" the food is actually 「シチュー」 "Shi-chu").

Now that we've gotten that sorted out, let me explain why I'm writing this. At TOKYOPOP, we decided to start a new column in our manga called "TOKYOPOP Insider" where some of our staff can write something casually – whatever's on their mind. I guess it's sort of a paper-based blog. I thought I'd be the first one to give it a go and see what you guys thought.

It may be hard to believe but it's been 13 years since I founded TOKYOPOP. Wow, time flies! Along with me, you manga readers have matured as well. We've seen some of our favorite series end, others begin, lots of content go online, and books evolve. Many more people know and love Japanese culture than when I first started – and I'm proud that I was a part of making that happen.

So, let me say ありがとう！("arigatou" - "thank you") to all of you for being interested in manga, Japan, and otaku culture overall. It's been a whirlwind of a ride over the past 13 years, but I've enjoyed every thrilling moment of it – working day and night for a passion that we all share.

This summer we're doing something I've wanted to do for years but never had the guts. I'm going on the road with Dice (from TOKYOPOP) and a very talented group of fans (the "Otaku Six") and we're going to search the nation for "America's Greatest Otaku" as well as give away lots of TOKYOPOP swag. Who knows what will happen – it's a crazy endeavor since we'll all be living on a humongous bus for 3 months – but my goal is to meet as many of you in person as I can (www.Americasgreatestotaku.com).

The details will be online but please come out and say hi if we're in your neighborhood – I'd love to meet you!

今後とも宜しくお願いします！("Kongo tomo Yoroshiku onegai-shimasu!"which roughly translates as "Looking forward to it!")

Cheers!
--Stu

A TOKYOPOP Manga
E-mail: info@TOKYOPOP.com
Come visit us online at www.TOKYOPOP.com

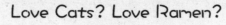

THE SMALLEST HERO!?
RATMAN
ラットマン

Shuto Katsuragi is a superhero otaku. Only problem is, he's a shrimp always getting teased for his height…especially when he tries to emulate his favorite superhero! To make matters worse, Shuto suddenly gets abducted by his classmate and tricked into participating in some rather sketchy and super-villainous experiments! Why is it always one step forward and a hundred steps back for this little guy?

ACTION

OT OLDER TEEN AGE 16+

The second epic trilogy continues!

Ai fights to escape the clutches of her mysterious and malevolent captors, not knowing whether Kent, left behind on the Other Side, is even still alive. A frantic rescue mission commences, and in the end, even Ai's magical voice may not be enough to protect her from the trials of the Black Forest.

Dark secrets are revealed, and Ai must use all her strength and courage to face off against the new threat to Ai-Land. But will she ever see Kent again...?

"A very intriguing read that will satisfy old fans and create new fans, too."
— Bookloons

TOKYOPOP MANGA SUPPLEMENT

DEADMAN WONDERLAND

Where survival comes at an unthinkable price.

Ten years have passed since the Great Tokyo Earthquake, and the people's memories of the disaster have faded. Ganta Igarashi, a middle school evacuee, has finally begun to live a normal life...That is, until the "Red Man" appears at his school and Ganta's fate is changed forever. His entire class is brutally murdered, and although innocent of the crime, Ganta is sentenced to death and sent to the bizarre prison known as "Deadman Wonderland.

Let the insane and brutal game of prison survival begin!

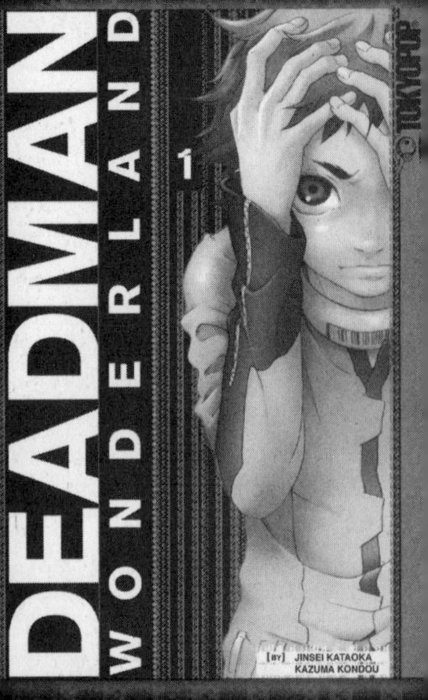
DEADMAN WONDERLAND
1
[BY] JINSEI KATAOKA
KAZUMA KONDOU
TOKYOPOP

WATCH THE TRAILER AT

www.TOKYOPOP.com/DeadmanTrailer

OT OLDER TEEN AGE 16+

ACTION

STO

This is the back of the book.
You wouldn't want to spoil a great ending!

This book is printed "manga-style," in the authentic Japanese right-to-left format. Since none of the artwork has been flipped or altered, readers get to experience the story just as the creator intended. You've been asking for it, so TOKYOPOP® delivered: authentic, hot-off-the-press, and far more fun!

1
2
3
4
5
6
7
8
9
10

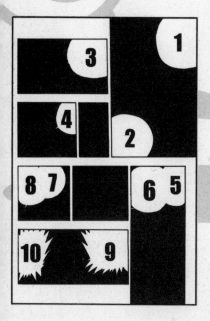

DIRECTIONS

If this is your first time reading manga-style, here's a quick guide to help you understand how it works.

It's easy... just start in the top right panel and follow the numbers. Have fun, and look for more 100% authentic manga from TOKYOPOP®!

THE MANGA REVOLUTION • LEADING THE MANGA REVOLUTION • LEADING

漫画革命